Shojo Beat

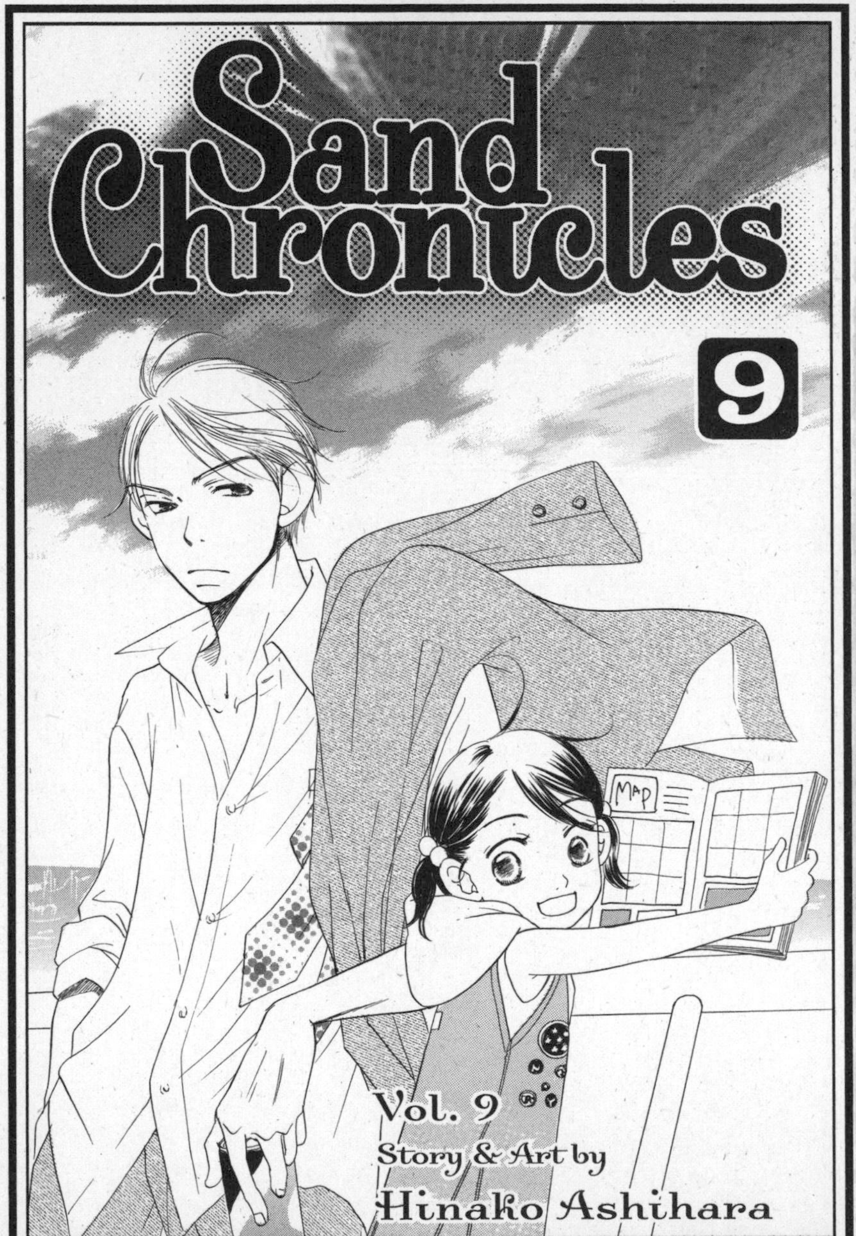
Sand Chronicles
9
Vol. 9
Story & Art by
Hinako Ashihara

Sand Chronicles
Volume 9

Contents

Bonus Episodes

Canary—5

~Thirty Years Ago~

Summer Vacation—107

The Present—169

Glossary—186

Story thus far...

It took years for Ann to come to terms with her mother Miwako's suicide. Now she is happily married to Daigo, her childhood boyfriend. These are the stories of their parents and their friends' parents, a generation before... Plus bonus side stories not included in the original series!

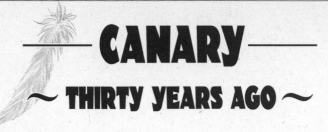

— CANARY —
~ THIRTY YEARS AGO ~

HATOYAMA BAKERY

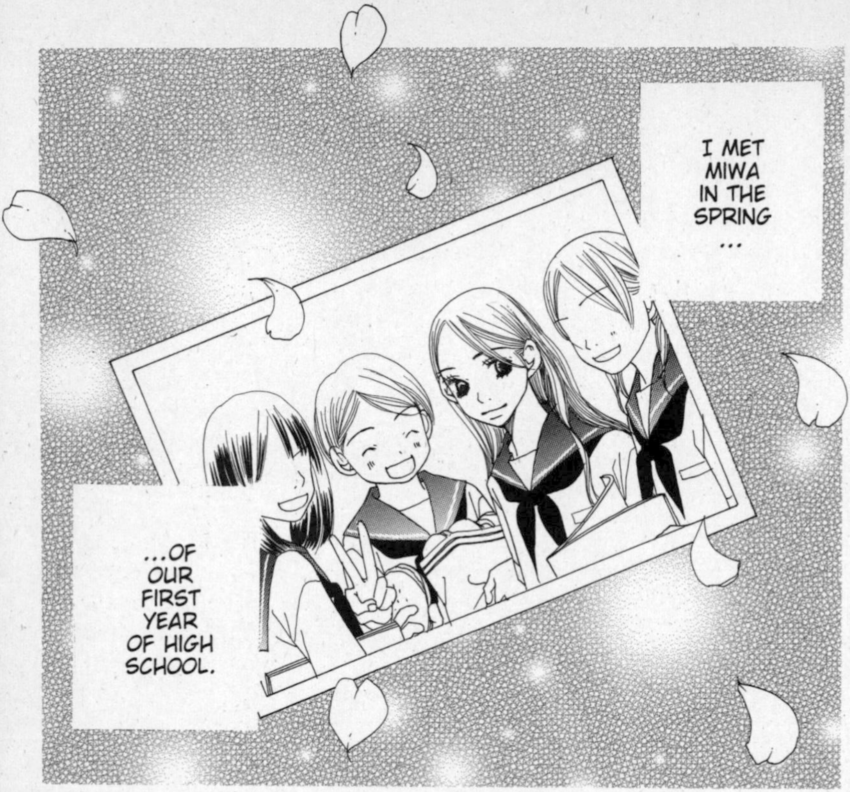
I MET MIWA IN THE SPRING ...
...OF OUR FIRST YEAR OF HIGH SCHOOL.

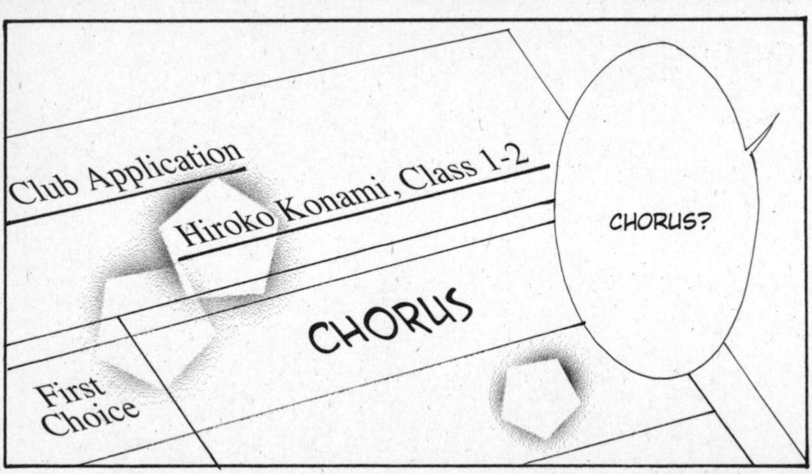
CHORUS?
Club Application
Hiroko Konami, Class 1-2
First Choice
CHORUS

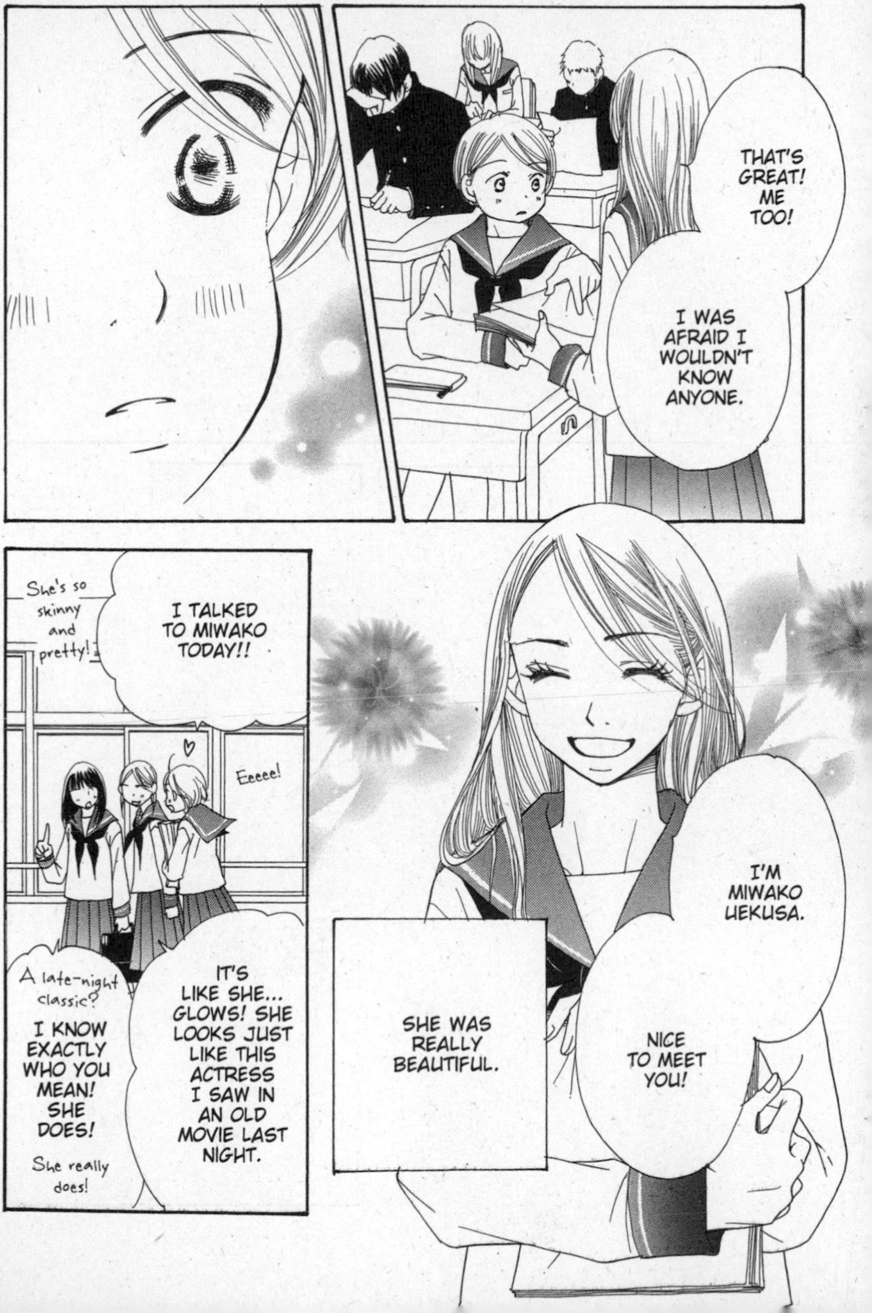
THAT'S GREAT! ME TOO!
I WAS AFRAID I WOULDN'T KNOW ANYONE.
I'M MIWAKO UEKUSA.
NICE TO MEET YOU!
SHE WAS REALLY BEAUTIFUL.
I TALKED TO MIWAKO TODAY!!
She's so skinny and pretty!
Eeeee!
IT'S LIKE SHE... GLOWS! SHE LOOKS JUST LIKE THIS ACTRESS I SAW IN AN OLD MOVIE LAST NIGHT.
A late-night classic?
I KNOW EXACTLY WHO YOU MEAN! SHE DOES!
She really does!

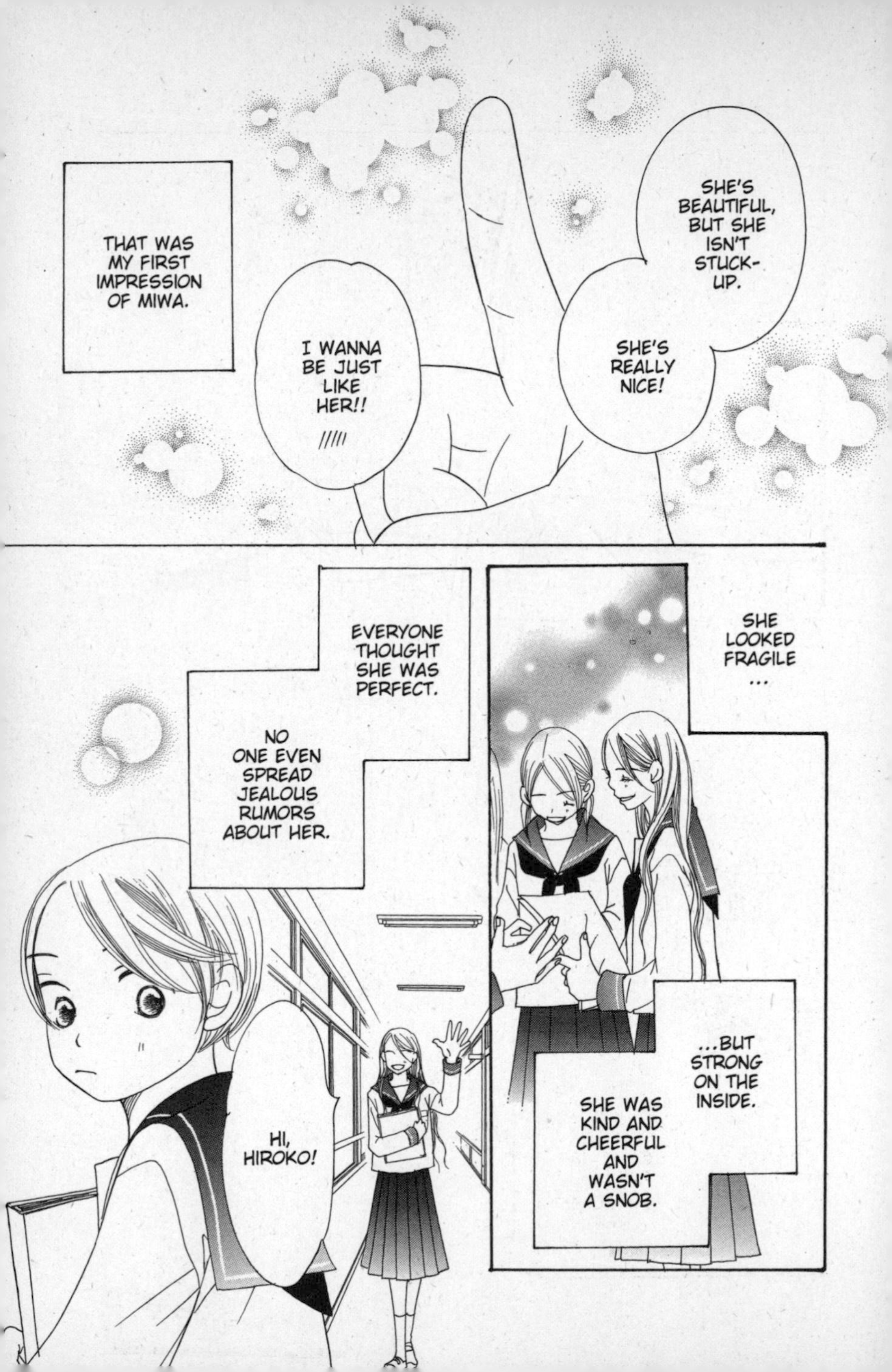
SHE'S BEAUTIFUL, BUT SHE ISN'T STUCK-UP.
SHE'S REALLY NICE!
I WANNA BE JUST LIKE HER!!
THAT WAS MY FIRST IMPRESSION OF MIWA.
SHE LOOKED FRAGILE...
...BUT STRONG ON THE INSIDE.
SHE WAS KIND AND CHEERFUL AND WASN'T A SNOB.
EVERYONE THOUGHT SHE WAS PERFECT.
NO ONE EVEN SPREAD JEALOUS RUMORS ABOUT HER.
HI, HIROKO!

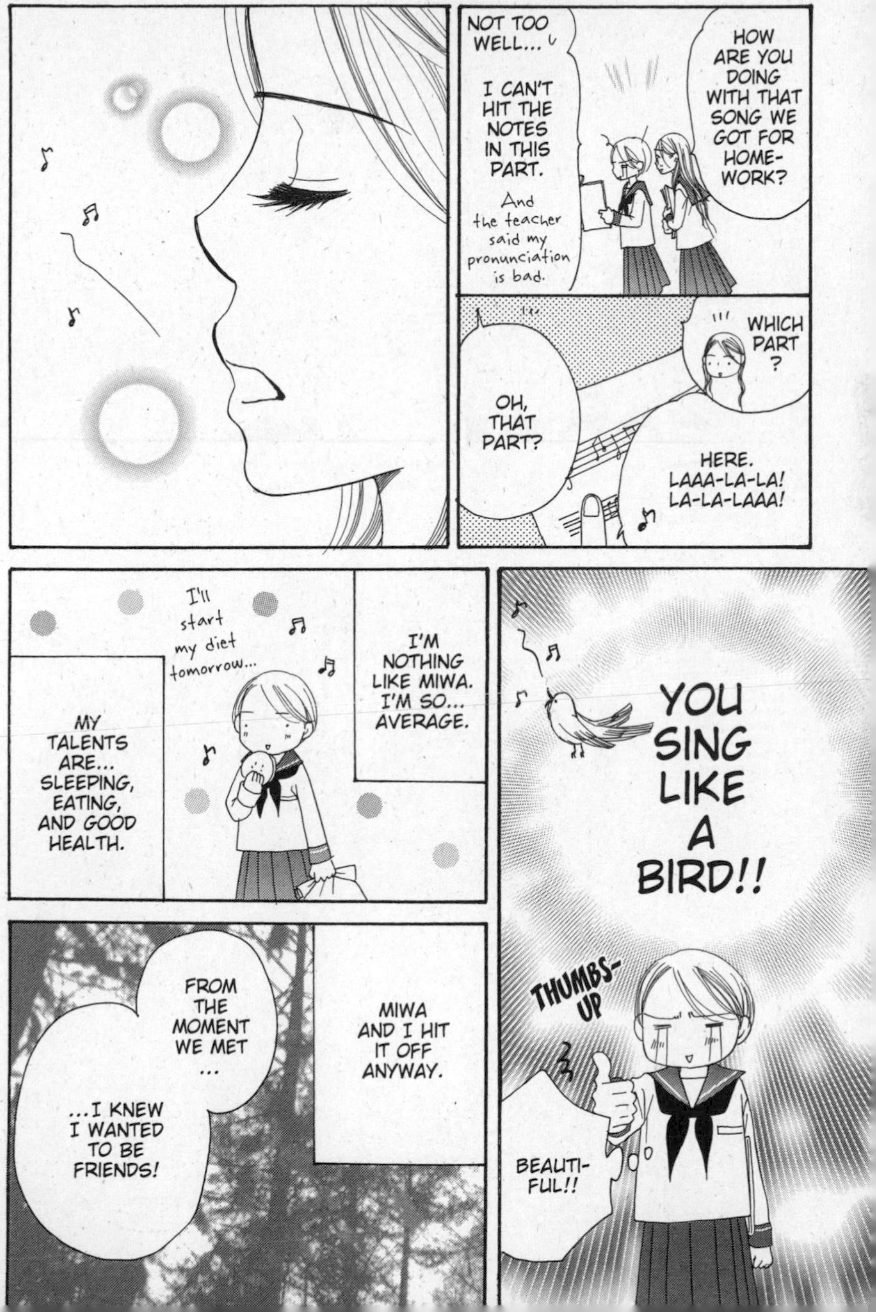
HOW ARE YOU DOING WITH THAT SONG WE GOT FOR HOME-WORK?
NOT TOO WELL...
I CAN'T HIT THE NOTES IN THIS PART.
And the teacher said my pronunciation is bad.
WHICH PART?
OH, THAT PART?
HERE. LAAA-LA-LA! LA-LA-LAAA!
YOU SING LIKE A BIRD!!
THUMBS-UP
BEAUTI-FUL!!
I'M NOTHING LIKE MIWA. I'M SO... AVERAGE.
I'll start my diet tomorrow...
MY TALENTS ARE... SLEEPING, EATING, AND GOOD HEALTH.
MIWA AND I HIT IT OFF ANYWAY.
FROM THE MOMENT WE MET...
...I KNEW I WANTED TO BE FRIENDS!

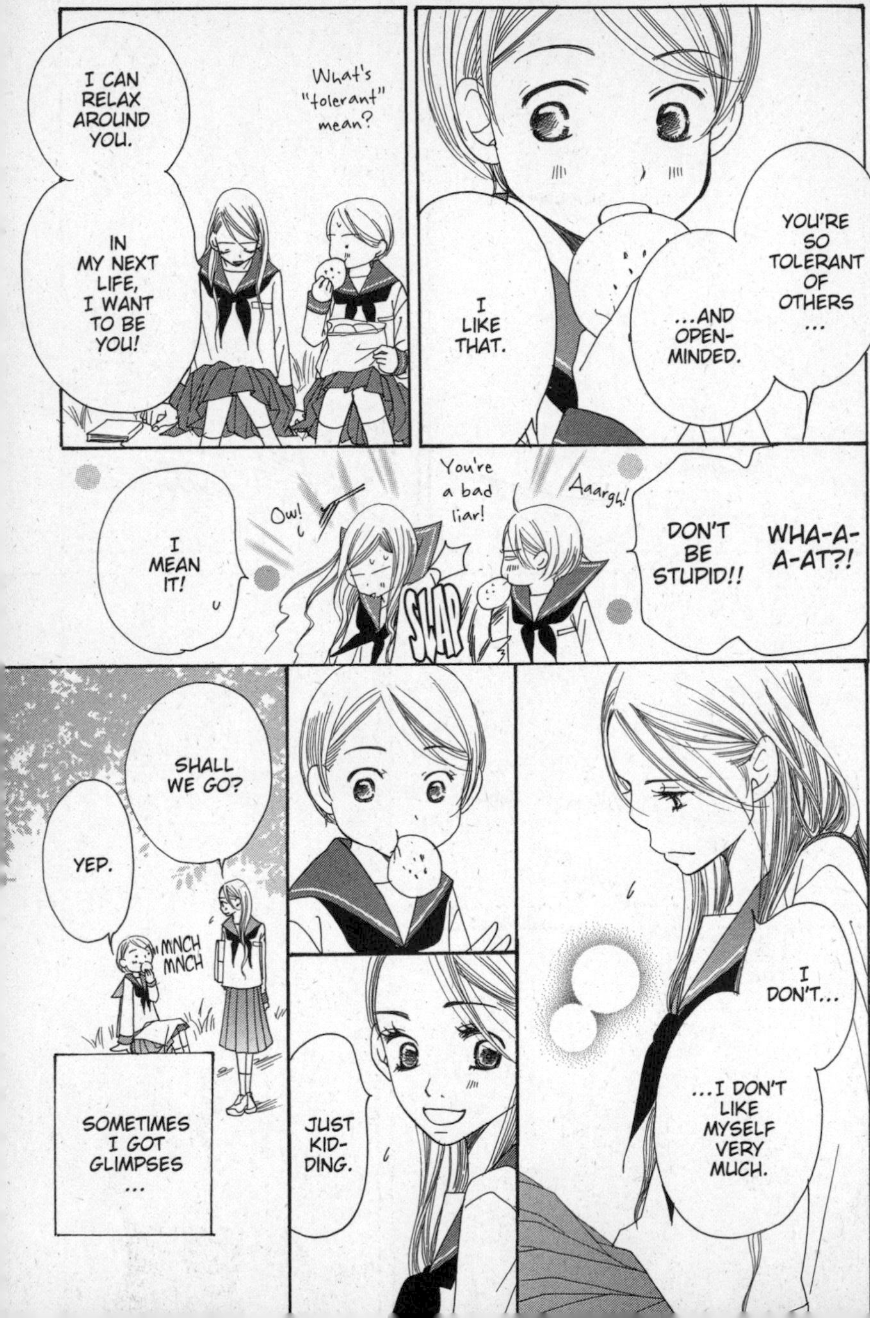
YOU'RE SO TOLERANT OF OTHERS...
...AND OPEN-MINDED.
I LIKE THAT.
What's "tolerant" mean?
I CAN RELAX AROUND YOU.
IN MY NEXT LIFE, I WANT TO BE YOU!
WHA-A-A-AT?!
DON'T BE STUPID!!
Aaargh!
You're a bad liar!
SLAP
Ow!
I MEAN IT!
I DON'T...
...I DON'T LIKE MYSELF VERY MUCH.
JUST KID-DING.
SHALL WE GO?
YEP.
MNCH MNCH
SOMETIMES I GOT GLIMPSES...

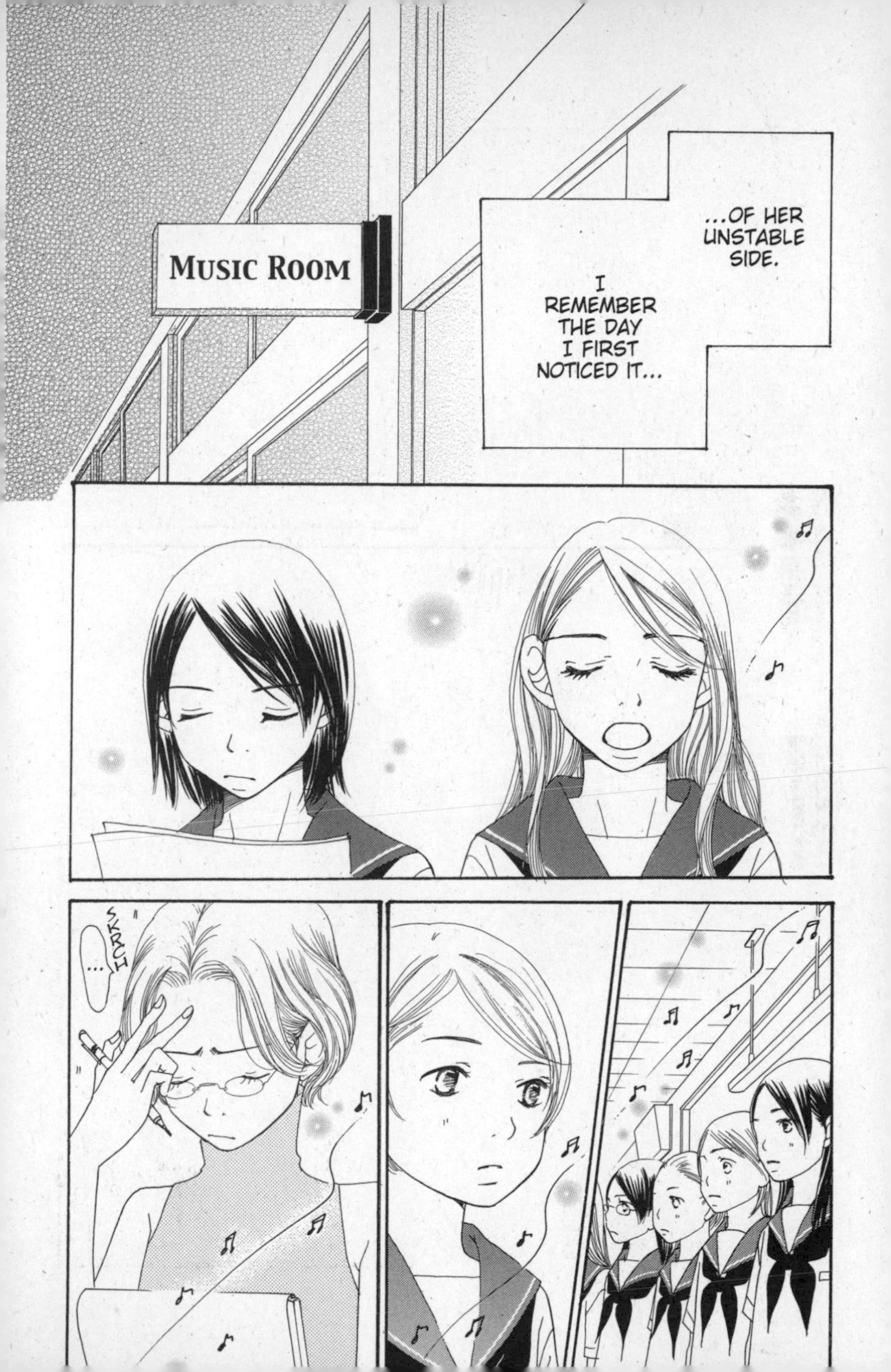
I REMEMBER THE DAY I FIRST NOTICED IT...
...OF HER UNSTABLE SIDE.
MUSIC ROOM
...
SKRCH

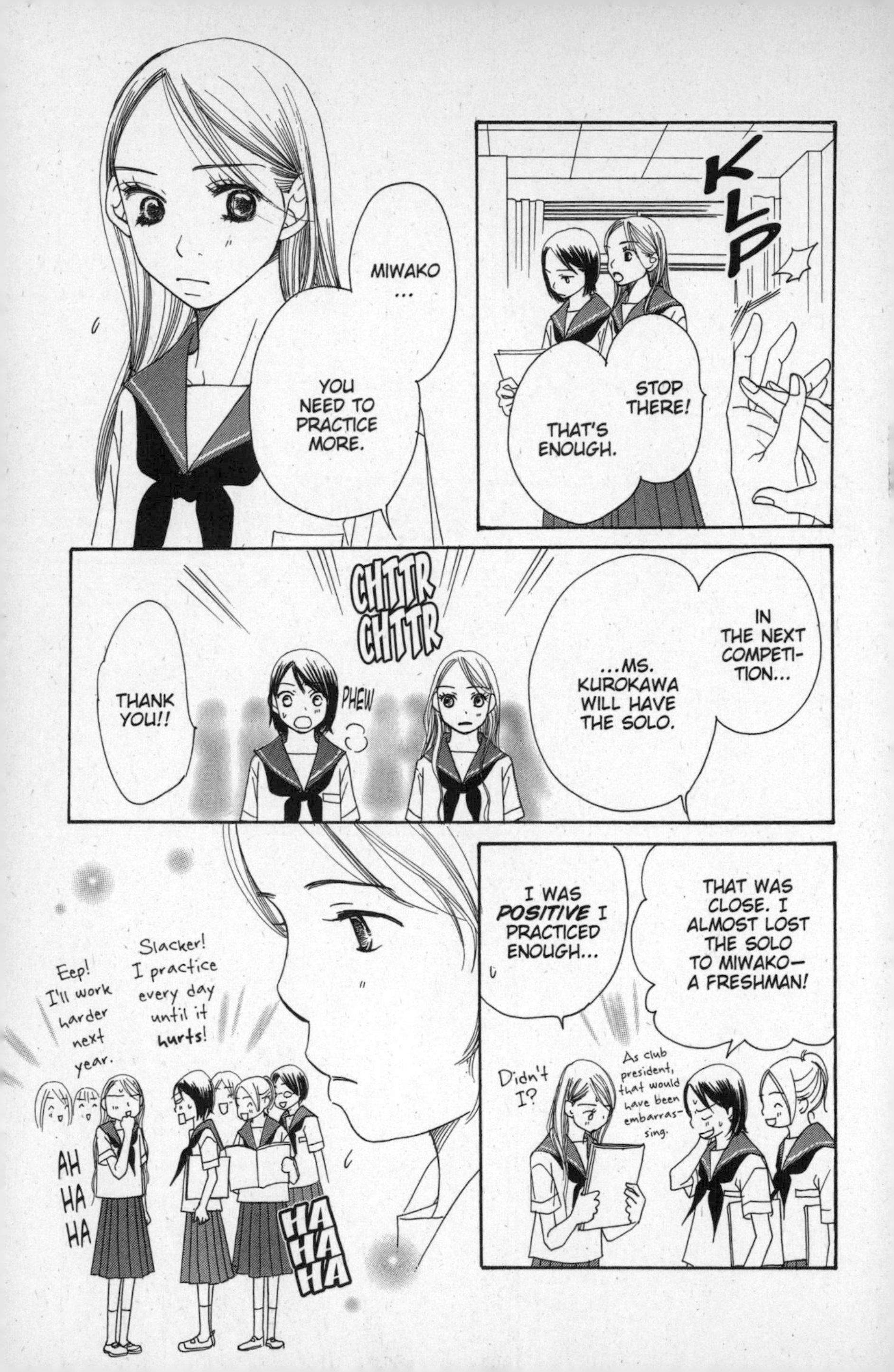
KLP
STOP THERE!
THAT'S ENOUGH.
MIWAKO ...
YOU NEED TO PRACTICE MORE.
IN THE NEXT COMPETITION...
...MS. KUROKAWA WILL HAVE THE SOLO.
CHTTR CHTTR
PHEW
THANK YOU!!
THAT WAS CLOSE. I ALMOST LOST THE SOLO TO MIWAKO—A FRESHMAN!
I WAS POSITIVE I PRACTICED ENOUGH...
As club president, that would have been embarrassing.
Didn't I?
Slacker! I practice every day until it hurts!
Eep! I'll work harder next year.
AH HA HA
HA HA HA

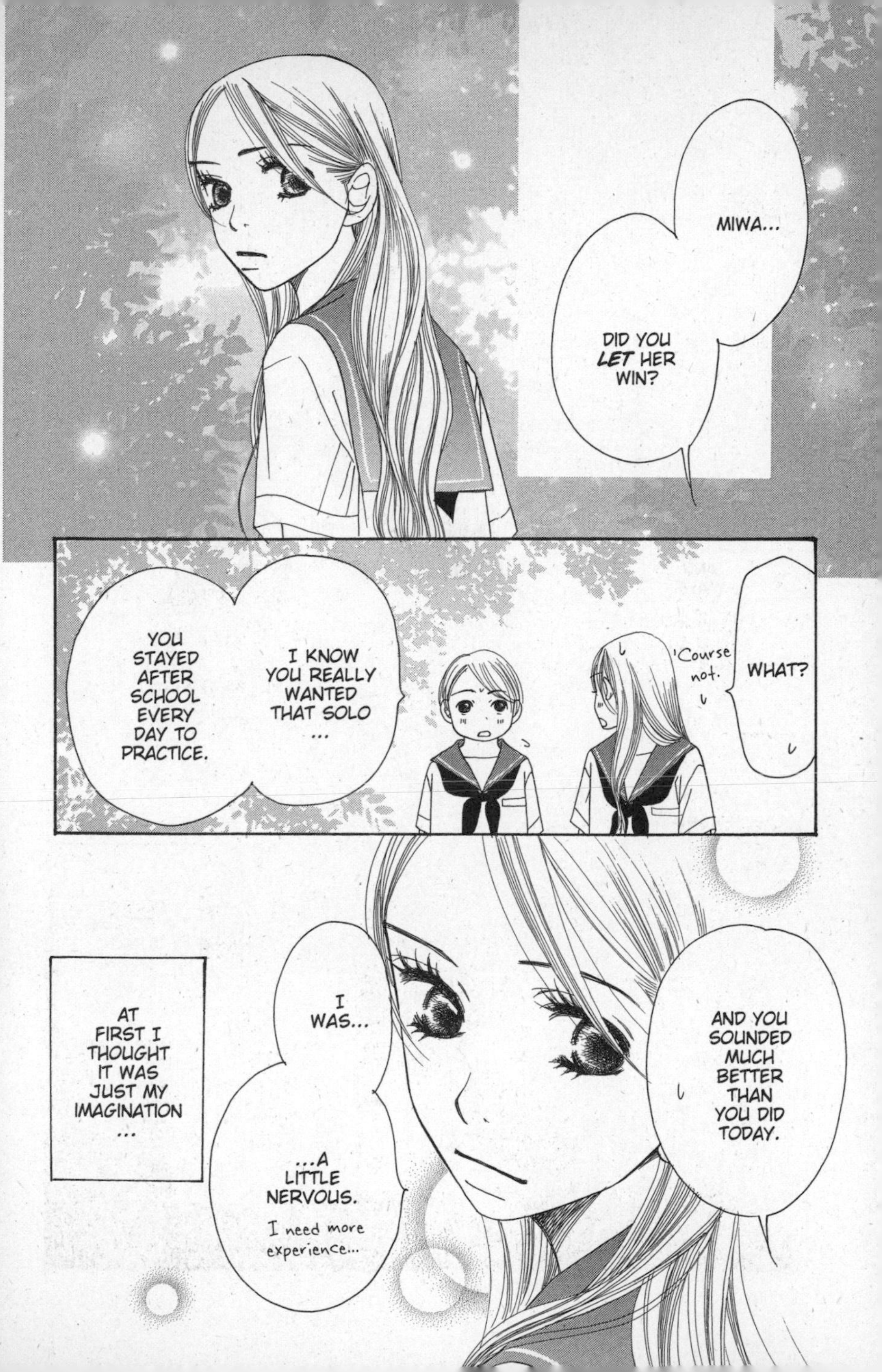
MIWA...
DID YOU *LET* HER WIN?
WHAT?
'Course not.
I KNOW YOU REALLY WANTED THAT SOLO ...
YOU STAYED AFTER SCHOOL EVERY DAY TO PRACTICE.
AND YOU SOUNDED MUCH BETTER THAN YOU DID TODAY.
I WAS... ...A LITTLE NERVOUS.
I need more experience...
AT FIRST I THOUGHT IT WAS JUST MY IMAGINATION ...

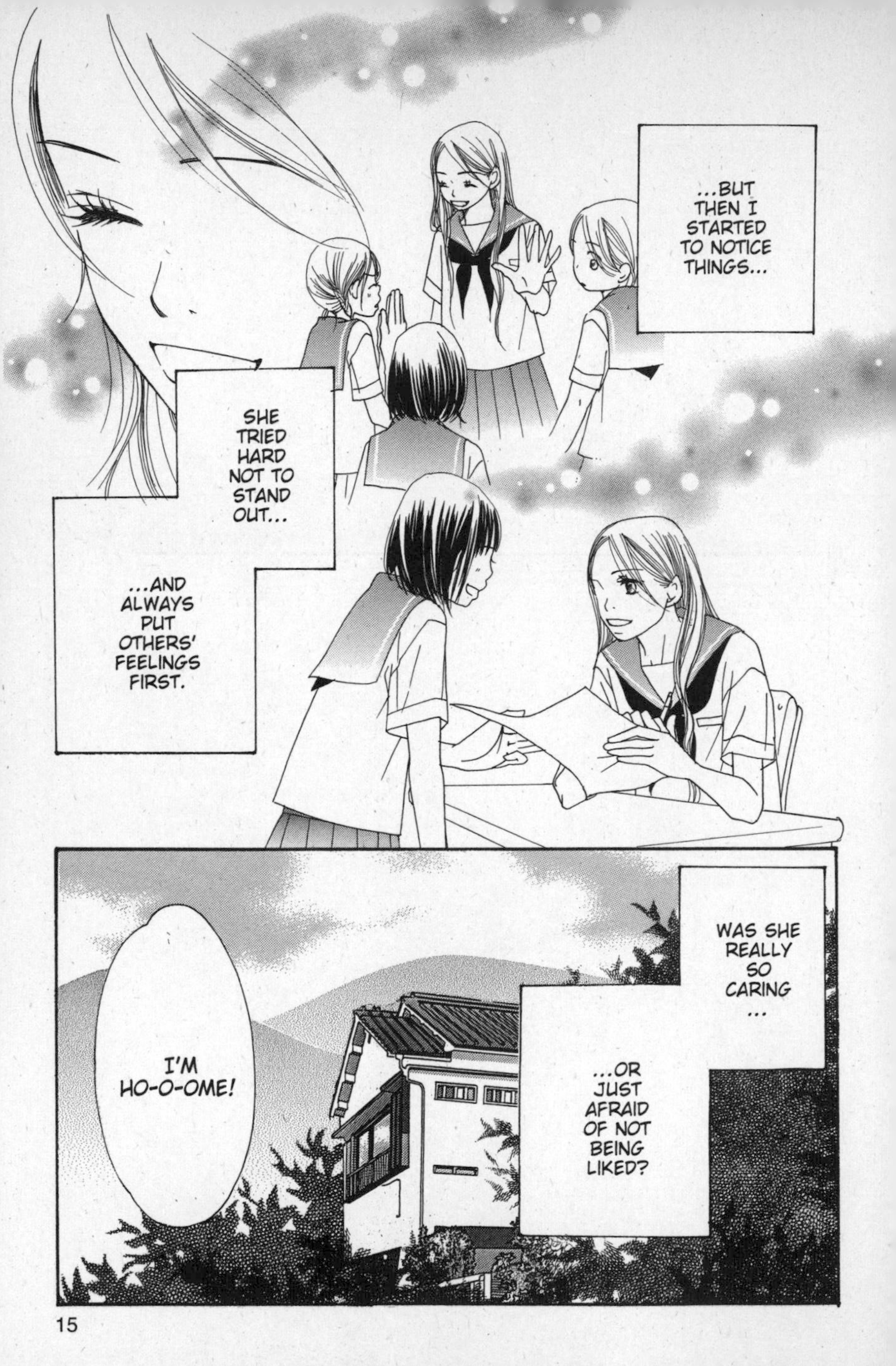
...BUT THEN I STARTED TO NOTICE THINGS...
SHE TRIED HARD NOT TO STAND OUT...
...AND ALWAYS PUT OTHERS' FEELINGS FIRST.
WAS SHE REALLY SO CARING...
...OR JUST AFRAID OF NOT BEING LIKED?
I'M HO-O-OME!

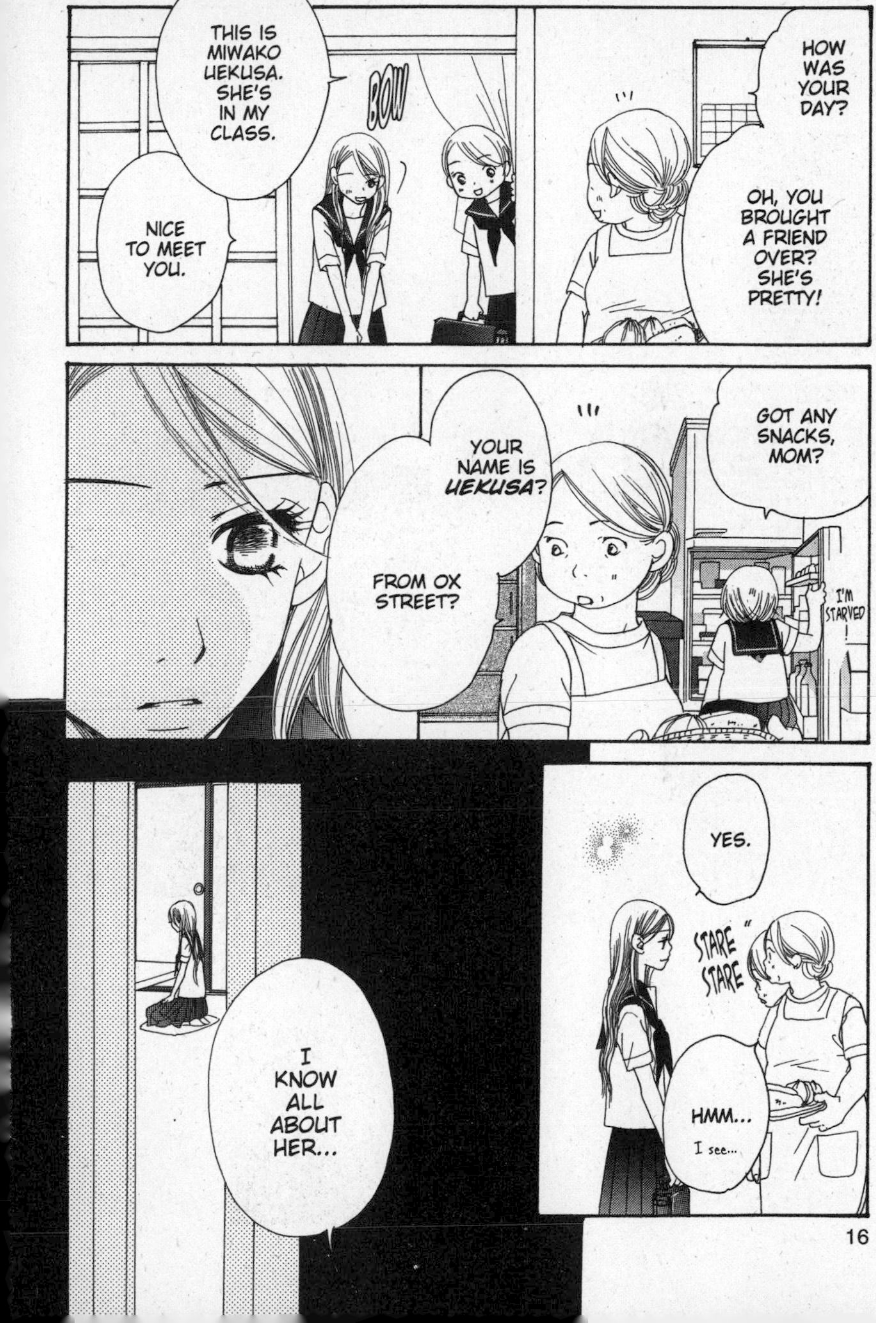
HOW WAS YOUR DAY?
OH, YOU BROUGHT A FRIEND OVER? SHE'S PRETTY!
THIS IS MIWAKO UEKUSA. SHE'S IN MY CLASS.
BOW
NICE TO MEET YOU.
GOT ANY SNACKS, MOM?
I'M STARVED!
YOUR NAME IS UEKUSA?
FROM OX STREET?
YES.
STARE STARE
HMM...
I see...
I KNOW ALL ABOUT HER...

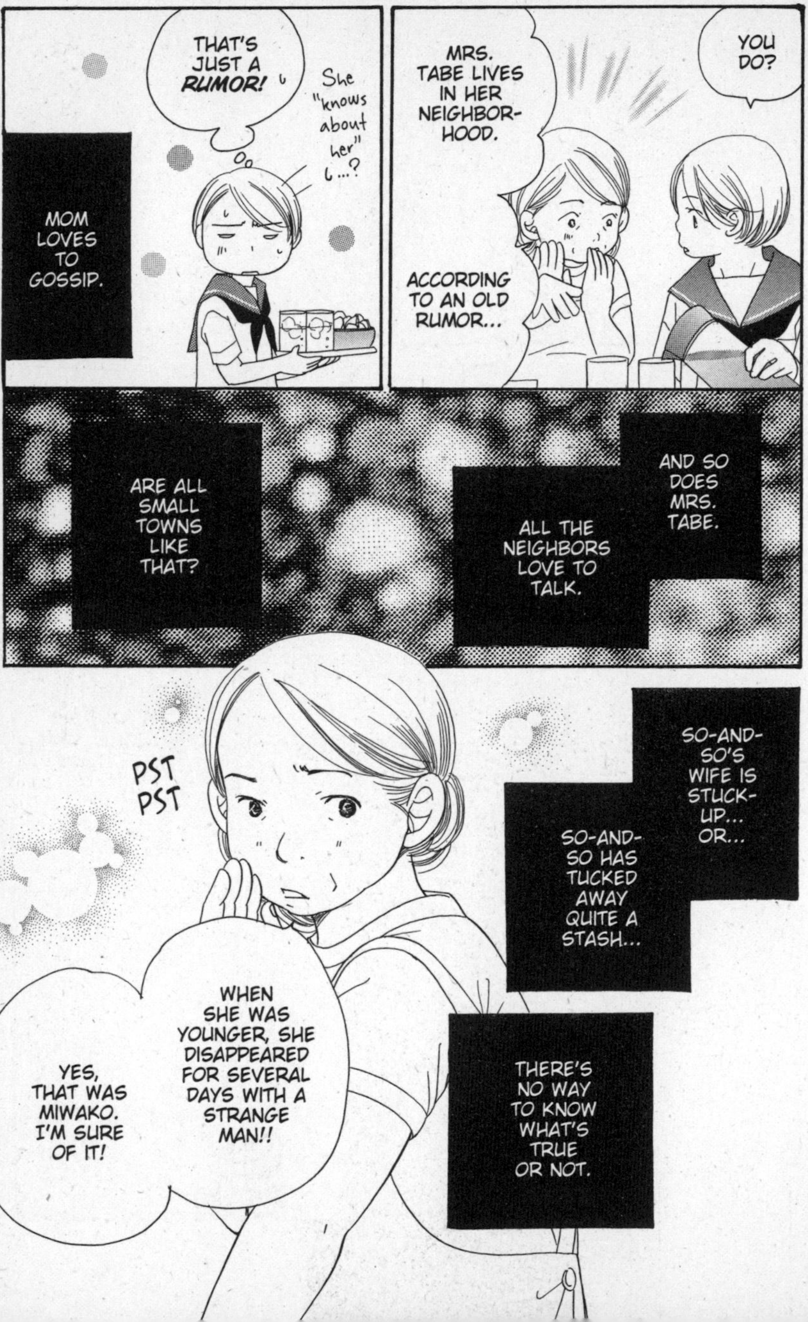
YOU DO?
MRS. TABE LIVES IN HER NEIGHBOR-HOOD.
ACCORDING TO AN OLD RUMOR...
THAT'S JUST A RUMOR!
She "knows about her"...?
MOM LOVES TO GOSSIP.
AND SO DOES MRS. TABE.
ALL THE NEIGHBORS LOVE TO TALK.
ARE ALL SMALL TOWNS LIKE THAT?
SO-AND-SO'S WIFE IS STUCK-UP... OR...
SO-AND-SO HAS TUCKED AWAY QUITE A STASH...
PST PST
THERE'S NO WAY TO KNOW WHAT'S TRUE OR NOT.
WHEN SHE WAS YOUNGER, SHE DISAPPEARED FOR SEVERAL DAYS WITH A STRANGE MAN!!
YES, THAT WAS MIWAKO. I'M SURE OF IT!

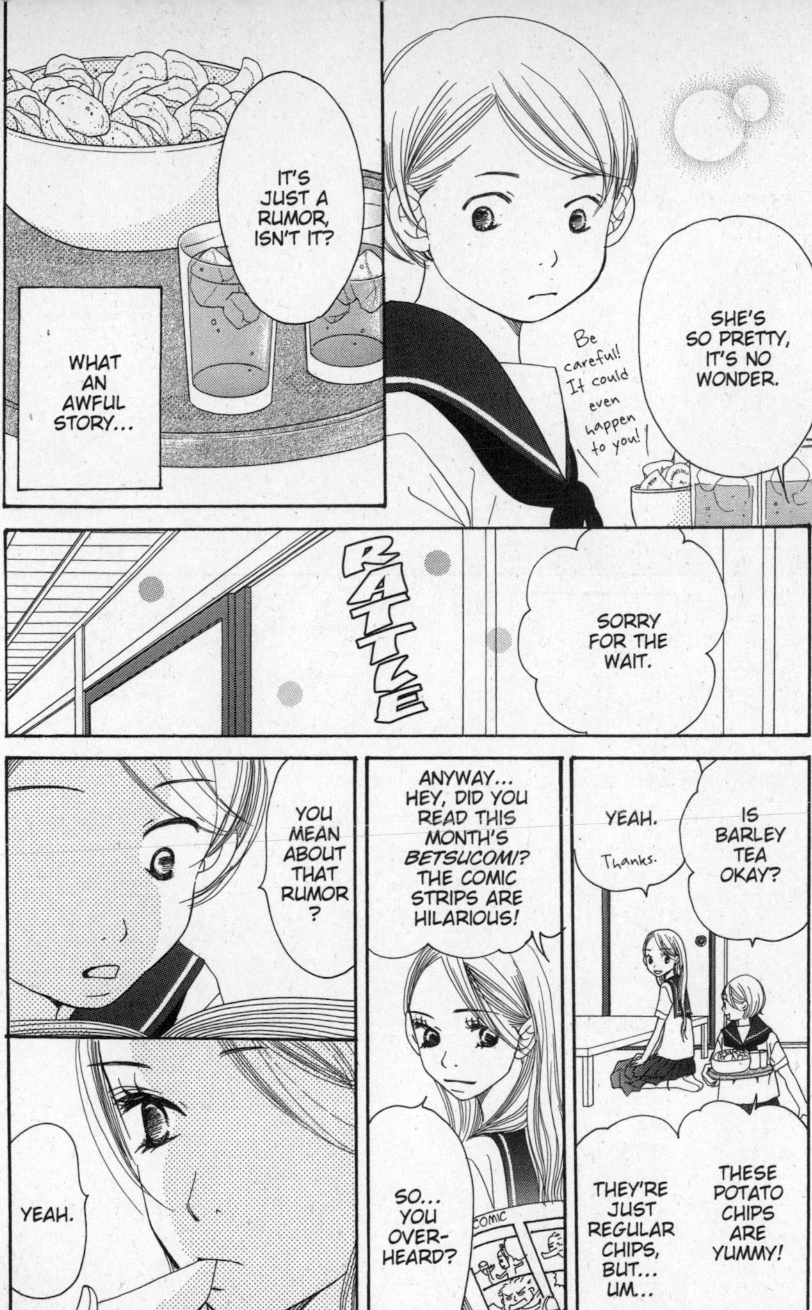
SHE'S SO PRETTY, IT'S NO WONDER.
Be careful! It could even happen to you!
IT'S JUST A RUMOR, ISN'T IT?
WHAT AN AWFUL STORY...
SORRY FOR THE WAIT.
RATTLE
IS BARLEY TEA OKAY?
YEAH.
Thanks.
THESE POTATO CHIPS ARE YUMMY!
THEY'RE JUST REGULAR CHIPS, BUT... UM...
ANYWAY... HEY, DID YOU READ THIS MONTH'S *BETSUCOMI*? THE COMIC STRIPS ARE HILARIOUS!
SO... YOU OVERHEARD?
COMIC
YOU MEAN ABOUT THAT RUMOR?
YEAH.

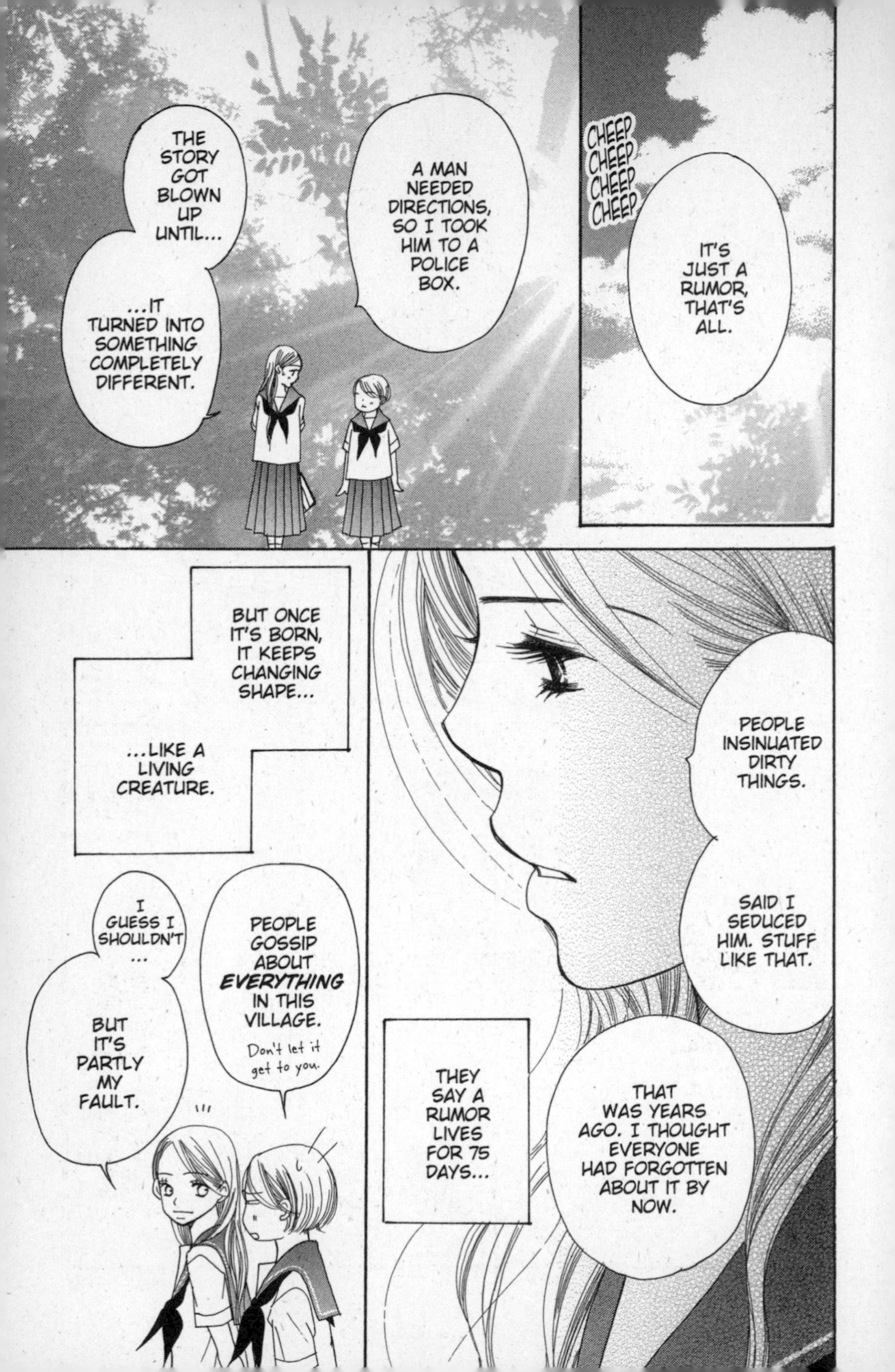
CHEEP CHEEP CHEEP CHEEP
IT'S JUST A RUMOR, THAT'S ALL.
A MAN NEEDED DIRECTIONS, SO I TOOK HIM TO A POLICE BOX.
THE STORY GOT BLOWN UP UNTIL...
...IT TURNED INTO SOMETHING COMPLETELY DIFFERENT.
PEOPLE INSINUATED DIRTY THINGS.
SAID I SEDUCED HIM. STUFF LIKE THAT.
THAT WAS YEARS AGO. I THOUGHT EVERYONE HAD FORGOTTEN ABOUT IT BY NOW.
THEY SAY A RUMOR LIVES FOR 75 DAYS...
BUT ONCE IT'S BORN, IT KEEPS CHANGING SHAPE...
...LIKE A LIVING CREATURE.
PEOPLE GOSSIP ABOUT EVERYTHING IN THIS VILLAGE.
Don't let it get to you.
I GUESS I SHOULDN'T...
BUT IT'S PARTLY MY FAULT.

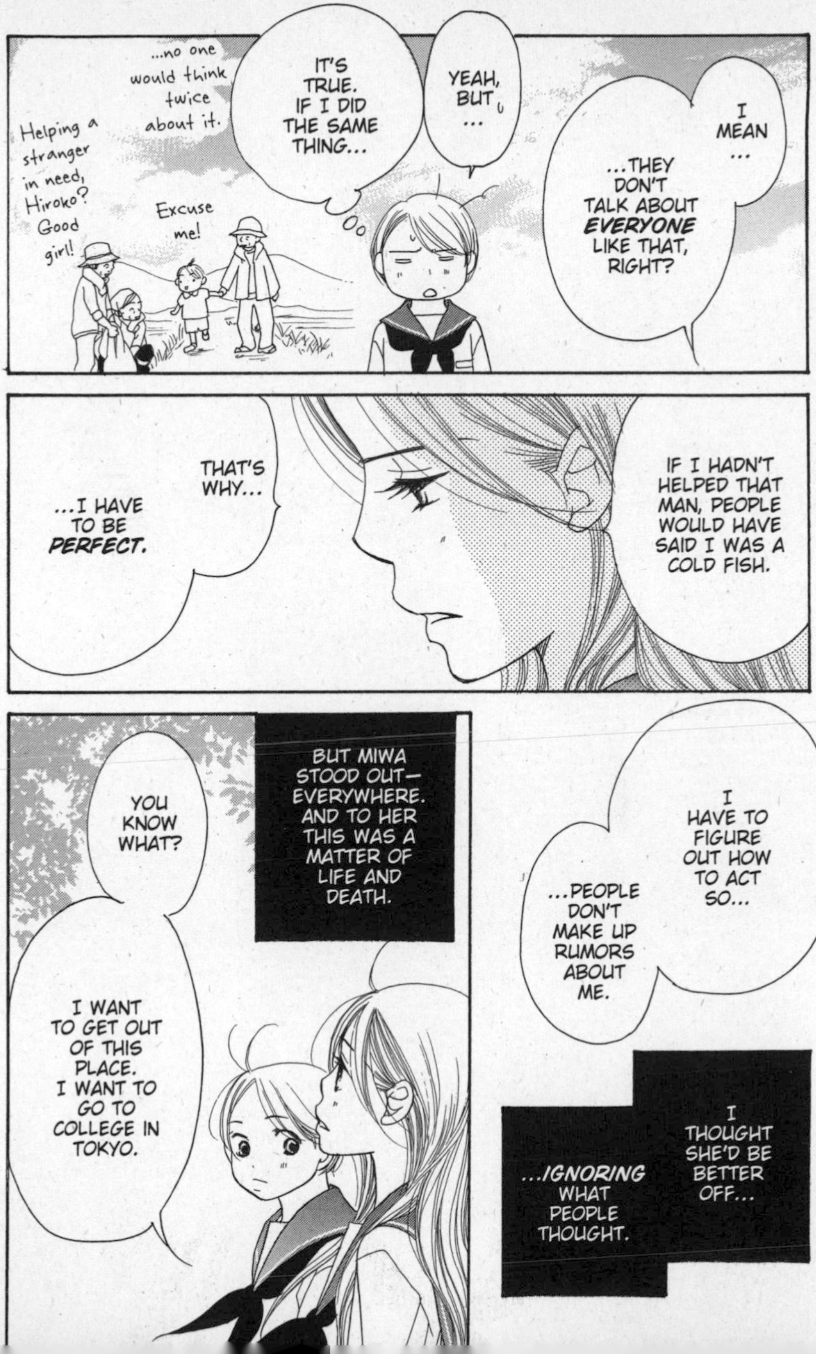
I MEAN...
...THEY DON'T TALK ABOUT **EVERYONE** LIKE THAT, RIGHT?
YEAH, BUT...
IT'S TRUE. IF I DID THE SAME THING...
...no one would think twice about it.
Helping a stranger in need, Hiroko? Good girl!
Excuse me!
IF I HADN'T HELPED THAT MAN, PEOPLE WOULD HAVE SAID I WAS A COLD FISH.
THAT'S WHY...
...I HAVE TO BE **PERFECT.**
I HAVE TO FIGURE OUT HOW TO ACT SO...
...PEOPLE DON'T MAKE UP RUMORS ABOUT ME.
I THOUGHT SHE'D BE BETTER OFF...
...*IGNORING* WHAT PEOPLE THOUGHT.
BUT MIWA STOOD OUT—EVERYWHERE. AND TO HER THIS WAS A MATTER OF LIFE AND DEATH.
YOU KNOW WHAT?
I WANT TO GET OUT OF THIS PLACE. I WANT TO GO TO COLLEGE IN TOKYO.

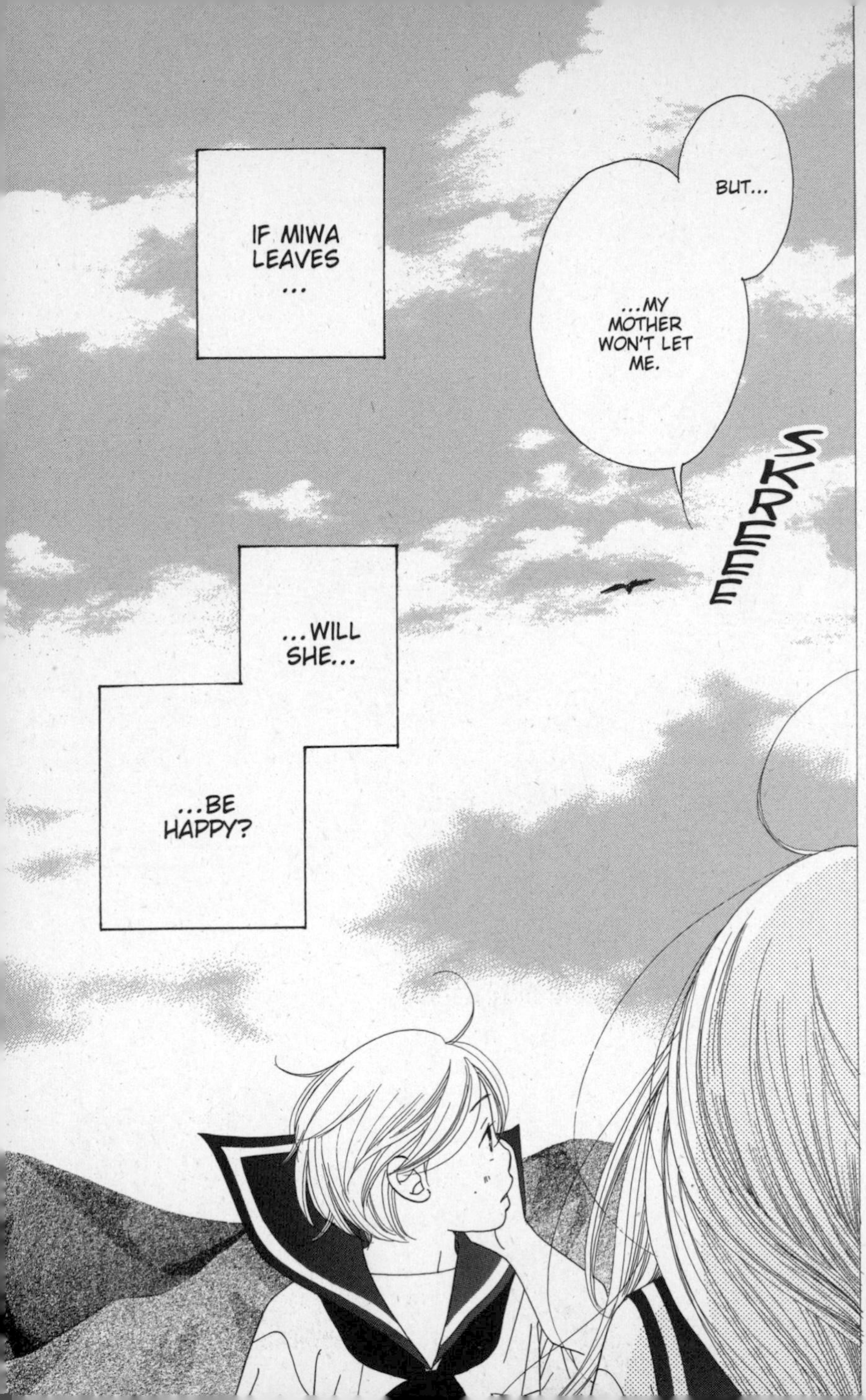
BUT...
...MY MOTHER WON'T LET ME.
IF MIWA LEAVES ...
SKREEE
...WILL SHE...
...BE HAPPY?

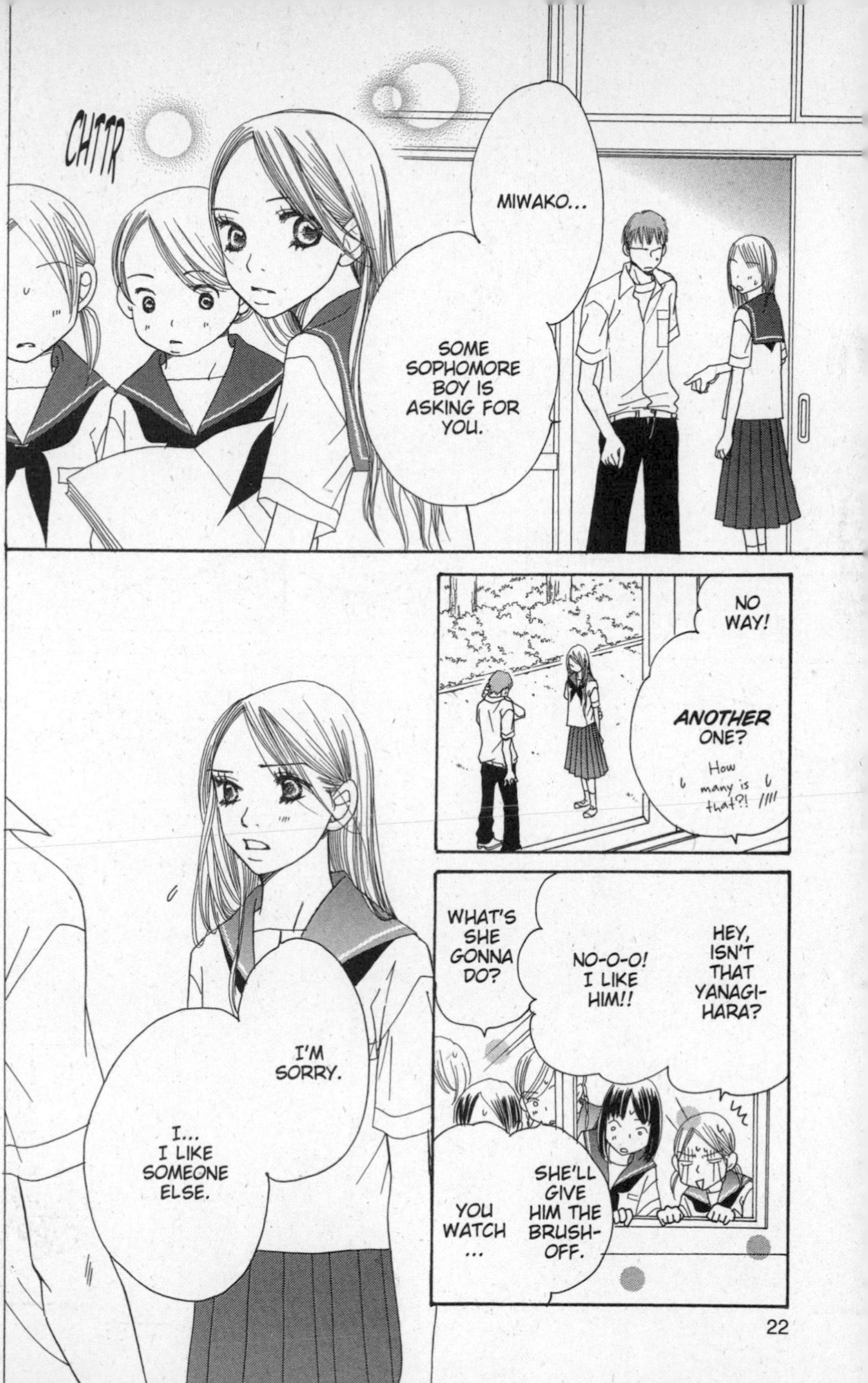
MIWAKO...
SOME SOPHOMORE BOY IS ASKING FOR YOU.
CHTTR
NO WAY!
ANOTHER ONE?
How many is that?!
HEY, ISN'T THAT YANAGI-HARA?
NO-O-O! I LIKE HIM!!
WHAT'S SHE GONNA DO?
SHE'LL GIVE HIM THE BRUSH-OFF.
YOU WATCH ...
I'M SORRY.
I... I LIKE SOMEONE ELSE.

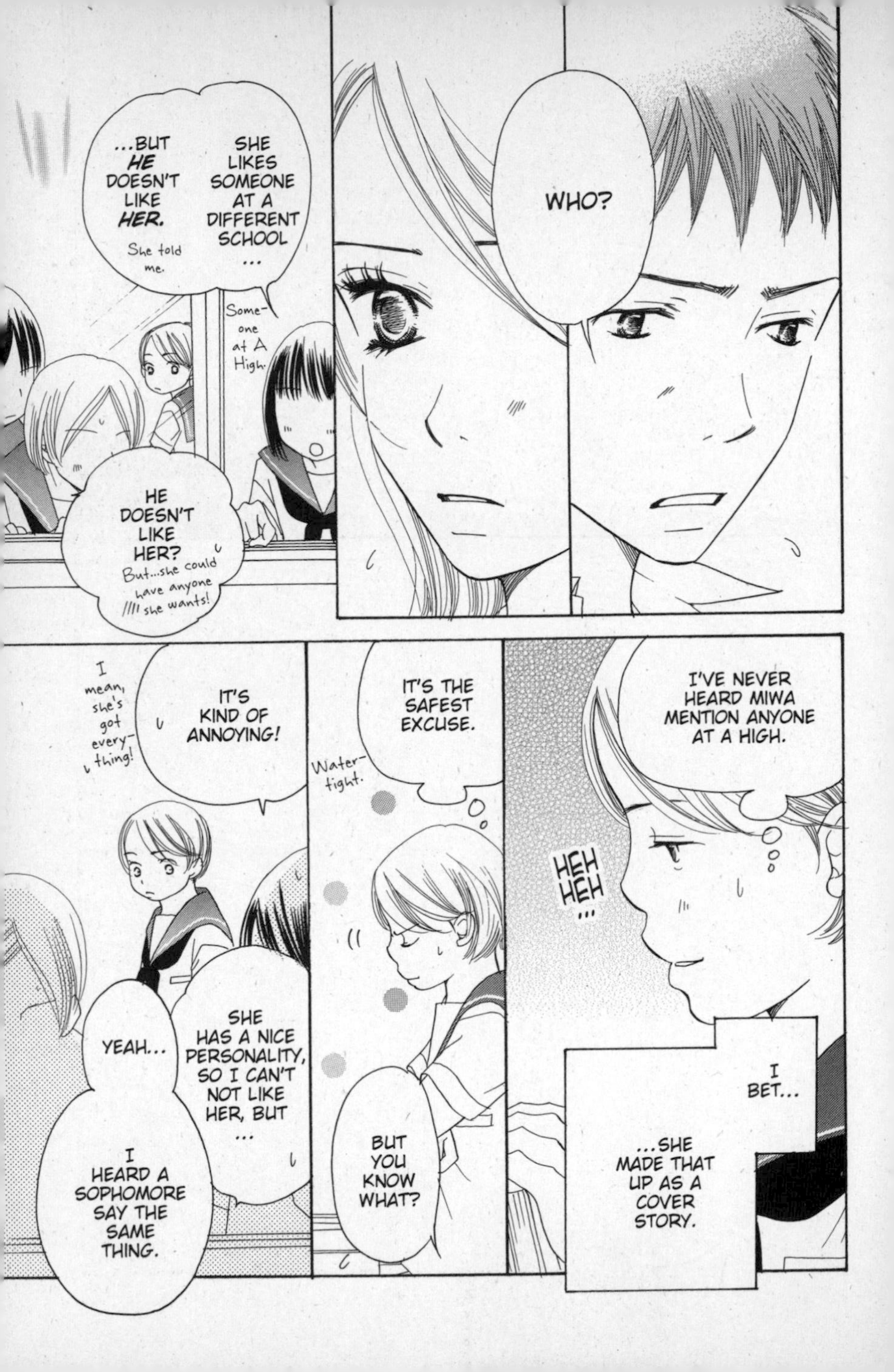
WHO?
SHE LIKES SOMEONE AT A DIFFERENT SCHOOL...
...BUT **HE** DOESN'T LIKE **HER.**
She told me.
Some-one at A High.
HE DOESN'T LIKE HER?
But...she could have anyone she wants!
I'VE NEVER HEARD MIWA MENTION ANYONE AT A HIGH.
HEH HEH...
I BET...
...SHE MADE THAT UP AS A COVER STORY.
IT'S THE SAFEST EXCUSE.
Water-tight.
BUT YOU KNOW WHAT?
IT'S KIND OF ANNOYING!
I mean, she's got every-thing!
SHE HAS A NICE PERSONALITY, SO I CAN'T NOT LIKE HER, BUT...
YEAH...
I HEARD A SOPHOMORE SAY THE SAME THING.

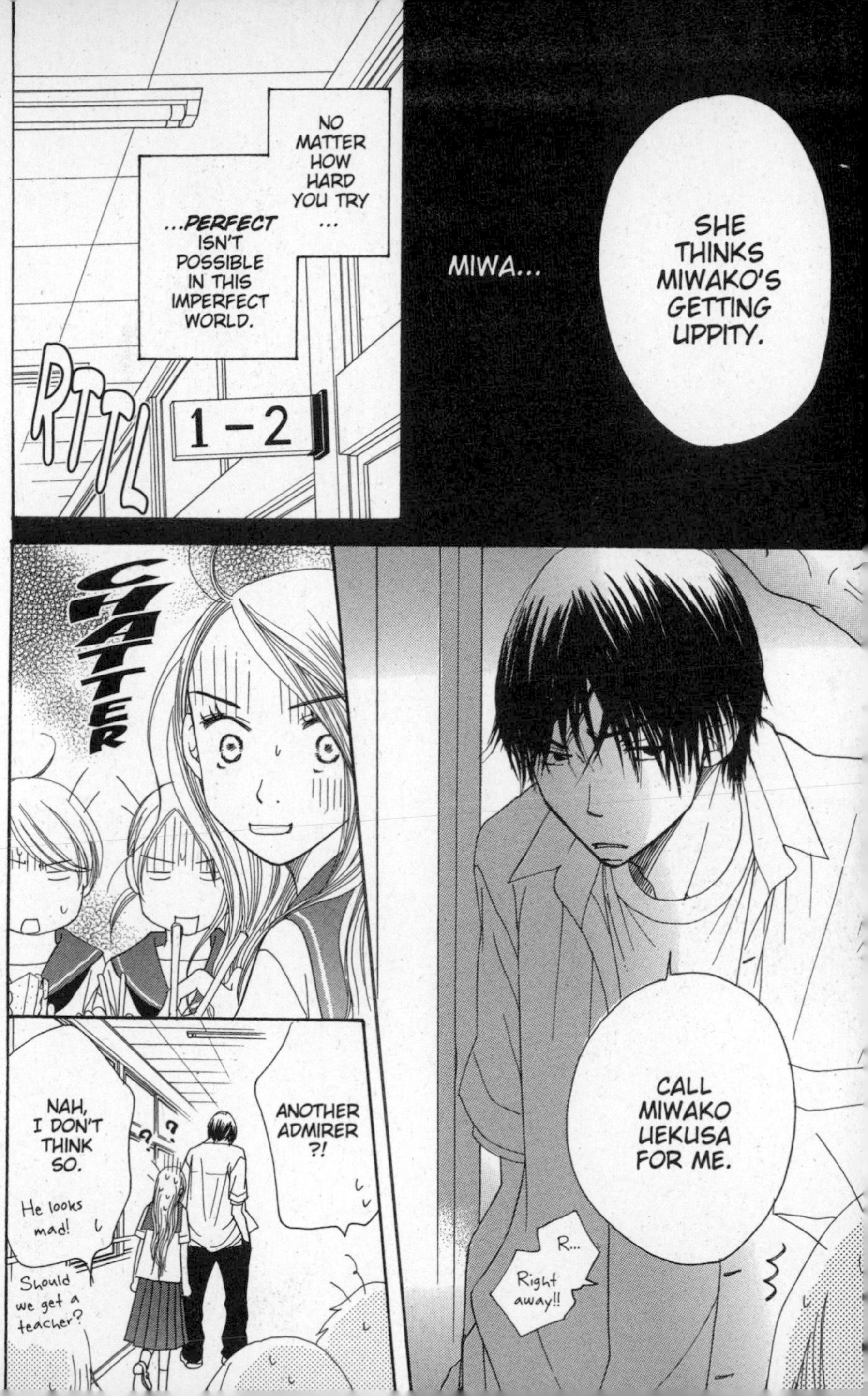
SHE THINKS MIWAKO'S GETTING UPPITY.
MIWA...
NO MATTER HOW HARD YOU TRY ...
...PERFECT ISN'T POSSIBLE IN THIS IMPERFECT WORLD.
RTTL
1－2
CALL MIWAKO UEKUSA FOR ME.
R...
Right away!!
CLATTER
ANOTHER ADMIRER ?!
NAH, I DON'T THINK SO.
He looks mad!
Should we get a teacher?

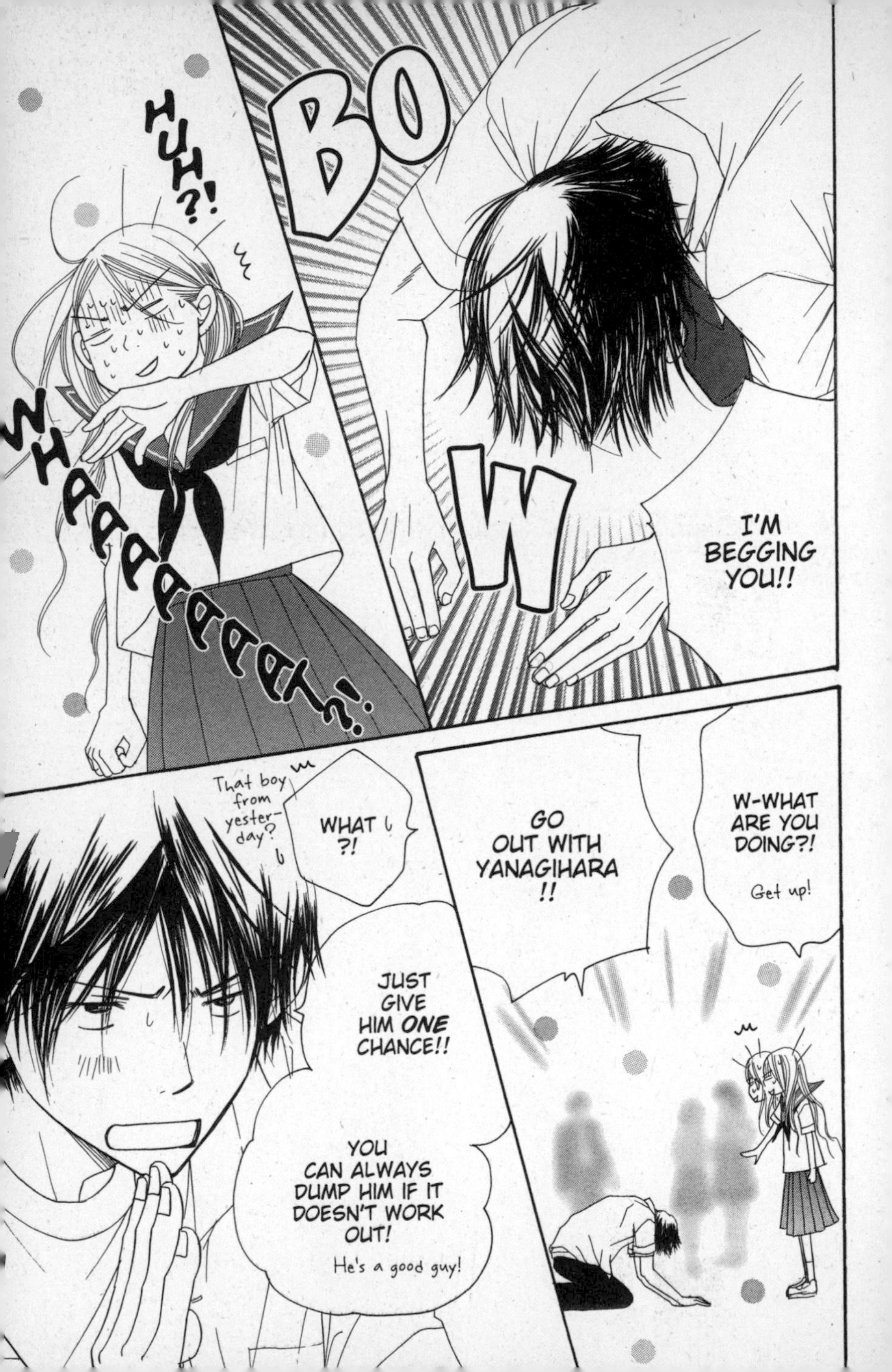
BOW
I'M BEGGING YOU!!
HUH?!
WHAAAAAAAT?!
W-WHAT ARE YOU DOING?!
Get up!
GO OUT WITH YANAGIHARA!!
WHAT?!
That boy from yester-day?
JUST GIVE HIM ONE CHANCE!!
YOU CAN ALWAYS DUMP HIM IF IT DOESN'T WORK OUT!
He's a good guy!

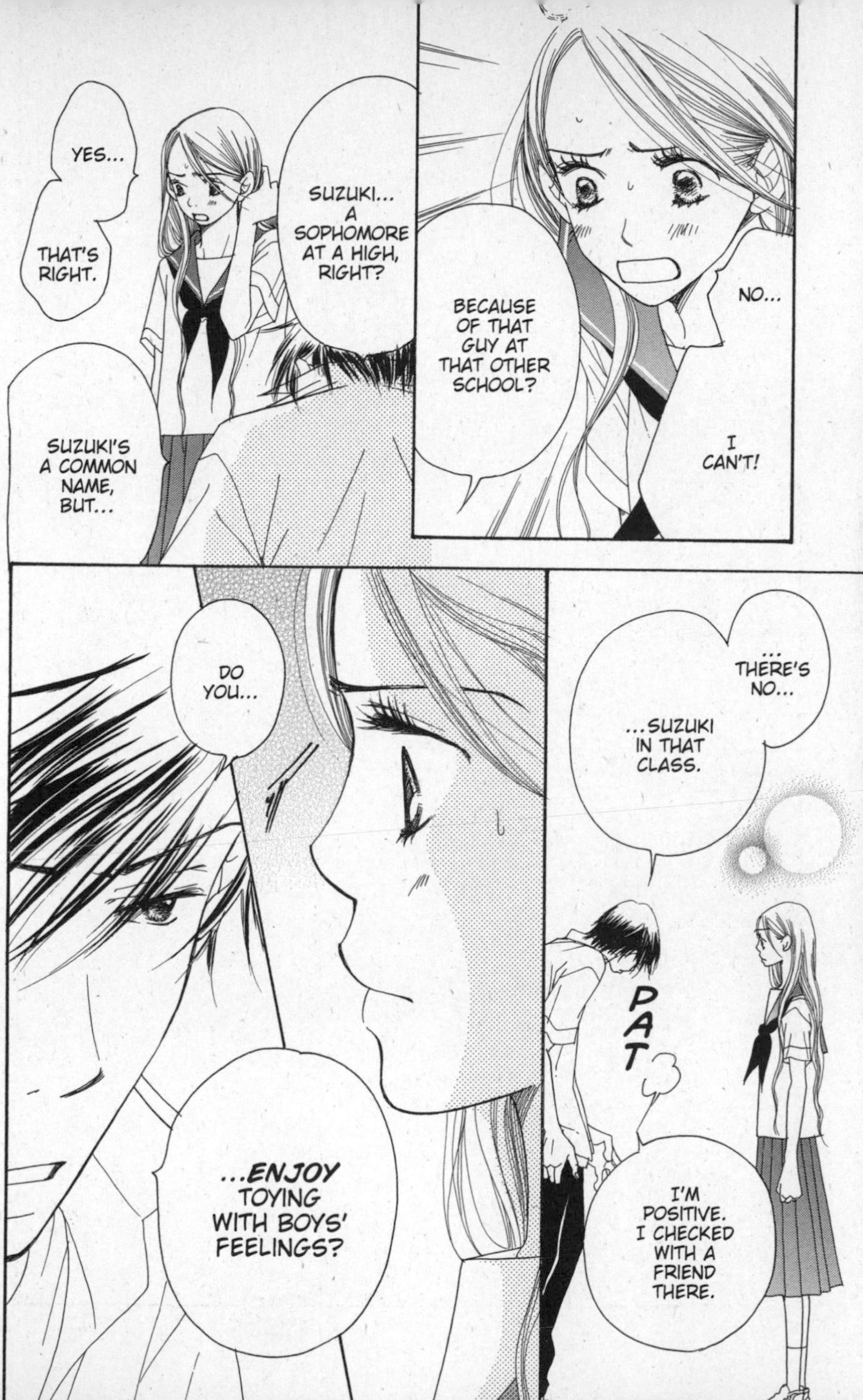
NO...
BECAUSE OF THAT GUY AT THAT OTHER SCHOOL?
I CAN'T!
SUZUKI... A SOPHOMORE AT A HIGH, RIGHT?
YES...
THAT'S RIGHT.
SUZUKI'S A COMMON NAME, BUT...
... THERE'S NO...
...SUZUKI IN THAT CLASS.
PAT
I'M POSITIVE. I CHECKED WITH A FRIEND THERE.
DO YOU...
...*ENJOY* TOYING WITH BOYS' FEELINGS?

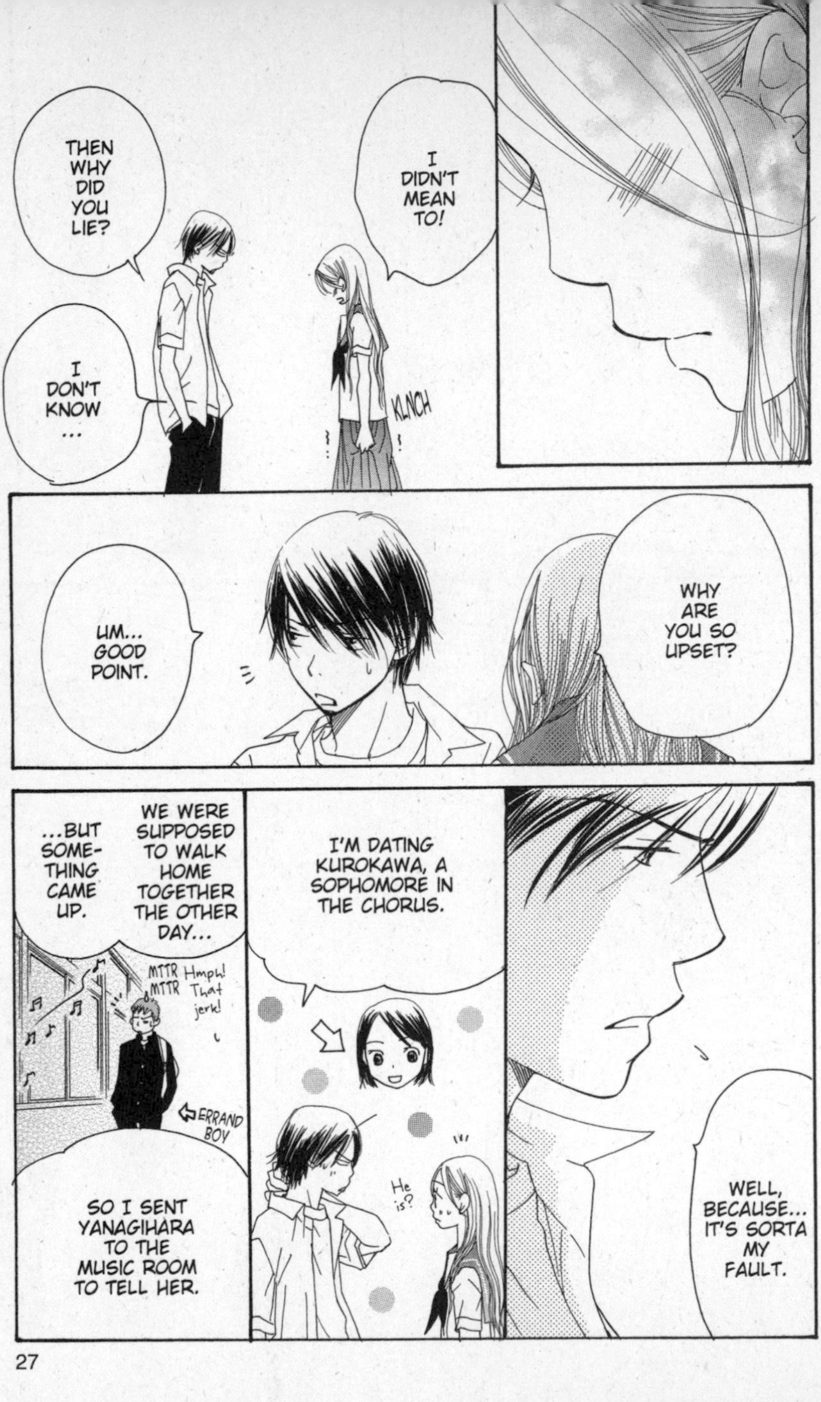
I DIDN'T MEAN TO!
THEN WHY DID YOU LIE?
KLNCH
I DON'T KNOW ...
WHY ARE YOU SO UPSET?
UM... GOOD POINT.
WELL, BECAUSE... IT'S SORTA MY FAULT.
I'M DATING KUROKAWA, A SOPHOMORE IN THE CHORUS.
He is?
WE WERE SUPPOSED TO WALK HOME TOGETHER THE OTHER DAY...
...BUT SOMETHING CAME UP.
MTTR MTTR
Hmph! That jerk!
ERRAND BOY
SO I SENT YANAGIHARA TO THE MUSIC ROOM TO TELL HER.

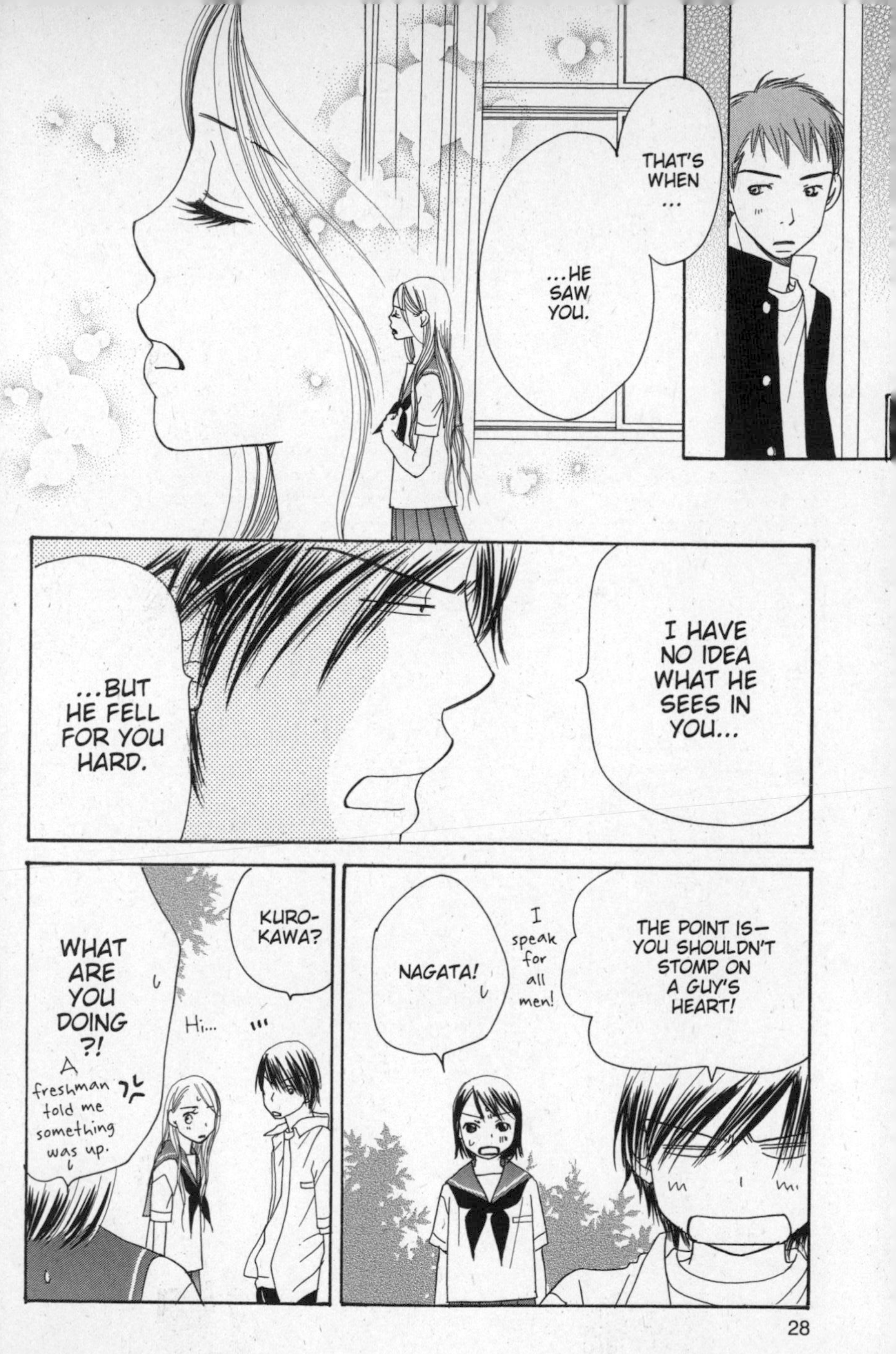
THAT'S WHEN ...
...HE SAW YOU.
I HAVE NO IDEA WHAT HE SEES IN YOU...
...BUT HE FELL FOR YOU HARD.
THE POINT IS— YOU SHOULDN'T STOMP ON A GUY'S HEART!
I speak for all men!
NAGATA!
KURO-KAWA?
WHAT ARE YOU DOING ?!
A freshman told me something was up.
Hi...

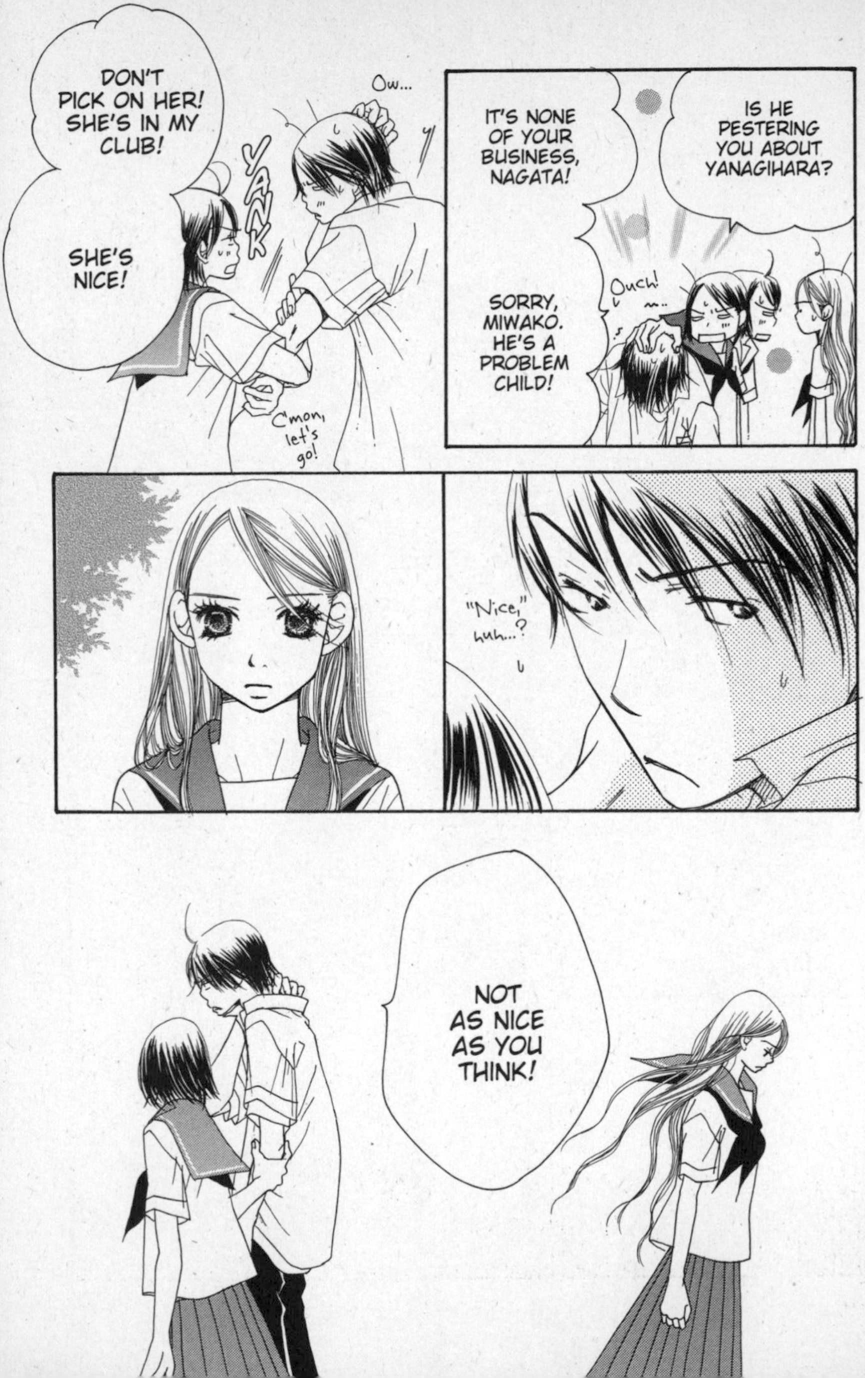

IS HE PESTERING YOU ABOUT YANAGIHARA?
IT'S NONE OF YOUR BUSINESS, NAGATA!
Ouch!
SORRY, MIWAKO. HE'S A PROBLEM CHILD!
Ow...
YANK
DON'T PICK ON HER! SHE'S IN MY CLUB!
SHE'S NICE!
C'mon, let's go!
"Nice," huh...?
NOT AS NICE AS YOU THINK!

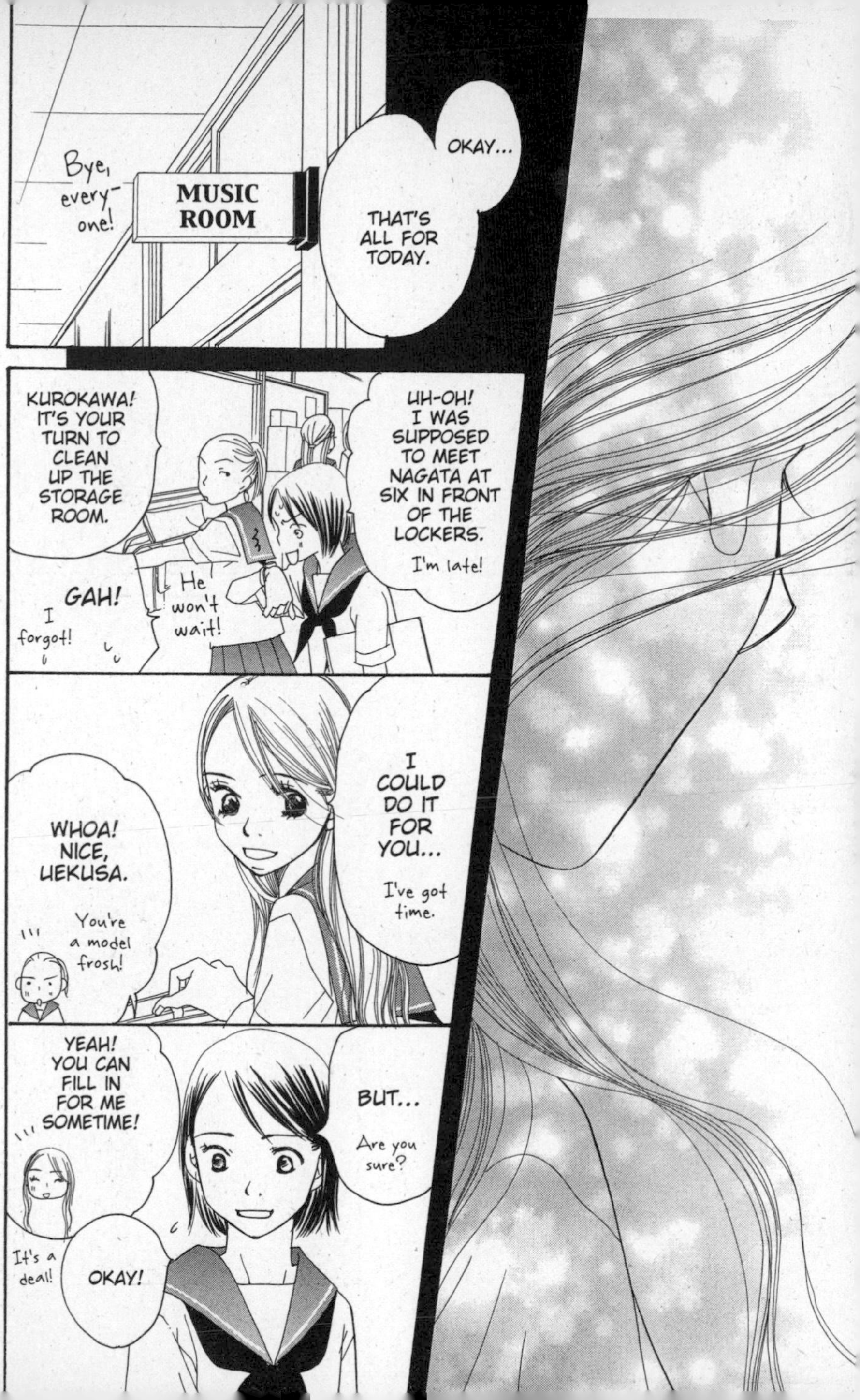
OKAY...
THAT'S ALL FOR TODAY.
MUSIC ROOM
Bye, every-one!
UH-OH! I WAS SUPPOSED TO MEET NAGATA AT SIX IN FRONT OF THE LOCKERS.
I'm late!
KUROKAWA! IT'S YOUR TURN TO CLEAN UP THE STORAGE ROOM.
He won't wait!
GAH!
I forgot!
I COULD DO IT FOR YOU...
I've got time.
WHOA! NICE, UEKUSA.
You're a model frosh!
BUT...
Are you sure?
YEAH! YOU CAN FILL IN FOR ME SOMETIME!
OKAY!
It's a deal!

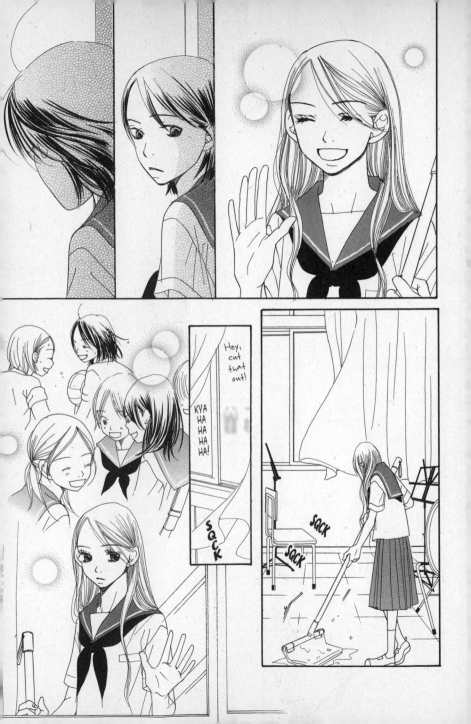

Hey, cut that out!

KYA HA HA HA HA!

SQCK

SQCK

SQCK

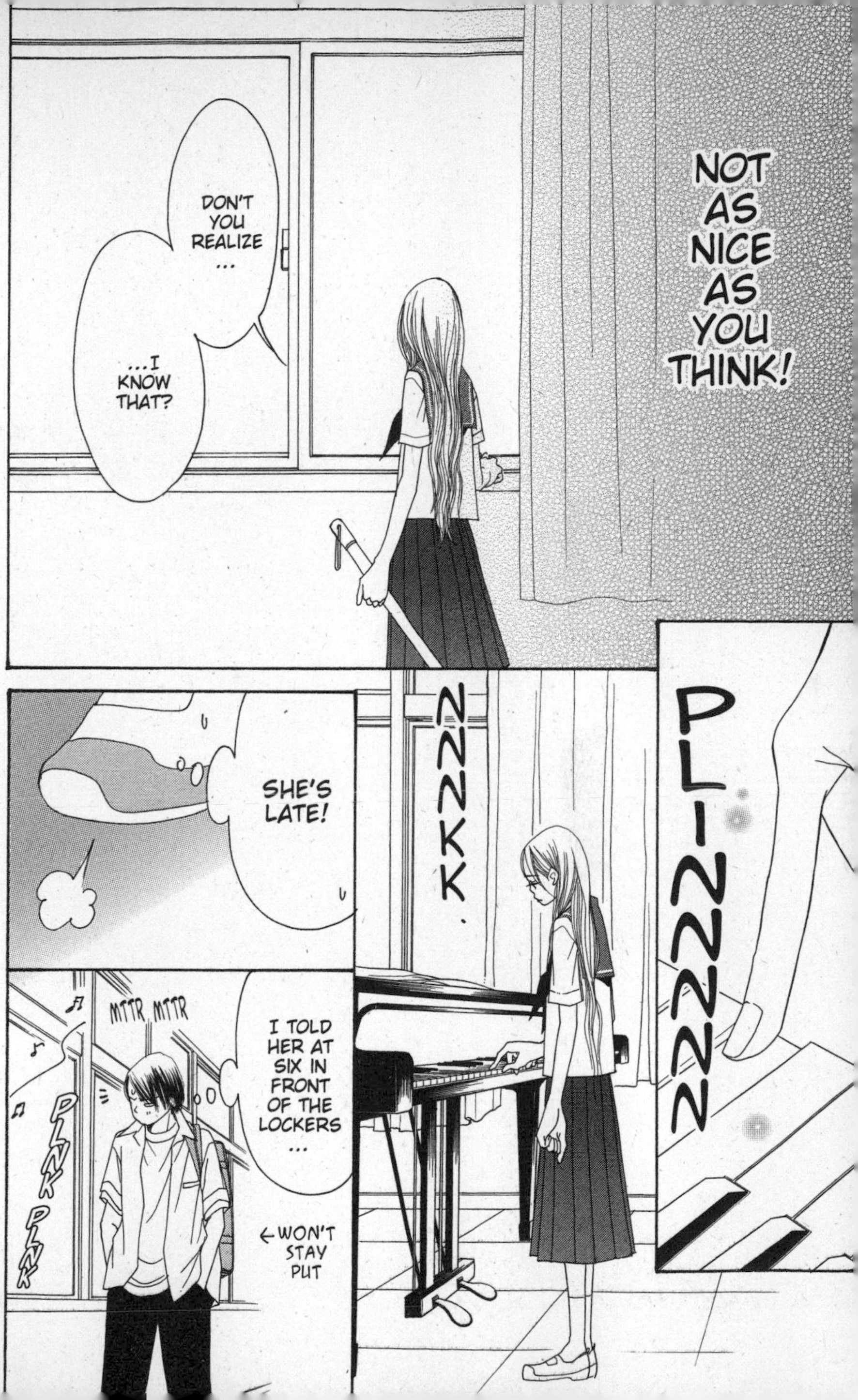
NOT AS NICE AS YOU THINK!
DON'T YOU REALIZE...
...I KNOW THAT?
PLINNNN
NNNKK
SHE'S LATE!
I TOLD HER AT SIX IN FRONT OF THE LOCKERS...
MTTR MTTR
PLINK PLINK
←WON'T STAY PUT

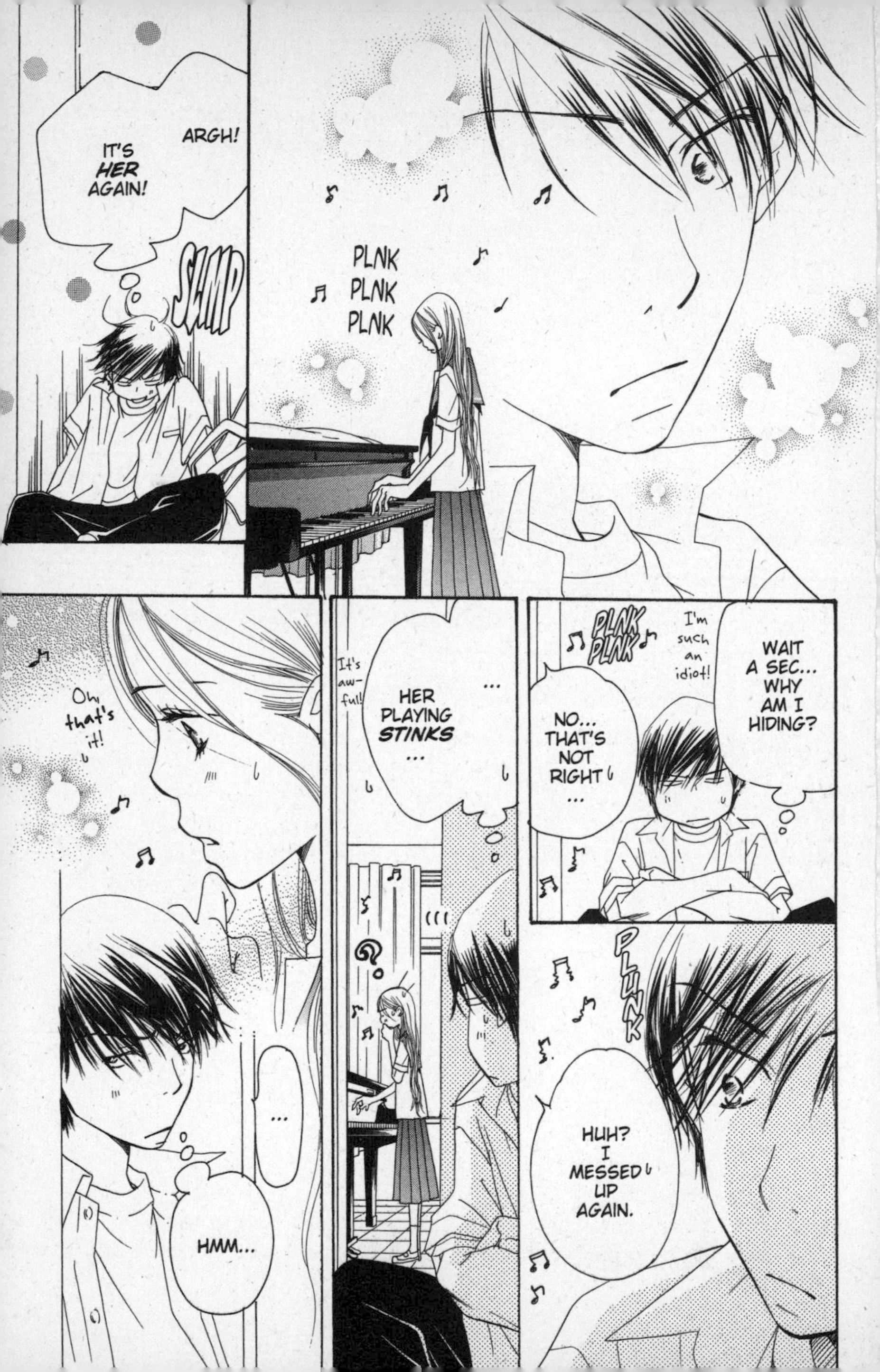
PLNK PLNK PLNK
ARGH!
IT'S HER AGAIN!
SLUMP
WAIT A SEC... WHY AM I HIDING?
I'm such an idiot!
PLNK PLNK
NO... THAT'S NOT RIGHT...
PLUNK
HUH? I MESSED UP AGAIN.
HER PLAYING STINKS...
...
It's awful!
Oh that's it!
...
HMM...

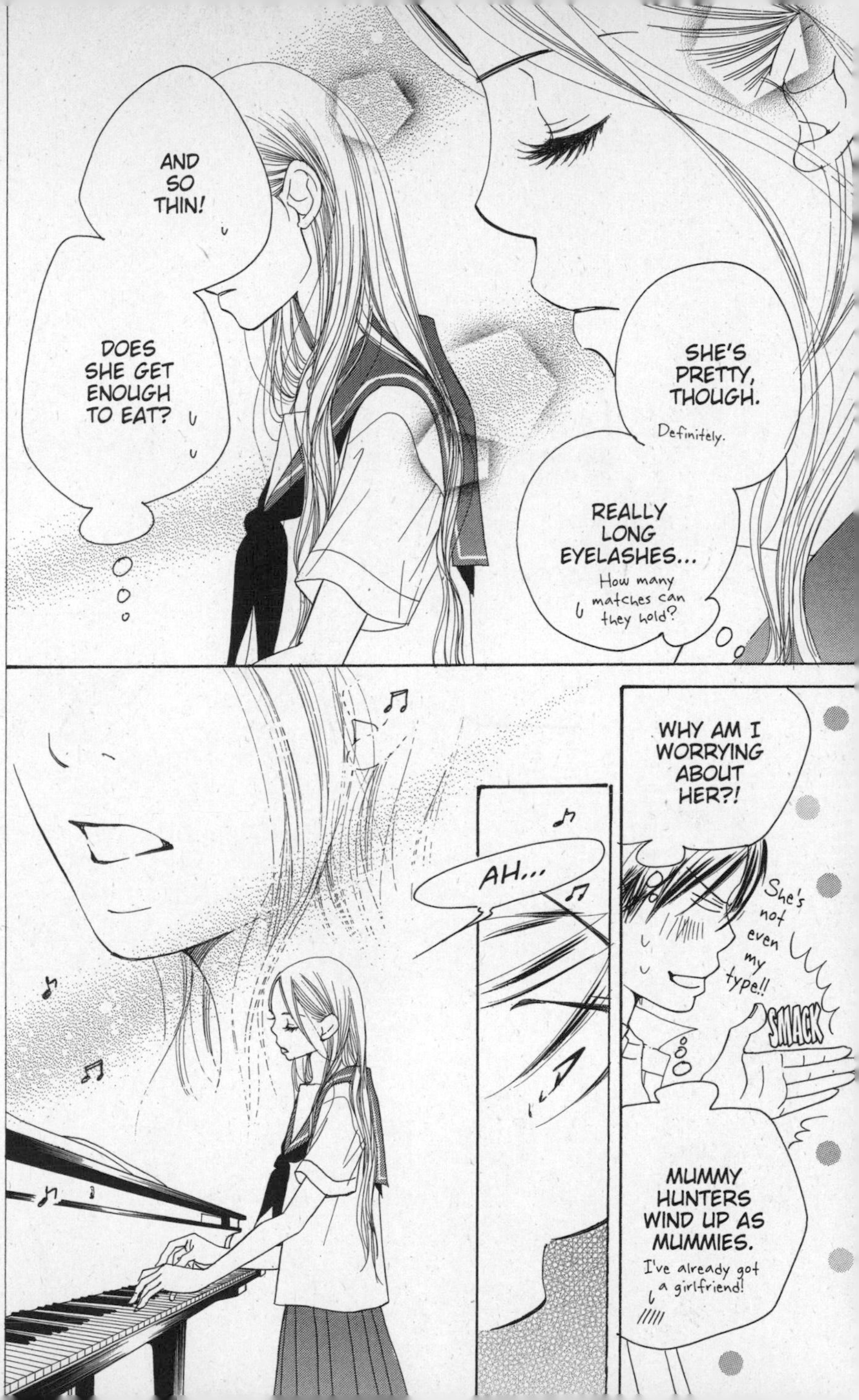
SHE'S PRETTY, THOUGH.
Definitely.
REALLY LONG EYELASHES...
How many matches can they hold?
AND SO THIN!
DOES SHE GET ENOUGH TO EAT?
WHY AM I WORRYING ABOUT HER?!
She's not even my type!!
SMACK
MUMMY HUNTERS WIND UP AS MUMMIES.
I've already got a girlfriend!
AH...

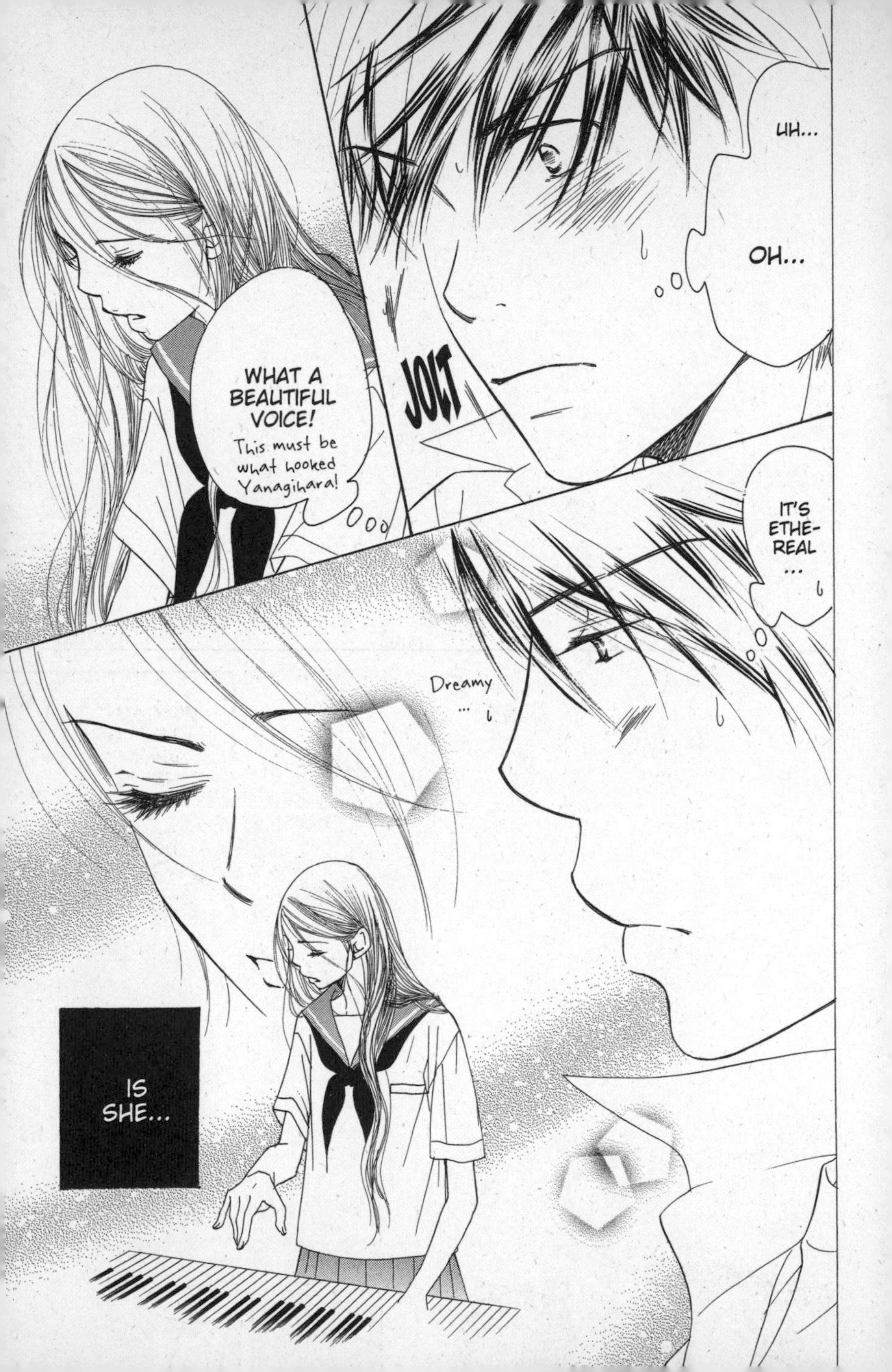
UH...
OH...
JOLT
WHAT A BEAUTIFUL VOICE!
This must be what hooked Yanagihara!
IT'S ETHEREAL...
Dreamy...
IS SHE...

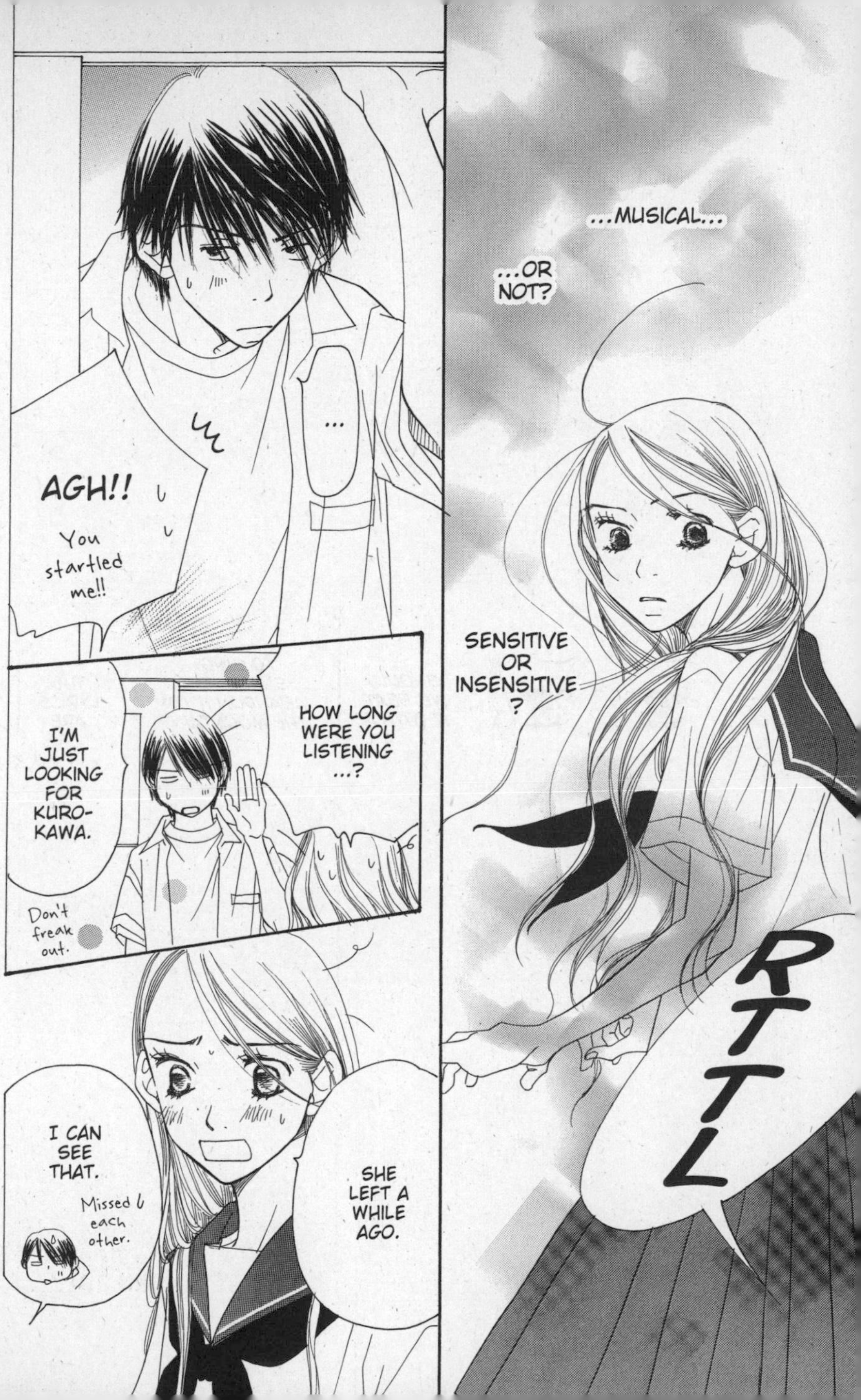
...MUSICAL...
...OR NOT?
SENSITIVE OR INSENSITIVE?
RTTL
...
AGH!!
You startled me!!
HOW LONG WERE YOU LISTENING ...?
I'M JUST LOOKING FOR KURO-KAWA.
Don't freak out.
SHE LEFT A WHILE AGO.
I CAN SEE THAT.
Missed each other.

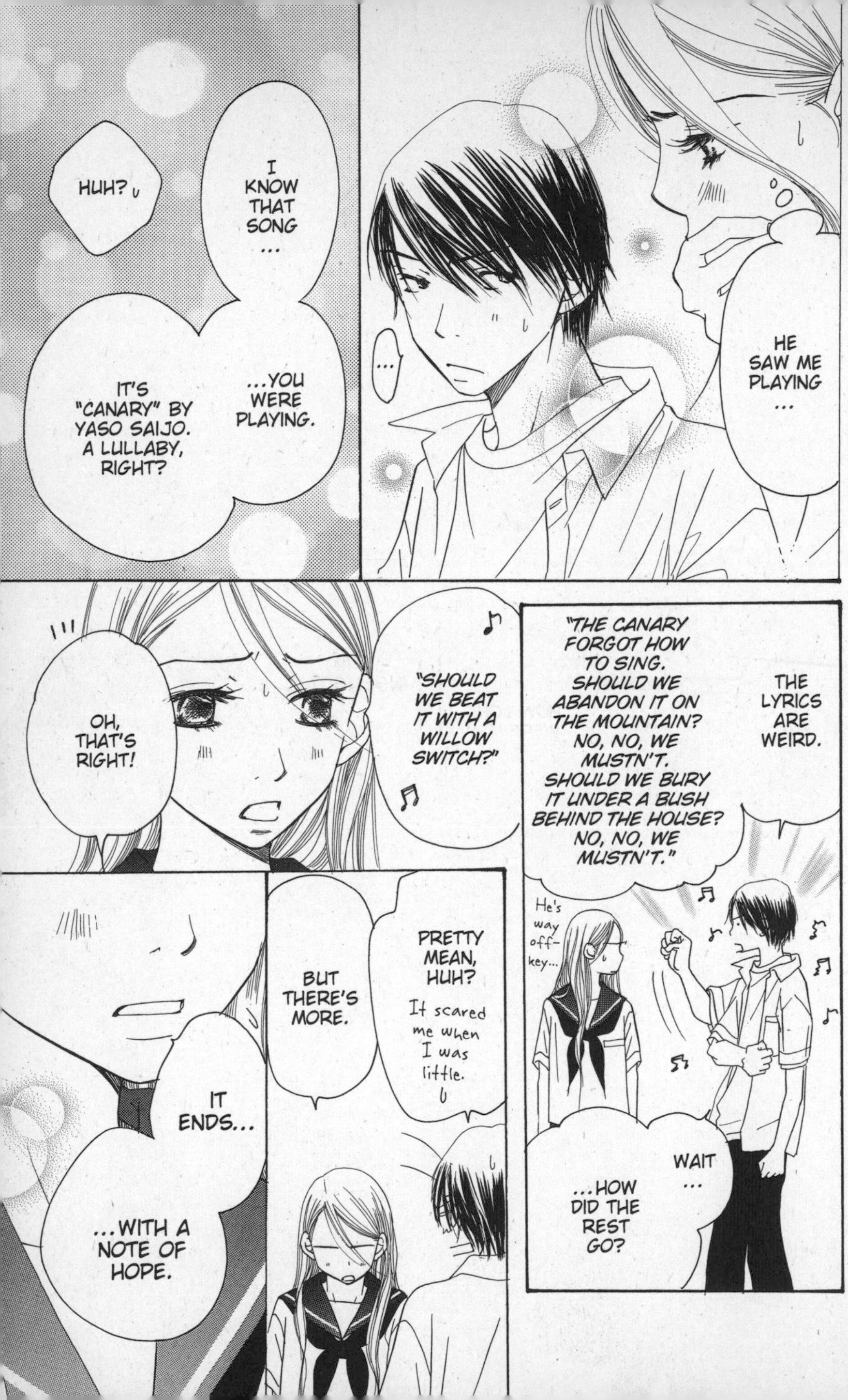
HE SAW ME PLAYING ...
...
I KNOW THAT SONG ...
...YOU WERE PLAYING.
HUH?
IT'S "CANARY" BY YASO SAIJO. A LULLABY, RIGHT?
THE LYRICS ARE WEIRD.
"THE CANARY FORGOT HOW TO SING. SHOULD WE ABANDON IT ON THE MOUNTAIN? NO, NO, WE MUSTN'T. SHOULD WE BURY IT UNDER A BUSH BEHIND THE HOUSE? NO, NO, WE MUSTN'T."
He's way off-key...
WAIT ...
...HOW DID THE REST GO?
"SHOULD WE BEAT IT WITH A WILLOW SWITCH?"
OH, THAT'S RIGHT!
PRETTY MEAN, HUH?
It scared me when I was little.
BUT THERE'S MORE.
IT ENDS...
...WITH A NOTE OF HOPE.

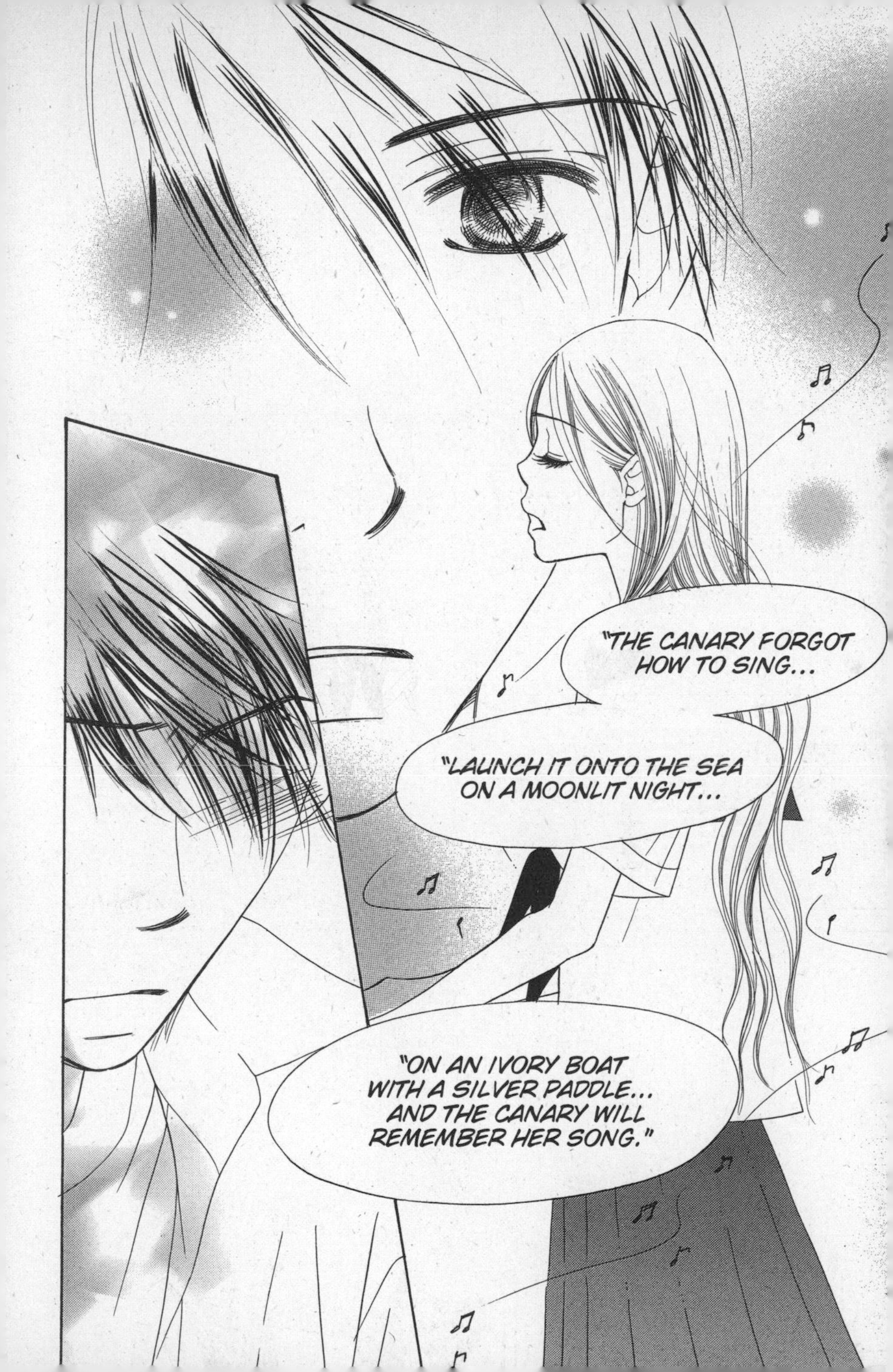
"THE CANARY FORGOT HOW TO SING...
"LAUNCH IT ONTO THE SEA ON A MOONLIT NIGHT...
"ON AN IVORY BOAT WITH A SILVER PADDLE... AND THE CANARY WILL REMEMBER HER SONG."

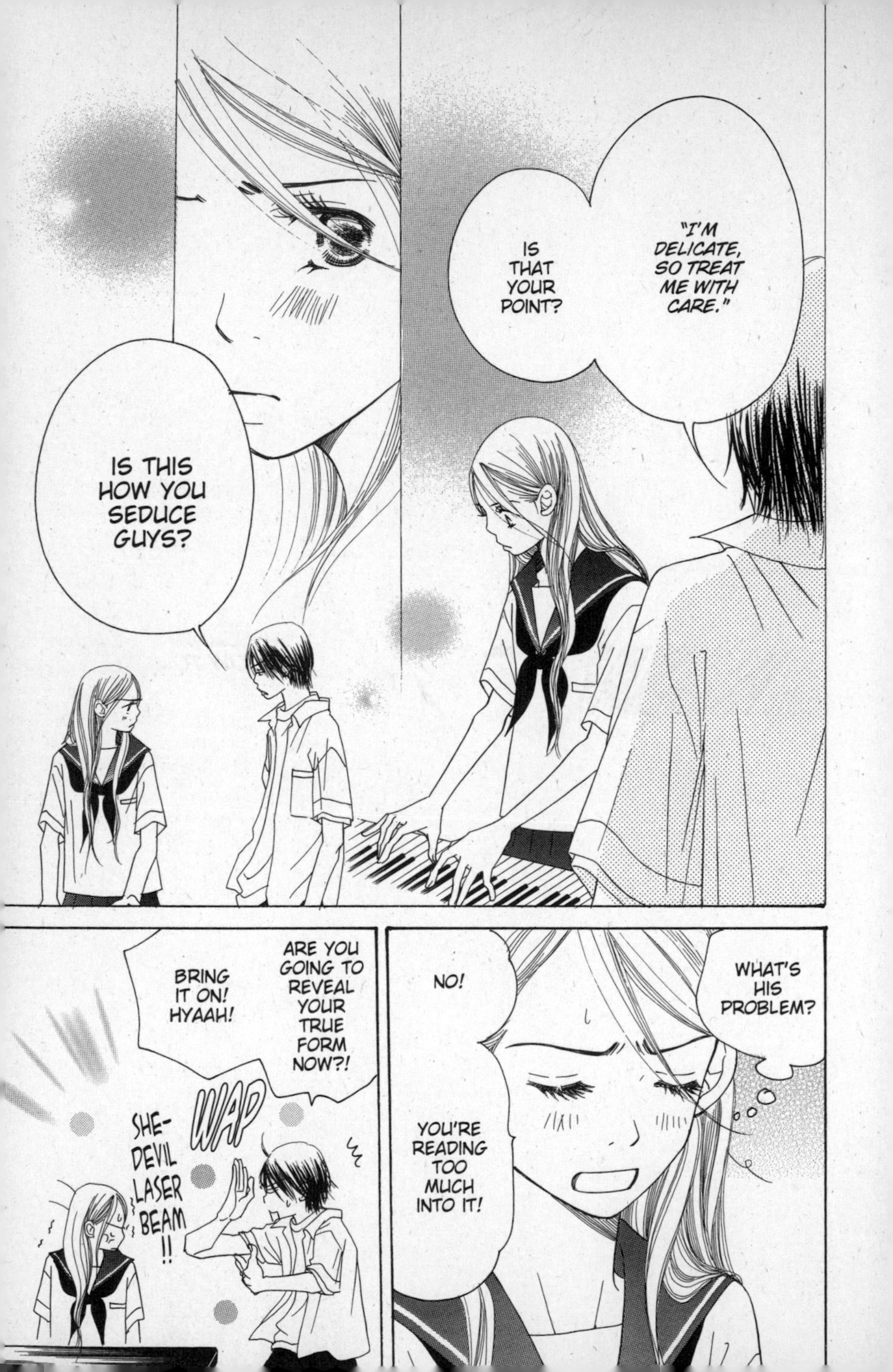
"I'M DELICATE, SO TREAT ME WITH CARE."
IS THAT YOUR POINT?
IS THIS HOW YOU SEDUCE GUYS?
WHAT'S HIS PROBLEM?
NO!
YOU'RE READING TOO MUCH INTO IT!
ARE YOU GOING TO REVEAL YOUR TRUE FORM NOW?!
BRING IT ON! HYAAH!
WAP
SHE-DEVIL LASER BEAM!!

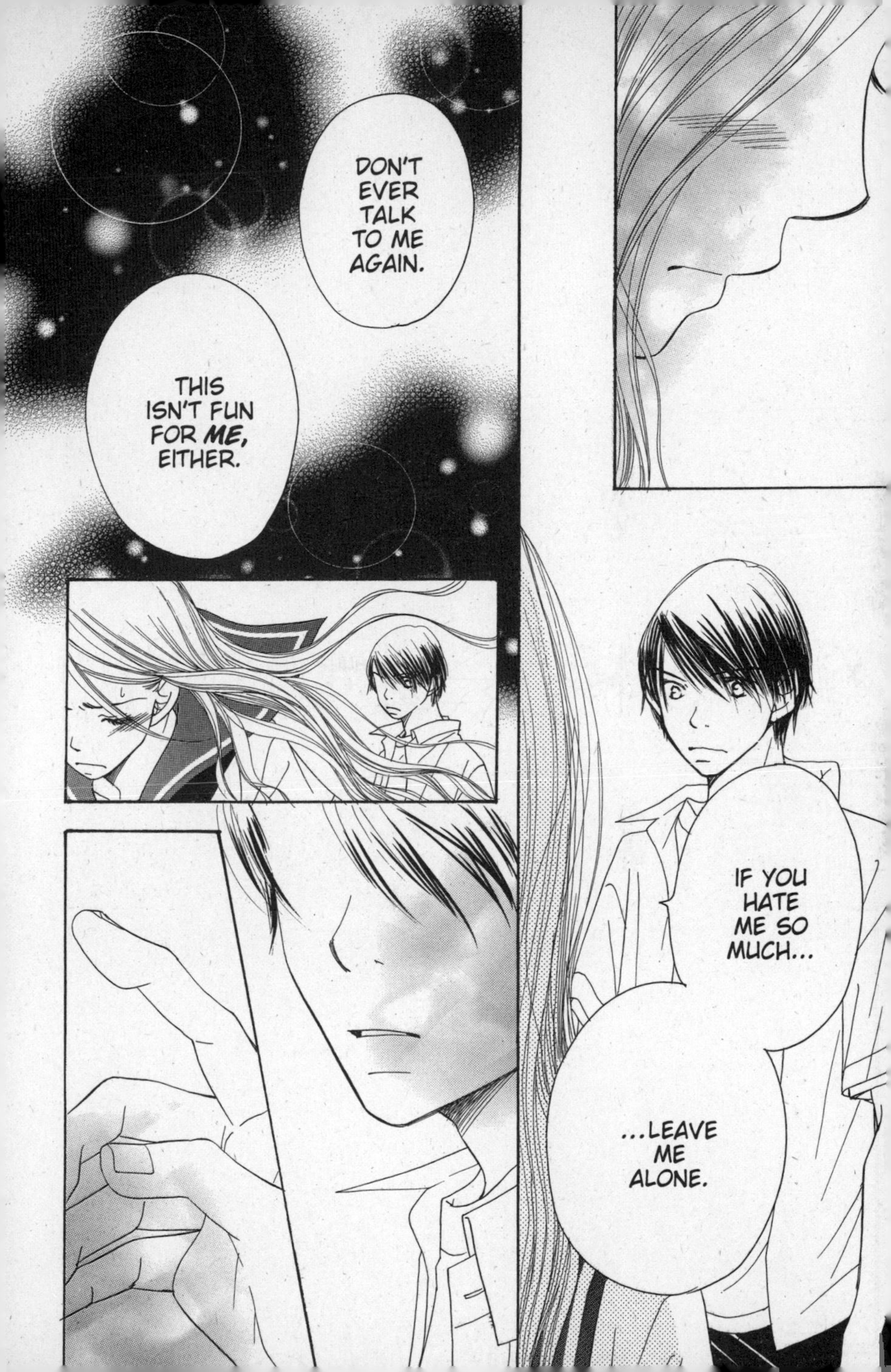
DON'T EVER TALK TO ME AGAIN.
THIS ISN'T FUN FOR *ME*, EITHER.
IF YOU HATE ME SO MUCH...
...LEAVE ME ALONE.

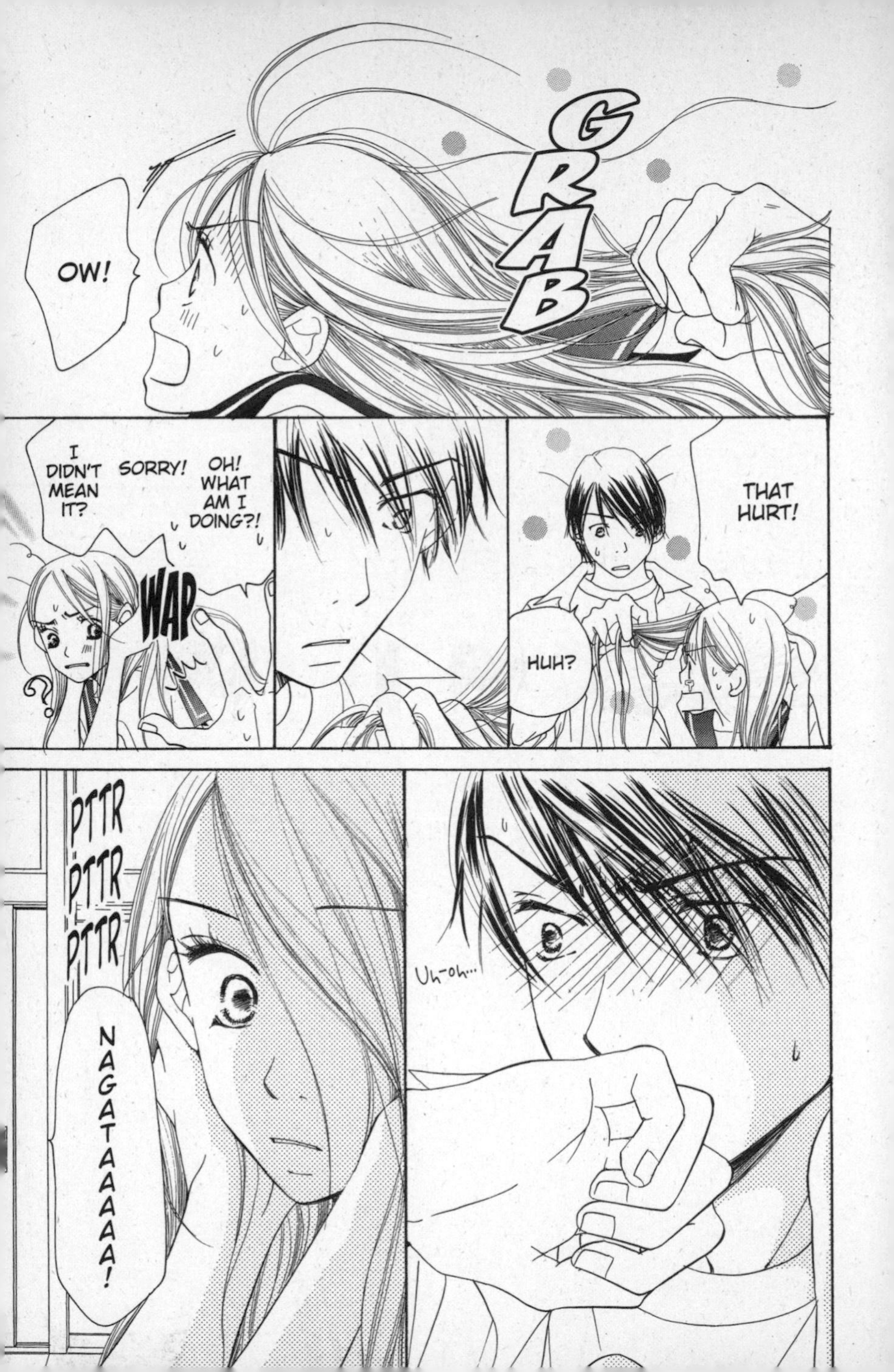
GRAB
OW!
THAT HURT!
HUH?
OH! WHAT AM I DOING?!
SORRY!
I DIDN'T MEAN IT?
WAP
Uh-oh...
PTTR PTTR PTTR
NAGATAAAAAA!

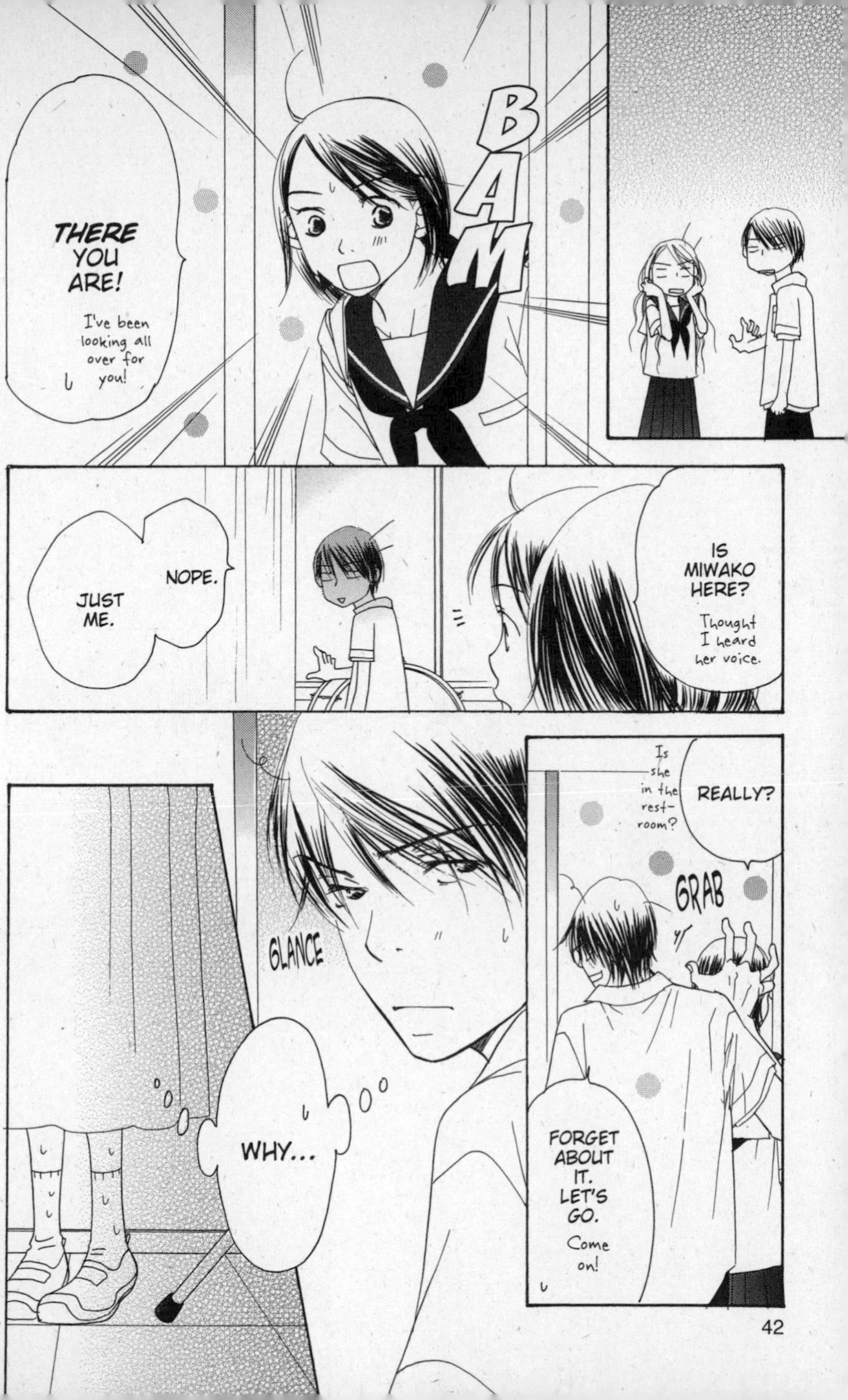
BAM
THERE YOU ARE!
I've been looking all over for you!
IS MIWAKO HERE?
Thought I heard her voice.
NOPE. JUST ME.
REALLY?
Is she in the rest-room?
GRAB
FORGET ABOUT IT. LET'S GO.
Come on!
GLANCE
WHY...

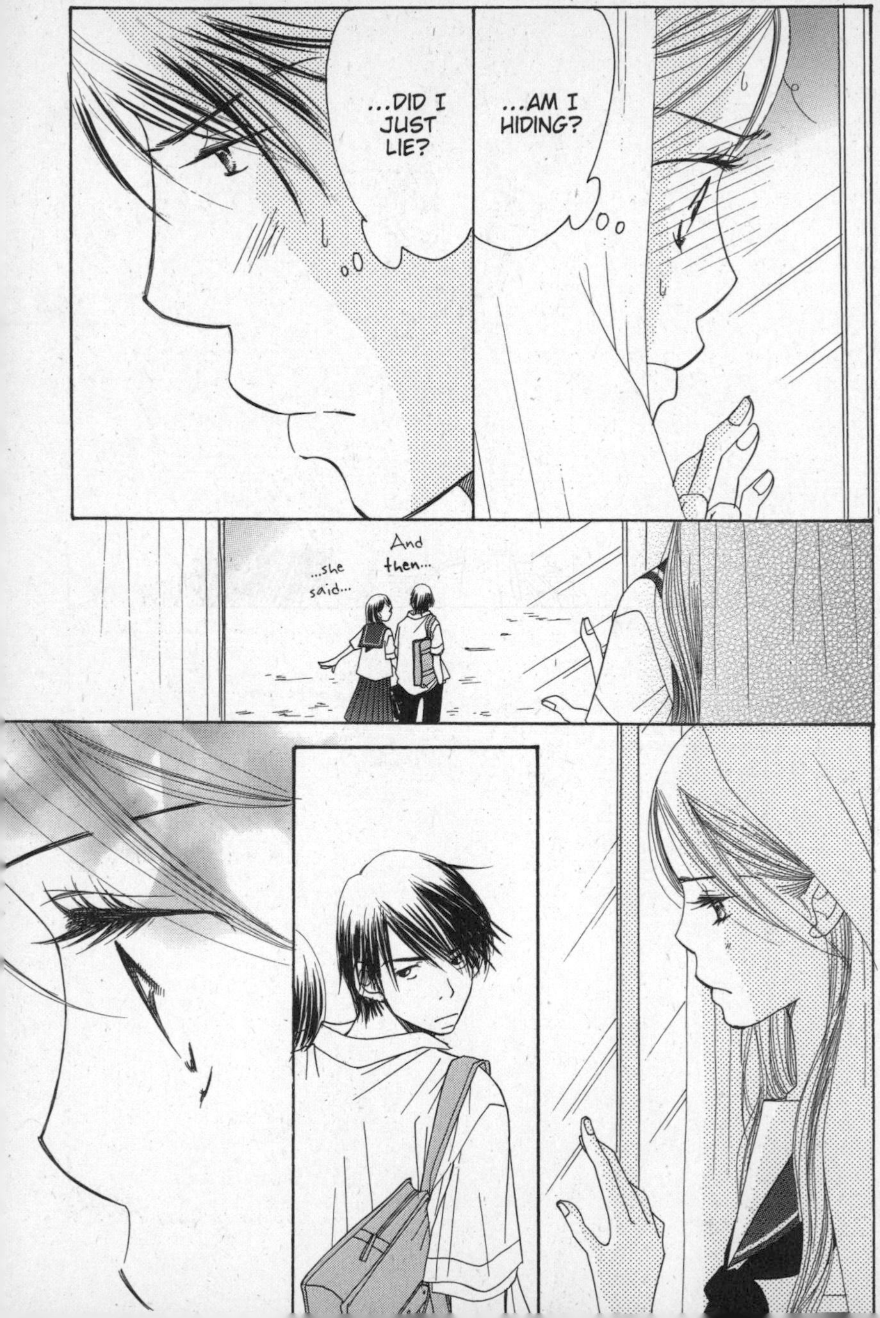
...AM I HIDING?
...DID I JUST LIE?
And then...
...she said...

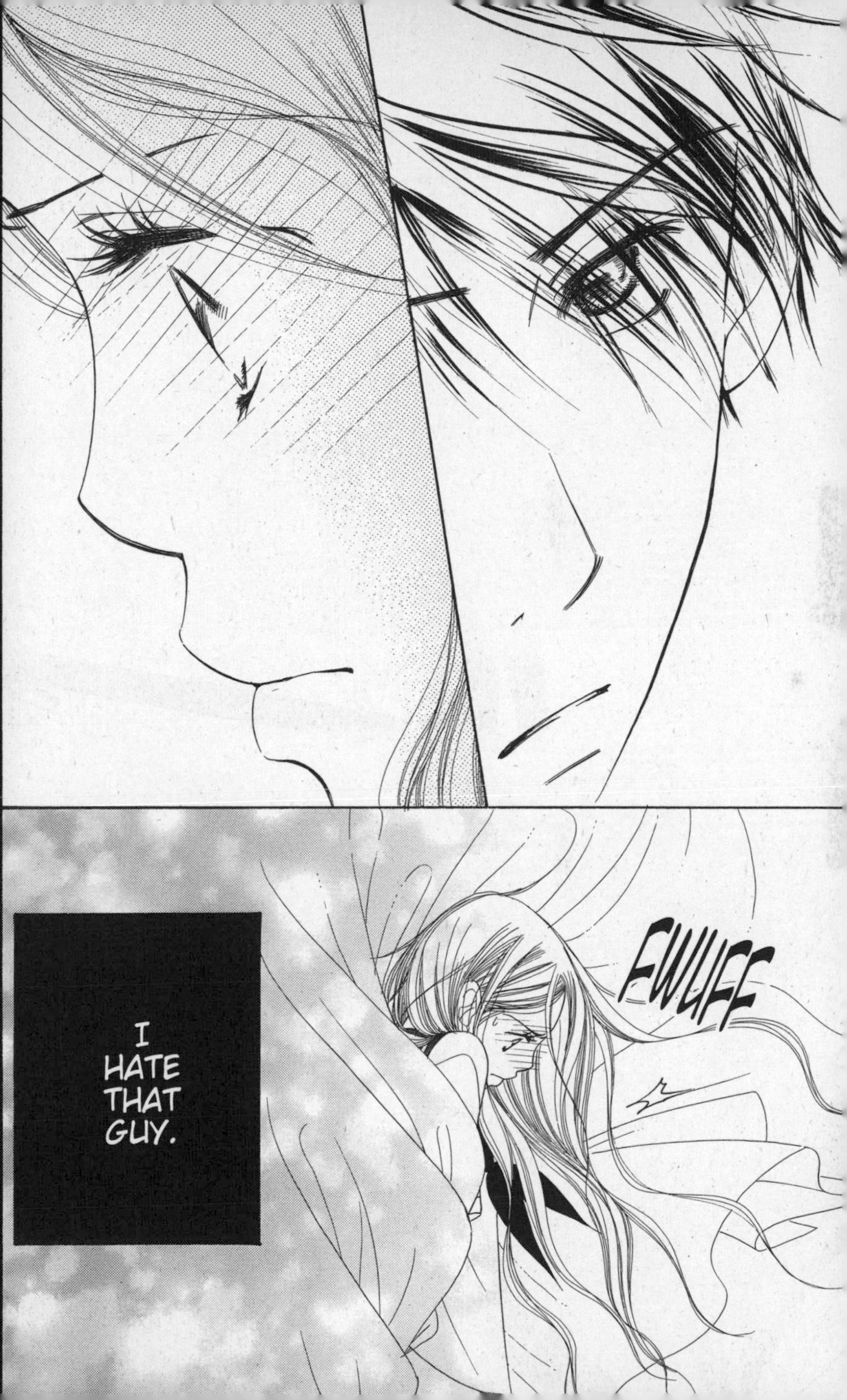
FWUFF
I HATE THAT GUY.

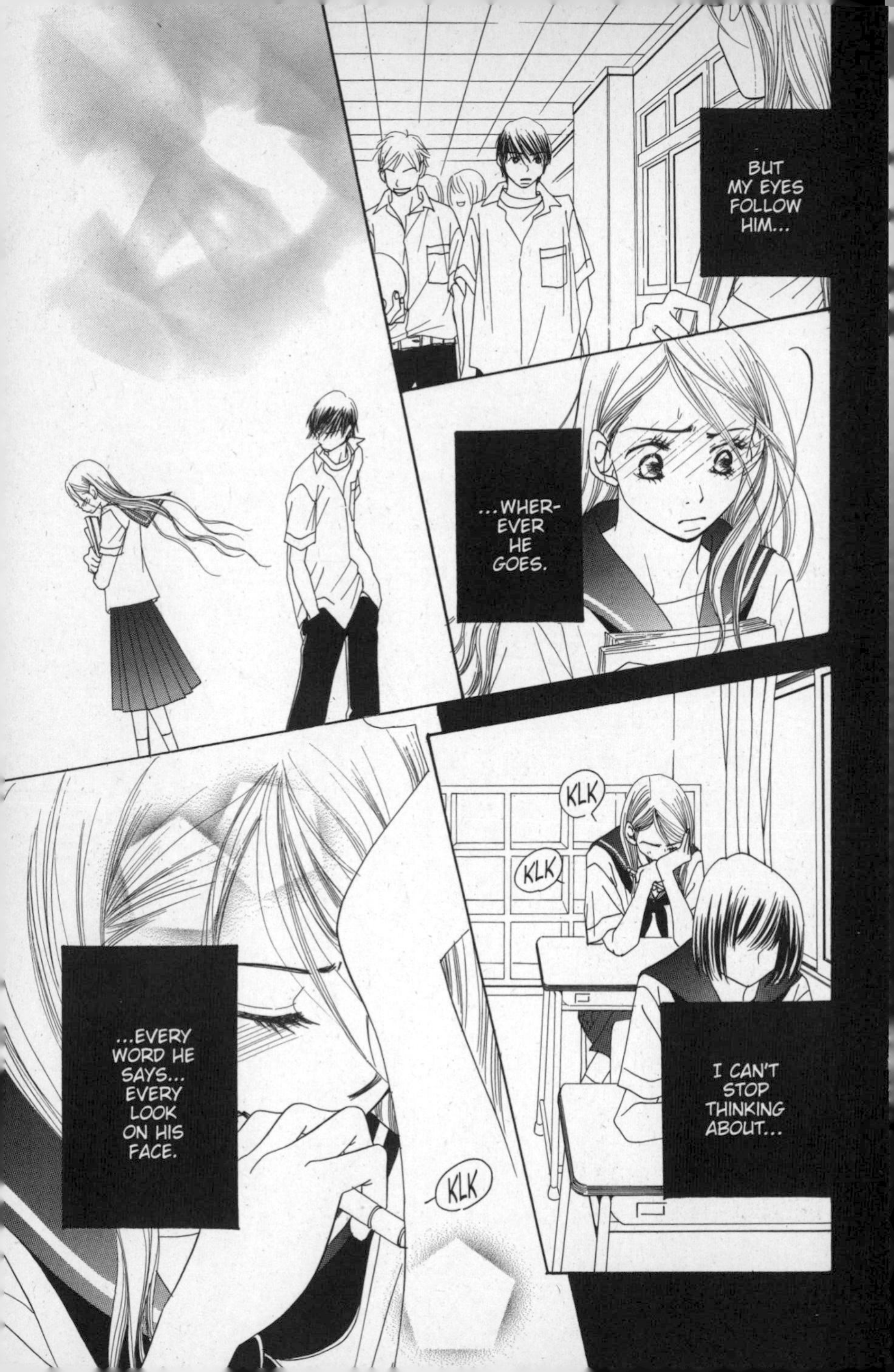
BUT MY EYES FOLLOW HIM...
...WHEREVER HE GOES.
KLK
KLK
I CAN'T STOP THINKING ABOUT...
...EVERY WORD HE SAYS... EVERY LOOK ON HIS FACE.
KLK

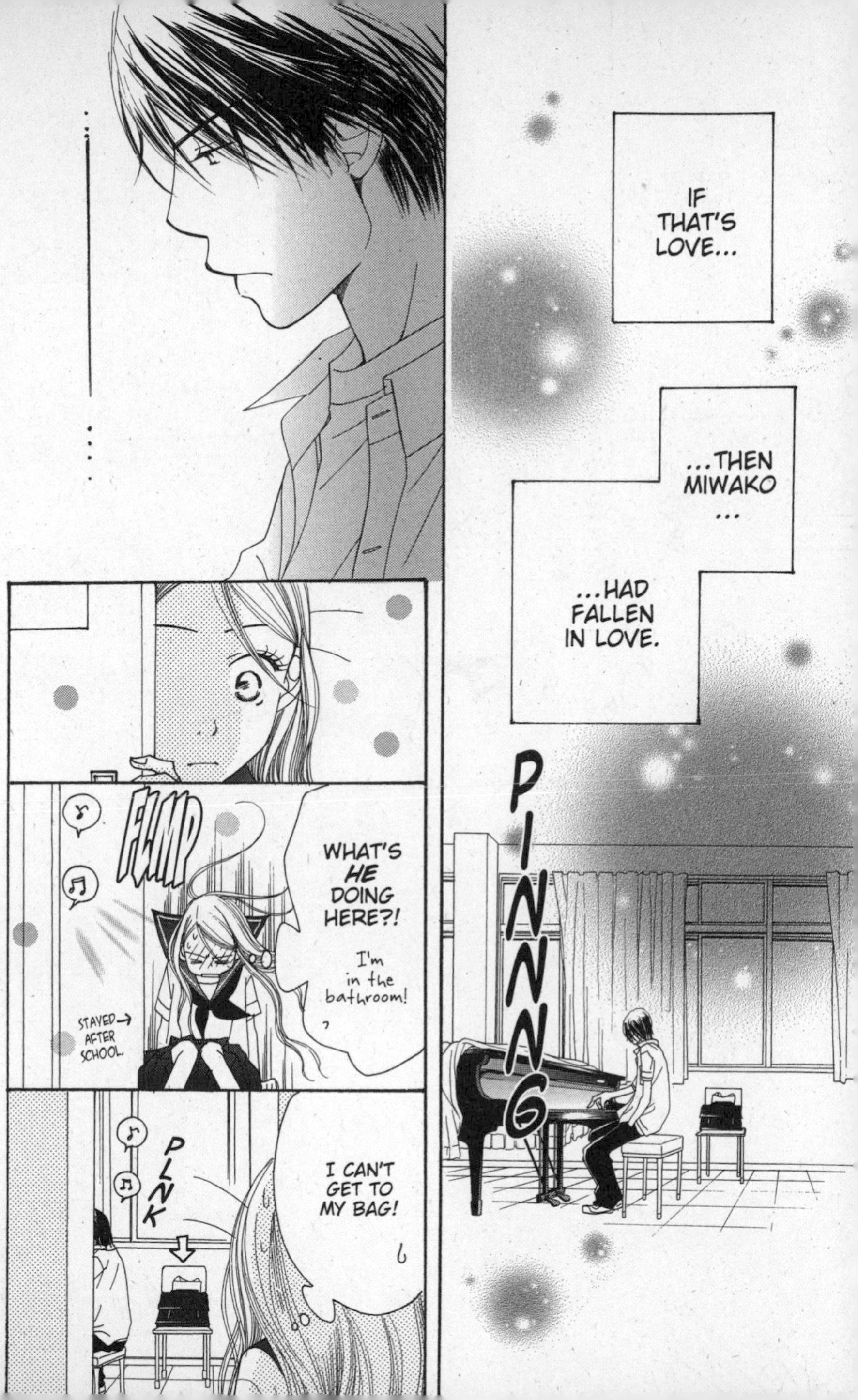
IF THAT'S LOVE...
...THEN MIWAKO ...
...HAD FALLEN IN LOVE.
PINNNG
FLMP
WHAT'S HE DOING HERE?!
I'm in the bathroom!
STAYED AFTER SCHOOL.
PLNK
I CAN'T GET TO MY BAG!

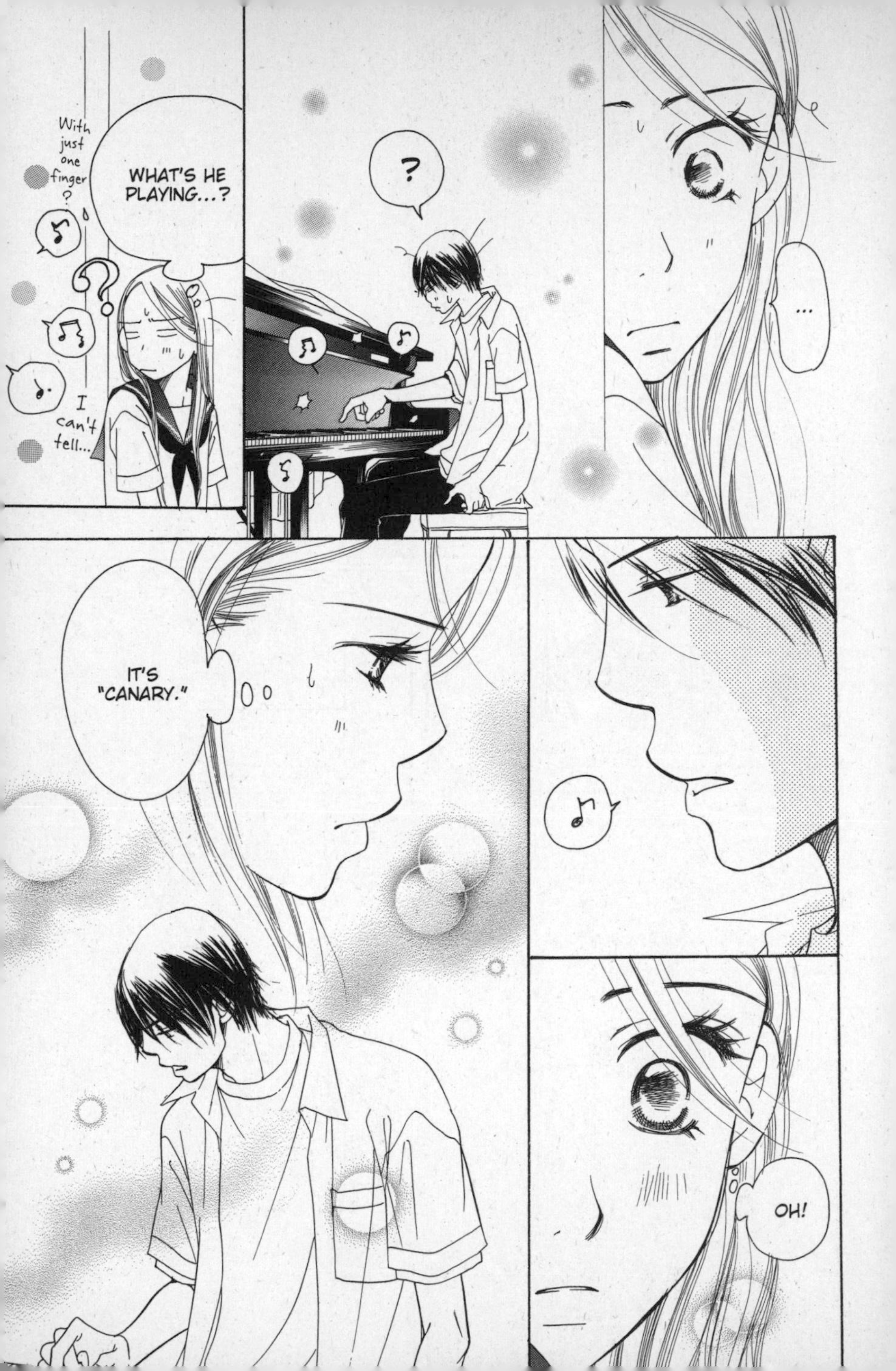
...
?
WHAT'S HE PLAYING...?
With just one finger?
I can't tell...
OH!
IT'S "CANARY."

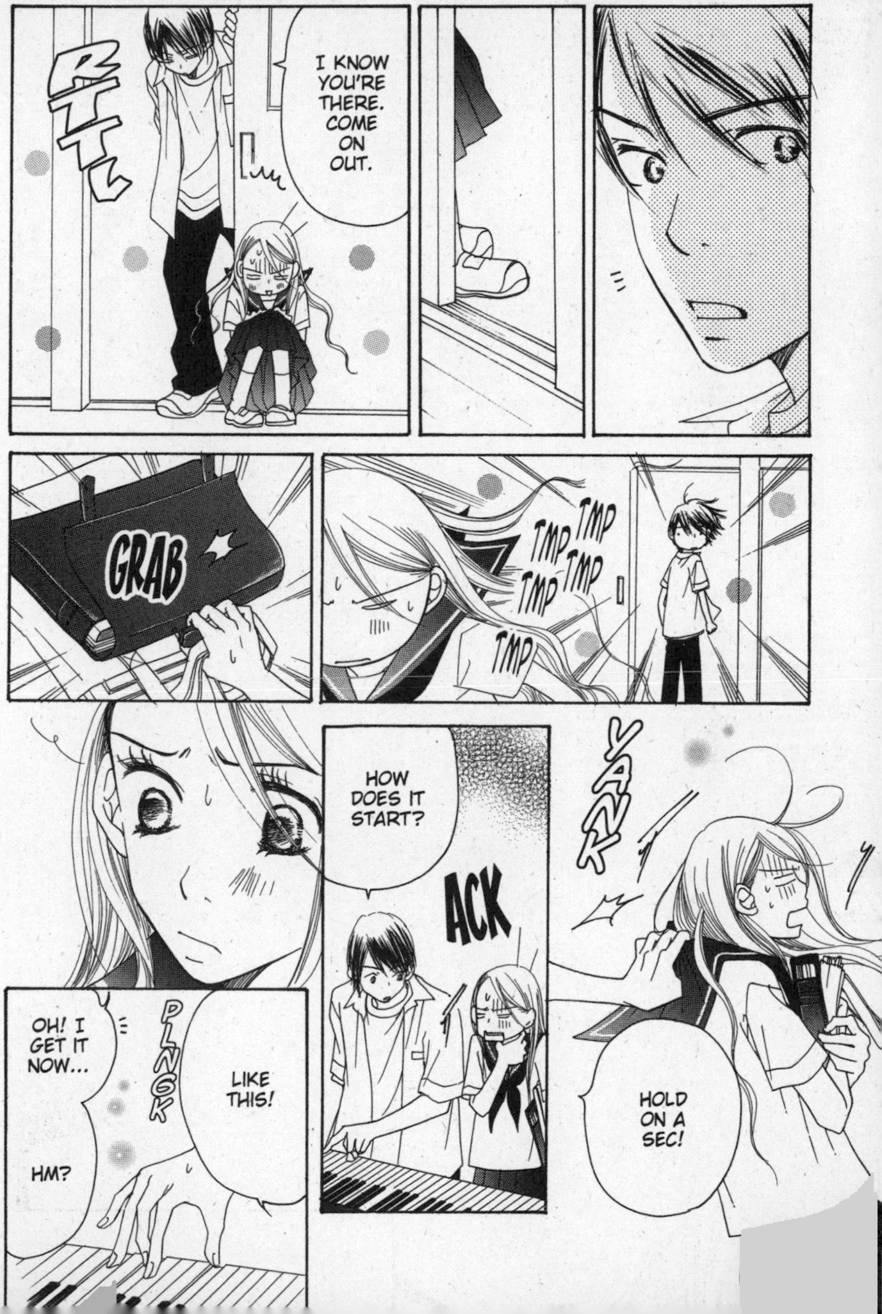
I KNOW YOU'RE THERE. COME ON OUT.
RITTL
TMP TMP TMP TMP TMP
GRAB
YANK
HOLD ON A SEC!
HOW DOES IT START?
ACK
LIKE THIS!
PLNGK
OH! I GET IT NOW...
HM?

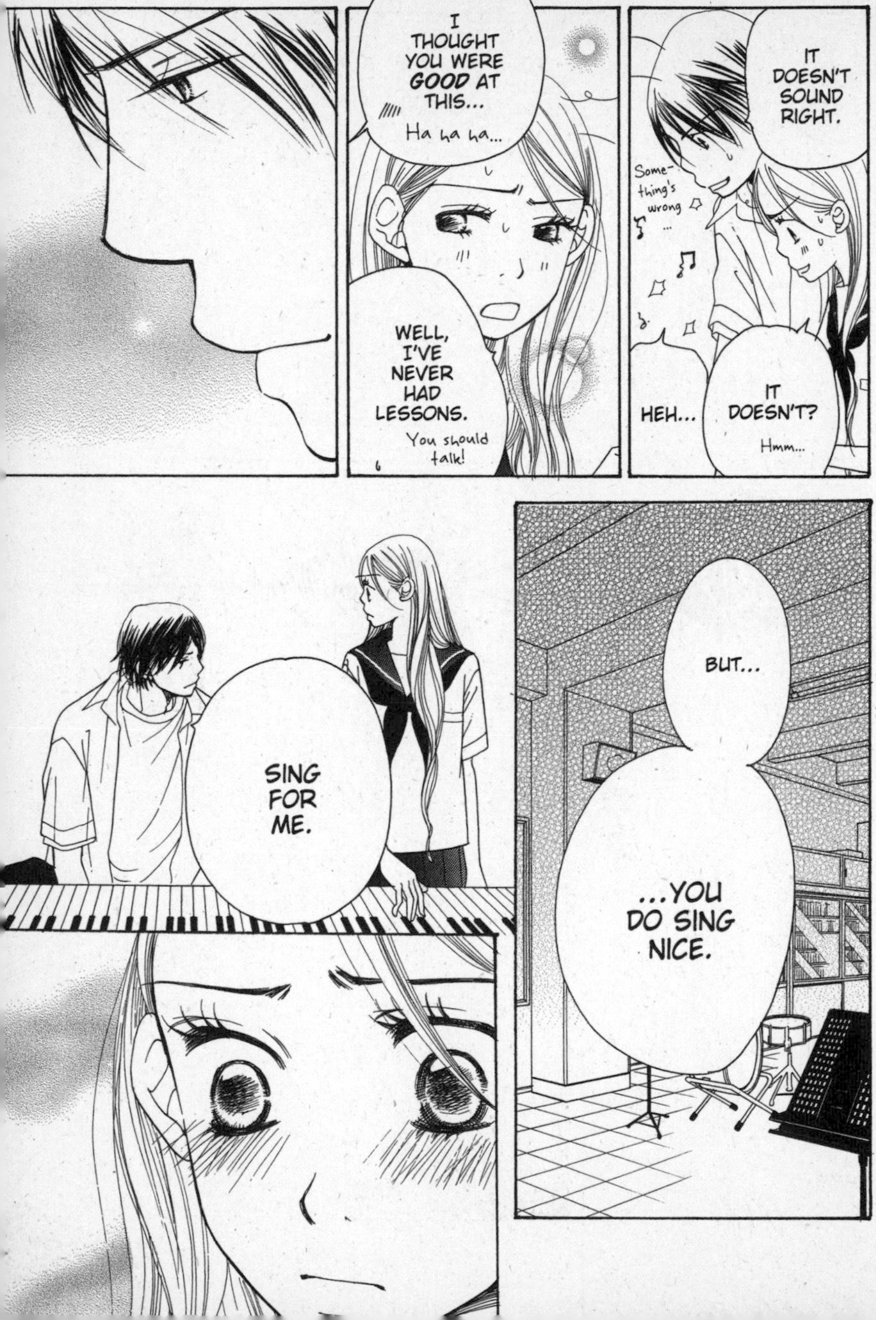
IT DOESN'T SOUND RIGHT.
Some-thing's wrong...
IT DOESN'T?
Hmm...
HEH...
I THOUGHT YOU WERE GOOD AT THIS...
Ha ha ha...
WELL, I'VE NEVER HAD LESSONS.
You should talk!
BUT...
...YOU DO SING NICE.
SING FOR ME.

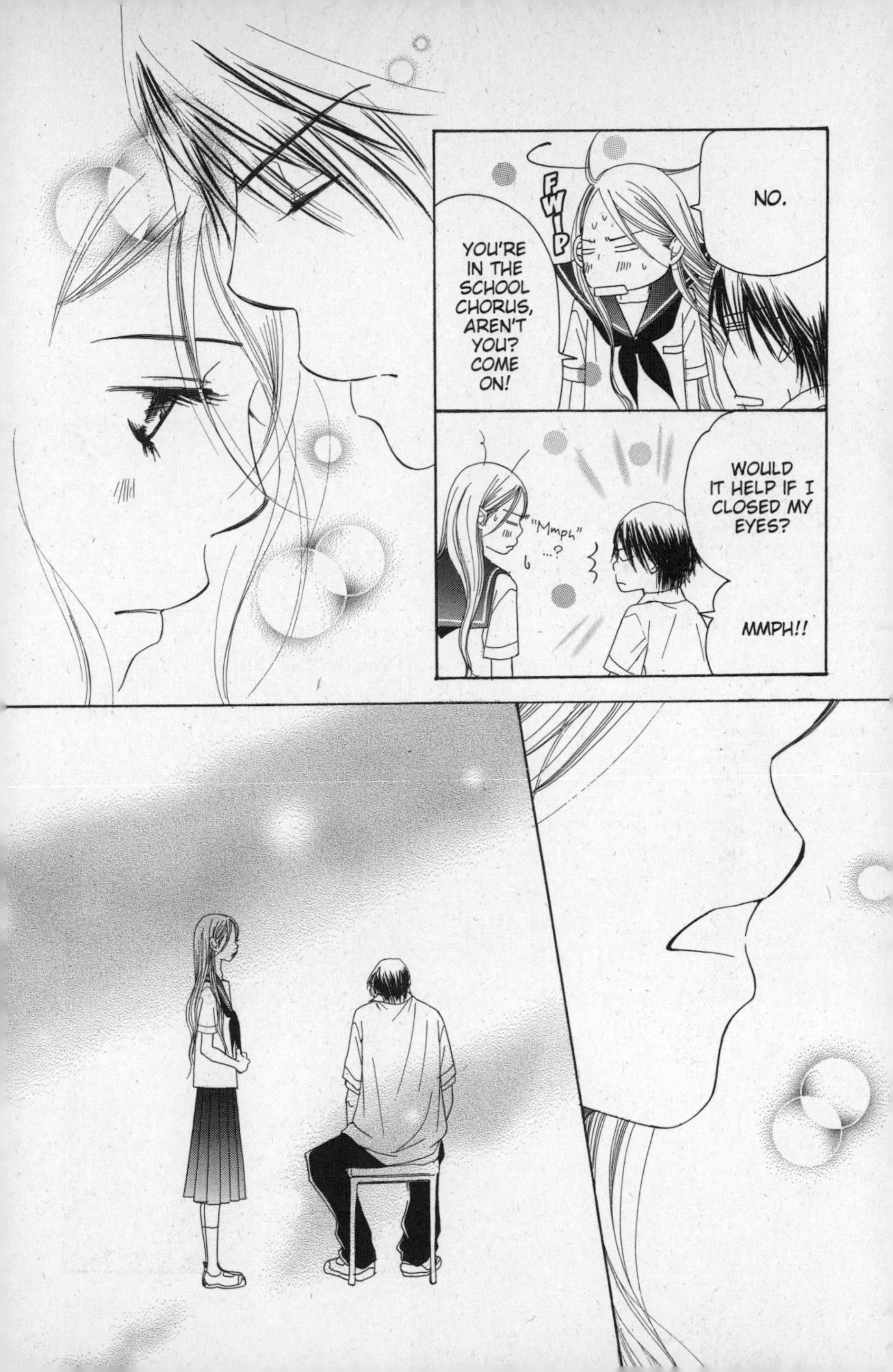
NO.
FWIP
YOU'RE IN THE SCHOOL CHORUS, AREN'T YOU? COME ON!
WOULD IT HELP IF I CLOSED MY EYES?
MMPH!!
"Mmph"
...?

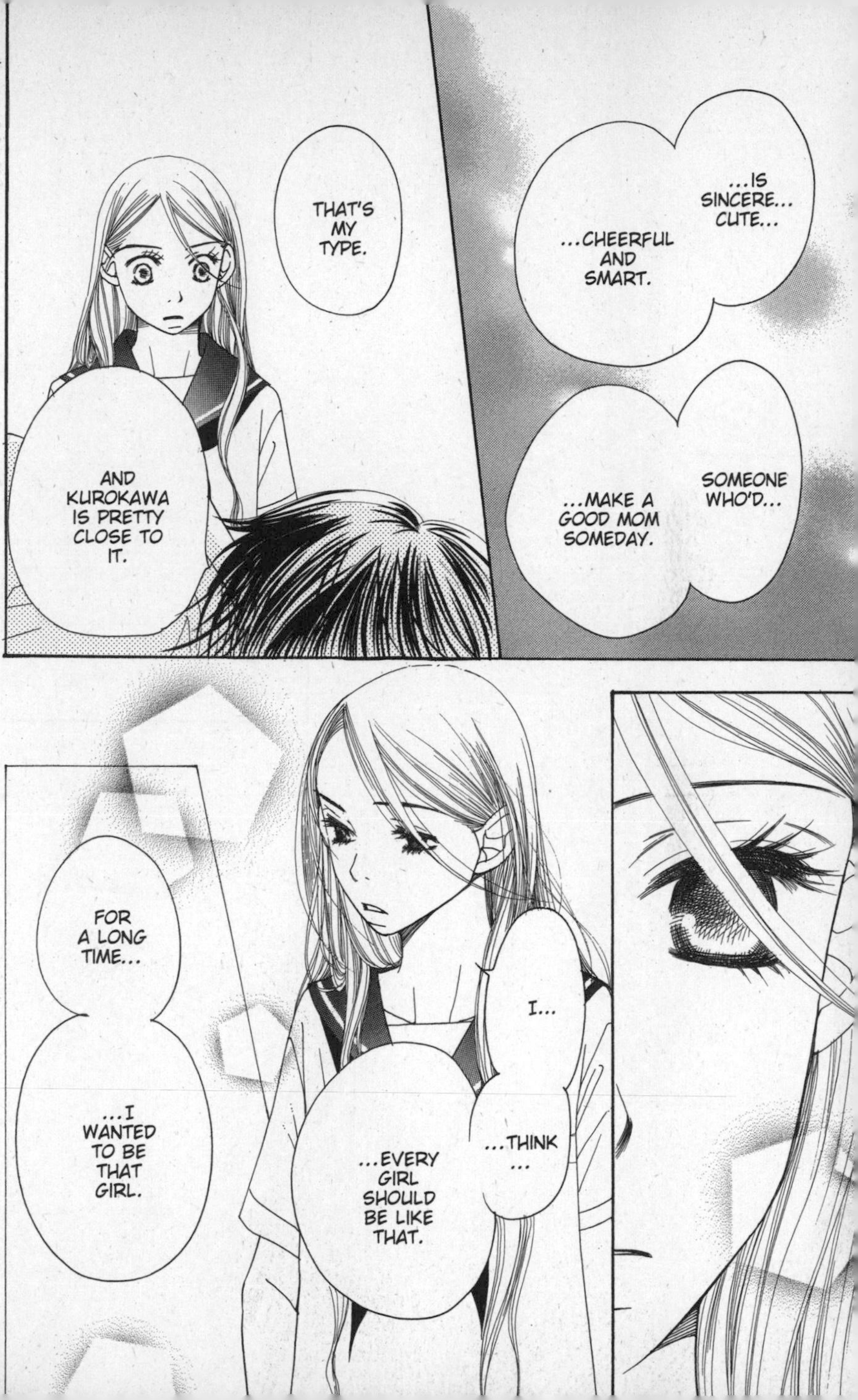

...IS SINCERE... CUTE...
...CHEERFUL AND SMART.
SOMEONE WHO'D...
...MAKE A GOOD MOM SOMEDAY.
THAT'S MY TYPE.
AND KUROKAWA IS PRETTY CLOSE TO IT.
I...
...THINK...
...EVERY GIRL SHOULD BE LIKE THAT.
FOR A LONG TIME...
...I WANTED TO BE THAT GIRL.

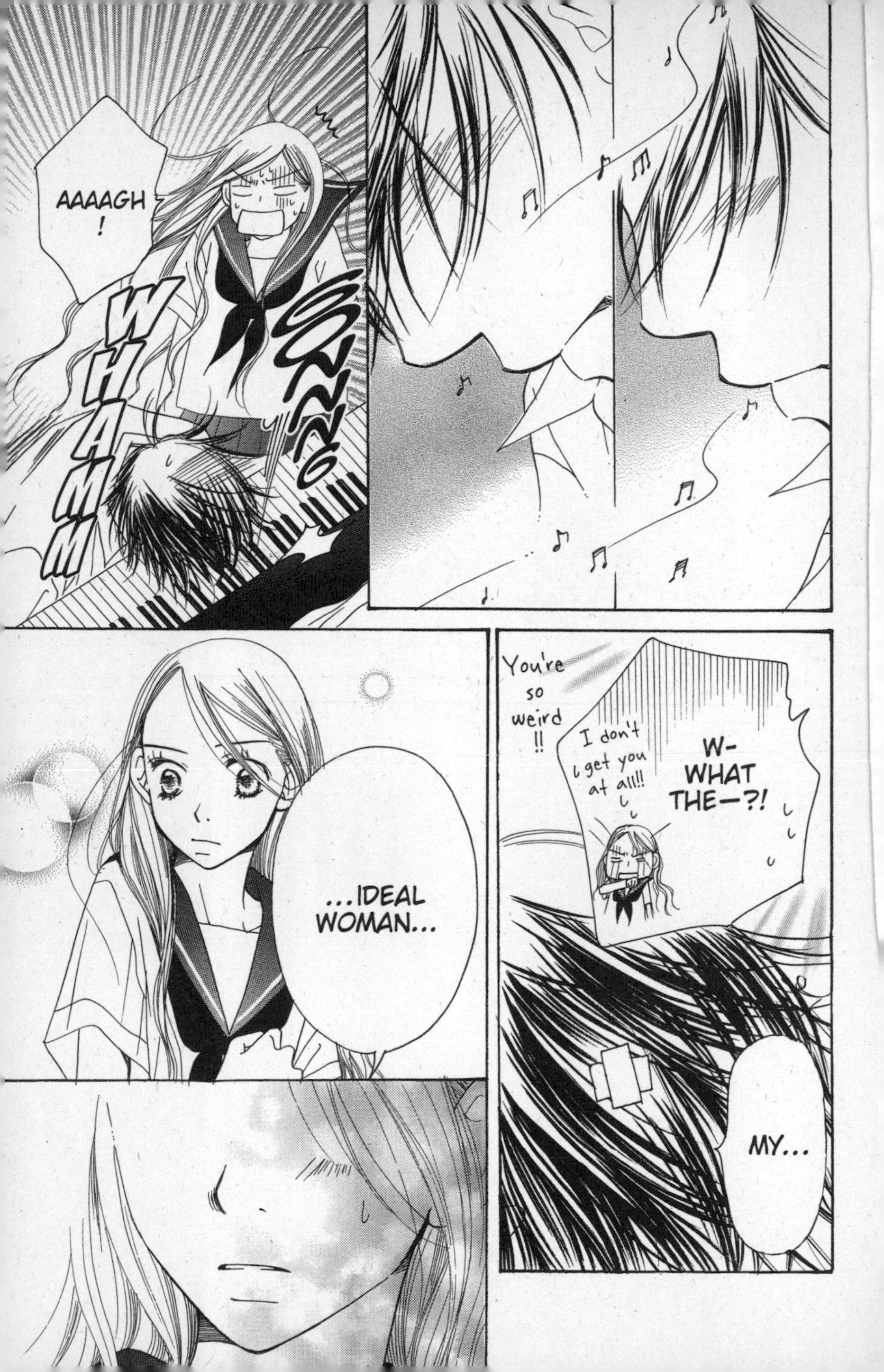

AAAAGH!
WHAMM
W-WHAT THE—?!
I don't get you at all!!
You're so weird!!
MY...
...IDEAL WOMAN...

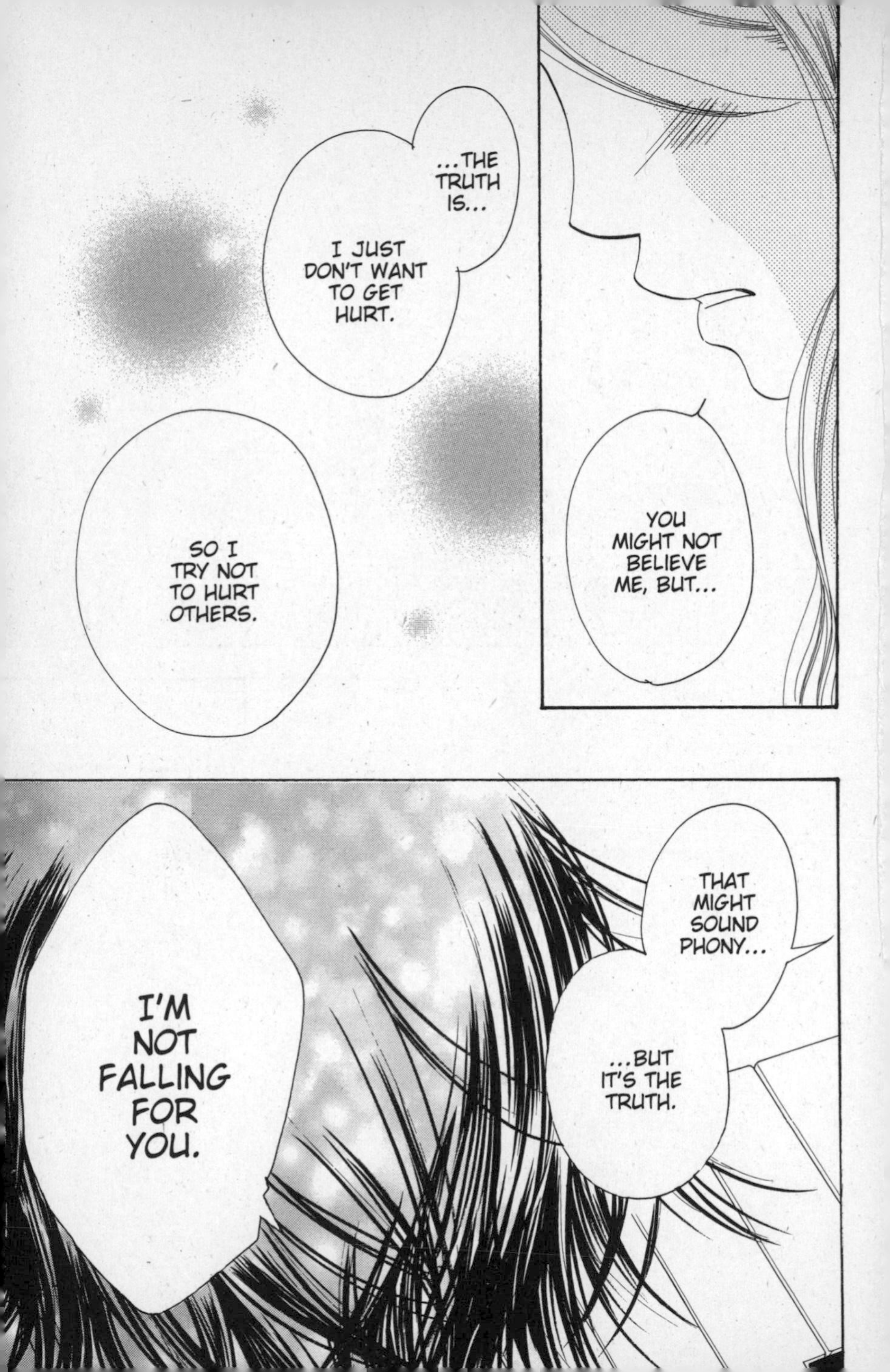
YOU MIGHT NOT BELIEVE ME, BUT...
...THE TRUTH IS...
I JUST DON'T WANT TO GET HURT.
SO I TRY NOT TO HURT OTHERS.
THAT MIGHT SOUND PHONY...
...BUT IT'S THE TRUTH.
I'M NOT FALLING FOR YOU.

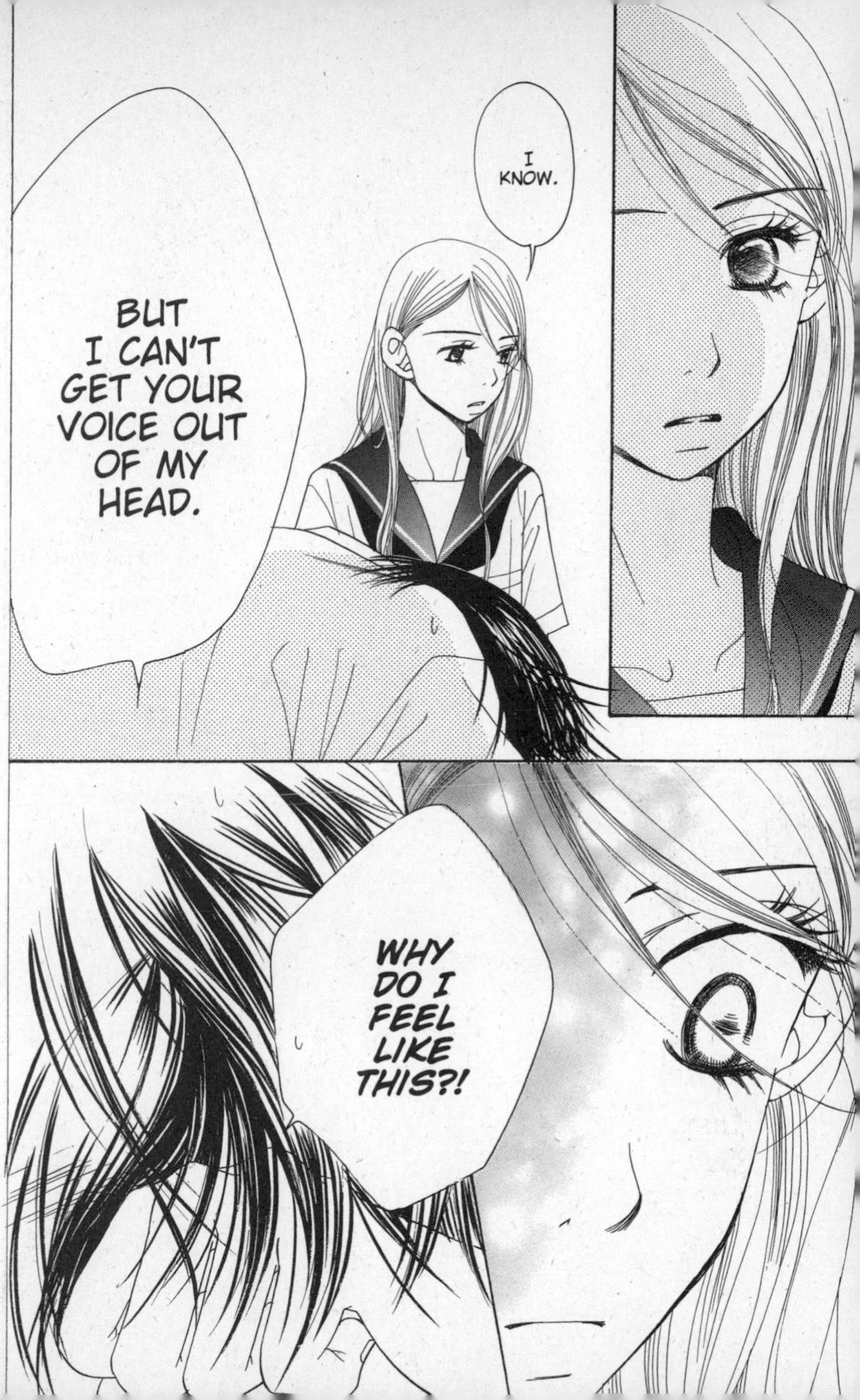
I KNOW.
BUT I CAN'T GET YOUR VOICE OUT OF MY HEAD.
WHY DO I FEEL LIKE THIS?!

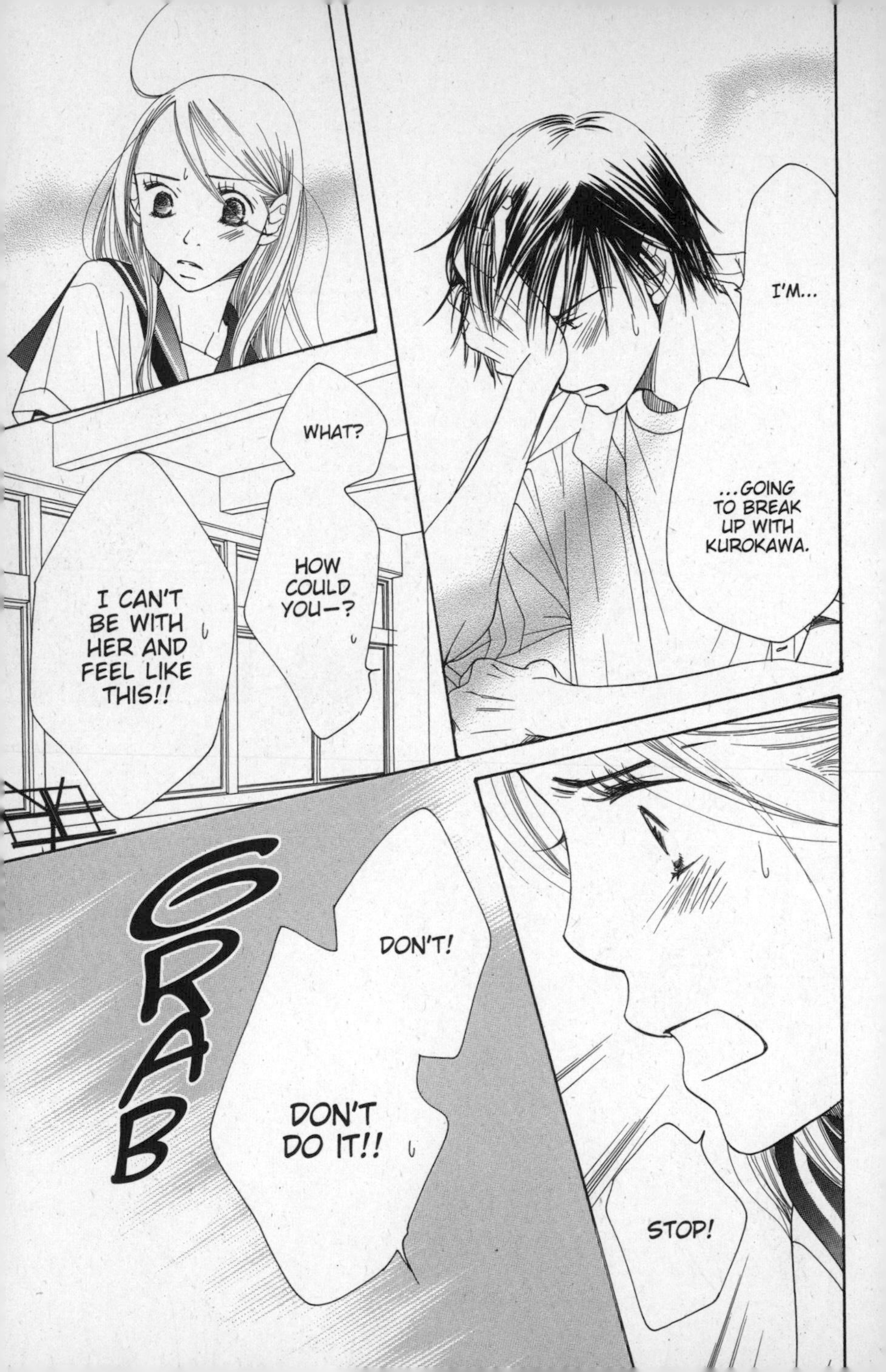
I'M...
...GOING TO BREAK UP WITH KUROKAWA.
WHAT?
HOW COULD YOU—?
I CAN'T BE WITH HER AND FEEL LIKE THIS!!
GRAB
DON'T!
DON'T DO IT!!
STOP!

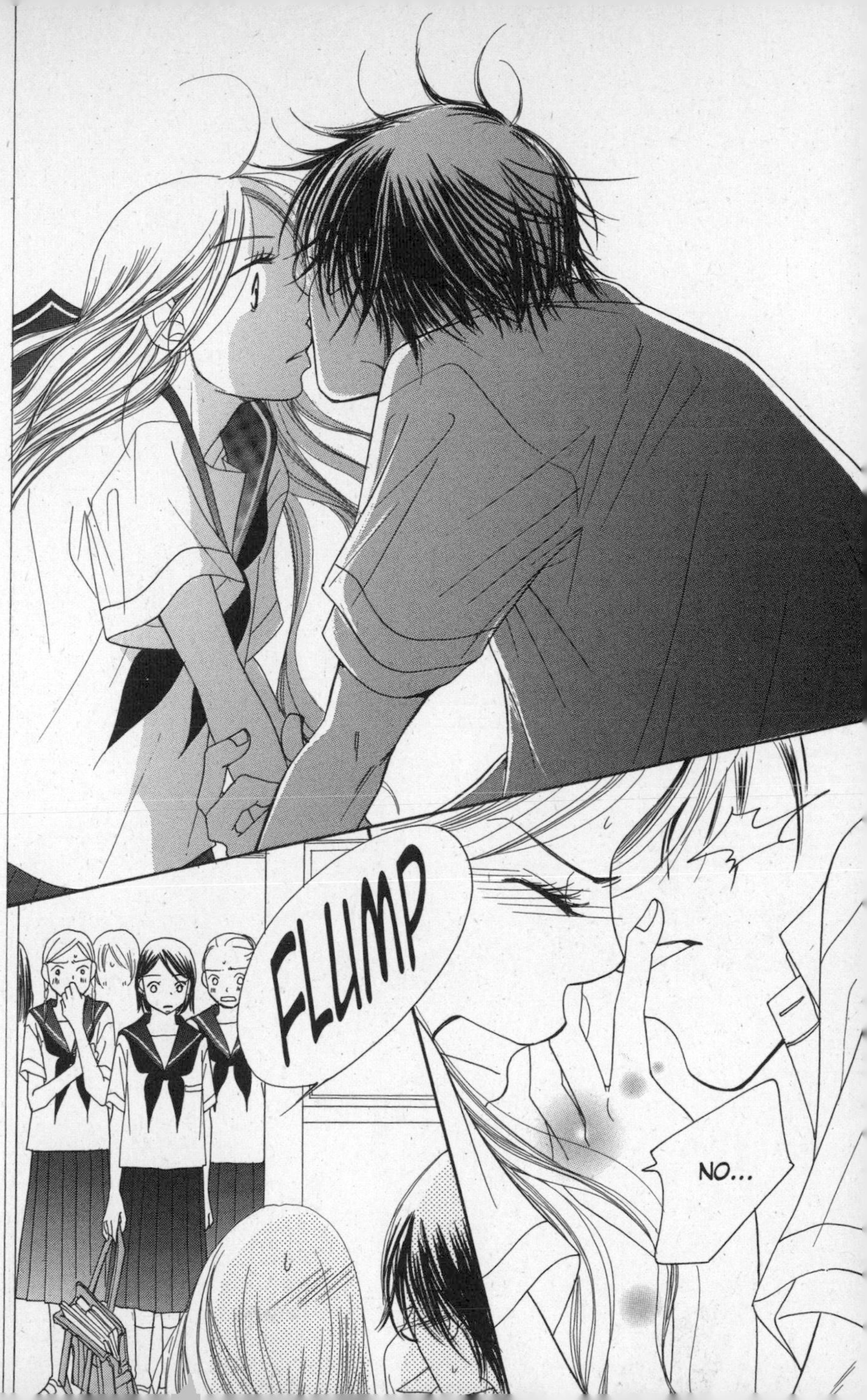
FLUMP
NO...

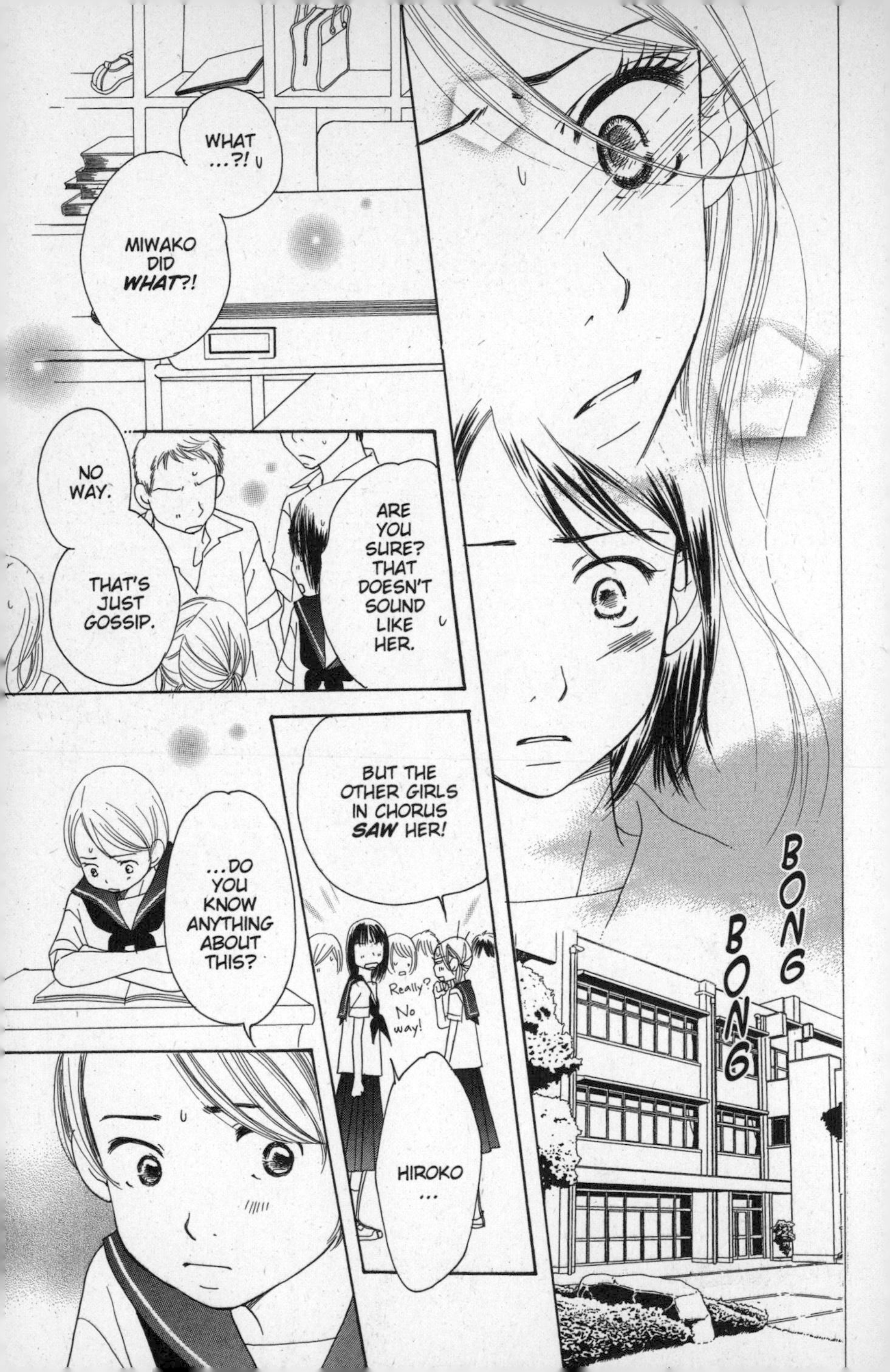
BONG
BONG
WHAT ...?!
MIWAKO DID WHAT?!
ARE YOU SURE? THAT DOESN'T SOUND LIKE HER.
NO WAY.
THAT'S JUST GOSSIP.
BUT THE OTHER GIRLS IN CHORUS SAW HER!
Really?
No way!
HIROKO ...
...DO YOU KNOW ANYTHING ABOUT THIS?

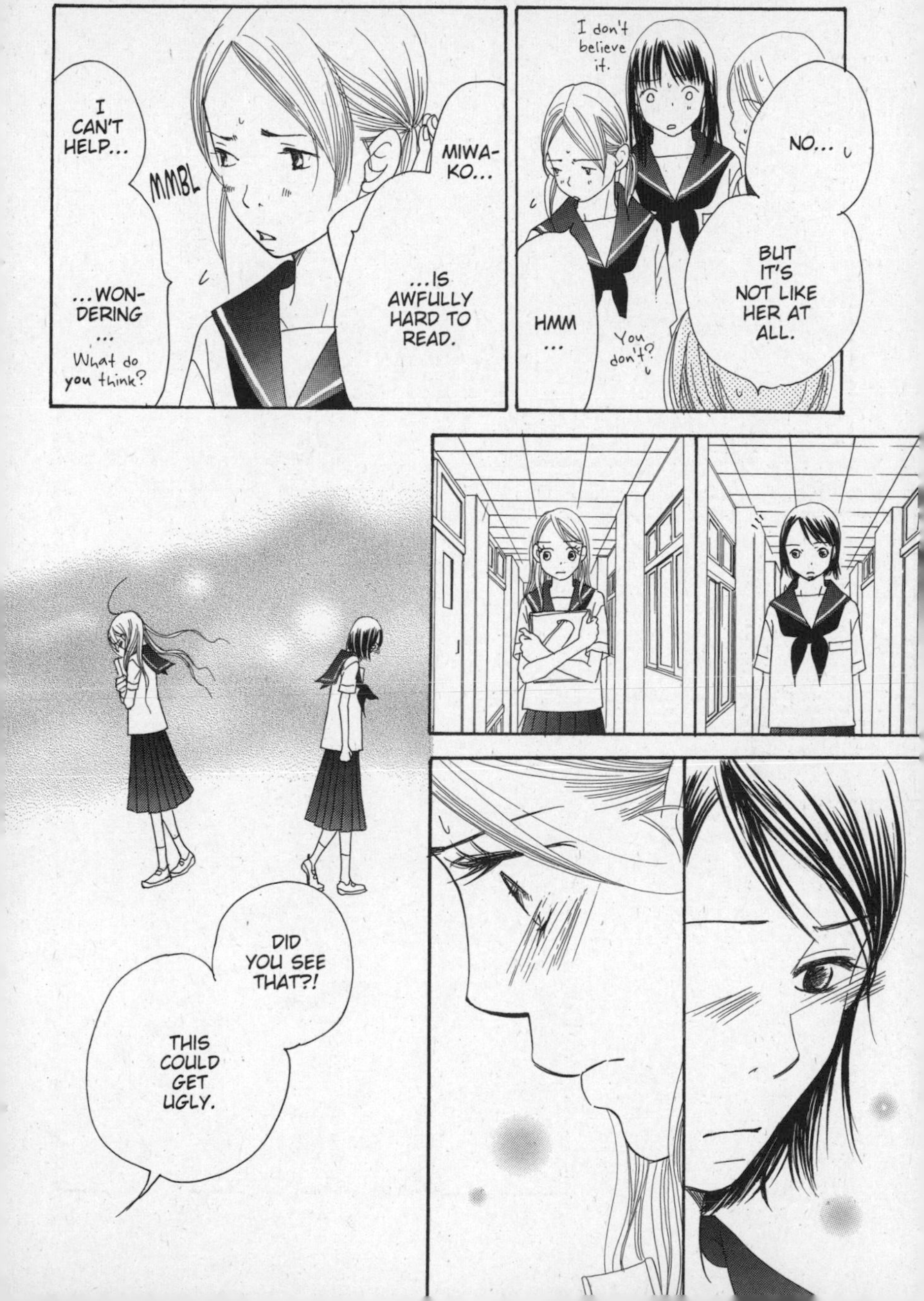
I don't believe it.
NO...
BUT IT'S NOT LIKE HER AT ALL.
HMM...
You don't?
MIWAKO...
...IS AWFULLY HARD TO READ.
I CAN'T HELP...
MMBL
...WONDERING...
What do you think?
DID YOU SEE THAT?!
THIS COULD GET UGLY.

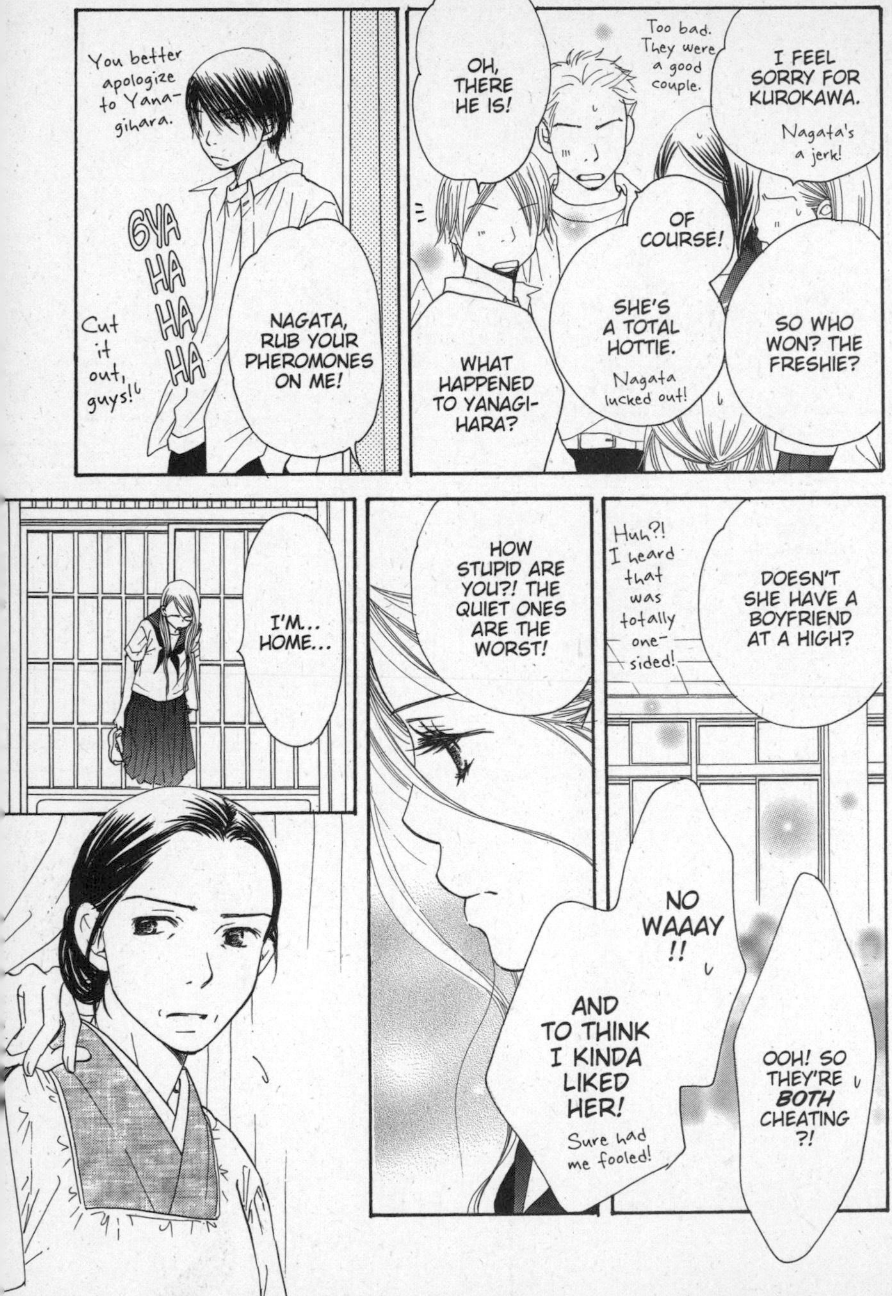
I FEEL SORRY FOR KUROKAWA.
Nagata's a jerk!
Too bad. They were a good couple.
OH, THERE HE IS!
SO WHO WON? THE FRESHIE?
OF COURSE!
SHE'S A TOTAL HOTTIE.
Nagata lucked out!
WHAT HAPPENED TO YANAGI-HARA?
NAGATA, RUB YOUR PHEROMONES ON ME!
GYA HA HA HA
You better apologize to Yana-gihara.
Cut it out, guys!
DOESN'T SHE HAVE A BOYFRIEND AT A HIGH?
Huh?! I heard that was totally one-sided!
HOW STUPID ARE YOU?! THE QUIET ONES ARE THE WORST!
OOH! SO THEY'RE *BOTH* CHEATING?!
NO WAAAY!!
AND TO THINK I KINDA LIKED HER!
Sure had me fooled!
I'M... HOME...

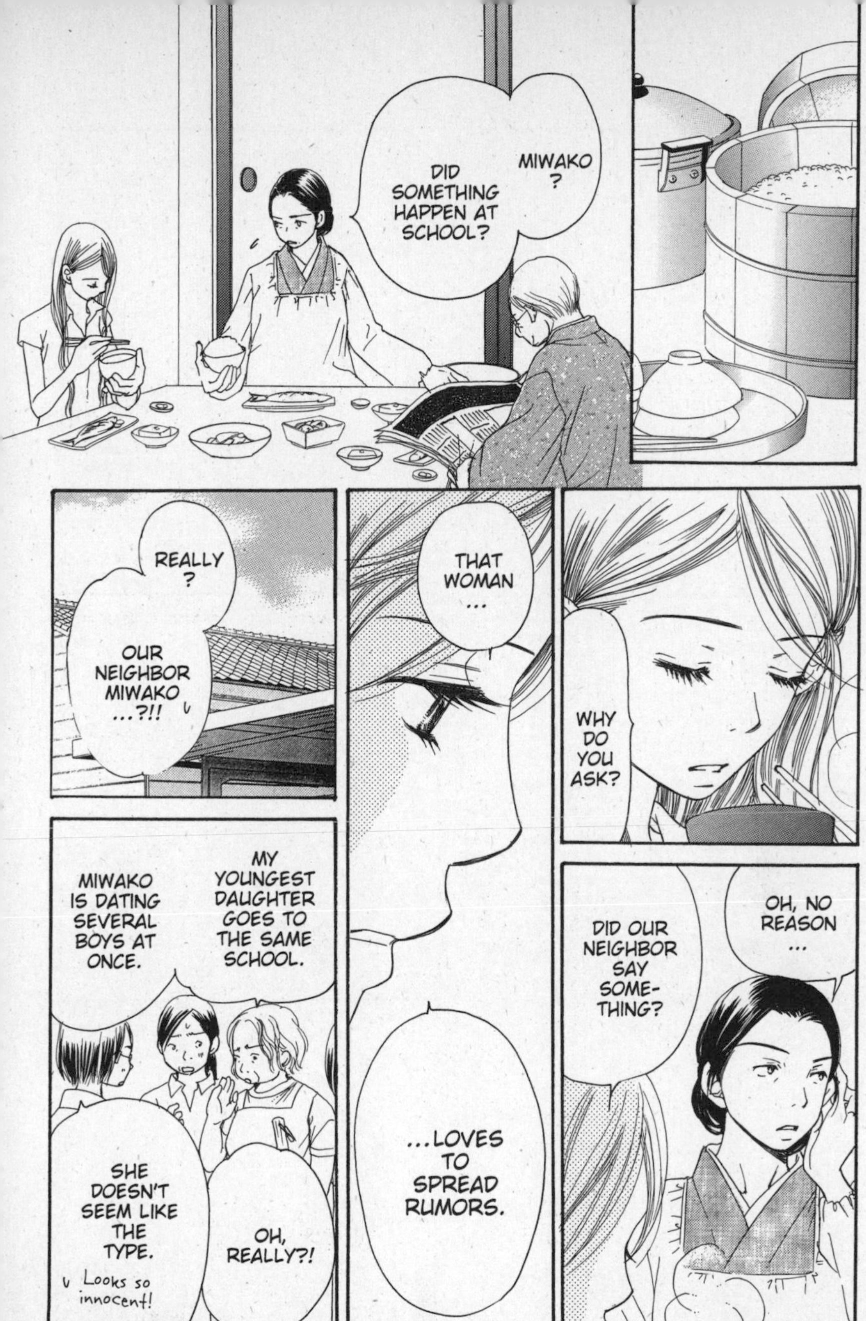
MIWAKO ?
DID SOMETHING HAPPEN AT SCHOOL?
WHY DO YOU ASK?
OH, NO REASON ...
DID OUR NEIGHBOR SAY SOME-THING?
THAT WOMAN ...
...LOVES TO SPREAD RUMORS.
REALLY ?
OUR NEIGHBOR MIWAKO ...?!!
MY YOUNGEST DAUGHTER GOES TO THE SAME SCHOOL.
MIWAKO IS DATING SEVERAL BOYS AT ONCE.
OH, REALLY?!
SHE DOESN'T SEEM LIKE THE TYPE.
Looks so innocent!

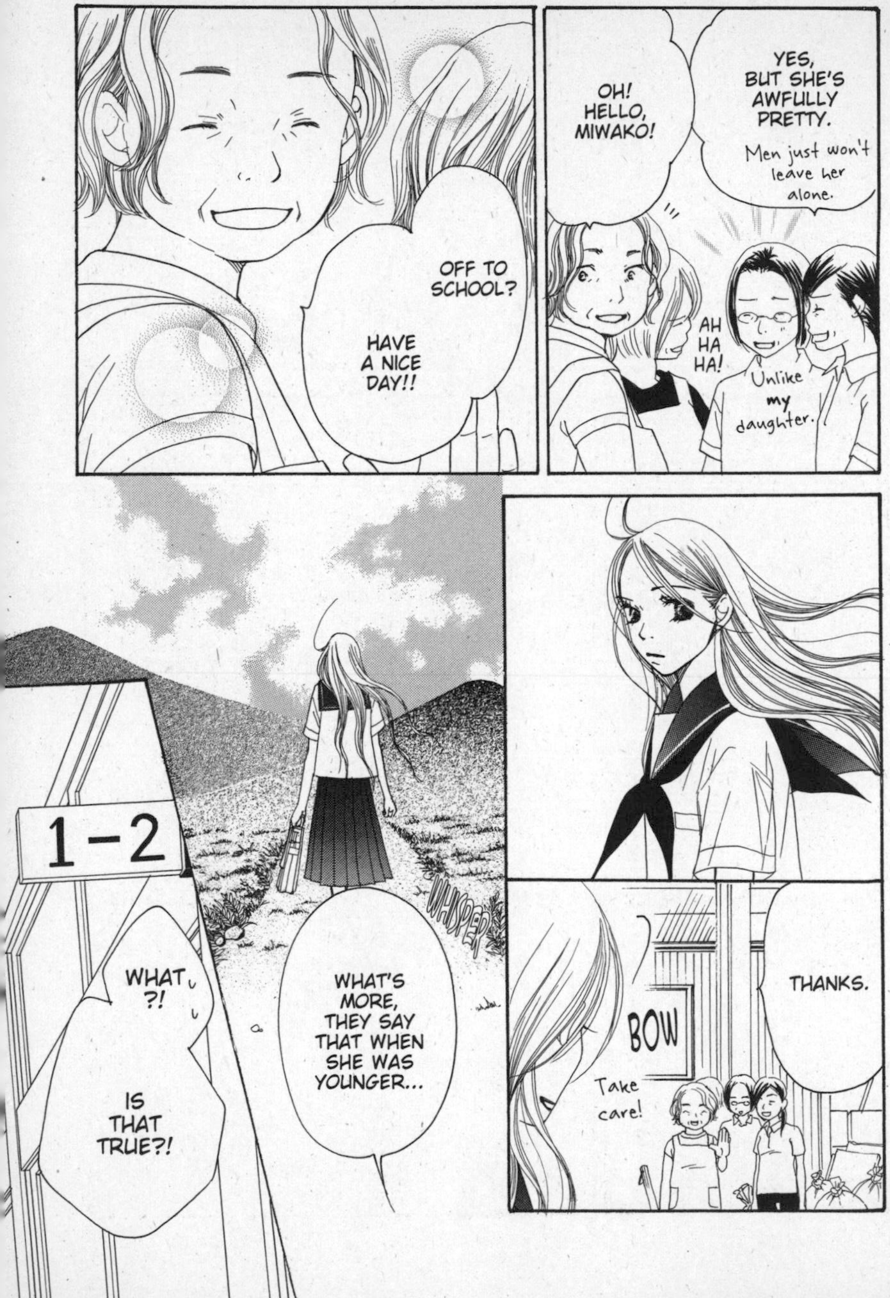
YES, BUT SHE'S AWFULLY PRETTY.
Men just won't leave her alone.
OH! HELLO, MIWAKO!
AH HA HA!
Unlike my daughter.
OFF TO SCHOOL?
HAVE A NICE DAY!!
THANKS.
BOW
Take care!
WHISPER
WHAT'S MORE, THEY SAY THAT WHEN SHE WAS YOUNGER...
1-2
WHAT?!
IS THAT TRUE?!

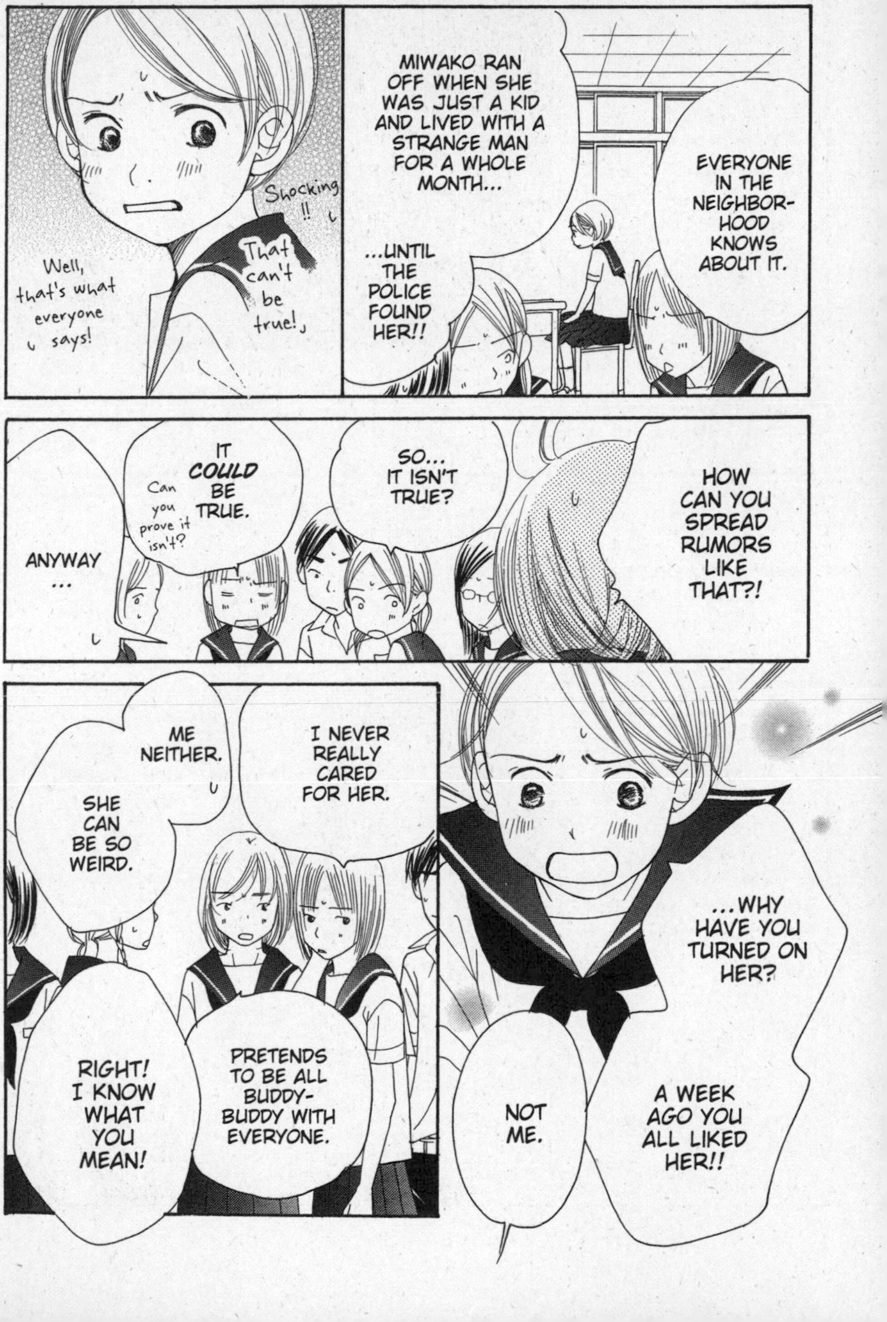
MIWAKO RAN OFF WHEN SHE WAS JUST A KID AND LIVED WITH A STRANGE MAN FOR A WHOLE MONTH...
...UNTIL THE POLICE FOUND HER!!
EVERYONE IN THE NEIGHBOR-HOOD KNOWS ABOUT IT.
Shocking!!
That can't be true!
Well, that's what everyone says!
HOW CAN YOU SPREAD RUMORS LIKE THAT?!
SO... IT ISN'T TRUE?
IT **COULD** BE TRUE.
Can you prove it isn't?
ANYWAY...
...WHY HAVE YOU TURNED ON HER?
A WEEK AGO YOU ALL LIKED HER!!
NOT ME.
I NEVER REALLY CARED FOR HER.
ME NEITHER.
SHE CAN BE SO WEIRD.
PRETENDS TO BE ALL BUDDY-BUDDY WITH EVERYONE.
RIGHT! I KNOW WHAT YOU MEAN!

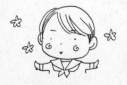

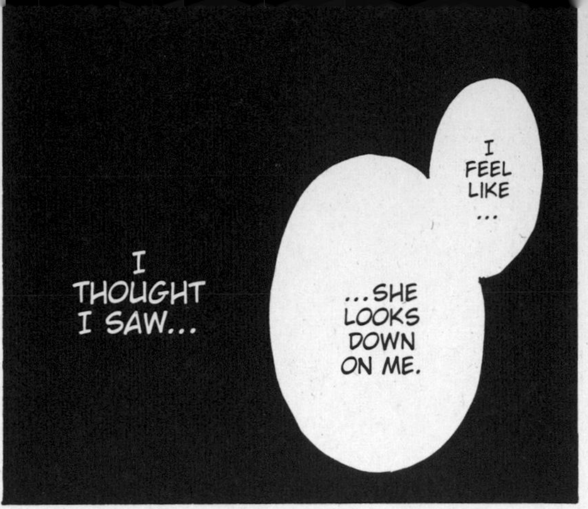
I FEEL LIKE ...
...SHE LOOKS DOWN ON ME.
I THOUGHT I SAW...

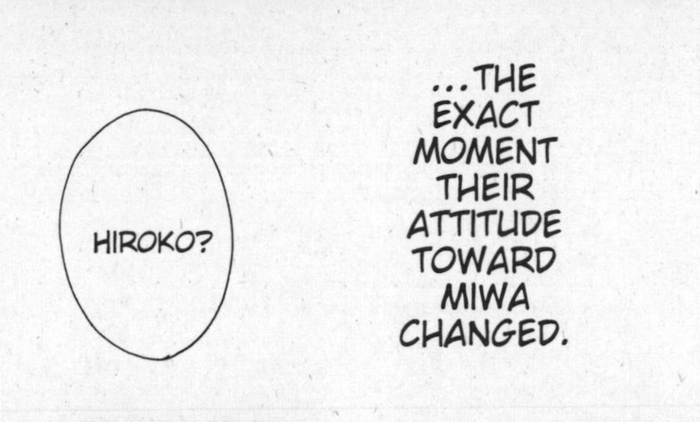
...THE EXACT MOMENT THEIR ATTITUDE TOWARD MIWA CHANGED.
HIROKO?

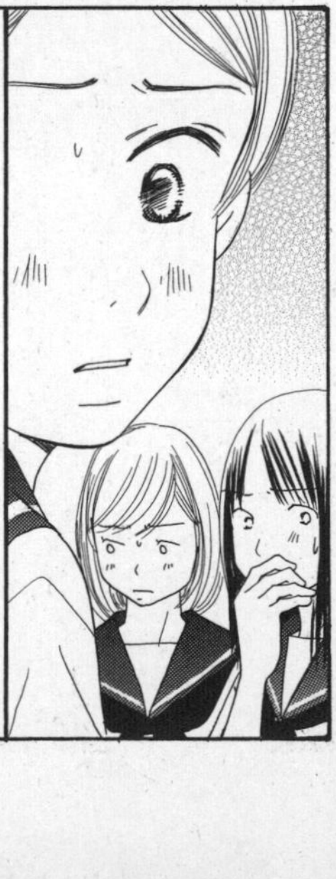

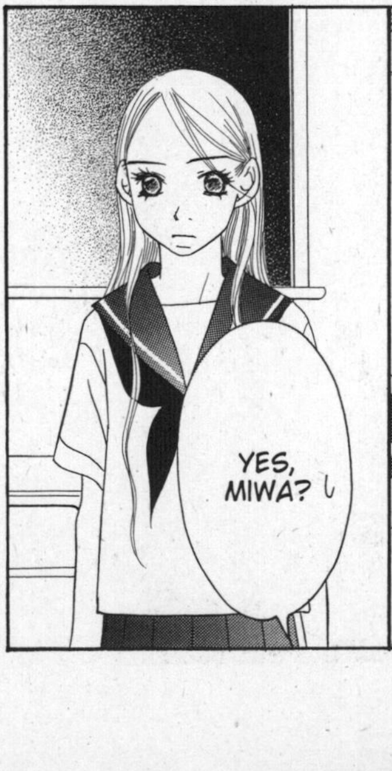
YES, MIWA?

"Canary"

I wanted to use the title "Canary" in the main series, but I didn't get the chance, so it ended up in this bonus episode... I hadn't written a stand-alone story for a long time, so it was fun.

A friend of mine couldn't remember what Yaso Saijo's song "Canary" sounded like and asked me to sing it. When I obliged, my friend said I was off-key... It's a hard song to sing! Or am I just tone-deaf...?

I considered making Shizuyo Tsukishima the main character, but I knew that would make it like a soap opera, so I gave that up.

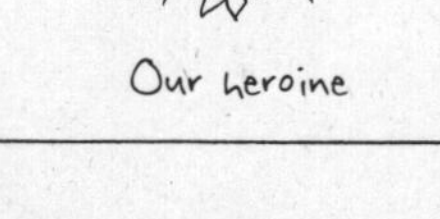

Our heroine

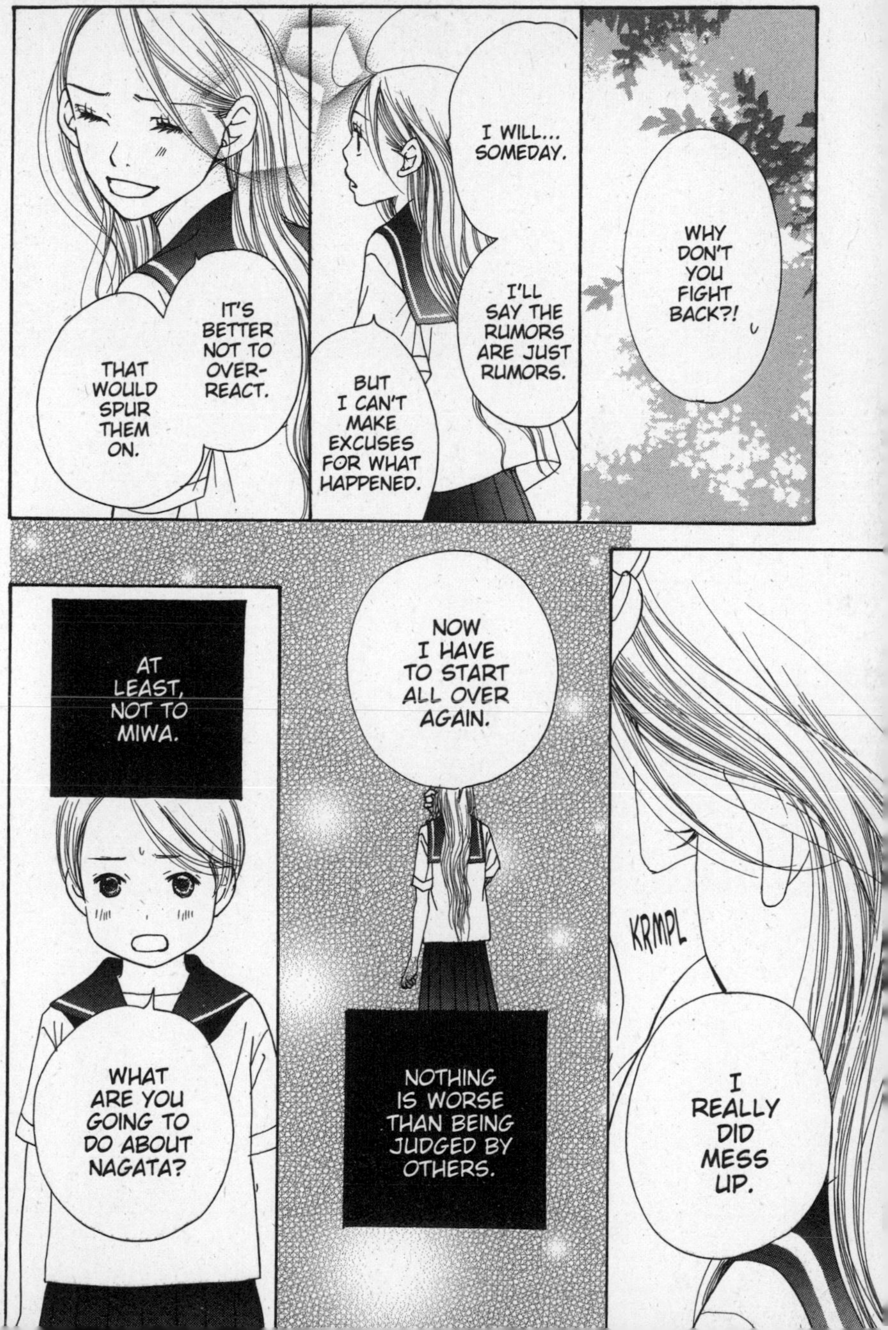

WHY DON'T YOU FIGHT BACK?!
I WILL... SOMEDAY.
I'LL SAY THE RUMORS ARE JUST RUMORS.
BUT I CAN'T MAKE EXCUSES FOR WHAT HAPPENED.
IT'S BETTER NOT TO OVER-REACT.
THAT WOULD SPUR THEM ON.
KRMPL
I REALLY DID MESS UP.
NOW I HAVE TO START ALL OVER AGAIN.
NOTHING IS WORSE THAN BEING JUDGED BY OTHERS.
AT LEAST, NOT TO MIWA.
WHAT ARE YOU GOING TO DO ABOUT NAGATA?

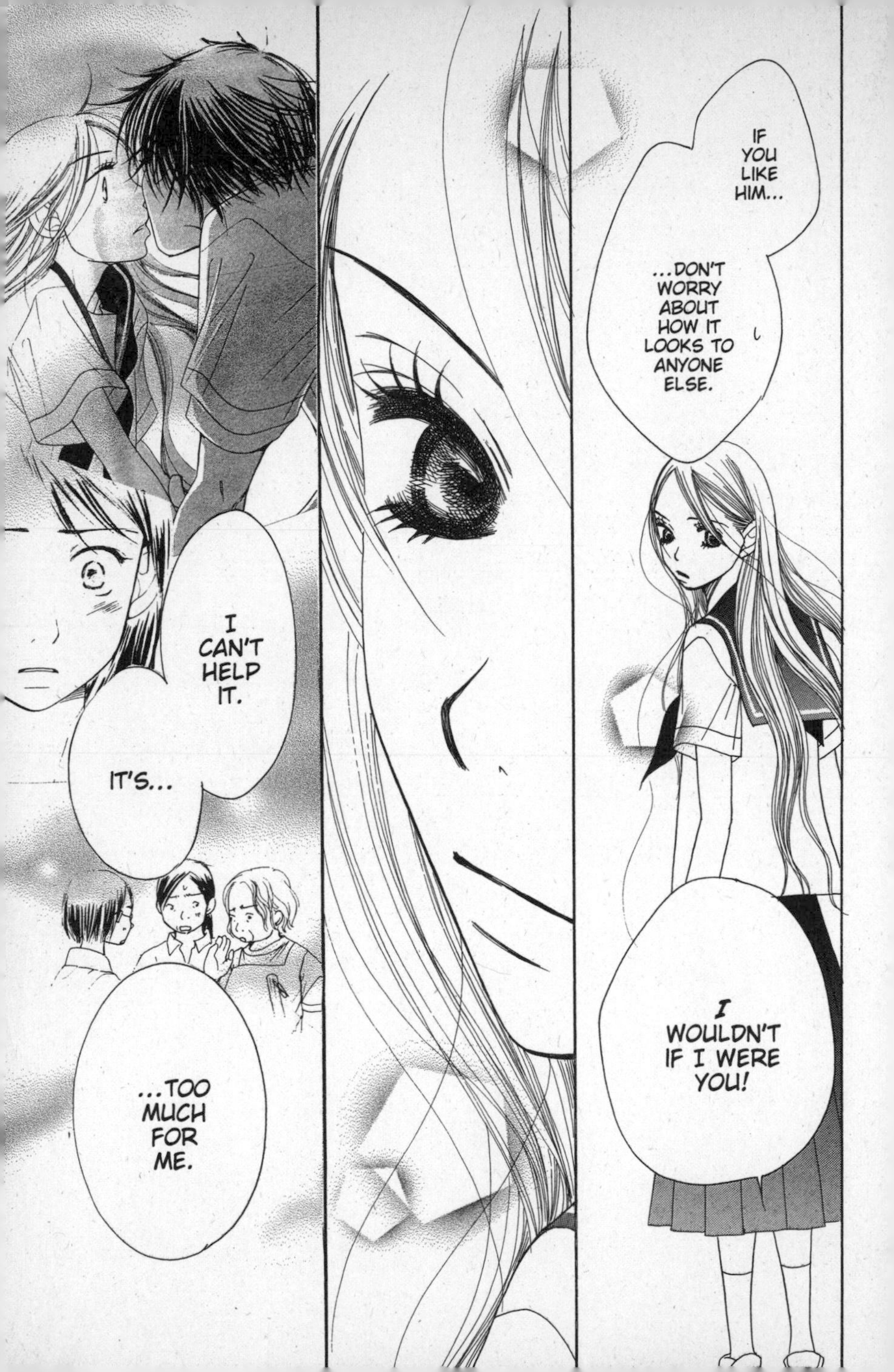

IF YOU LIKE HIM...
...DON'T WORRY ABOUT HOW IT LOOKS TO ANYONE ELSE.
I WOULDN'T IF I WERE YOU!
I CAN'T HELP IT.
IT'S...
...TOO MUCH FOR ME.

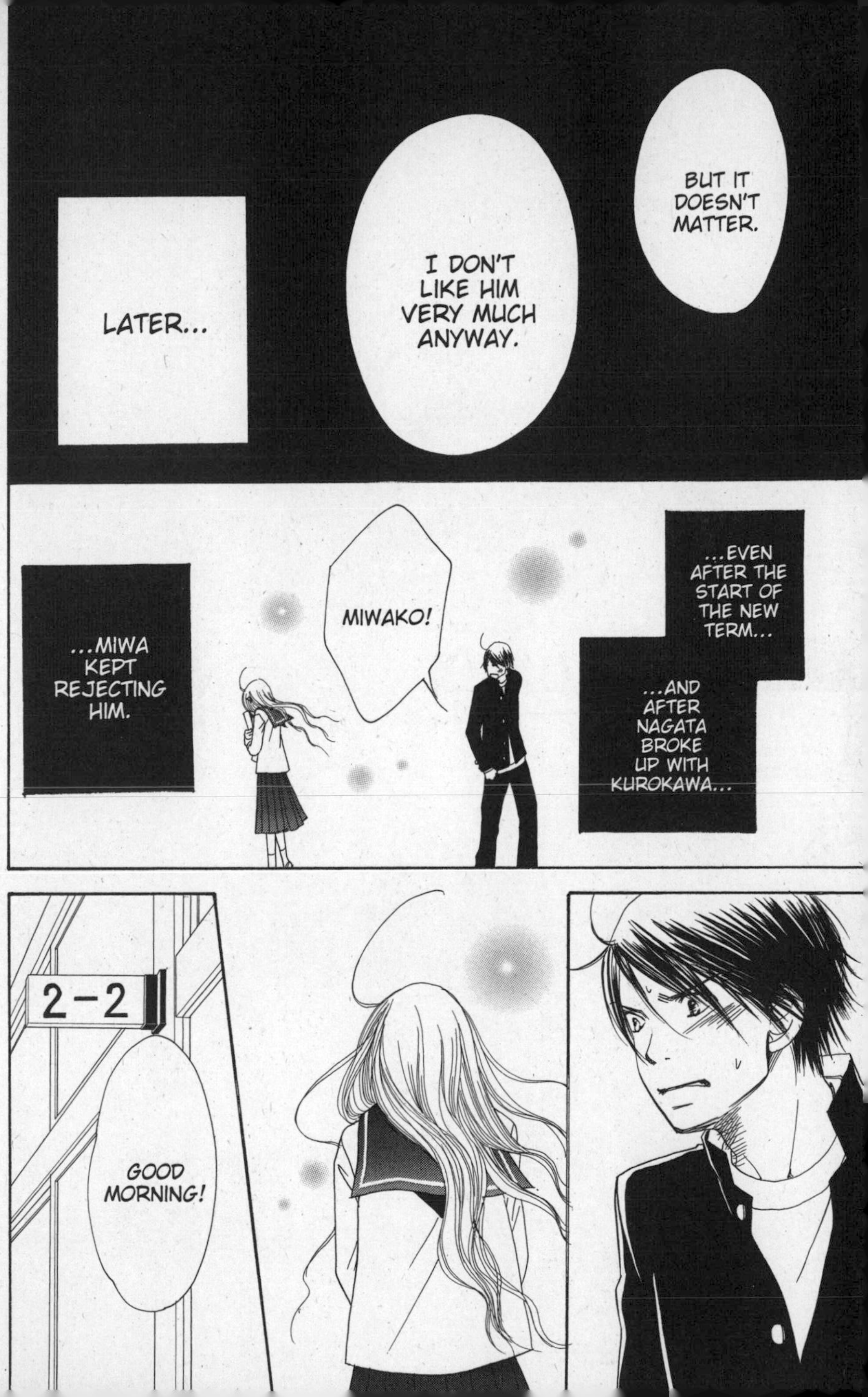
BUT IT DOESN'T MATTER.
I DON'T LIKE HIM VERY MUCH ANYWAY.
LATER...
...EVEN AFTER THE START OF THE NEW TERM...
...AND AFTER NAGATA BROKE UP WITH KUROKAWA...
MIWAKO!
...MIWA KEPT REJECTING HIM.
2-2
GOOD MORNING!

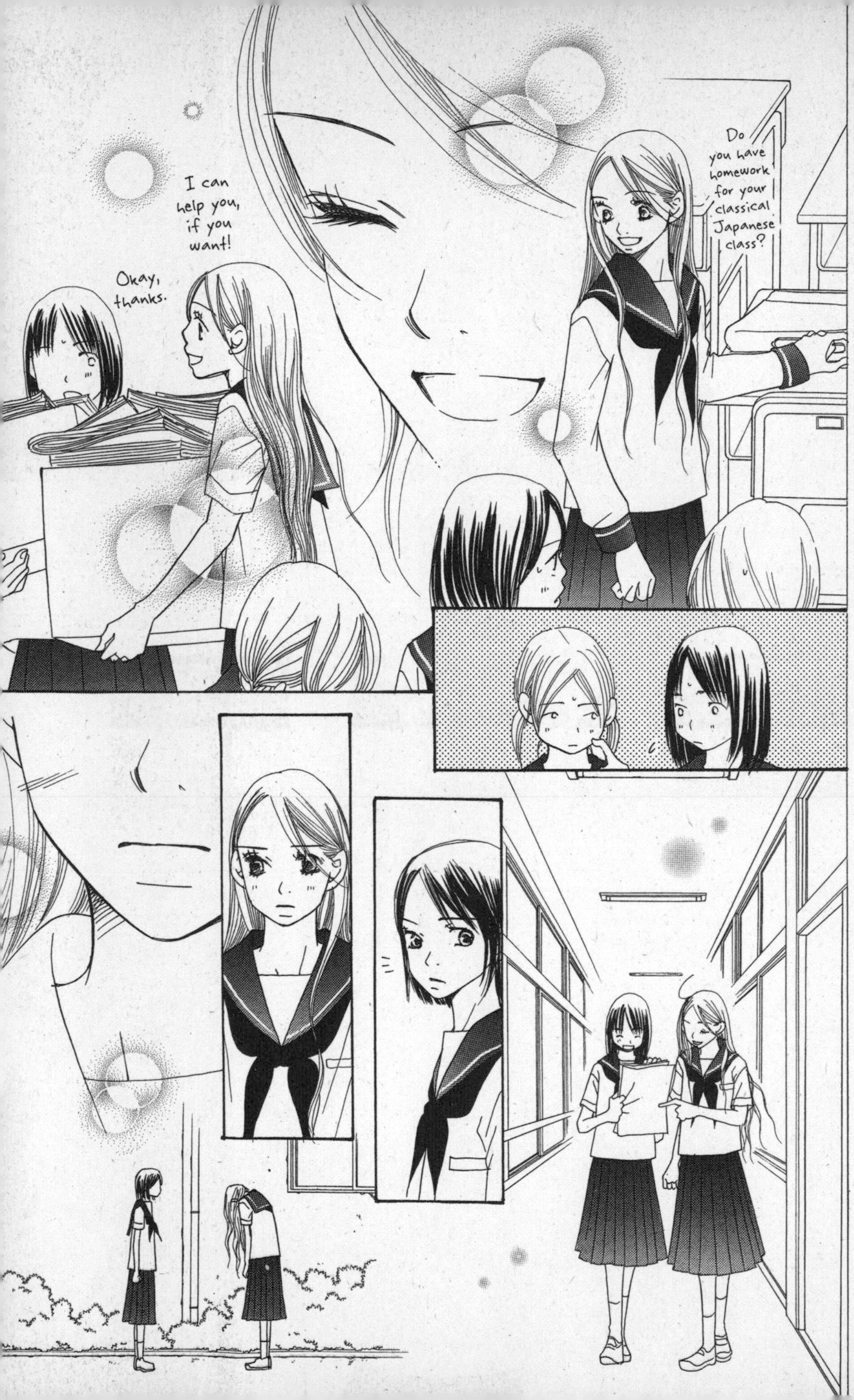
Do you have homework for your classical Japanese class?
I can help you, if you want!
Okay, thanks.

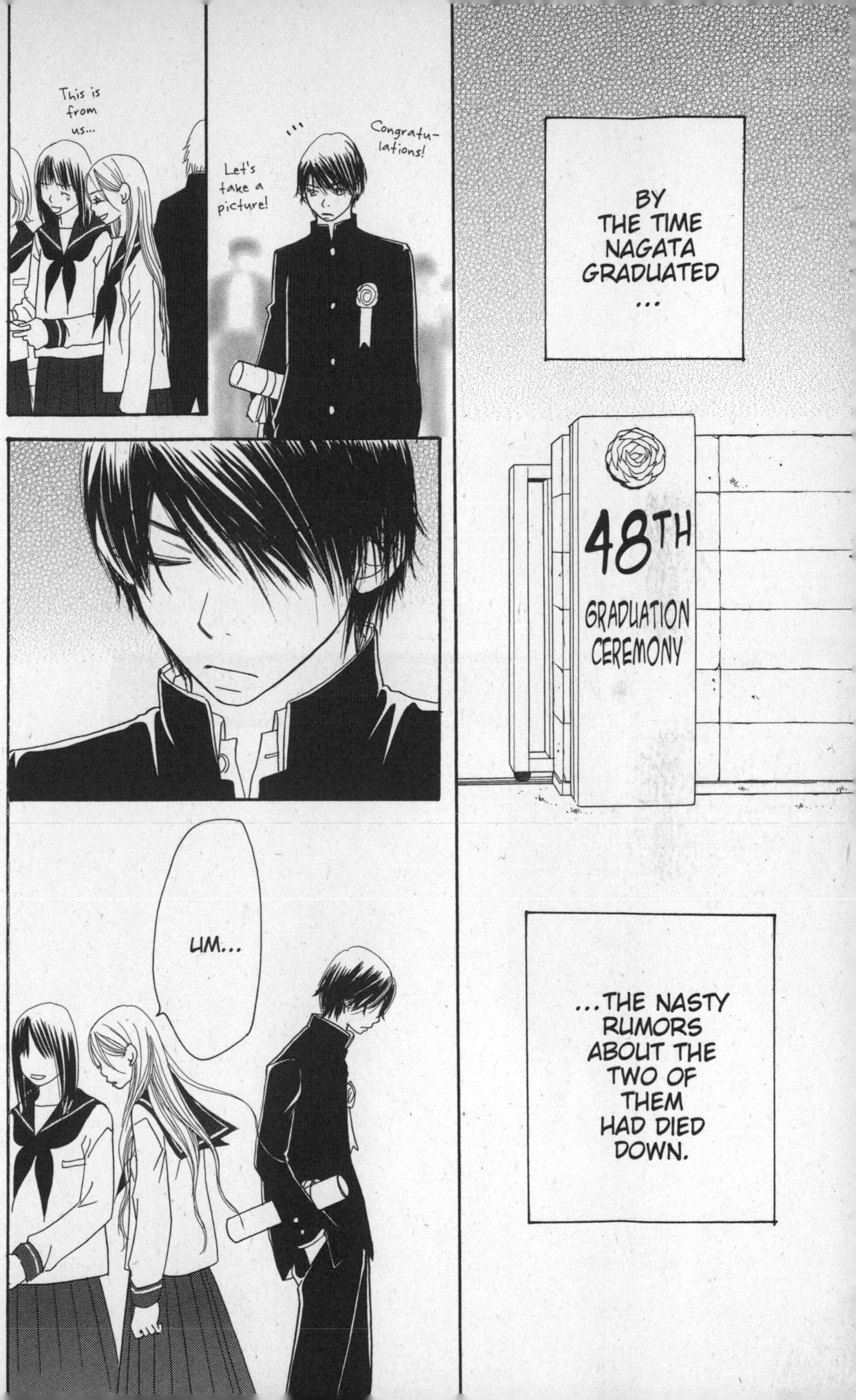
BY THE TIME NAGATA GRADUATED ...
48TH
GRADUATION CEREMONY
...THE NASTY RUMORS ABOUT THE TWO OF THEM HAD DIED DOWN.
Congratu-lations!
...
Let's take a picture!
This is from us...
UM...

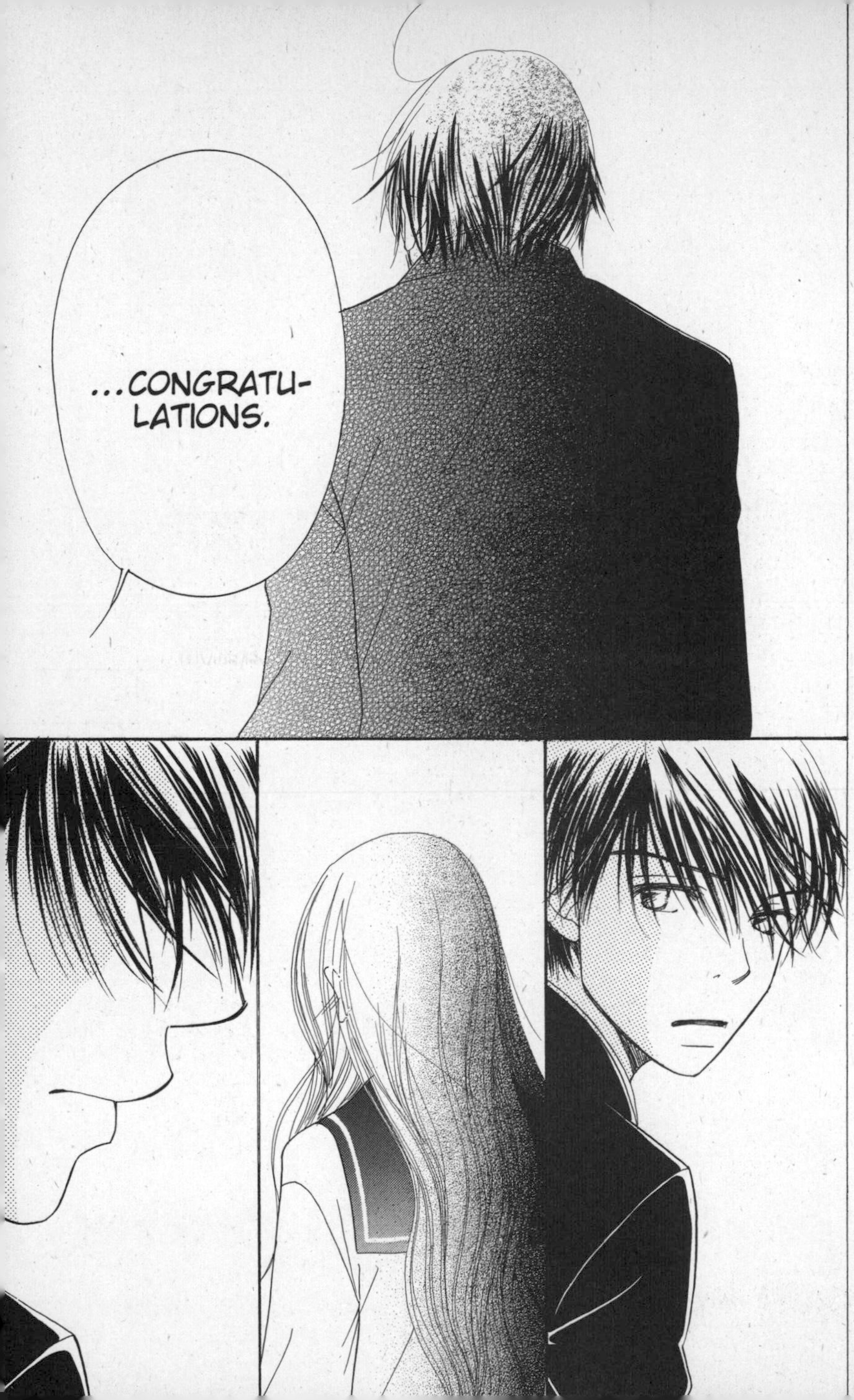
...CONGRATU-
LATIONS.

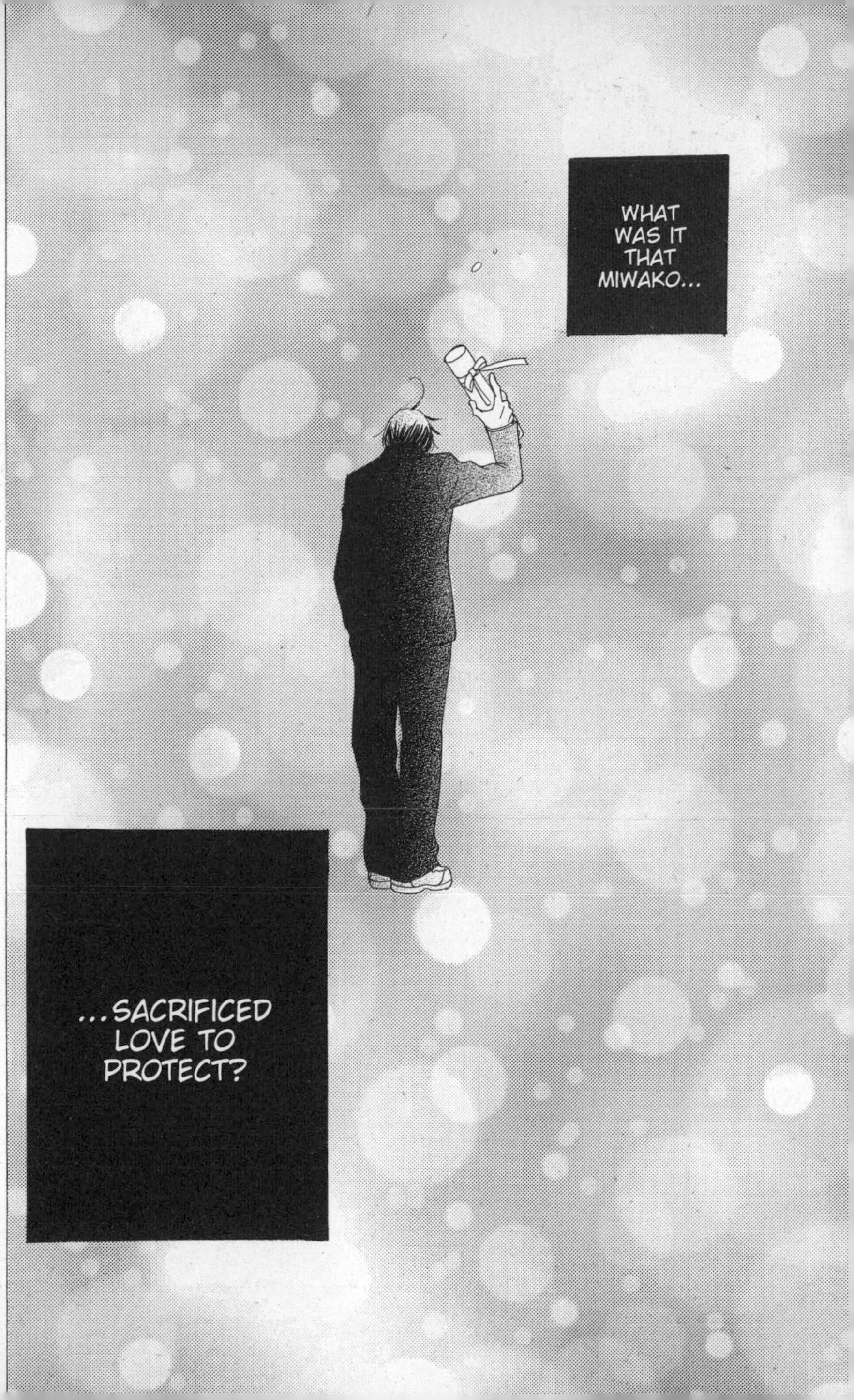
WHAT WAS IT THAT MIWAKO...
...SACRIFICED LOVE TO PROTECT?

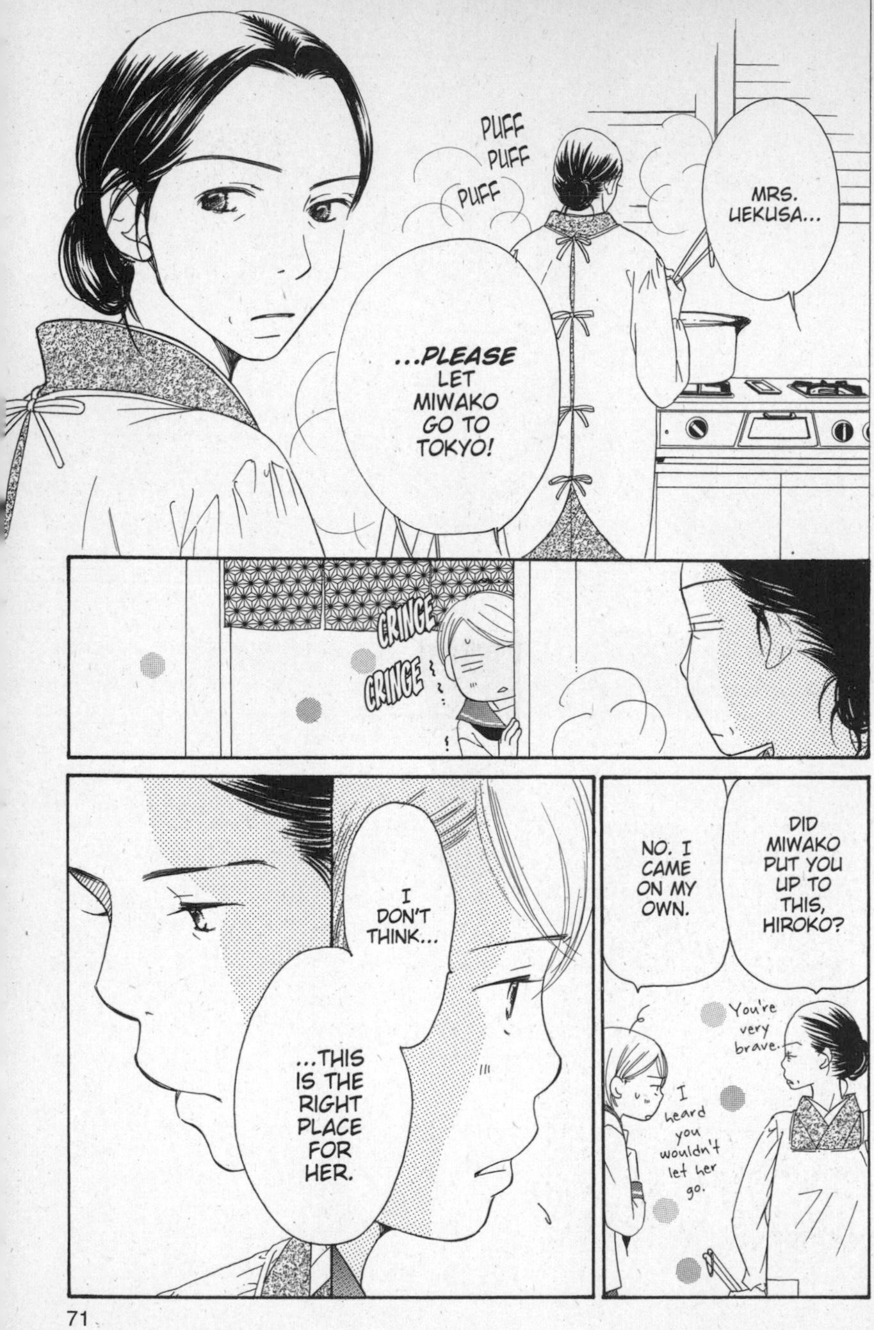
MRS. UEKUSA...
PUFF PUFF PUFF
...PLEASE LET MIWAKO GO TO TOKYO!
CRINGE CRINGE
DID MIWAKO PUT YOU UP TO THIS, HIROKO?
NO. I CAME ON MY OWN.
You're very brave.
I heard you wouldn't let her go.
I DON'T THINK...
...THIS IS THE RIGHT PLACE FOR HER.

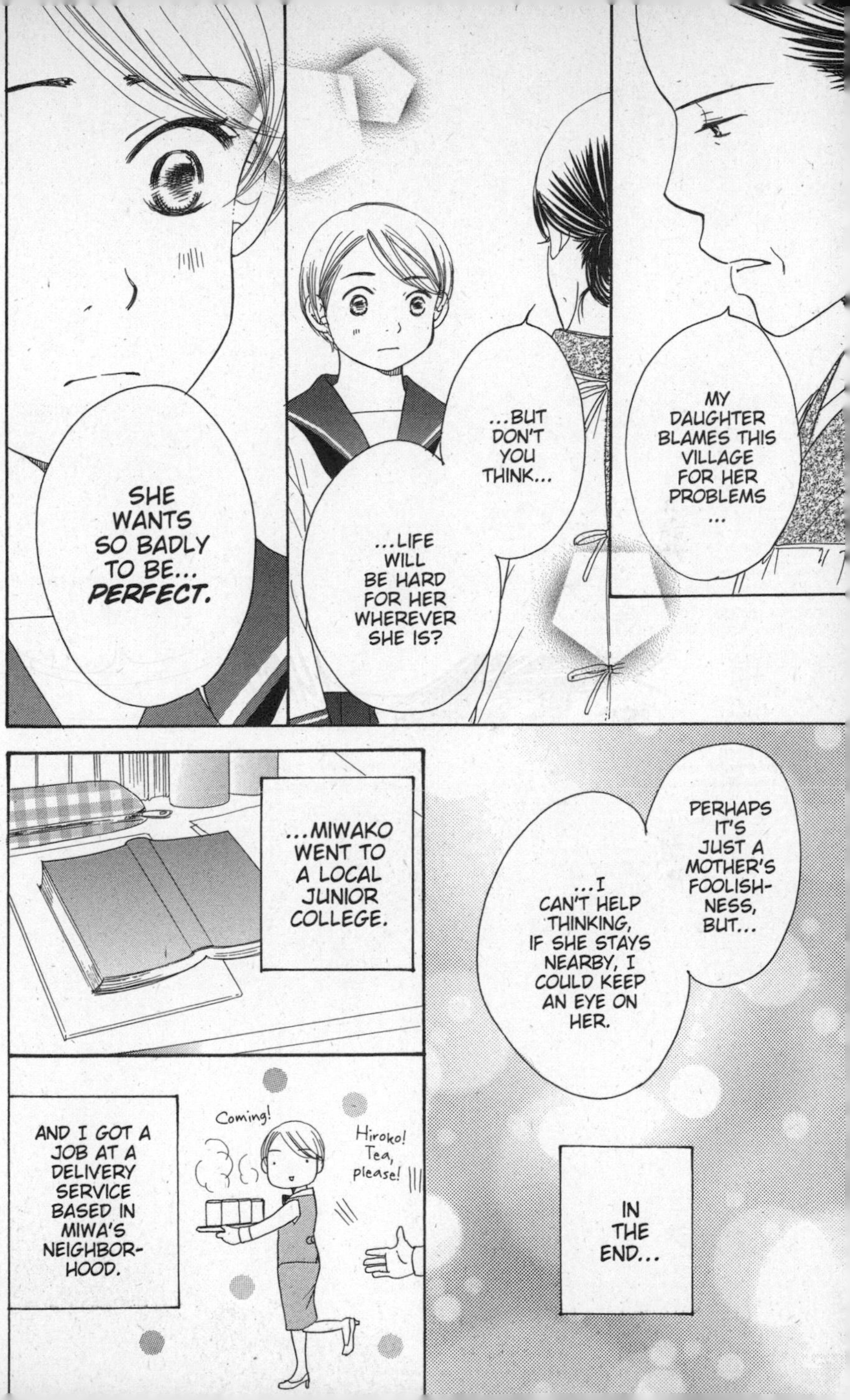
MY DAUGHTER BLAMES THIS VILLAGE FOR HER PROBLEMS ...
...BUT DON'T YOU THINK...
...LIFE WILL BE HARD FOR HER WHEREVER SHE IS?
SHE WANTS SO BADLY TO BE... *PERFECT.*
PERHAPS IT'S JUST A MOTHER'S FOOLISH-NESS, BUT...
...I CAN'T HELP THINKING, IF SHE STAYS NEARBY, I COULD KEEP AN EYE ON HER.
IN THE END...
...MIWAKO WENT TO A LOCAL JUNIOR COLLEGE.
AND I GOT A JOB AT A DELIVERY SERVICE BASED IN MIWA'S NEIGHBOR-HOOD.
Hiroko! Tea, please!
Coming!

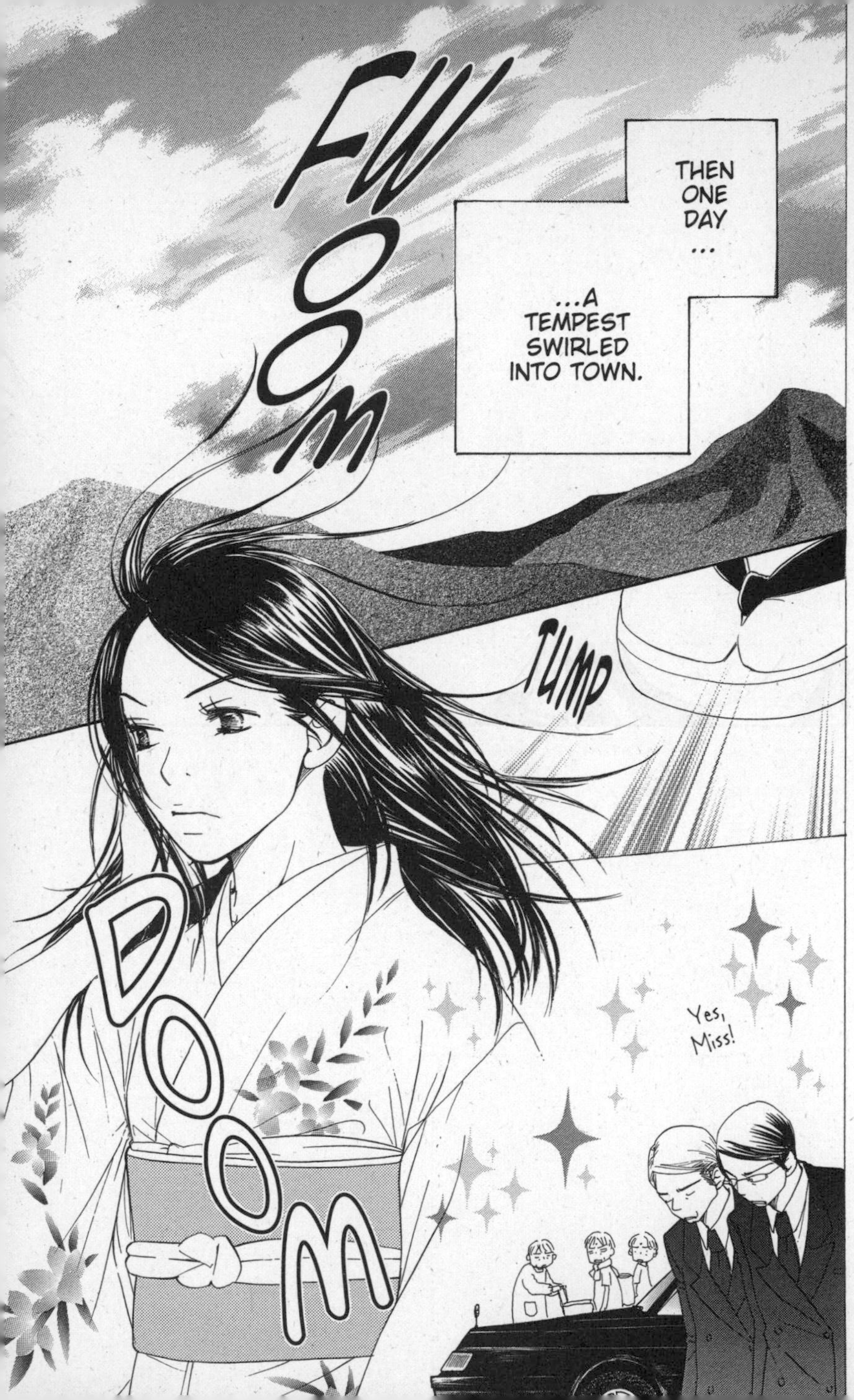
THEN ONE DAY ...
...A TEMPEST SWIRLED INTO TOWN.
FWOOM
TUMP
Yes, Miss!
DOOOM

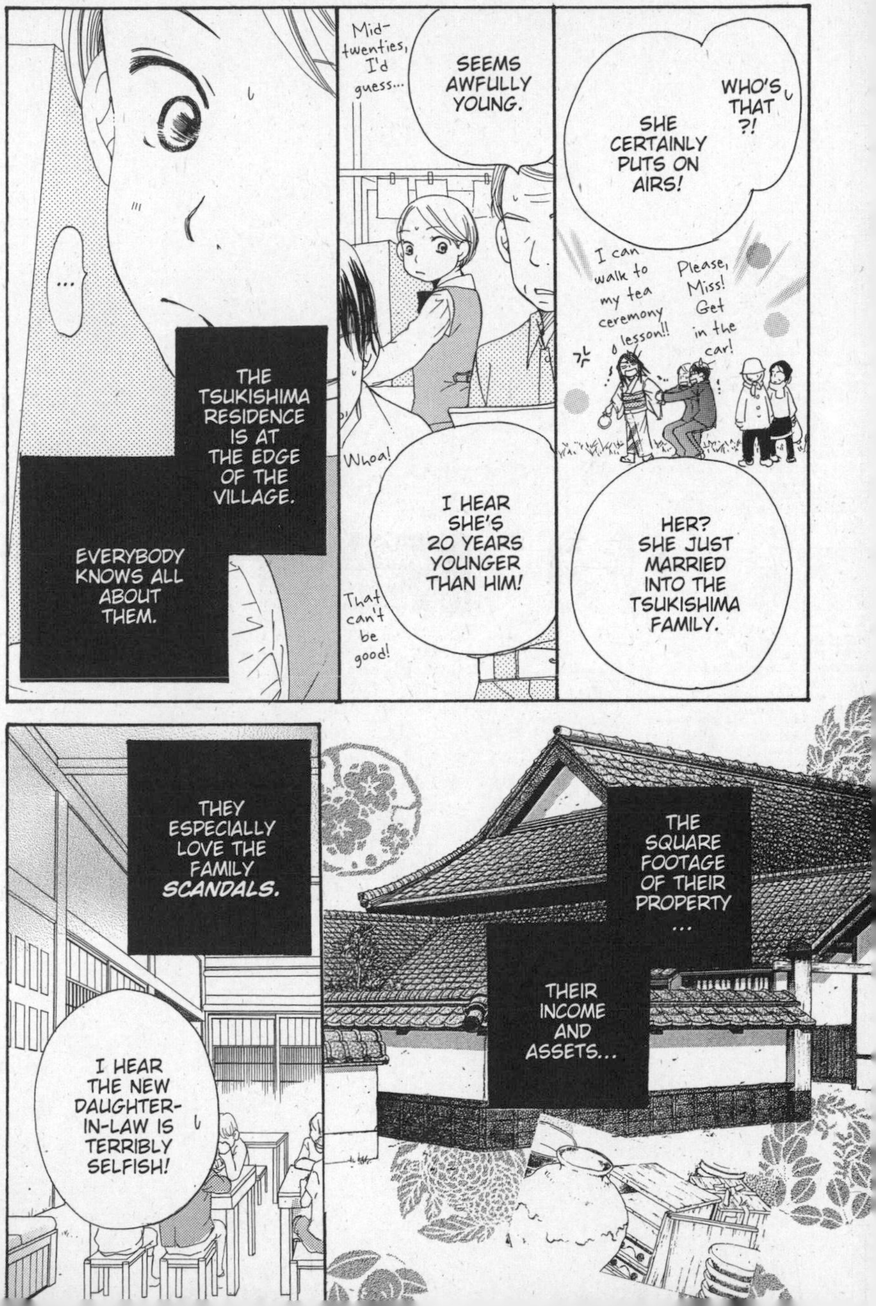
WHO'S THAT ?!
SHE CERTAINLY PUTS ON AIRS!
I can walk to my tea ceremony lesson!!
Please, Miss! Get in the car!
HER? SHE JUST MARRIED INTO THE TSUKISHIMA FAMILY.
Mid-twenties, I'd guess...
SEEMS AWFULLY YOUNG.
Whoa!
I HEAR SHE'S 20 YEARS YOUNGER THAN HIM!
That can't be good!
...
THE TSUKISHIMA RESIDENCE IS AT THE EDGE OF THE VILLAGE.
EVERYBODY KNOWS ALL ABOUT THEM.
THE SQUARE FOOTAGE OF THEIR PROPERTY ...
THEIR INCOME AND ASSETS...
THEY ESPECIALLY LOVE THE FAMILY *SCANDALS.*
I HEAR THE NEW DAUGHTER-IN-LAW IS TERRIBLY SELFISH!

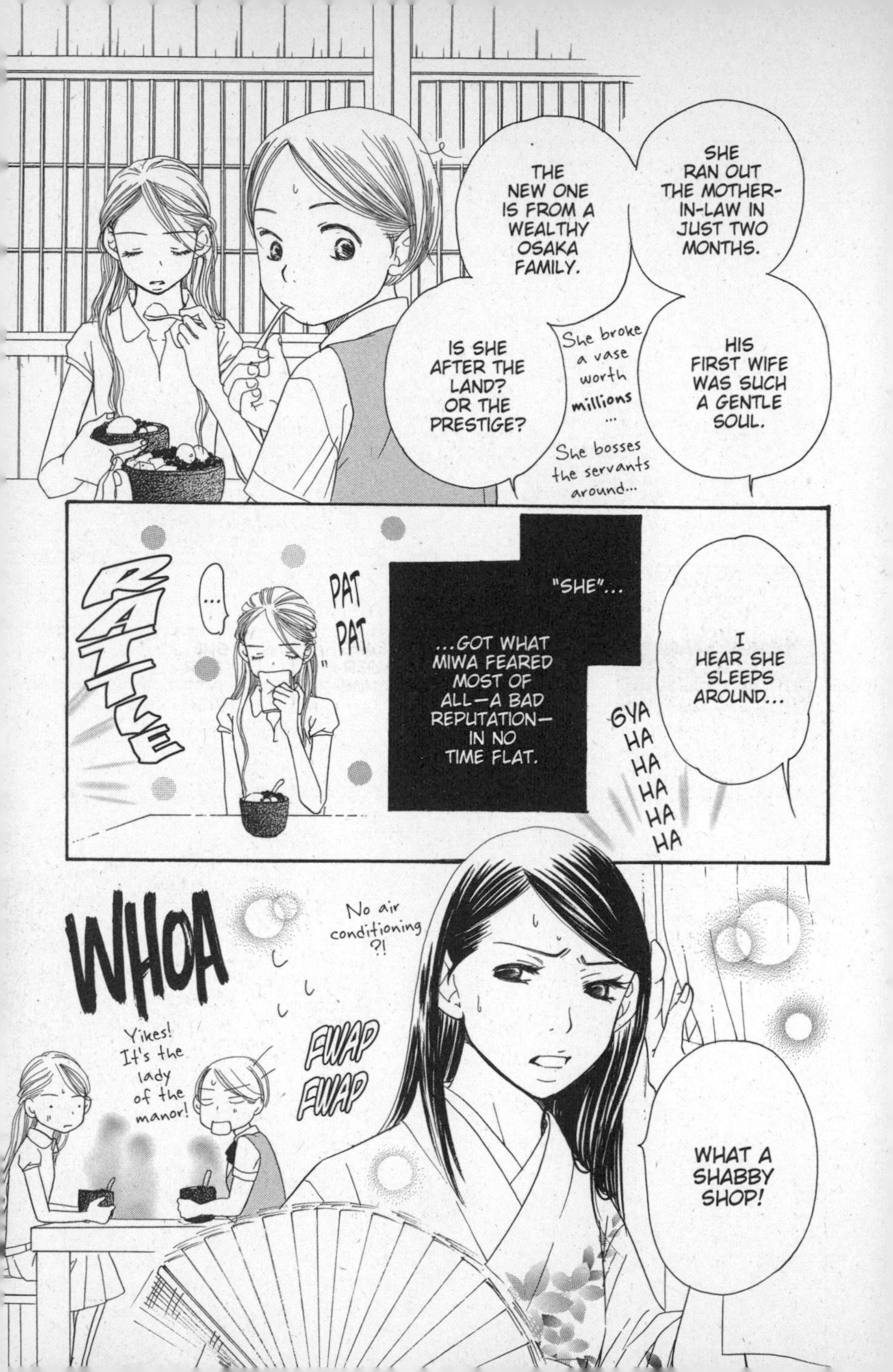
SHE RAN OUT THE MOTHER-IN-LAW IN JUST TWO MONTHS.
THE NEW ONE IS FROM A WEALTHY OSAKA FAMILY.
HIS FIRST WIFE WAS SUCH A GENTLE SOUL.
She broke a vase worth millions...
She bosses the servants around...
IS SHE AFTER THE LAND? OR THE PRESTIGE?
I HEAR SHE SLEEPS AROUND...
GYA HA HA HA HA HA HA
"SHE"...
...GOT WHAT MIWA FEARED MOST OF ALL—A BAD REPUTATION—IN NO TIME FLAT.
PAT PAT
...
RATTLE
WHAT A SHABBY SHOP!
No air conditioning?!
WHOA
FWAP FWAP
Yikes! It's the lady of the manor!

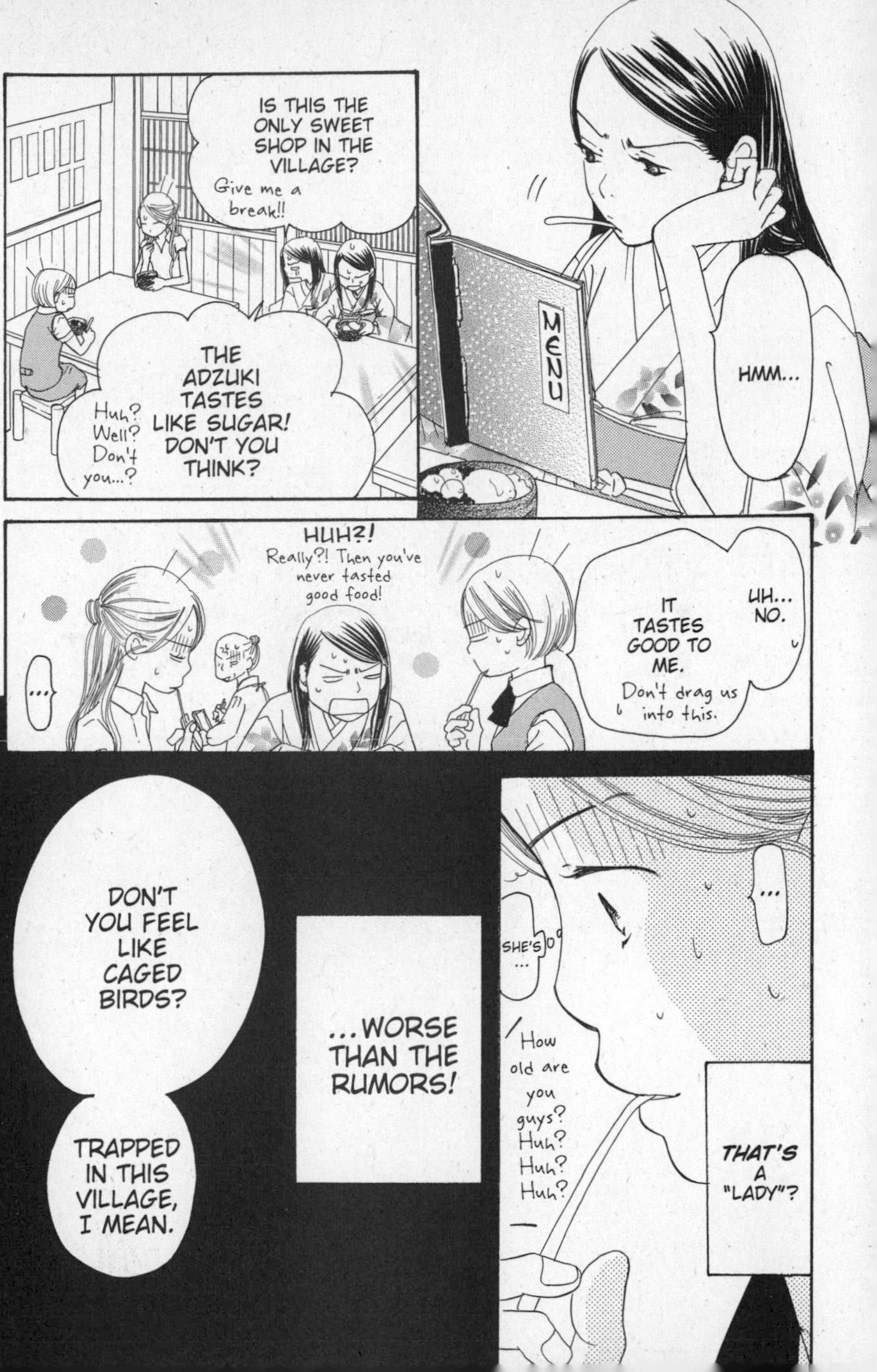
HMM...
IS THIS THE ONLY SWEET SHOP IN THE VILLAGE?
Give me a break!!
THE ADZUKI TASTES LIKE SUGAR! DON'T YOU THINK?
Huh? Well? Don't you...?
UH... NO.
IT TASTES GOOD TO ME.
Don't drag us into this.
HUH?!
Really?! Then you've never tasted good food!
...
...
THAT'S A "LADY"?
SHE'S...
How old are you guys? Huh? Huh? Huh?
...WORSE THAN THE RUMORS!
DON'T YOU FEEL LIKE CAGED BIRDS?
TRAPPED IN THIS VILLAGE, I MEAN.

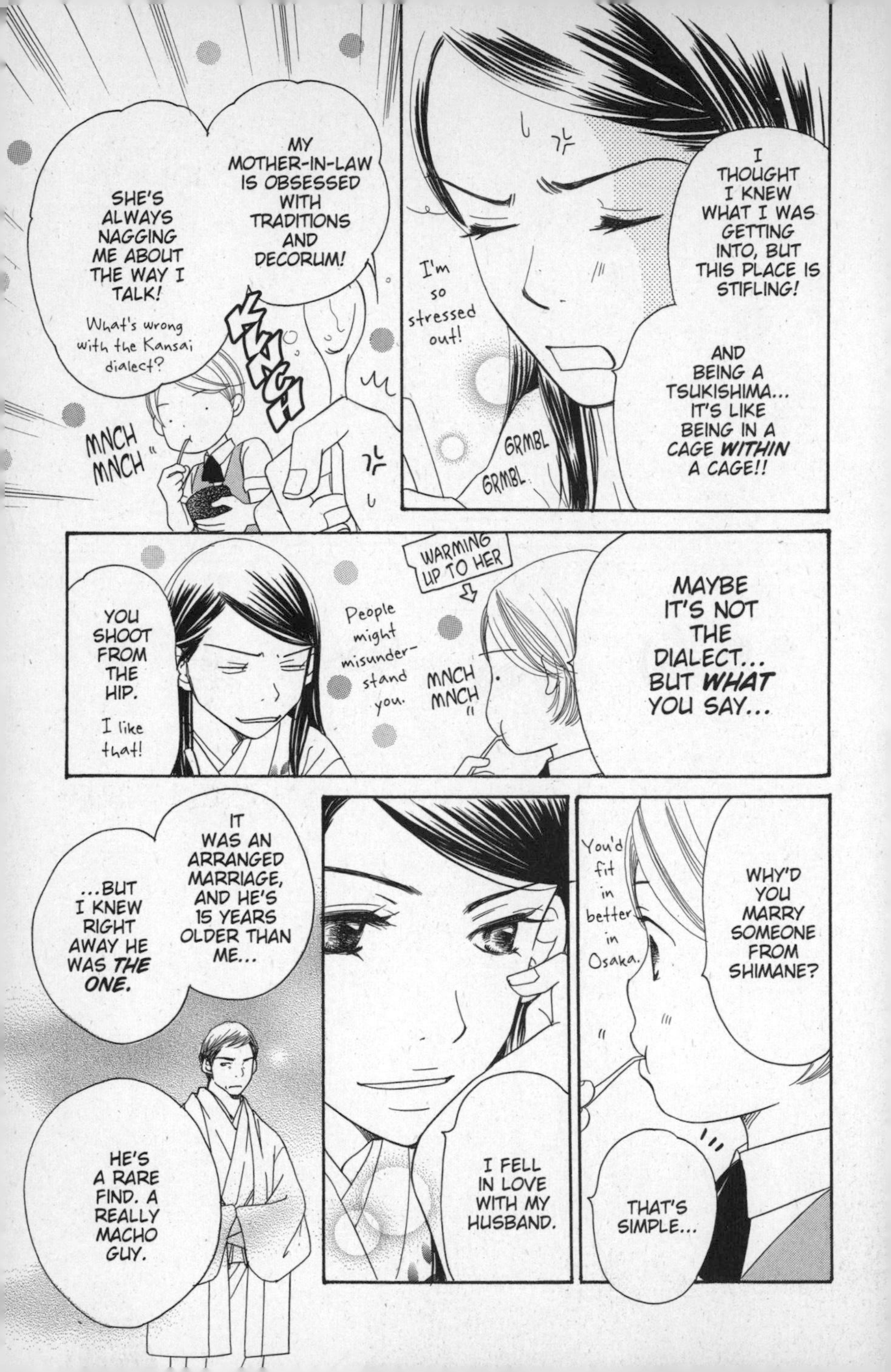
I THOUGHT I KNEW WHAT I WAS GETTING INTO, BUT THIS PLACE IS STIFLING!
AND BEING A TSUKISHIMA... IT'S LIKE BEING IN A CAGE *WITHIN* A CAGE!!
I'm so stressed out!
GRMBL
GRMBL
MY MOTHER-IN-LAW IS OBSESSED WITH TRADITIONS AND DECORUM!
SHE'S ALWAYS NAGGING ME ABOUT THE WAY I TALK!
What's wrong with the Kansai dialect?
MNCH MNCH
MAYBE IT'S NOT THE DIALECT... BUT *WHAT* YOU SAY...
WARMING UP TO HER
MNCH MNCH
People might misunder-stand you.
YOU SHOOT FROM THE HIP.
I like that!
WHY'D YOU MARRY SOMEONE FROM SHIMANE?
You'd fit in better in Osaka.
THAT'S SIMPLE...
I FELL IN LOVE WITH MY HUSBAND.
IT WAS AN ARRANGED MARRIAGE, AND HE'S 15 YEARS OLDER THAN ME...
...BUT I KNEW RIGHT AWAY HE WAS *THE ONE.*
HE'S A RARE FIND. A REALLY MACHO GUY.

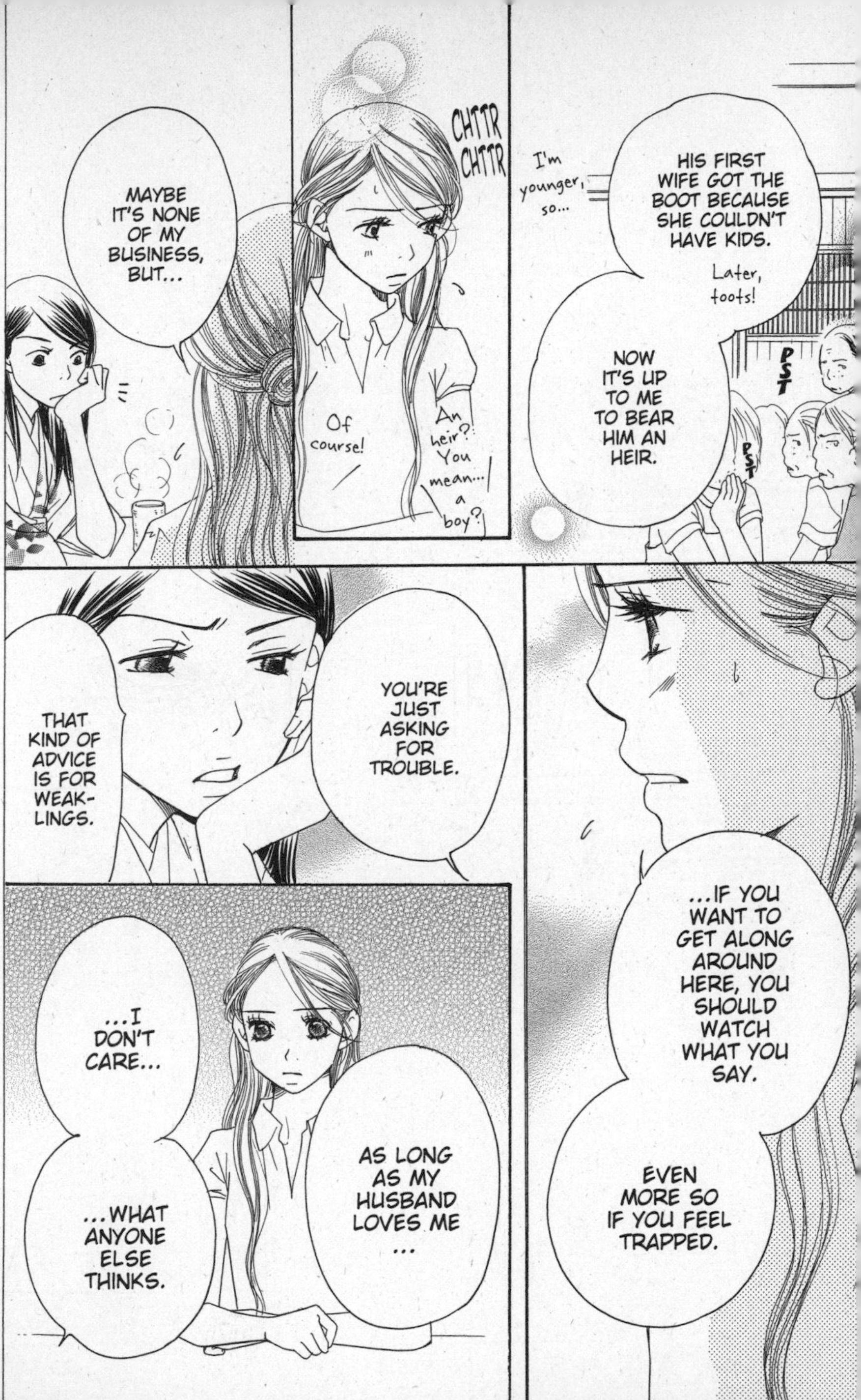
HIS FIRST WIFE GOT THE BOOT BECAUSE SHE COULDN'T HAVE KIDS.
Later, toots!
PST
PST
NOW IT'S UP TO ME TO BEAR HIM AN HEIR.
I'm younger, so...
CHTTR CHTTR
An heir?! You mean... a boy?!
Of course!
MAYBE IT'S NONE OF MY BUSINESS, BUT...
...IF YOU WANT TO GET ALONG AROUND HERE, YOU SHOULD WATCH WHAT YOU SAY.
EVEN MORE SO IF YOU FEEL TRAPPED.
YOU'RE JUST ASKING FOR TROUBLE.
THAT KIND OF ADVICE IS FOR WEAK-LINGS.
AS LONG AS MY HUSBAND LOVES ME ...
...I DON'T CARE...
...WHAT ANYONE ELSE THINKS.

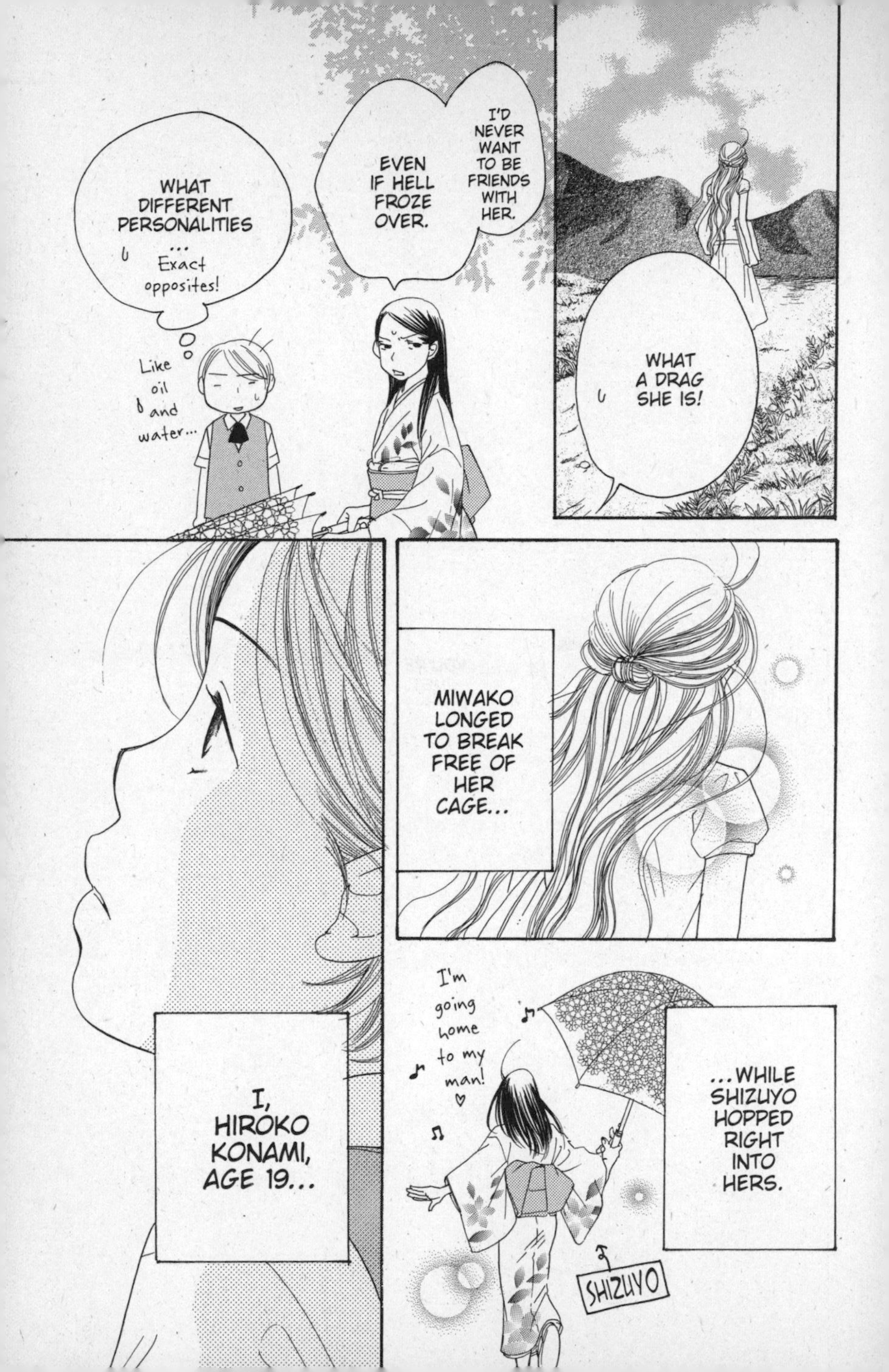
WHAT A DRAG SHE IS!
I'D NEVER WANT TO BE FRIENDS WITH HER.
EVEN IF HELL FROZE OVER.
WHAT DIFFERENT PERSONALITIES... Exact opposites!
Like oil and water...
MIWAKO LONGED TO BREAK FREE OF HER CAGE...
...WHILE SHIZUYO HOPPED RIGHT INTO HERS.
I'm going home to my man! ♡
SHIZUYO
I, HIROKO KONAMI, AGE 19...

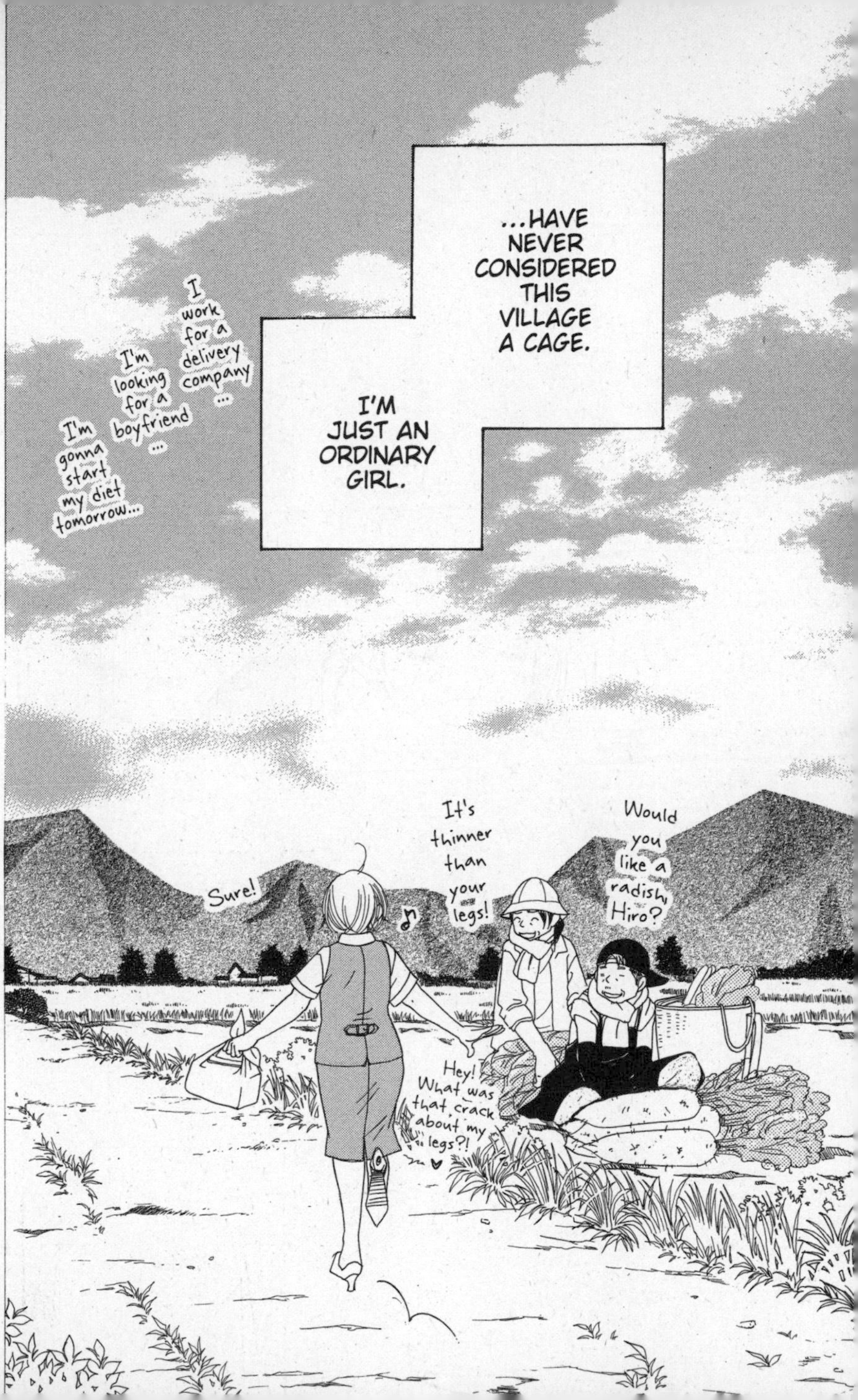
...HAVE NEVER CONSIDERED THIS VILLAGE A CAGE.
I'M JUST AN ORDINARY GIRL.
I work for a delivery company...
I'm looking for a boyfriend...
I'm gonna start my diet tomorrow...
Would you like a radish, Hiro?
It's thinner than your legs!
Hey! What was that crack about my legs?!
Sure!

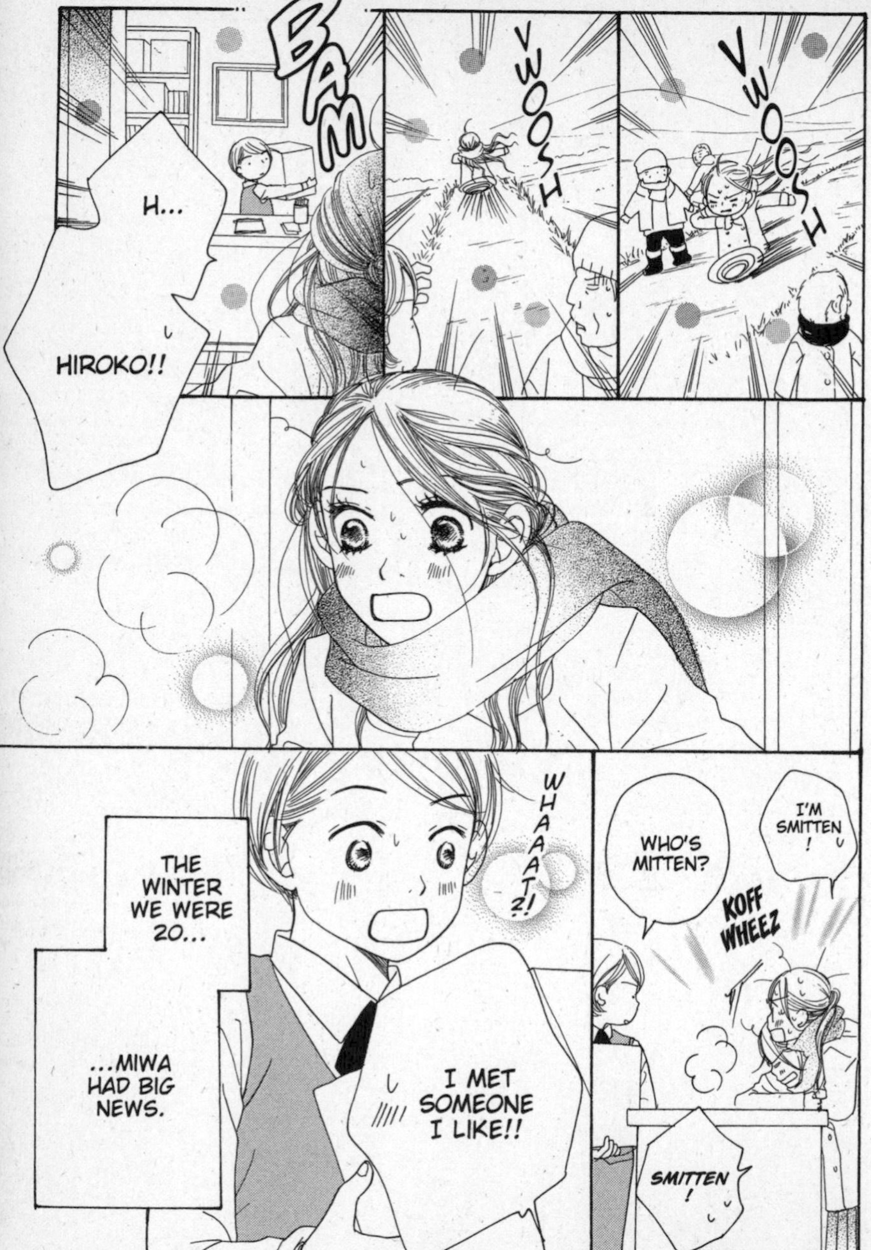
VWOOSH
VWOOSH
BAM
H...
HIROKO!!
I'M SMITTEN!
WHO'S MITTEN?
KOFF WHEEZ
SMITTEN!
WHAAAAT?!
THE WINTER WE WERE 20...
...MIWA HAD BIG NEWS.
I MET SOMEONE I LIKE!!

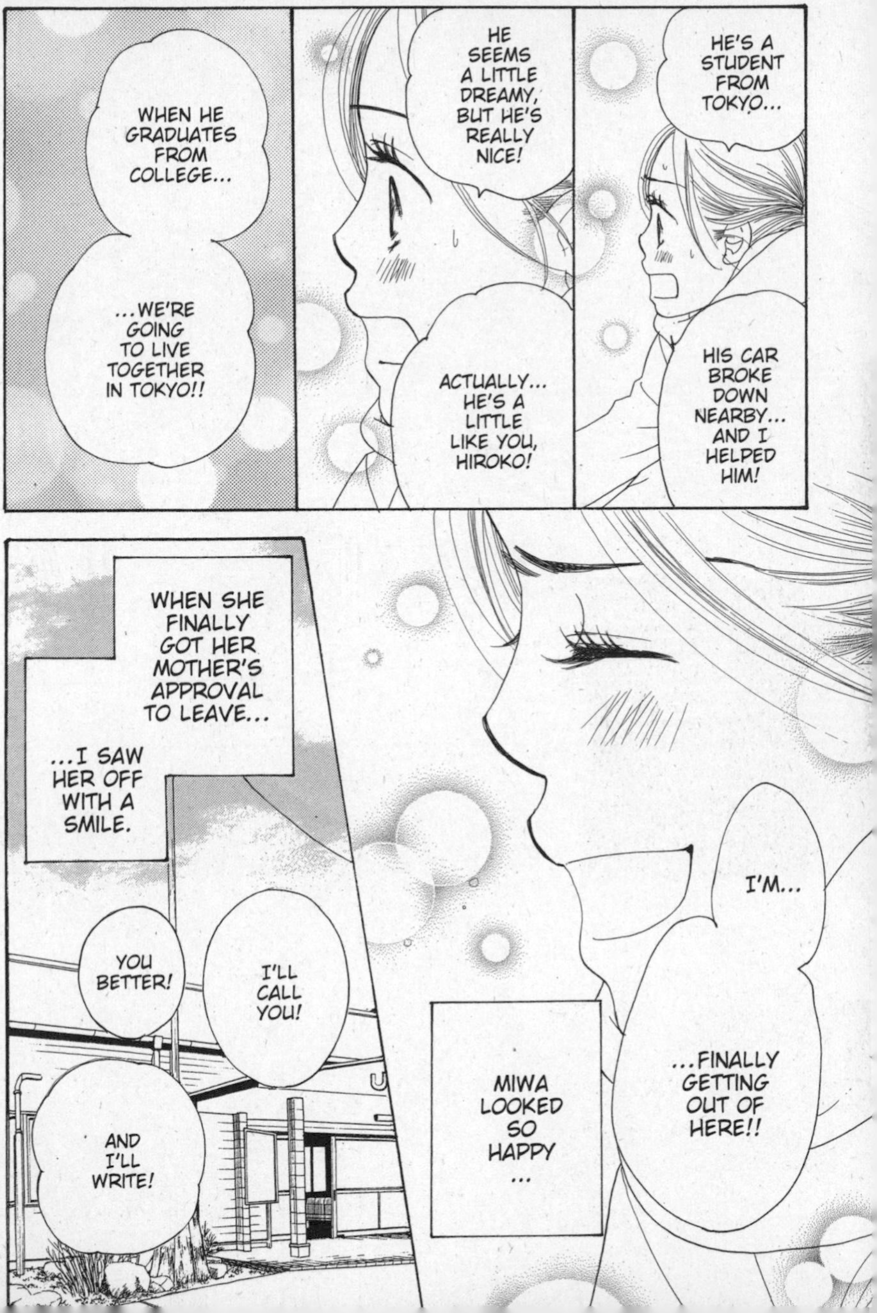
HE'S A STUDENT FROM TOKYO...
HIS CAR BROKE DOWN NEARBY... AND I HELPED HIM!
HE SEEMS A LITTLE DREAMY, BUT HE'S REALLY NICE!
ACTUALLY... HE'S A LITTLE LIKE YOU, HIROKO!
WHEN HE GRADUATES FROM COLLEGE...
...WE'RE GOING TO LIVE TOGETHER IN TOKYO!!
I'M...
...FINALLY GETTING OUT OF HERE!!
MIWA LOOKED SO HAPPY ...
WHEN SHE FINALLY GOT HER MOTHER'S APPROVAL TO LEAVE...
...I SAW HER OFF WITH A SMILE.
I'LL CALL YOU!
YOU BETTER!
AND I'LL WRITE!

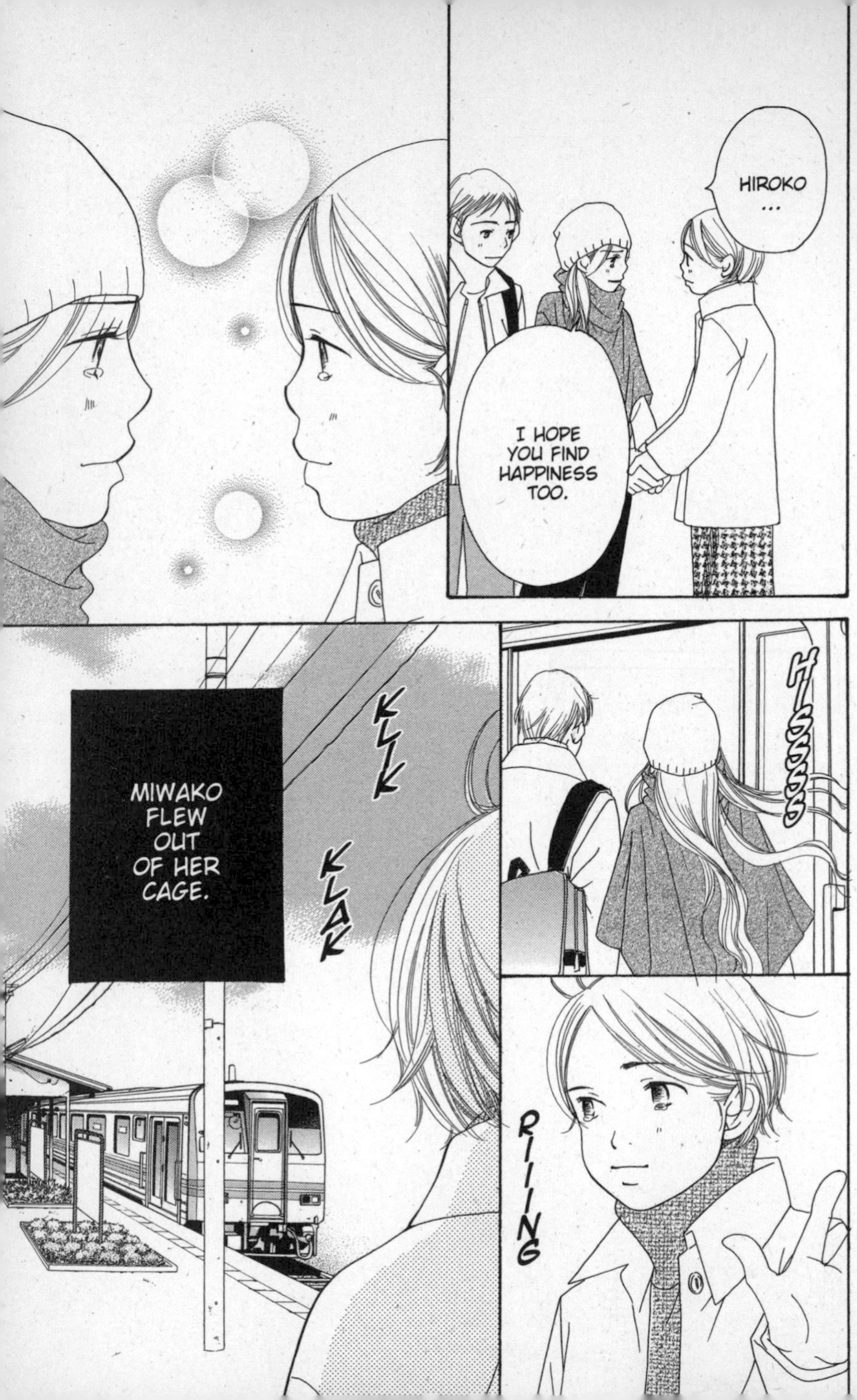
HIROKO ...
I HOPE YOU FIND HAPPINESS TOO.
HISSSS
RIIING
MIWAKO FLEW OUT OF HER CAGE.
KLIK
KLAK

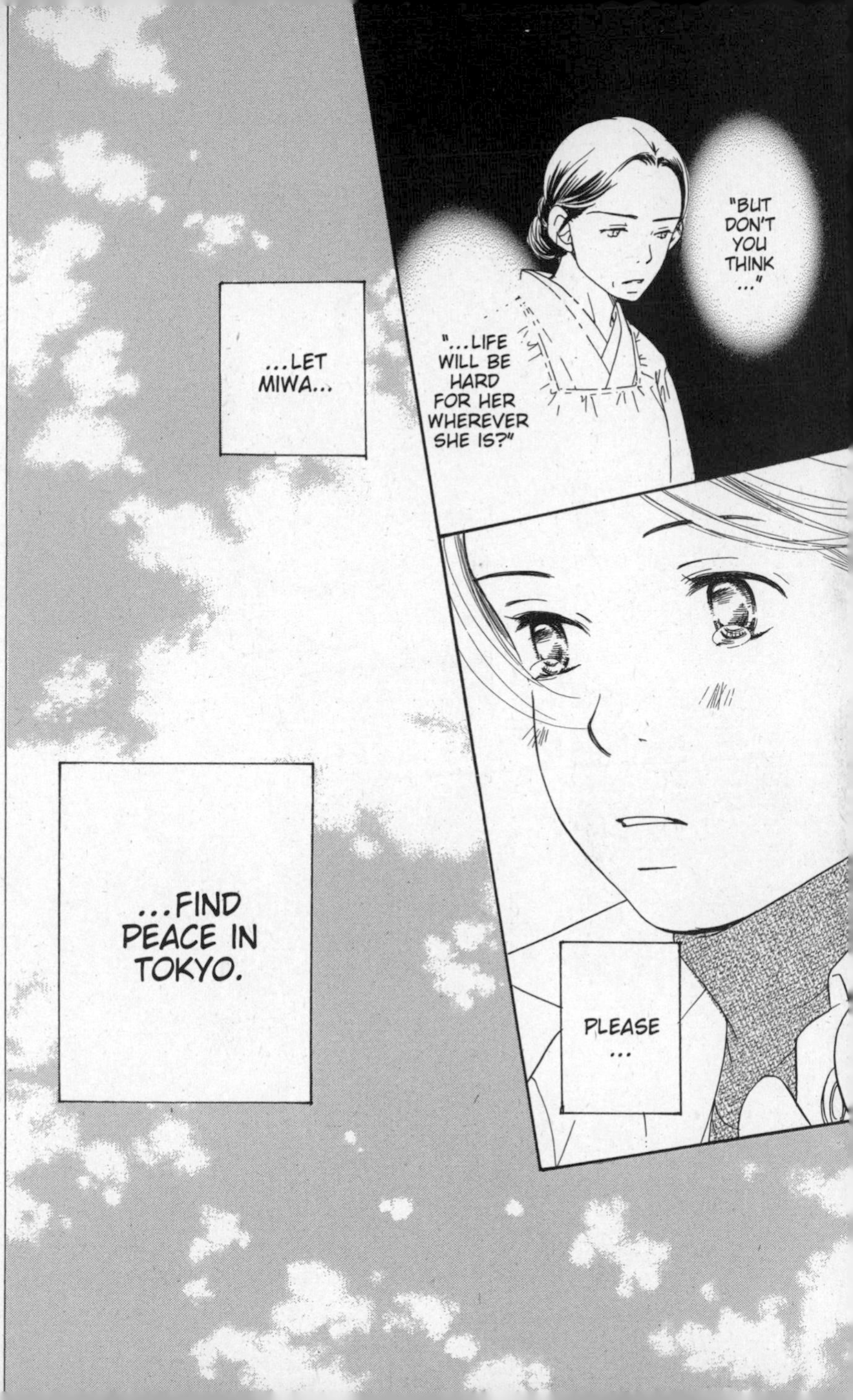
"BUT DON'T YOU THINK ..."
"...LIFE WILL BE HARD FOR HER WHEREVER SHE IS?"
PLEASE ...
...LET MIWA...
...FIND PEACE IN TOKYO.

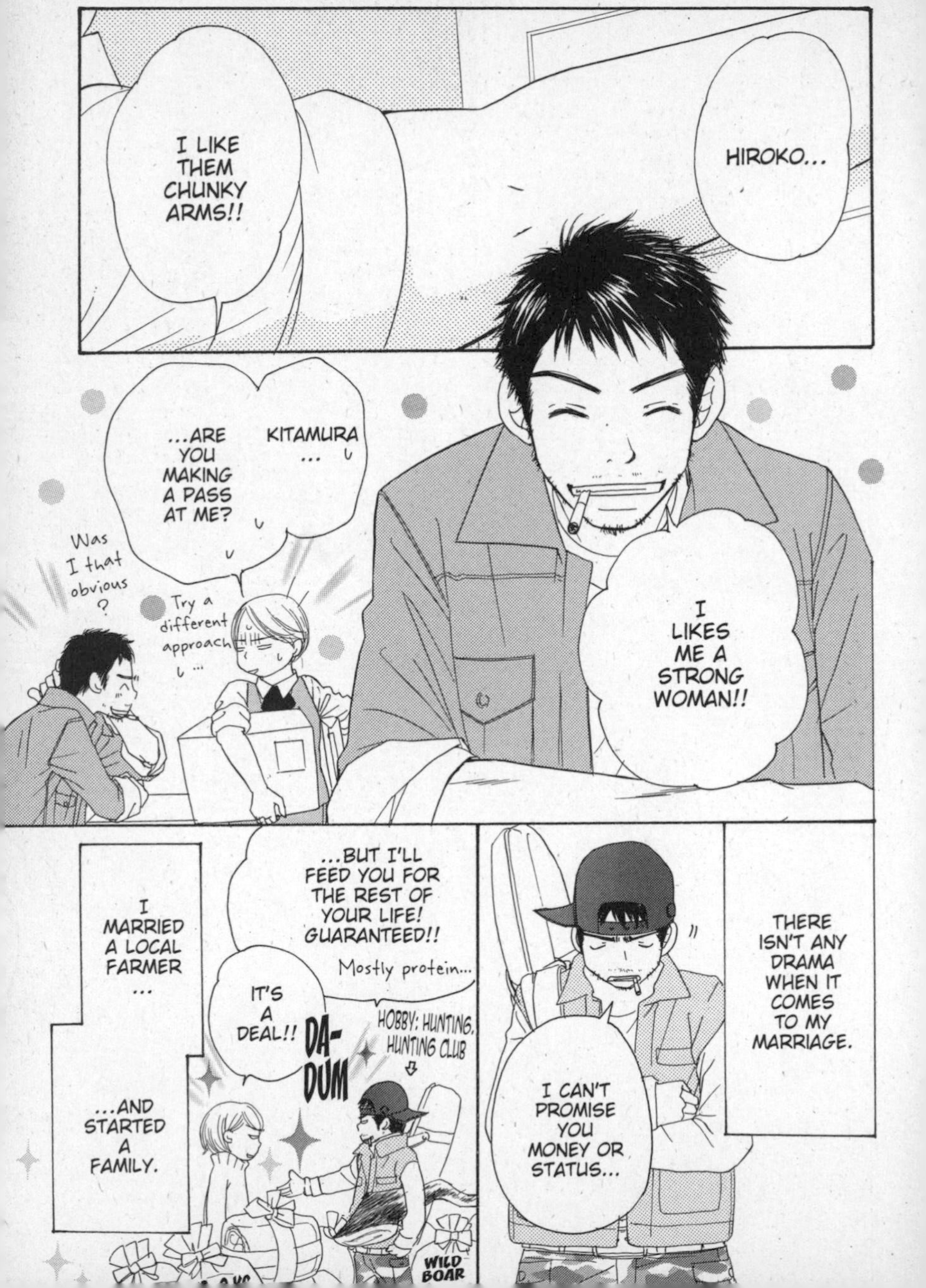
HIROKO...
I LIKE THEM CHUNKY ARMS!!
I LIKES ME A STRONG WOMAN!!
KITAMURA...
...ARE YOU MAKING A PASS AT ME?
Try a different approach...
Was I that obvious?
THERE ISN'T ANY DRAMA WHEN IT COMES TO MY MARRIAGE.
I CAN'T PROMISE YOU MONEY OR STATUS...
...BUT I'LL FEED YOU FOR THE REST OF YOUR LIFE! GUARANTEED!!
Mostly protein...
I MARRIED A LOCAL FARMER...
IT'S A DEAL!!
DA-DUM
HOBBY: HUNTING, HUNTING CLUB
...AND STARTED A FAMILY.
WILD BOAR

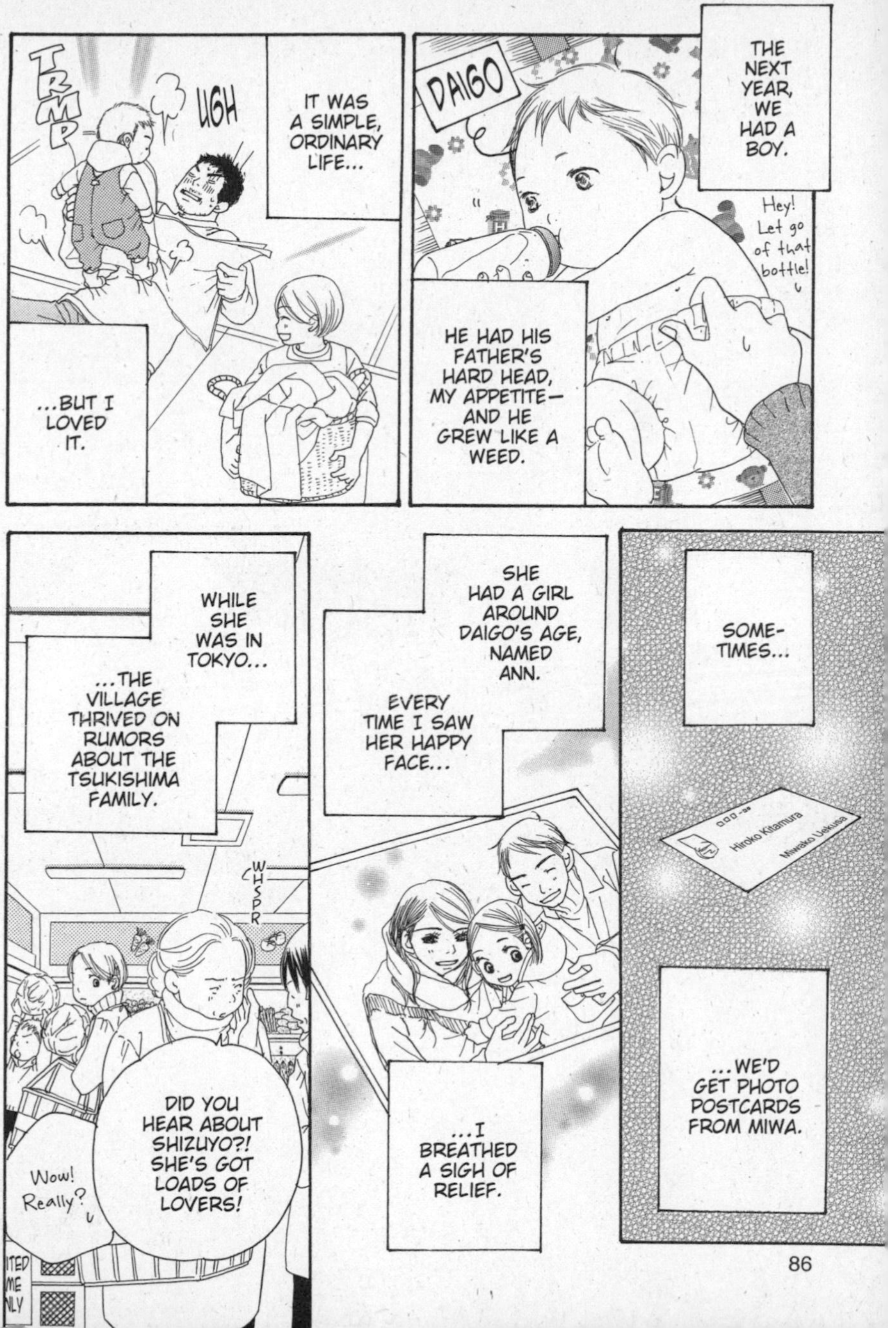
THE NEXT YEAR, WE HAD A BOY.
DAIGO
Hey! Let go of that bottle!
HE HAD HIS FATHER'S HARD HEAD, MY APPETITE—AND HE GREW LIKE A WEED.
IT WAS A SIMPLE, ORDINARY LIFE...
UGH
TRMP
...BUT I LOVED IT.
SOME-TIMES...
Hiroko Kitamura
Miwako Uekusa
...WE'D GET PHOTO POSTCARDS FROM MIWA.
SHE HAD A GIRL AROUND DAIGO'S AGE, NAMED ANN.
EVERY TIME I SAW HER HAPPY FACE...
...I BREATHED A SIGH OF RELIEF.
WHILE SHE WAS IN TOKYO...
...THE VILLAGE THRIVED ON RUMORS ABOUT THE TSUKISHIMA FAMILY.
WHSPR
DID YOU HEAR ABOUT SHIZUYO?! SHE'S GOT LOADS OF LOVERS!
Wow! Really?

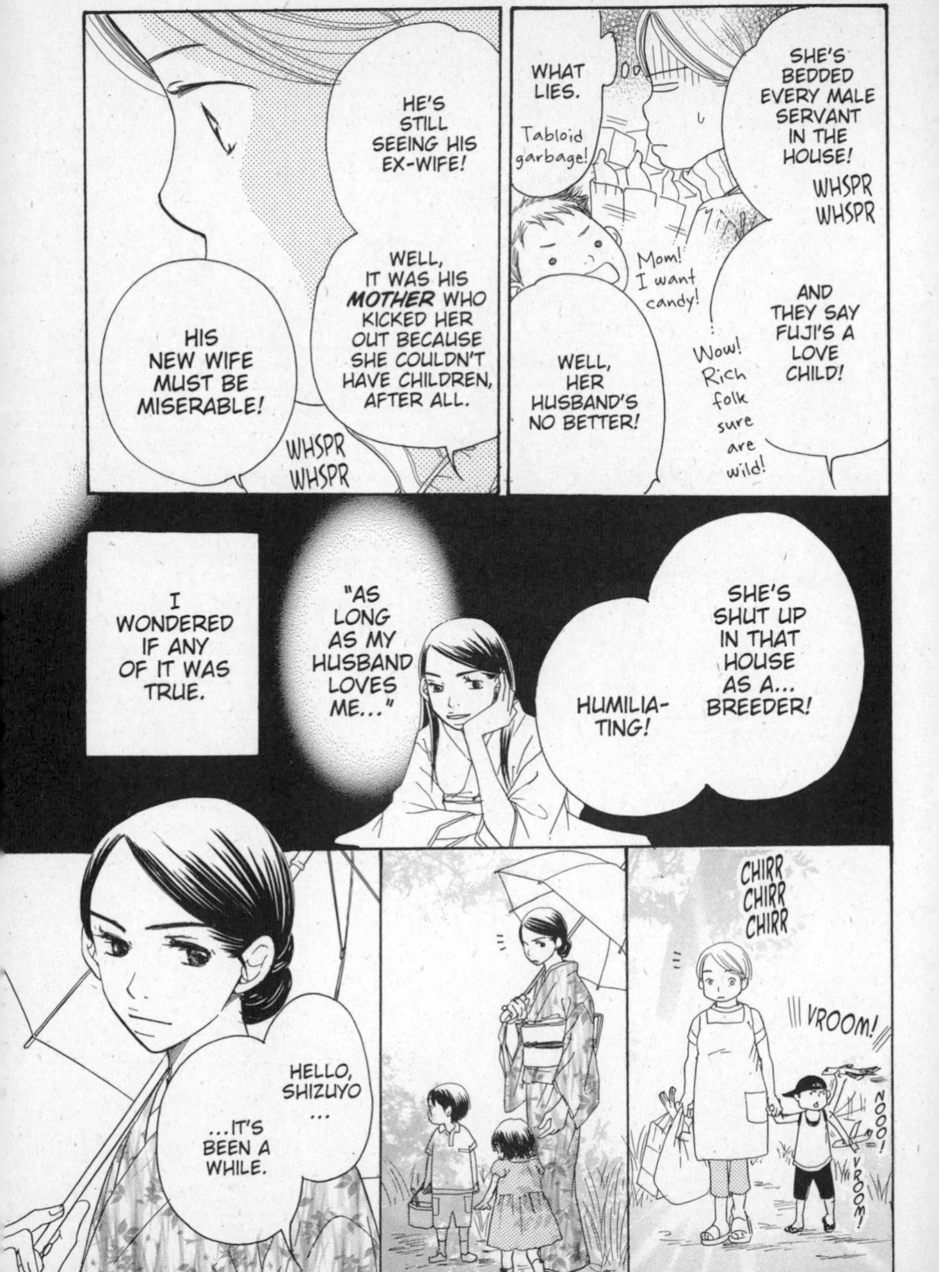
SHE'S BEDDED EVERY MALE SERVANT IN THE HOUSE!
WHSPR WHSPR
WHAT LIES.
Tabloid garbage!
AND THEY SAY FUJI'S A LOVE CHILD!
Wow! Rich folk sure are wild!
Mom! I want candy!
WELL, HER HUSBAND'S NO BETTER!
HE'S STILL SEEING HIS EX-WIFE!
WELL, IT WAS HIS *MOTHER* WHO KICKED HER OUT BECAUSE SHE COULDN'T HAVE CHILDREN, AFTER ALL.
HIS NEW WIFE MUST BE MISERABLE!
WHSPR WHSPR
SHE'S SHUT UP IN THAT HOUSE AS A... BREEDER!
HUMILIA-TING!
"AS LONG AS MY HUSBAND LOVES ME..."
I WONDERED IF ANY OF IT WAS TRUE.
CHIRR CHIRR CHIRR
VROOM!
NOOO!
VROOM!
HELLO, SHIZUYO ...
...IT'S BEEN A WHILE.

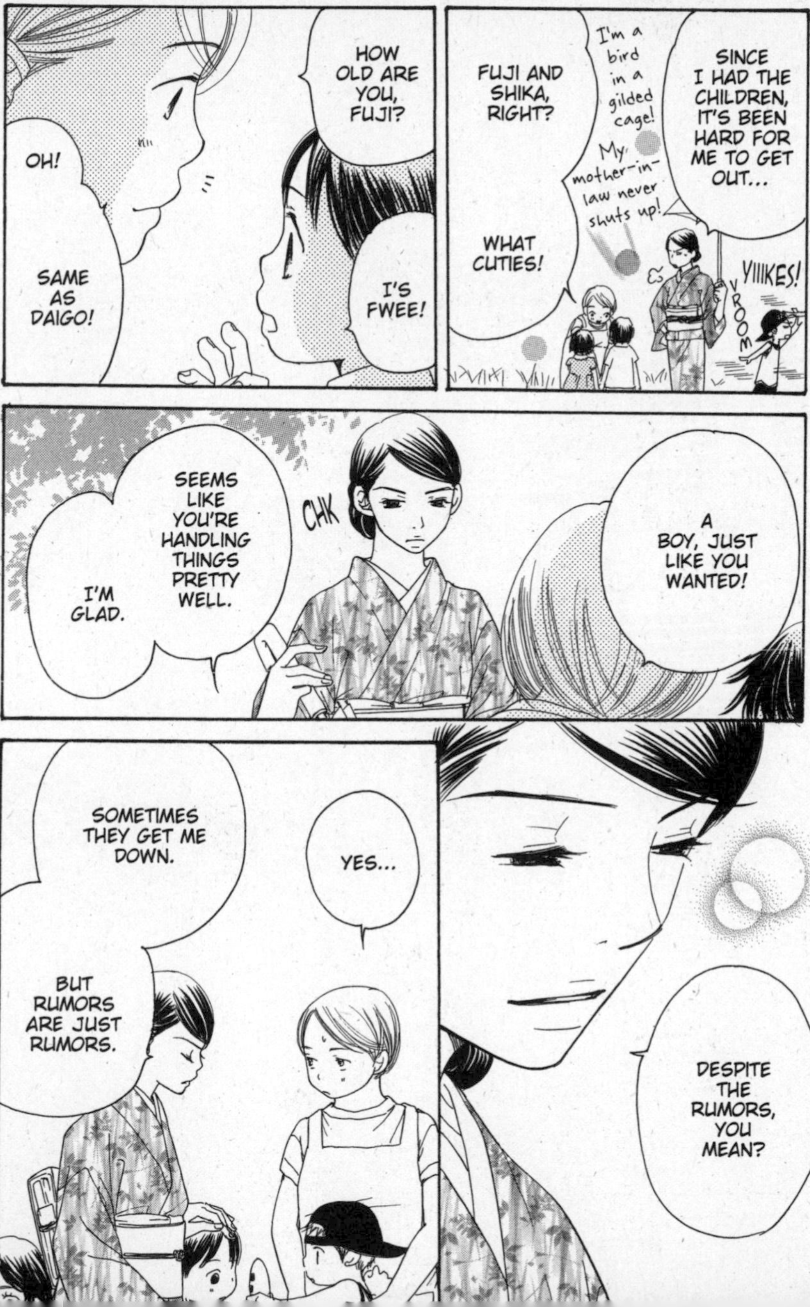
SINCE I HAD THE CHILDREN, IT'S BEEN HARD FOR ME TO GET OUT...
I'm a bird in a gilded cage!
My mother-in-law never shuts up!
YIIIKES!
VROOM
FUJI AND SHIKA, RIGHT?
WHAT CUTIES!
HOW OLD ARE YOU, FUJI?
I'S FWEE!
OH!
SAME AS DAIGO!
A BOY, JUST LIKE YOU WANTED!
CHK
SEEMS LIKE YOU'RE HANDLING THINGS PRETTY WELL.
I'M GLAD.
DESPITE THE RUMORS, YOU MEAN?
YES...
SOMETIMES THEY GET ME DOWN.
BUT RUMORS ARE JUST RUMORS.

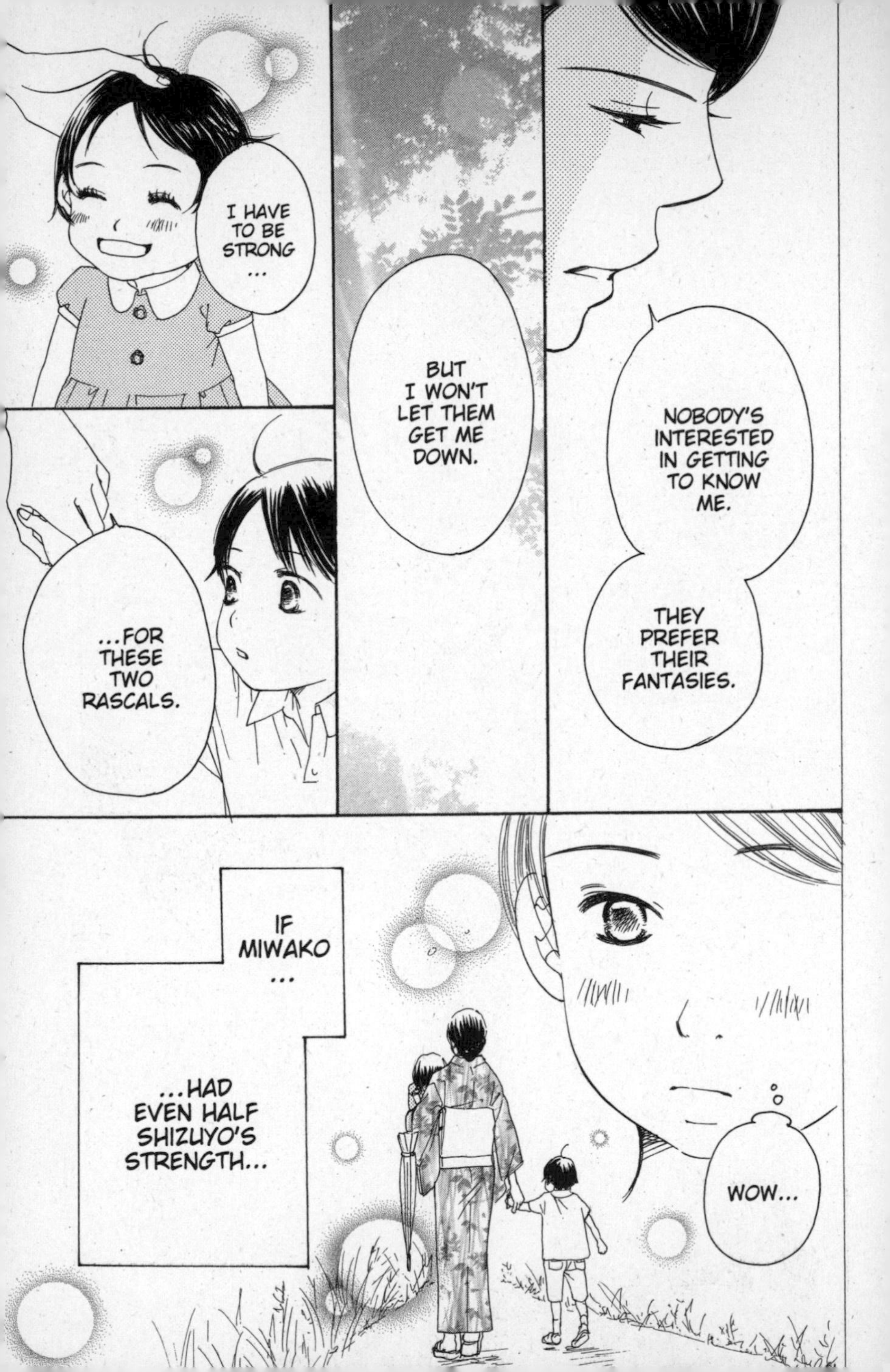

NOBODY'S INTERESTED IN GETTING TO KNOW ME.
THEY PREFER THEIR FANTASIES.
BUT I WON'T LET THEM GET ME DOWN.
I HAVE TO BE STRONG...
...FOR THESE TWO RASCALS.
WOW...
IF MIWAKO...
...HAD EVEN HALF SHIZUYO'S STRENGTH...

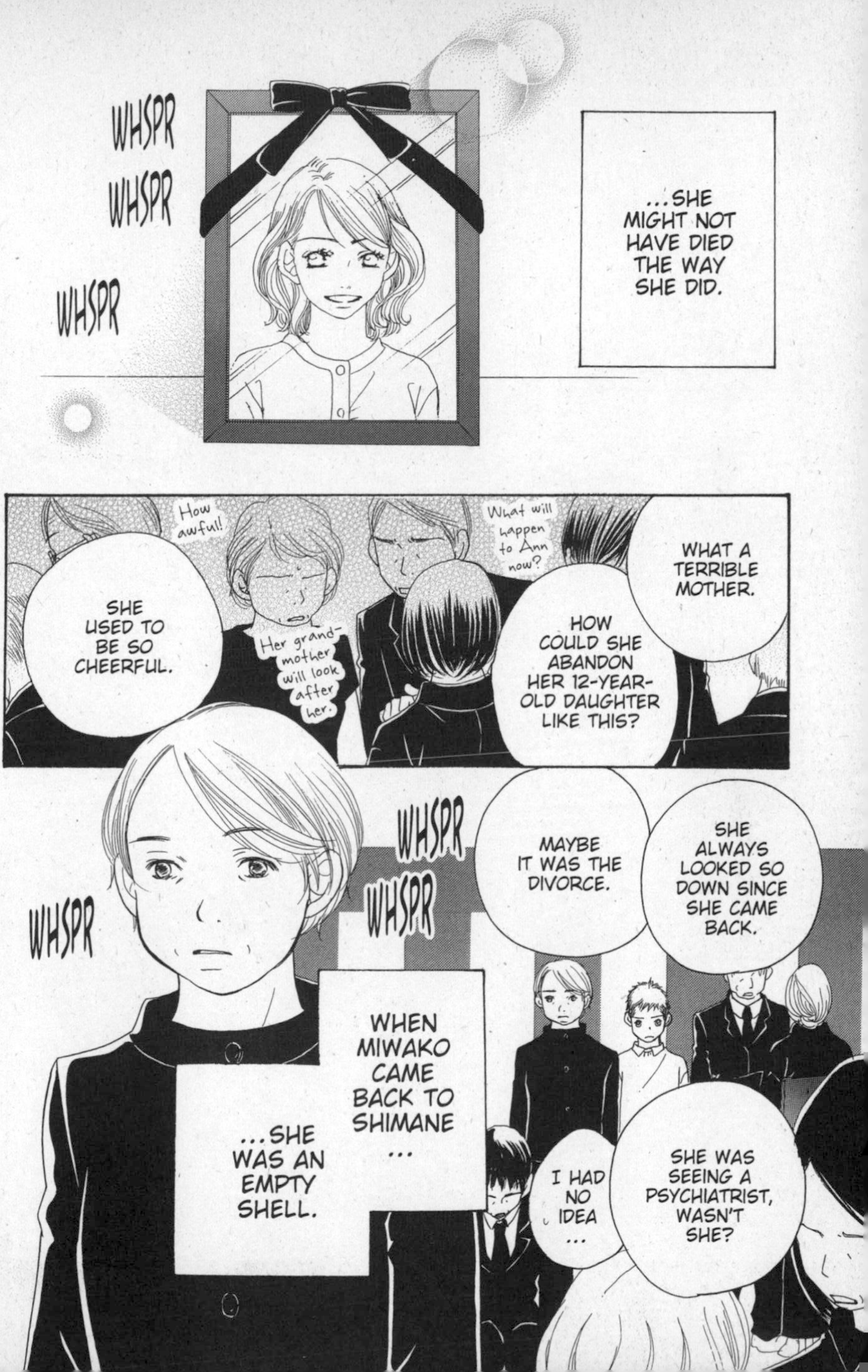
...SHE MIGHT NOT HAVE DIED THE WAY SHE DID.
WHSPR
WHSPR
WHSPR
WHAT A TERRIBLE MOTHER.
What will happen to Ann now?
HOW COULD SHE ABANDON HER 12-YEAR-OLD DAUGHTER LIKE THIS?
How awful!
Her grand-mother will look after her.
SHE USED TO BE SO CHEERFUL.
SHE ALWAYS LOOKED SO DOWN SINCE SHE CAME BACK.
MAYBE IT WAS THE DIVORCE.
WHSPR
WHSPR
WHEN MIWAKO CAME BACK TO SHIMANE...
SHE WAS SEEING A PSYCHIATRIST, WASN'T SHE?
I HAD NO IDEA...
...SHE WAS AN EMPTY SHELL.
WHSPR

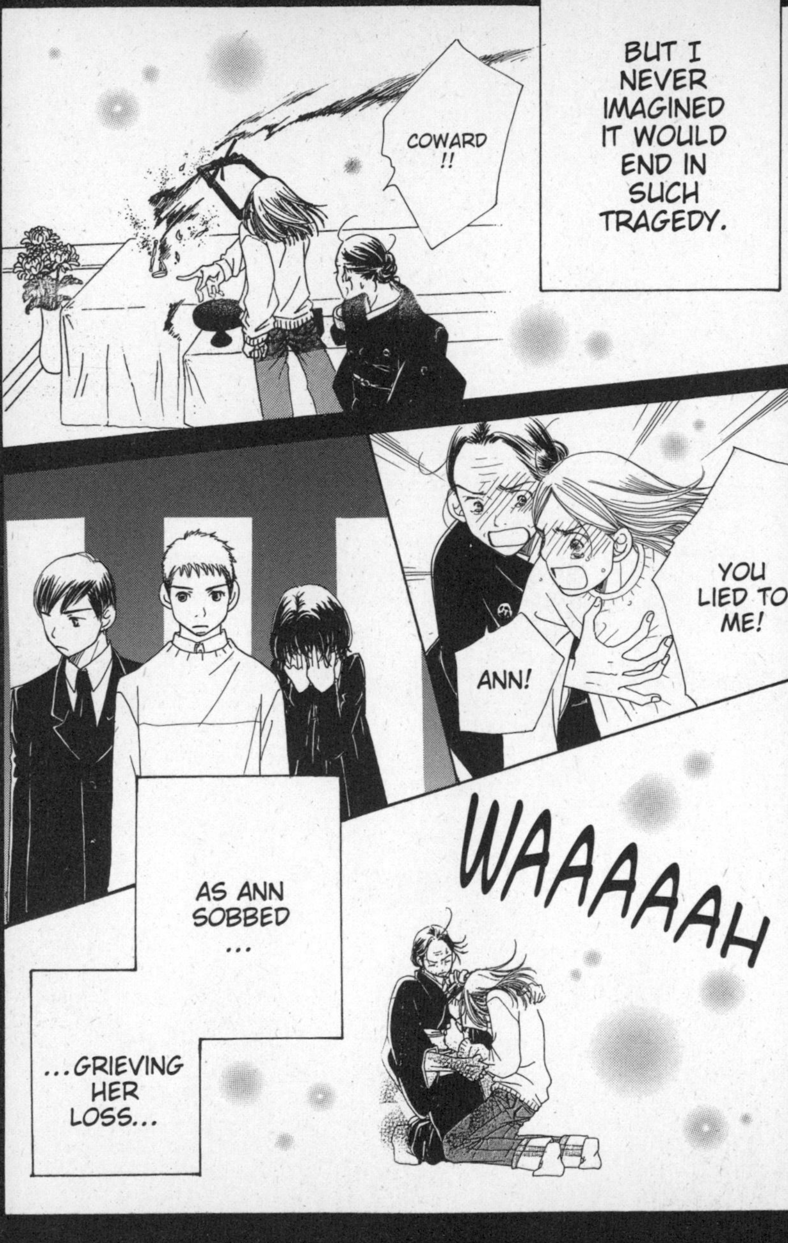
BUT I NEVER IMAGINED IT WOULD END IN SUCH TRAGEDY.
COWARD !!
YOU LIED TO ME!
ANN!
WAAAAAH
AS ANN SOBBED ...
...GRIEVING HER LOSS...

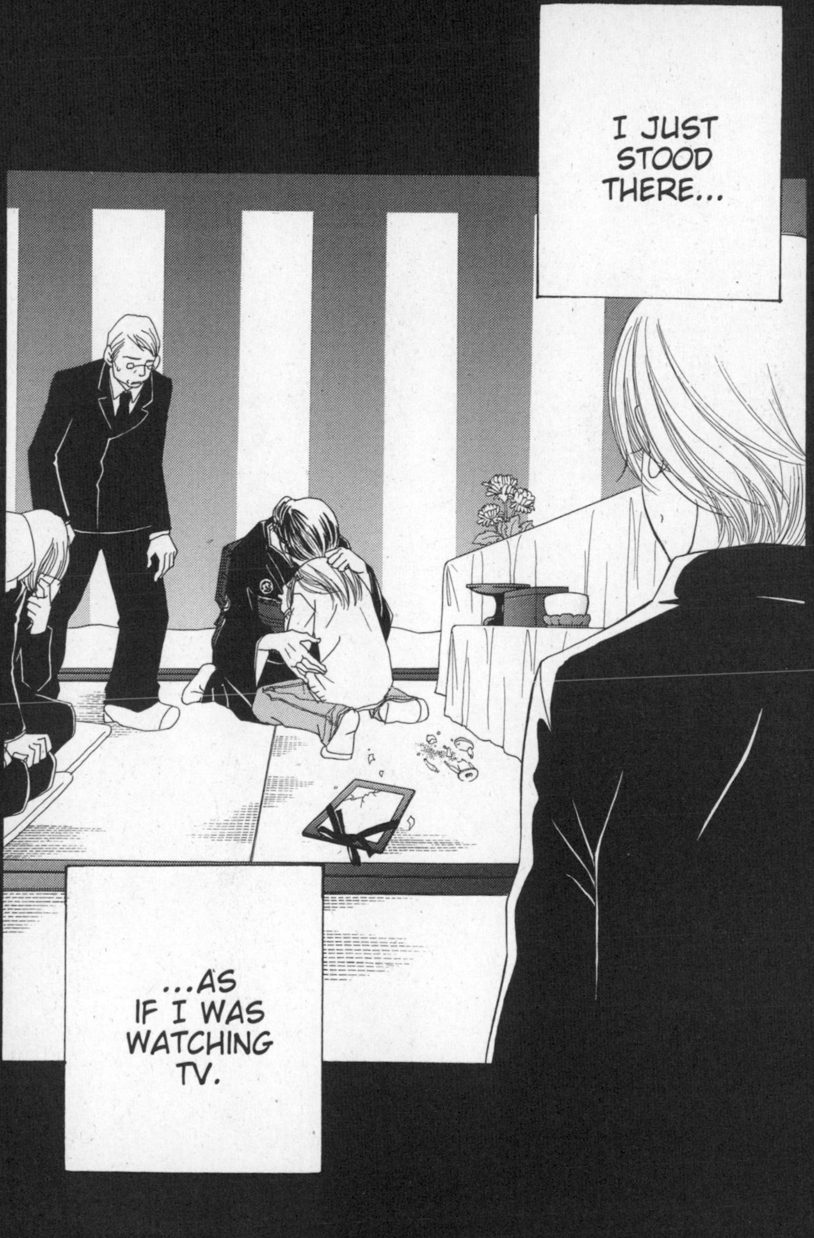
I JUST STOOD THERE...
...AS IF I WAS WATCHING TV.

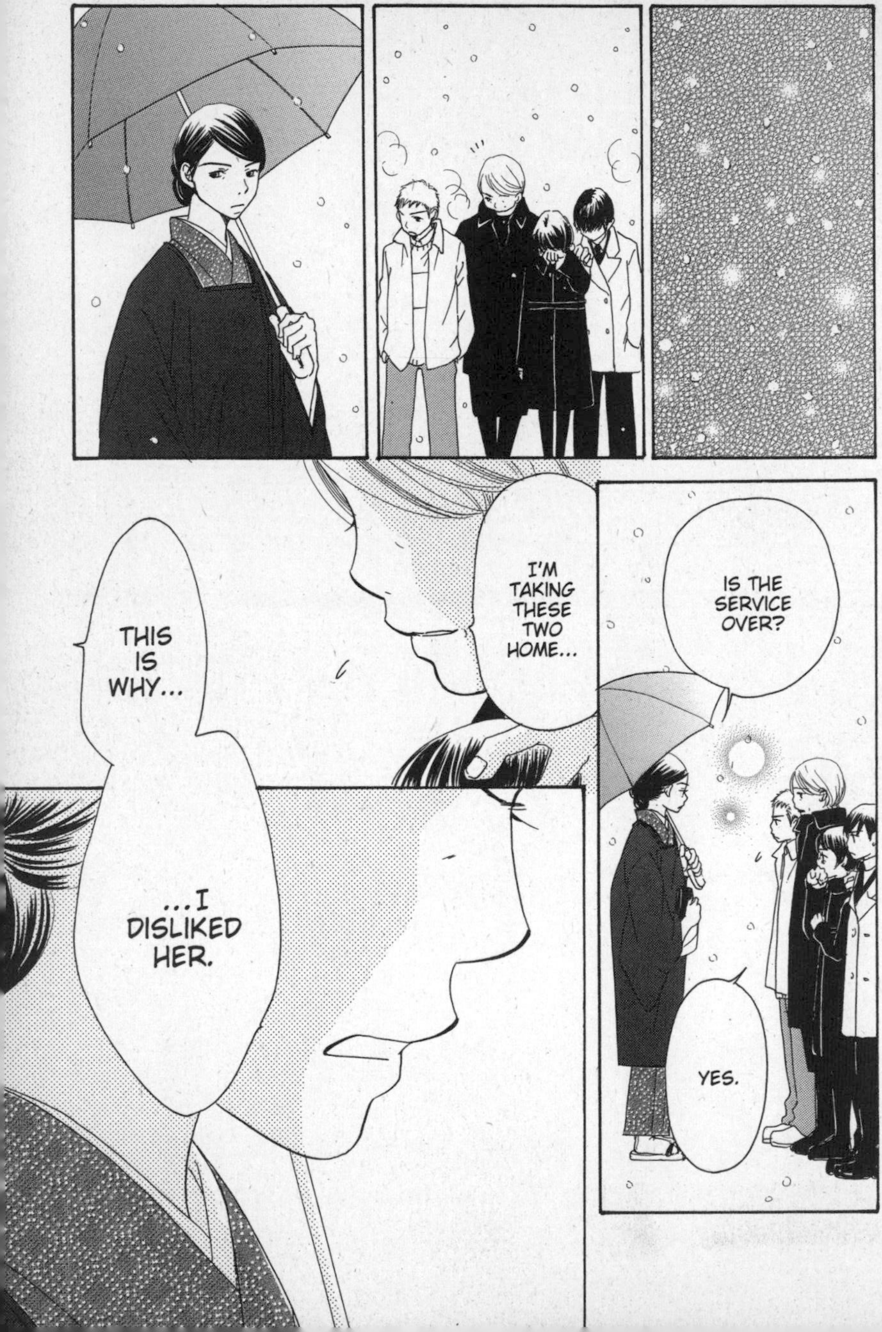
IS THE SERVICE OVER?
YES.
I'M TAKING THESE TWO HOME...
THIS IS WHY...
...I DISLIKED HER.

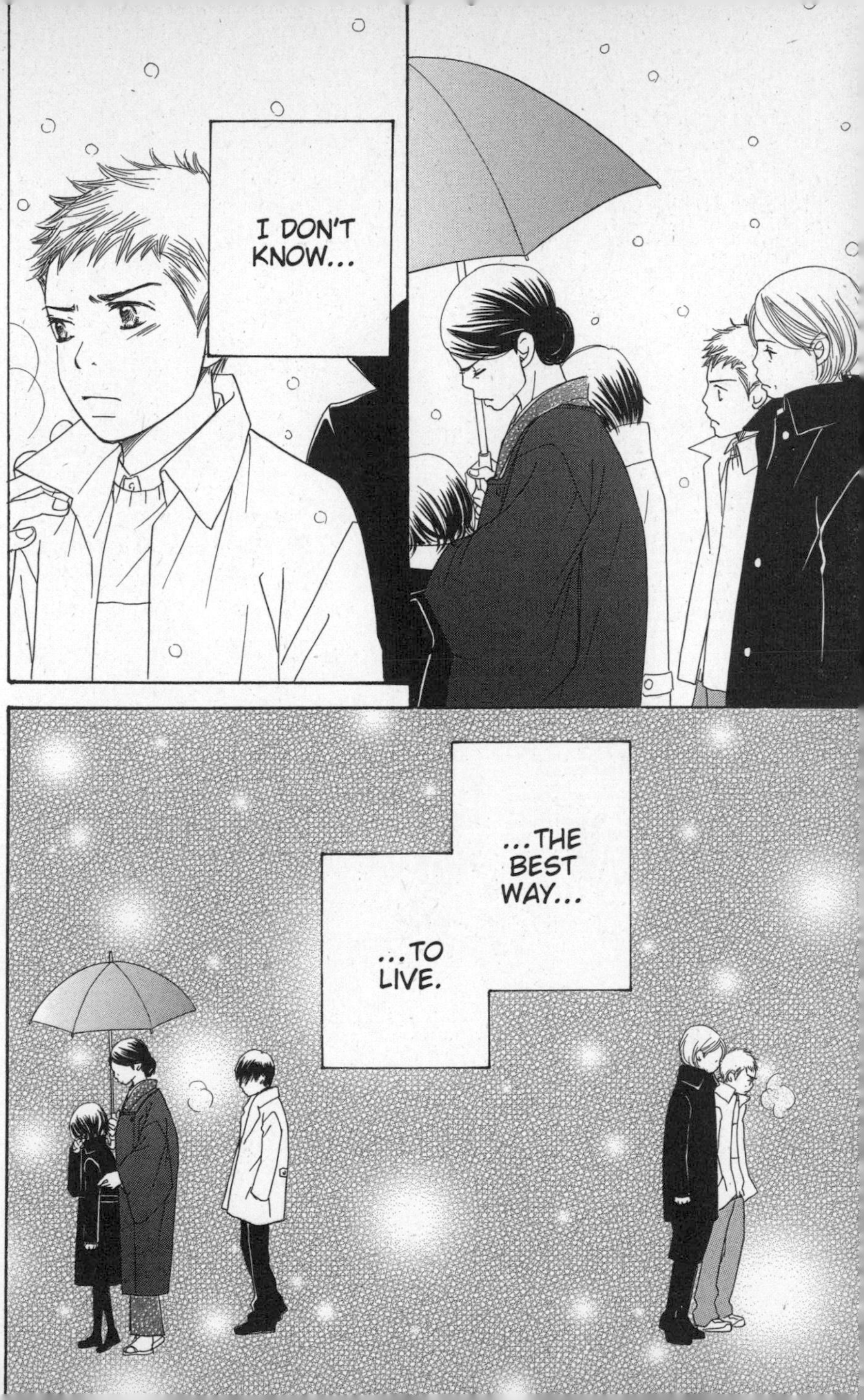
I DON'T KNOW...
...THE BEST WAY...
...TO LIVE.

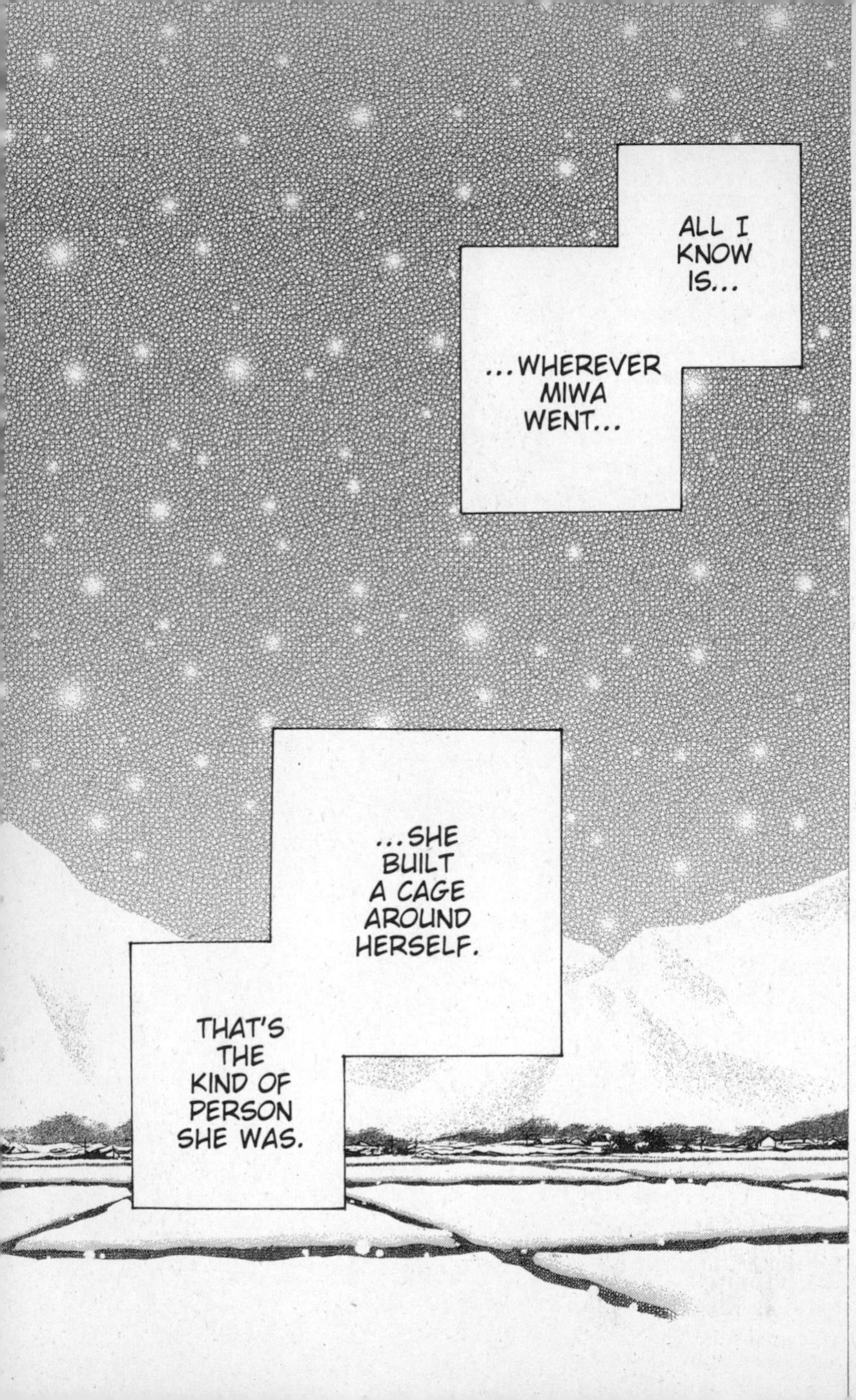
ALL I KNOW IS...
...WHEREVER MIWA WENT...
...SHE BUILT A CAGE AROUND HERSELF.
THAT'S THE KIND OF PERSON SHE WAS.

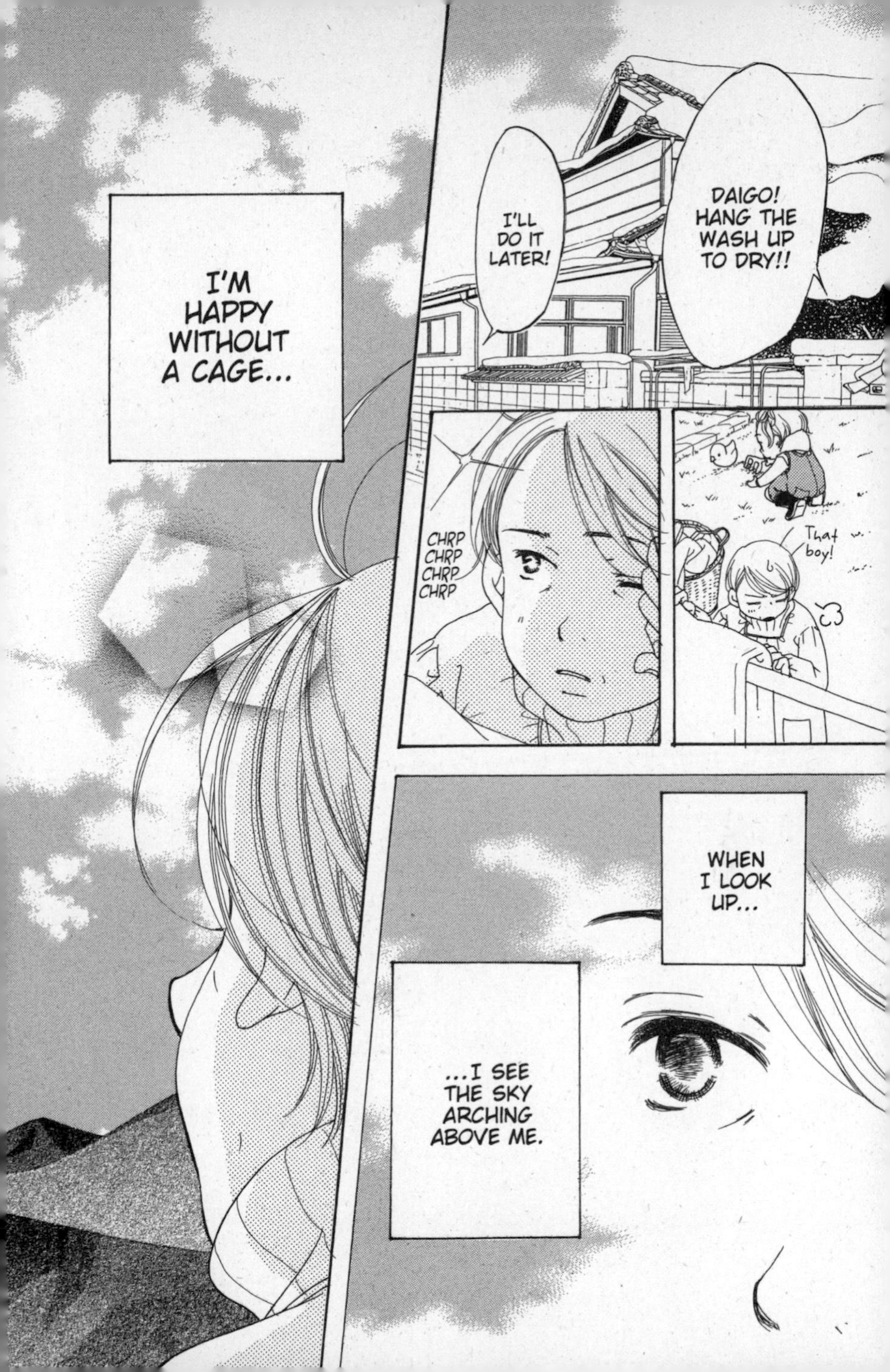
DAIGO! HANG THE WASH UP TO DRY!!
I'LL DO IT LATER!
That boy!
CHRP CHRP CHRP CHRP
WHEN I LOOK UP...
...I SEE THE SKY ARCHING ABOVE ME.
I'M HAPPY WITHOUT A CAGE...

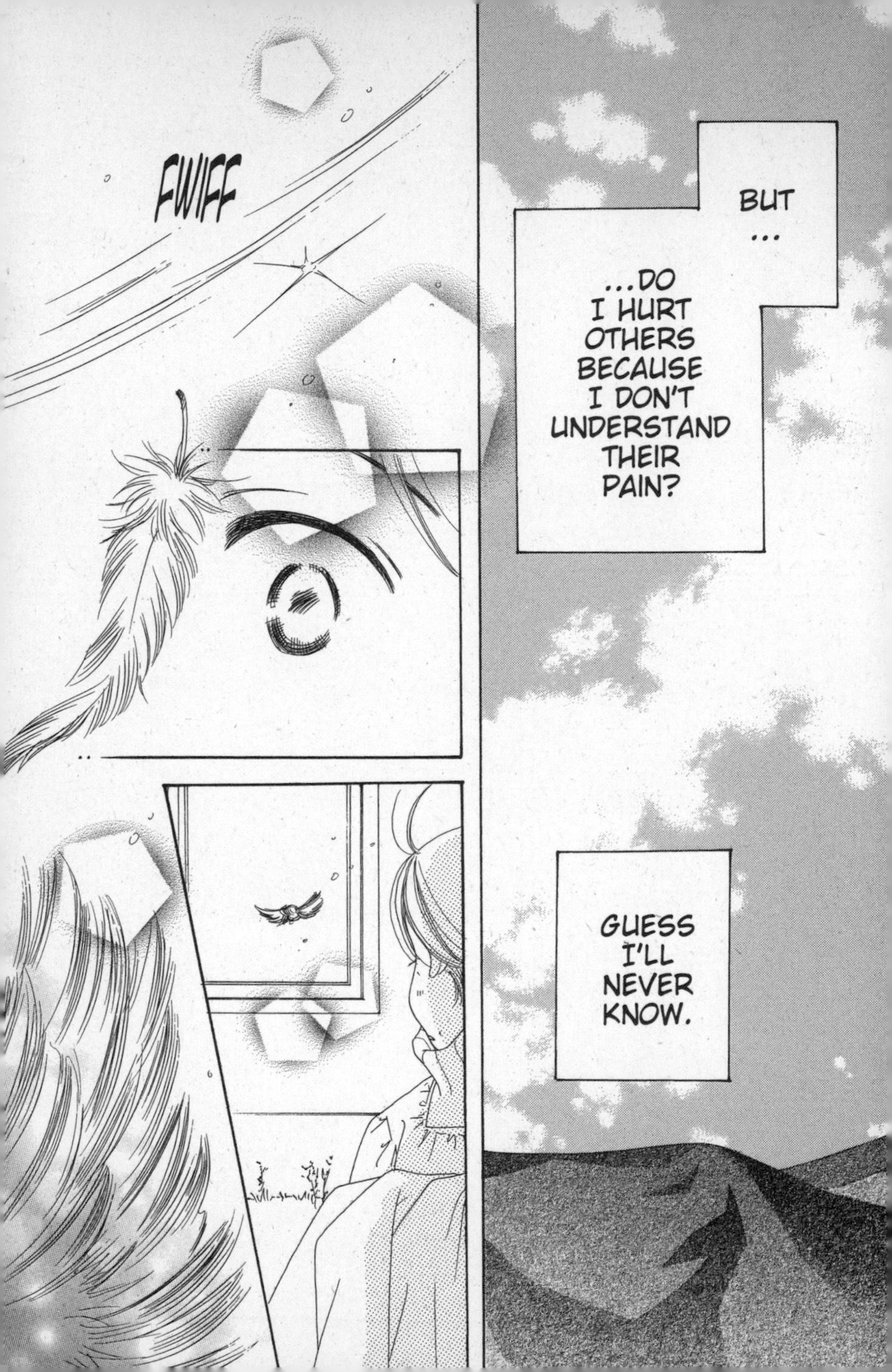
BUT ...
...DO I HURT OTHERS BECAUSE I DON'T UNDERSTAND THEIR PAIN?
GUESS I'LL NEVER KNOW.
FWIFF

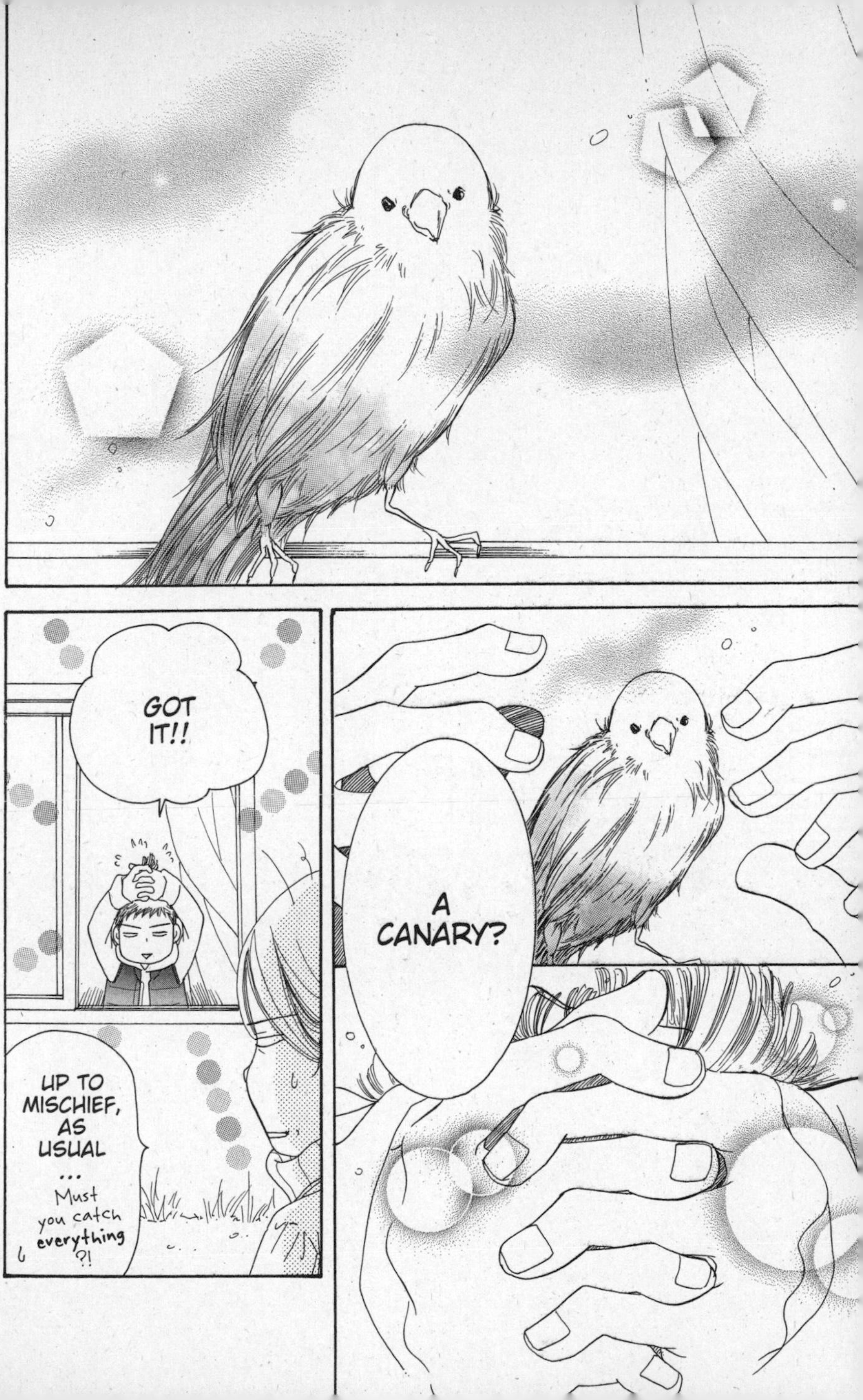
A CANARY?
GOT IT!!
UP TO MISCHIEF, AS USUAL ... Must you catch everything?!

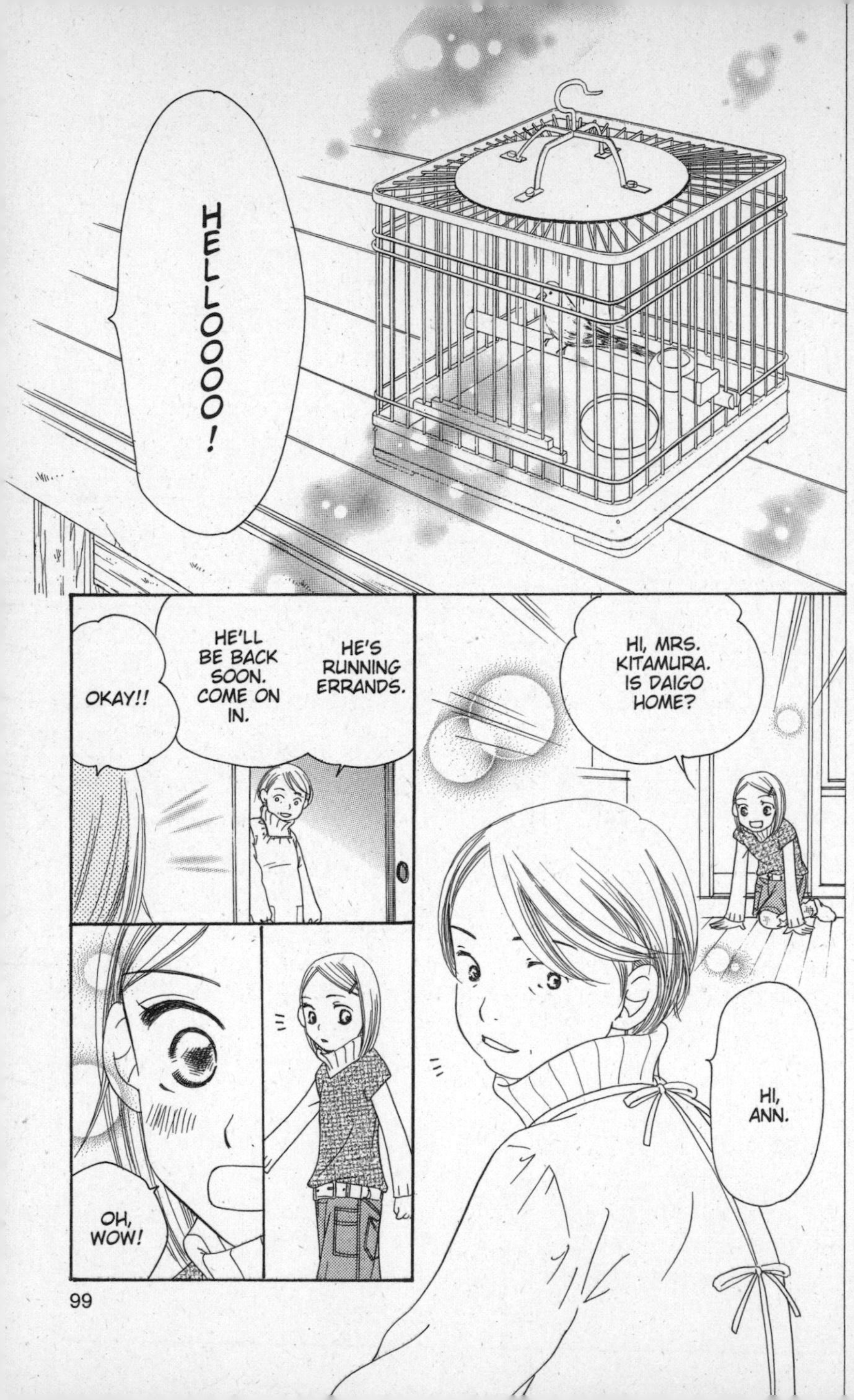
HELLOOOO!
HI, MRS. KITAMURA. IS DAIGO HOME?
HI, ANN.
HE'S RUNNING ERRANDS.
HE'LL BE BACK SOON. COME ON IN.
OKAY!!
OH, WOW!

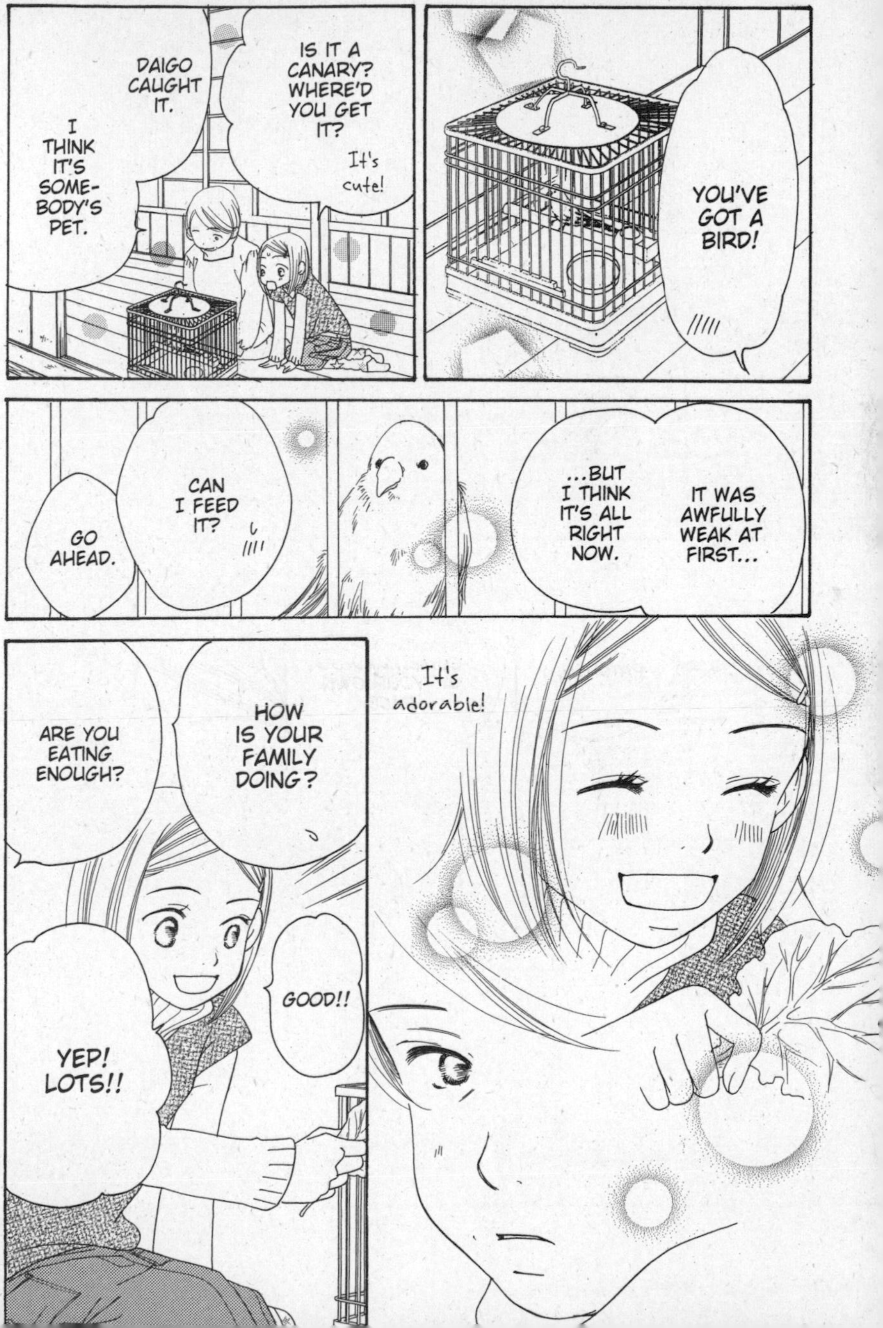
YOU'VE GOT A BIRD!
IS IT A CANARY? WHERE'D YOU GET IT?
It's cute!
DAIGO CAUGHT IT.
I THINK IT'S SOME-BODY'S PET.
IT WAS AWFULLY WEAK AT FIRST...
...BUT I THINK IT'S ALL RIGHT NOW.
CAN I FEED IT?
GO AHEAD.
It's adorable!
HOW IS YOUR FAMILY DOING?
ARE YOU EATING ENOUGH?
GOOD!!
YEP! LOTS!!

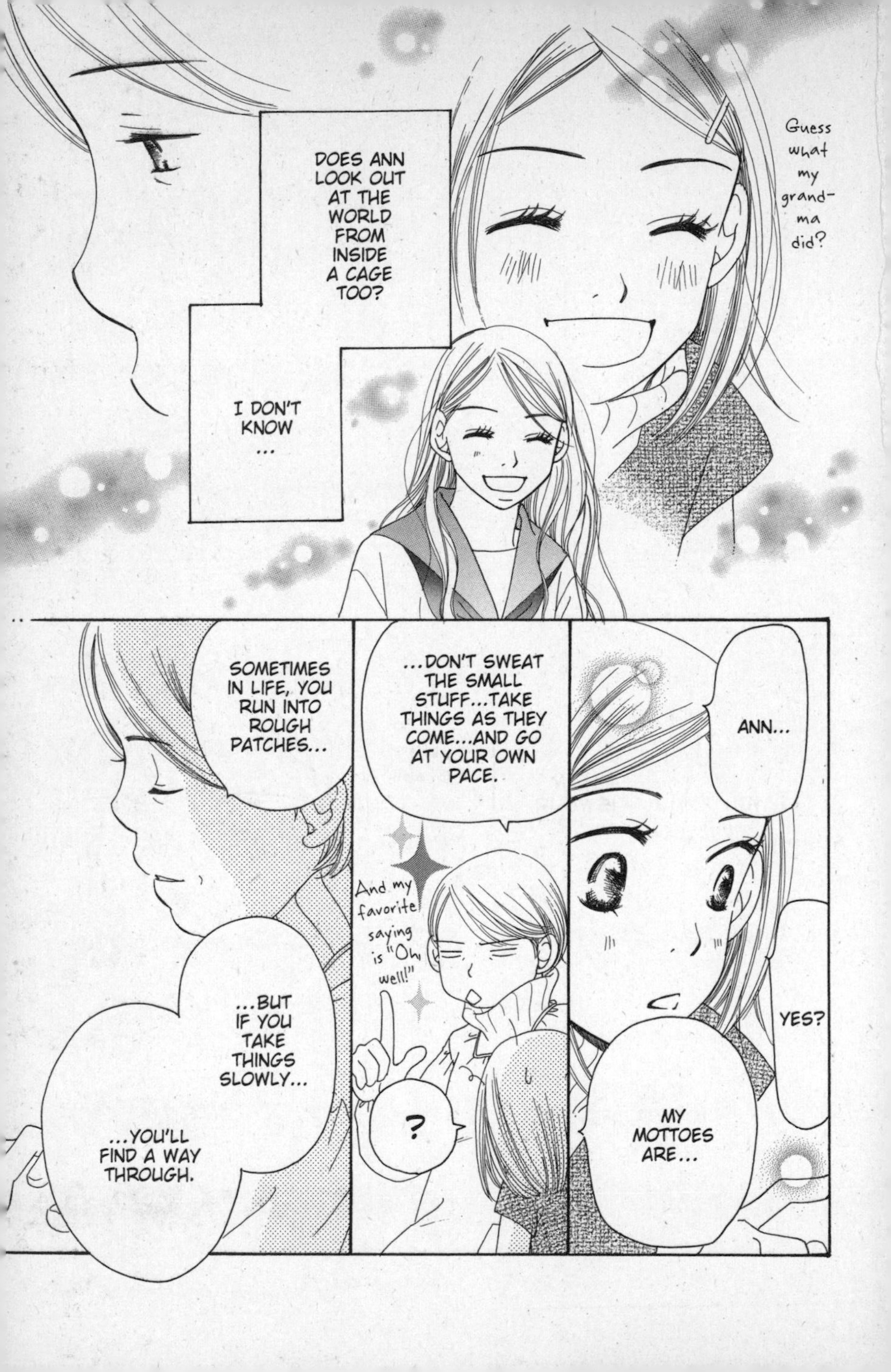
Guess what my grandma did?
DOES ANN LOOK OUT AT THE WORLD FROM INSIDE A CAGE TOO?
I DON'T KNOW...
ANN...
YES?
MY MOTTOES ARE...
...DON'T SWEAT THE SMALL STUFF...TAKE THINGS AS THEY COME...AND GO AT YOUR OWN PACE.
And my favorite saying is "Oh, well!"
?
SOMETIMES IN LIFE, YOU RUN INTO ROUGH PATCHES...
...BUT IF YOU TAKE THINGS SLOWLY...
...YOU'LL FIND A WAY THROUGH.

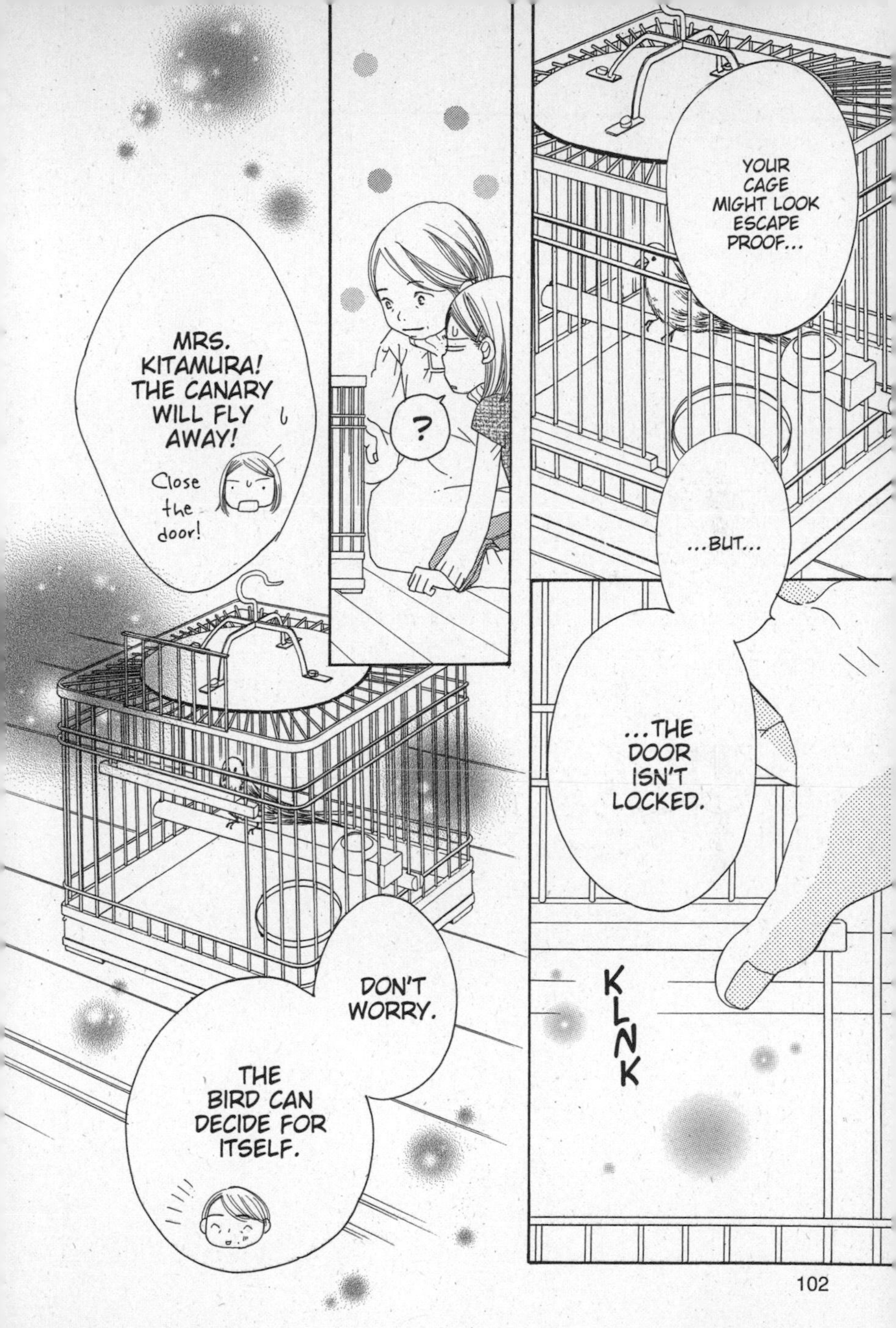
YOUR CAGE MIGHT LOOK ESCAPE PROOF...
...BUT...
...THE DOOR ISN'T LOCKED.
KLNK
?
MRS. KITAMURA! THE CANARY WILL FLY AWAY!
Close the door!
DON'T WORRY.
THE BIRD CAN DECIDE FOR ITSELF.

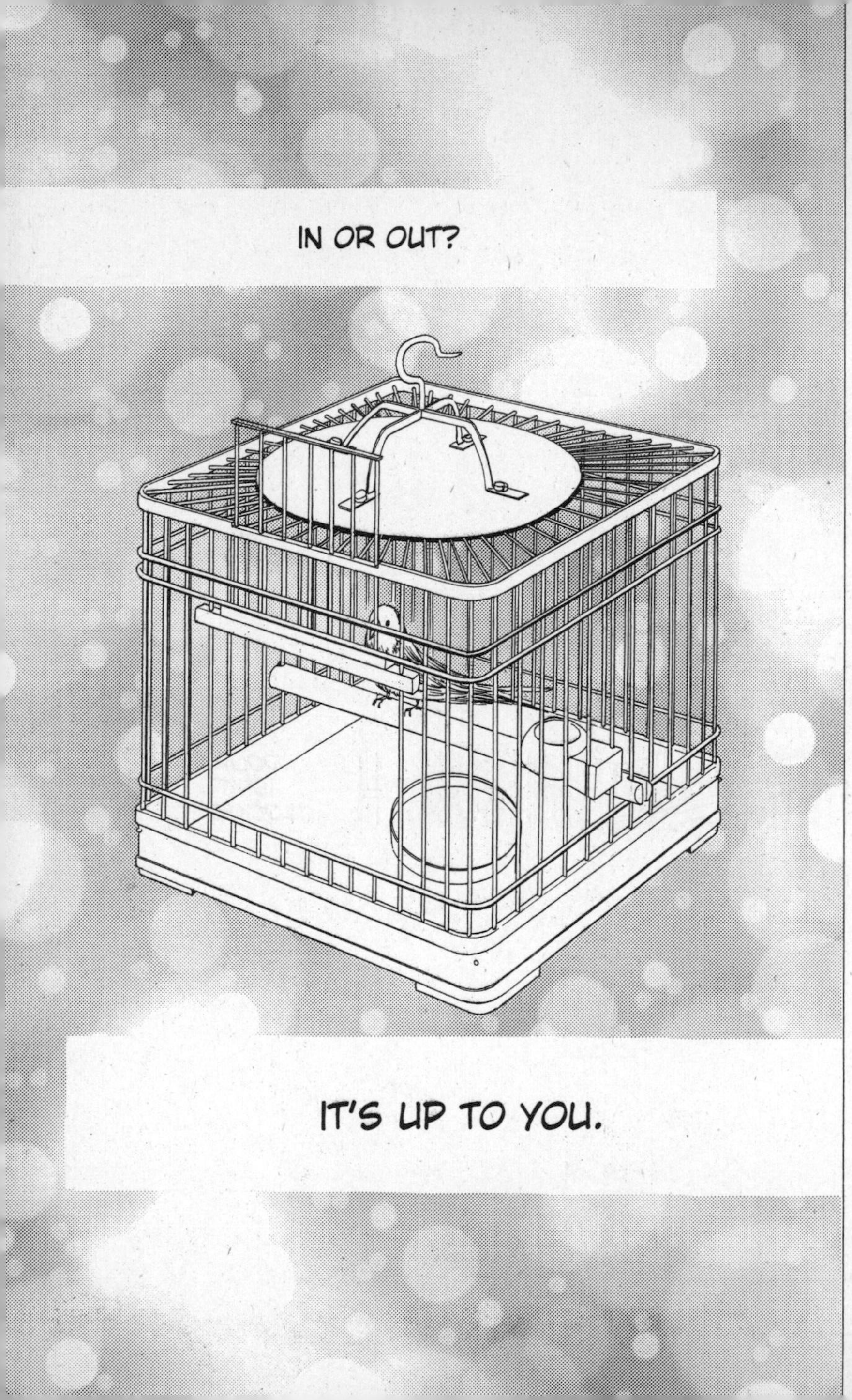
IN OR OUT?
IT'S UP TO YOU.

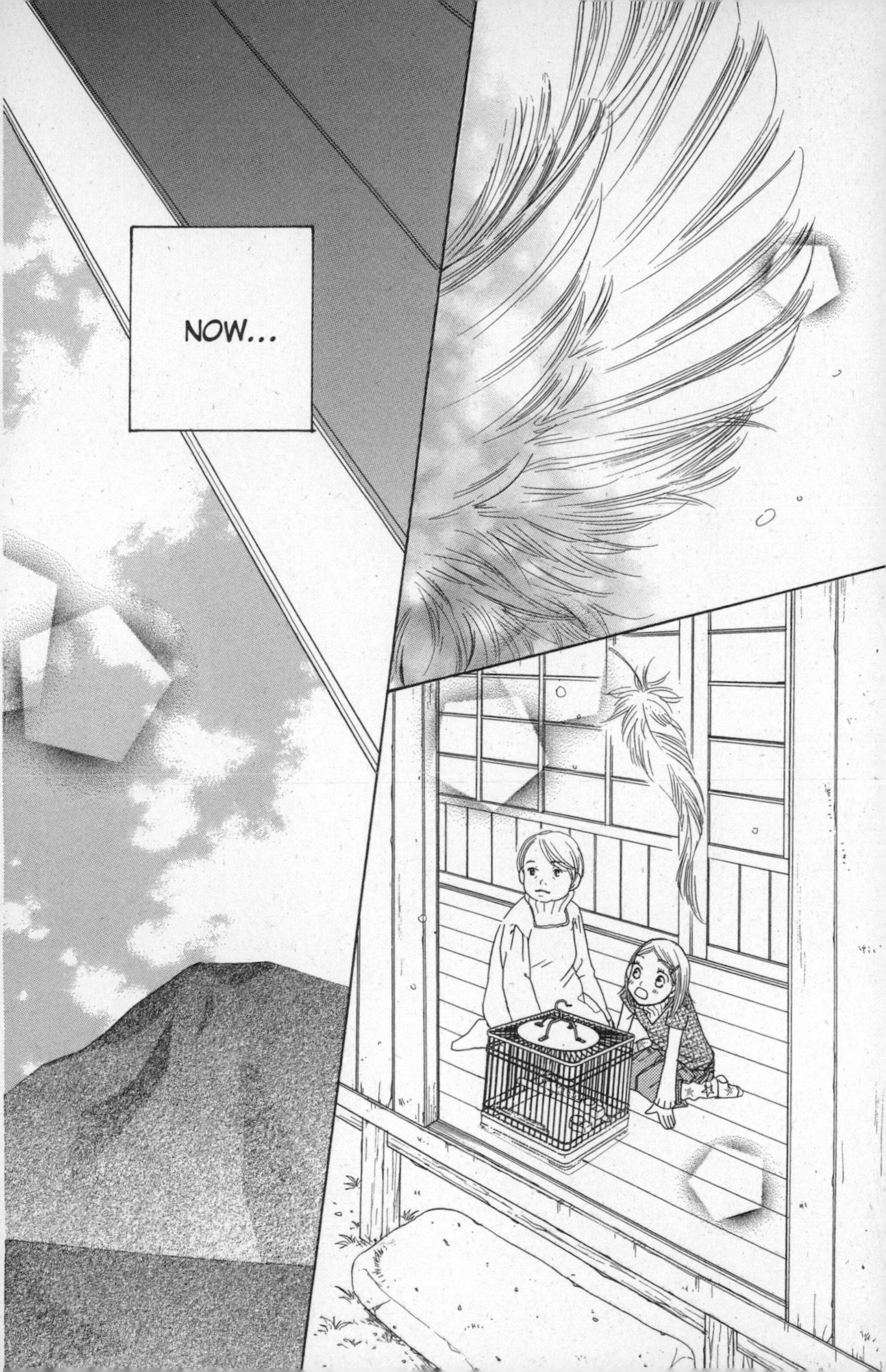
NOW...

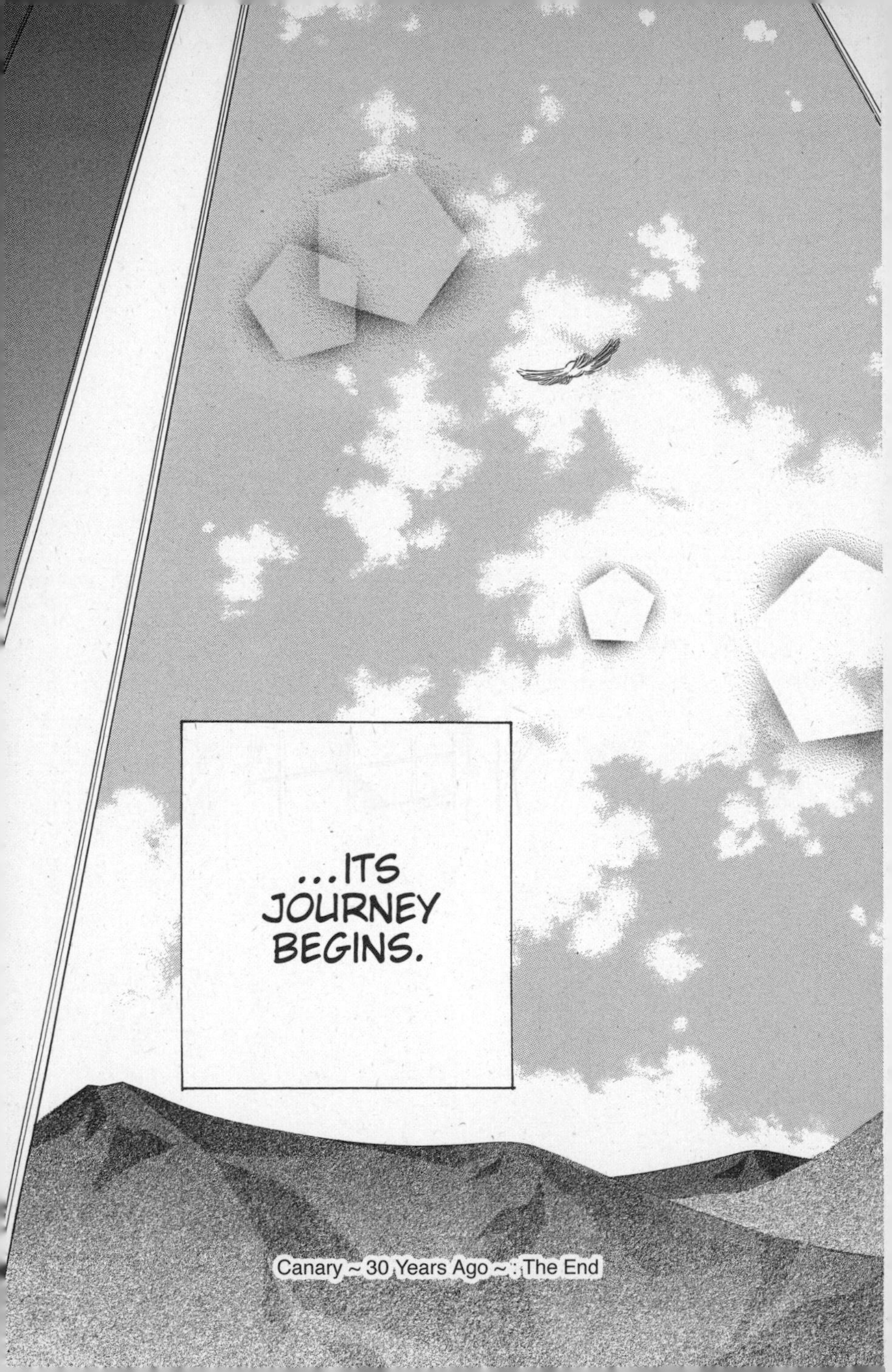
...ITS JOURNEY BEGINS.
Canary ~ 30 Years Ago ~ : The End

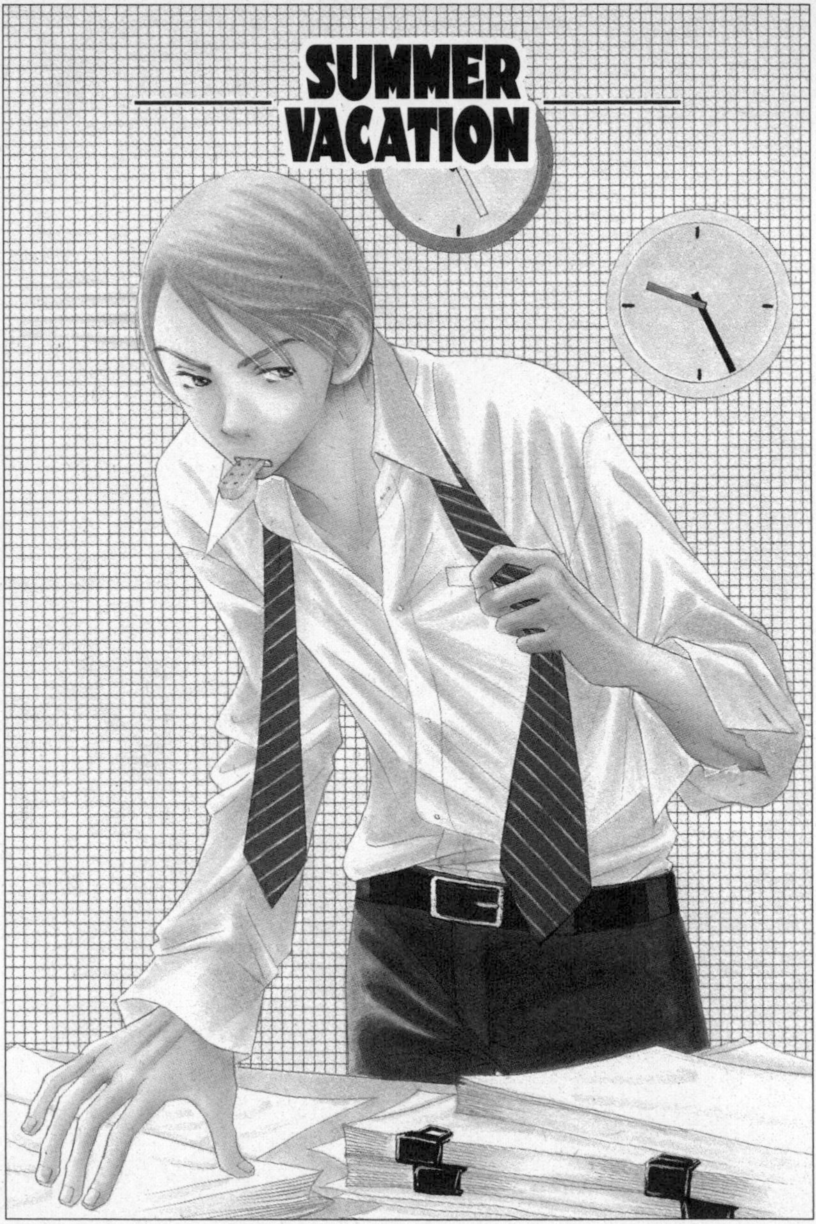
SUMMER
VACATION

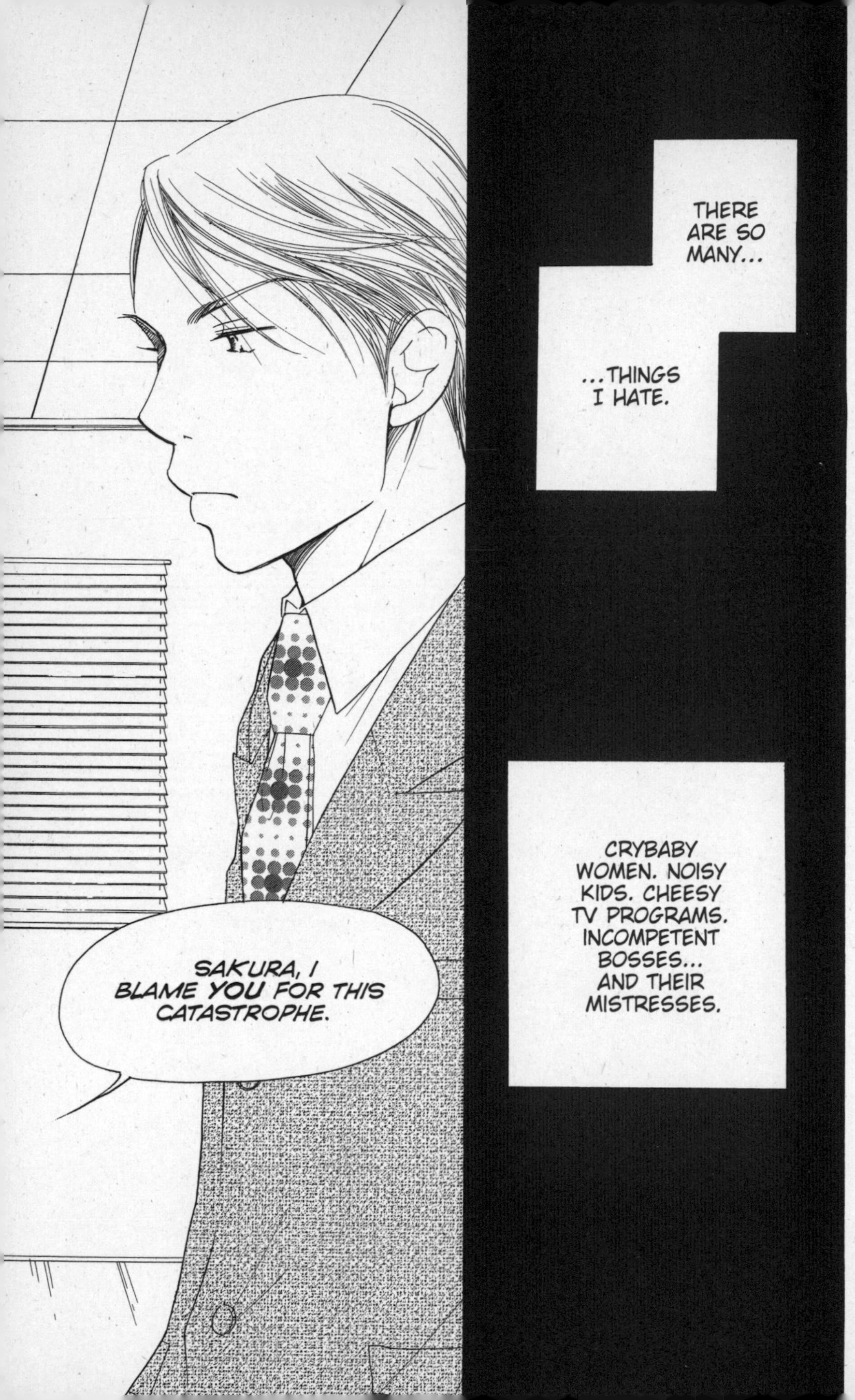
THERE ARE SO MANY...
...THINGS I HATE.
CRYBABY WOMEN. NOISY KIDS. CHEESY TV PROGRAMS. INCOMPETENT BOSSES... AND THEIR MISTRESSES.
SAKURA, I BLAME YOU FOR THIS CATASTROPHE.

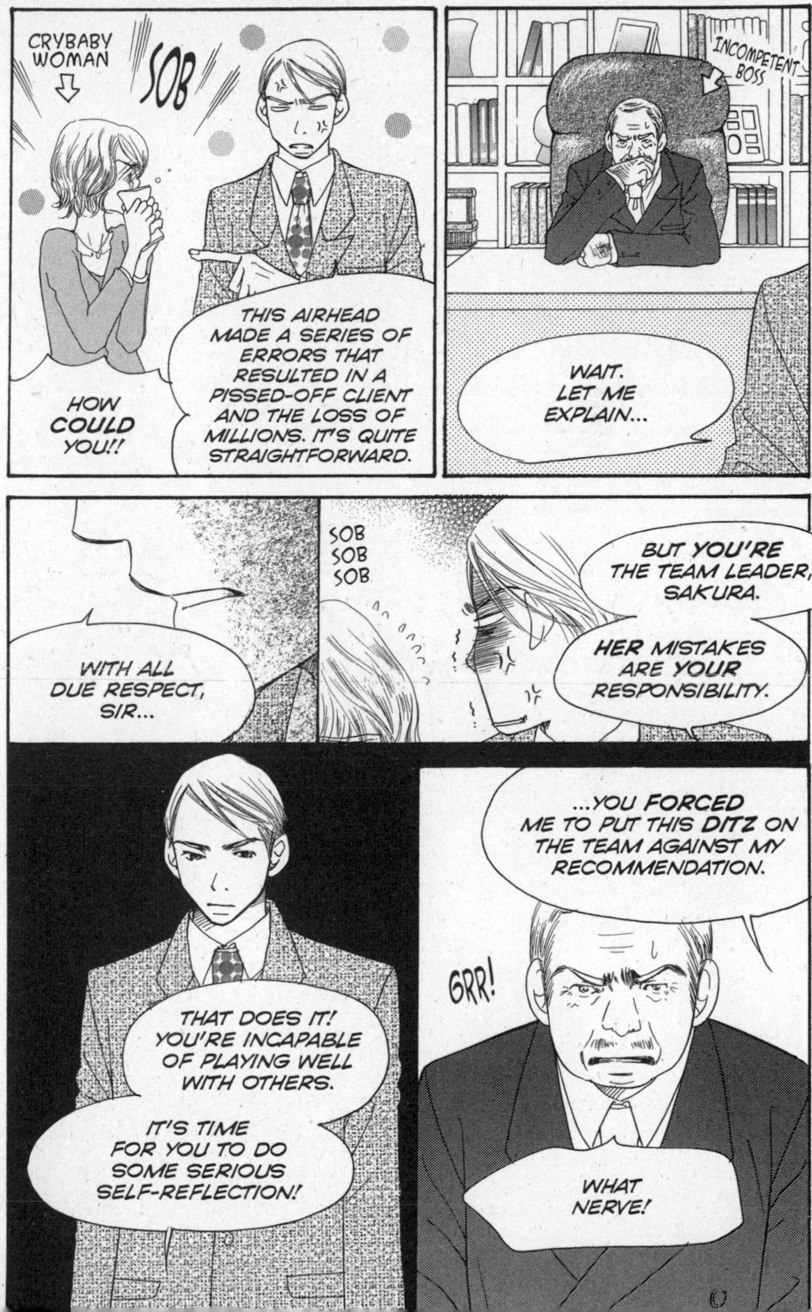
INCOMPETENT BOSS
WAIT. LET ME EXPLAIN...
CRYBABY WOMAN
SOB
THIS AIRHEAD MADE A SERIES OF ERRORS THAT RESULTED IN A PISSED-OFF CLIENT AND THE LOSS OF MILLIONS. IT'S QUITE STRAIGHTFORWARD.
HOW COULD YOU!!
BUT YOU'RE THE TEAM LEADER, SAKURA.
HER MISTAKES ARE YOUR RESPONSIBILITY.
SOB SOB SOB
WITH ALL DUE RESPECT, SIR...
...YOU FORCED ME TO PUT THIS DITZ ON THE TEAM AGAINST MY RECOMMENDATION.
GRR!
WHAT NERVE!
THAT DOES IT! YOU'RE INCAPABLE OF PLAYING WELL WITH OTHERS.
IT'S TIME FOR YOU TO DO SOME SERIOUS SELF-REFLECTION!

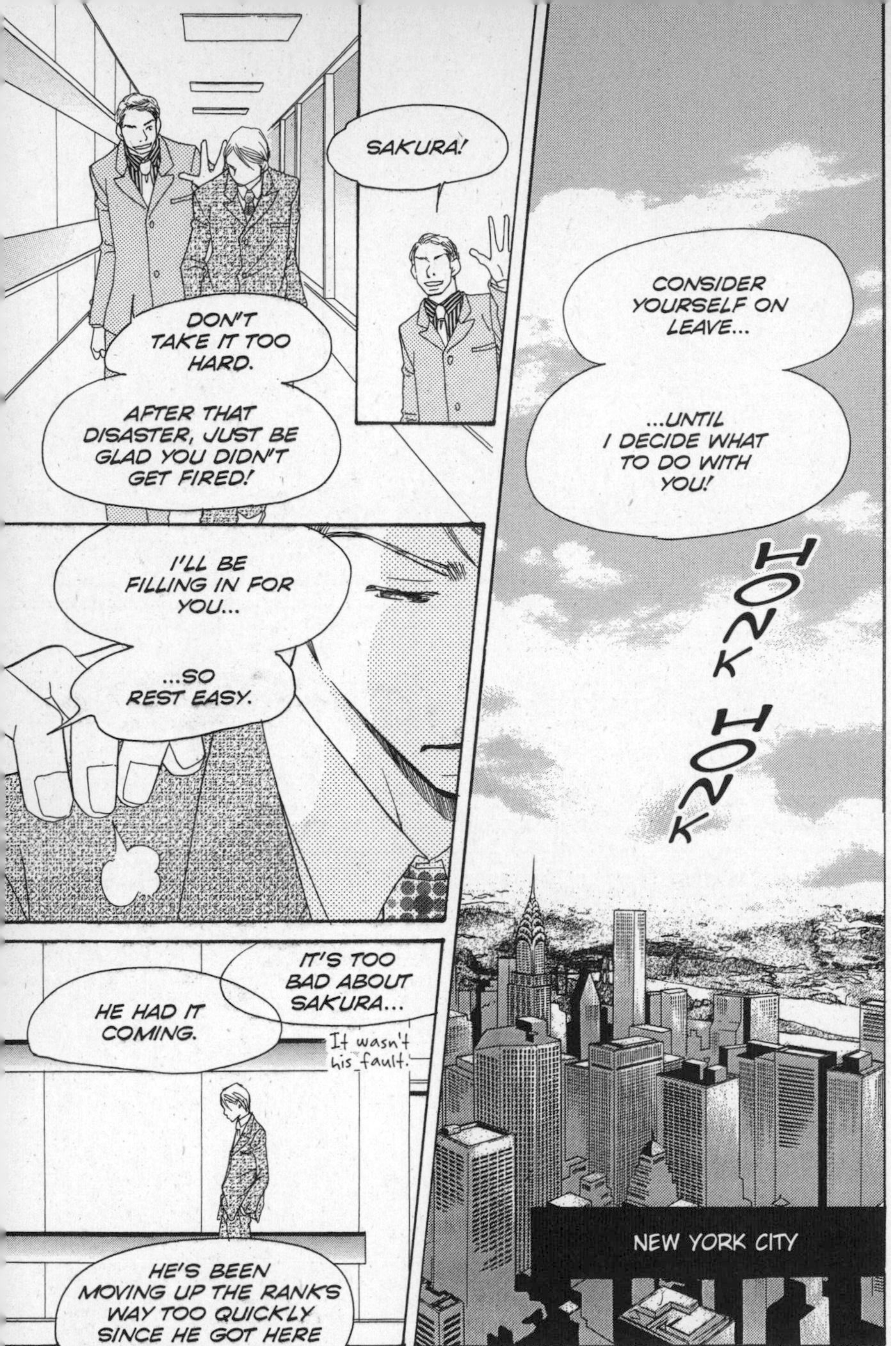

HONK HONK
CONSIDER YOURSELF ON LEAVE...
...UNTIL I DECIDE WHAT TO DO WITH YOU!
NEW YORK CITY
SAKURA!
DON'T TAKE IT TOO HARD.
AFTER THAT DISASTER, JUST BE GLAD YOU DIDN'T GET FIRED!
I'LL BE FILLING IN FOR YOU...
...SO REST EASY.
IT'S TOO BAD ABOUT SAKURA...
HE HAD IT COMING.
It wasn't his fault.
HE'S BEEN MOVING UP THE RANKS WAY TOO QUICKLY SINCE HE GOT HERE FROM JAPAN.

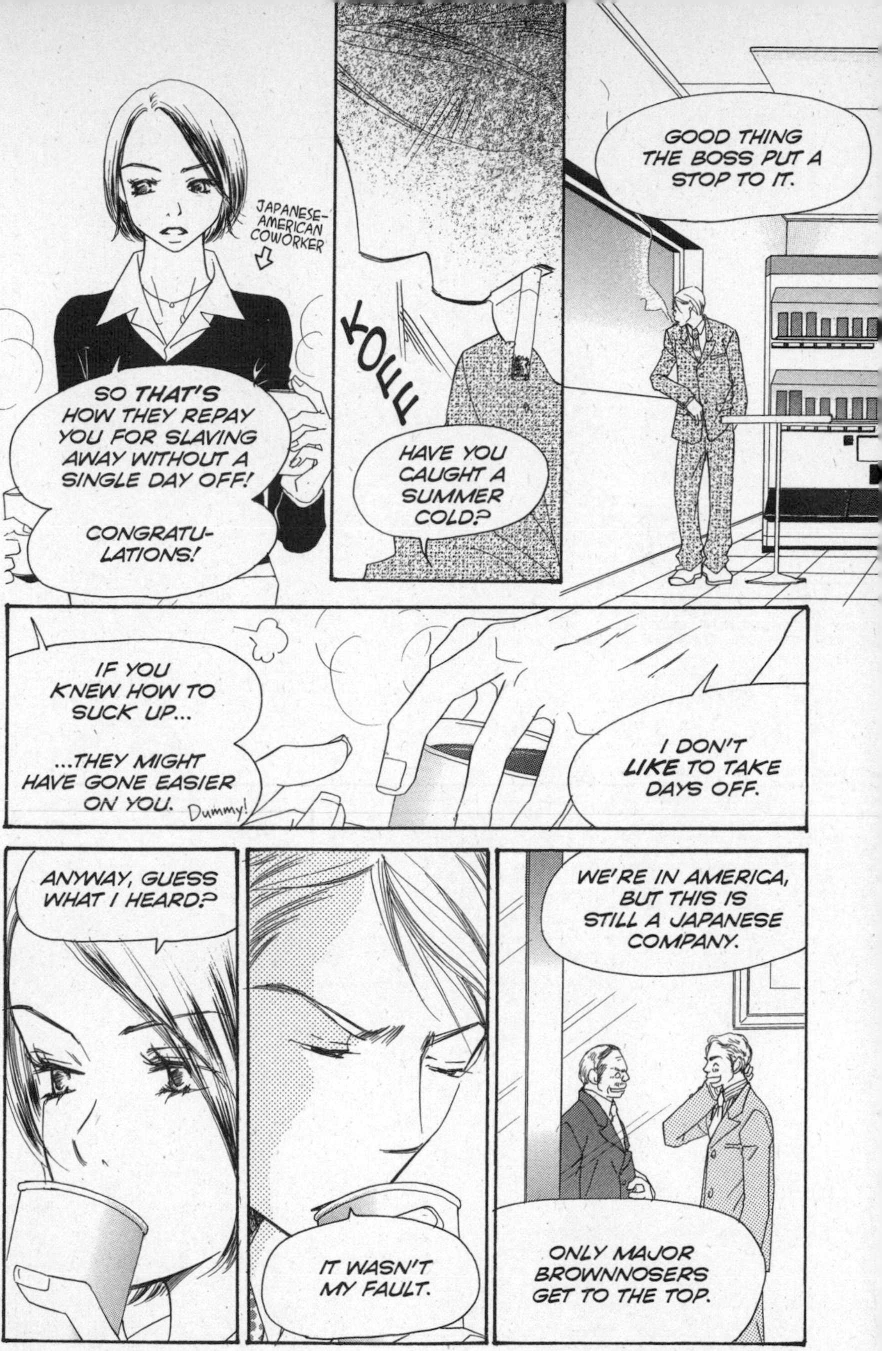
GOOD THING THE BOSS PUT A STOP TO IT.
KOFF
HAVE YOU CAUGHT A SUMMER COLD?
JAPANESE-AMERICAN COWORKER
SO THAT'S HOW THEY REPAY YOU FOR SLAVING AWAY WITHOUT A SINGLE DAY OFF!
CONGRATULATIONS!
I DON'T LIKE TO TAKE DAYS OFF.
IF YOU KNEW HOW TO SUCK UP...
...THEY MIGHT HAVE GONE EASIER ON YOU.
Dummy!
WE'RE IN AMERICA, BUT THIS IS STILL A JAPANESE COMPANY.
ONLY MAJOR BROWNNOSERS GET TO THE TOP.
IT WASN'T MY FAULT.
ANYWAY, GUESS WHAT I HEARD?

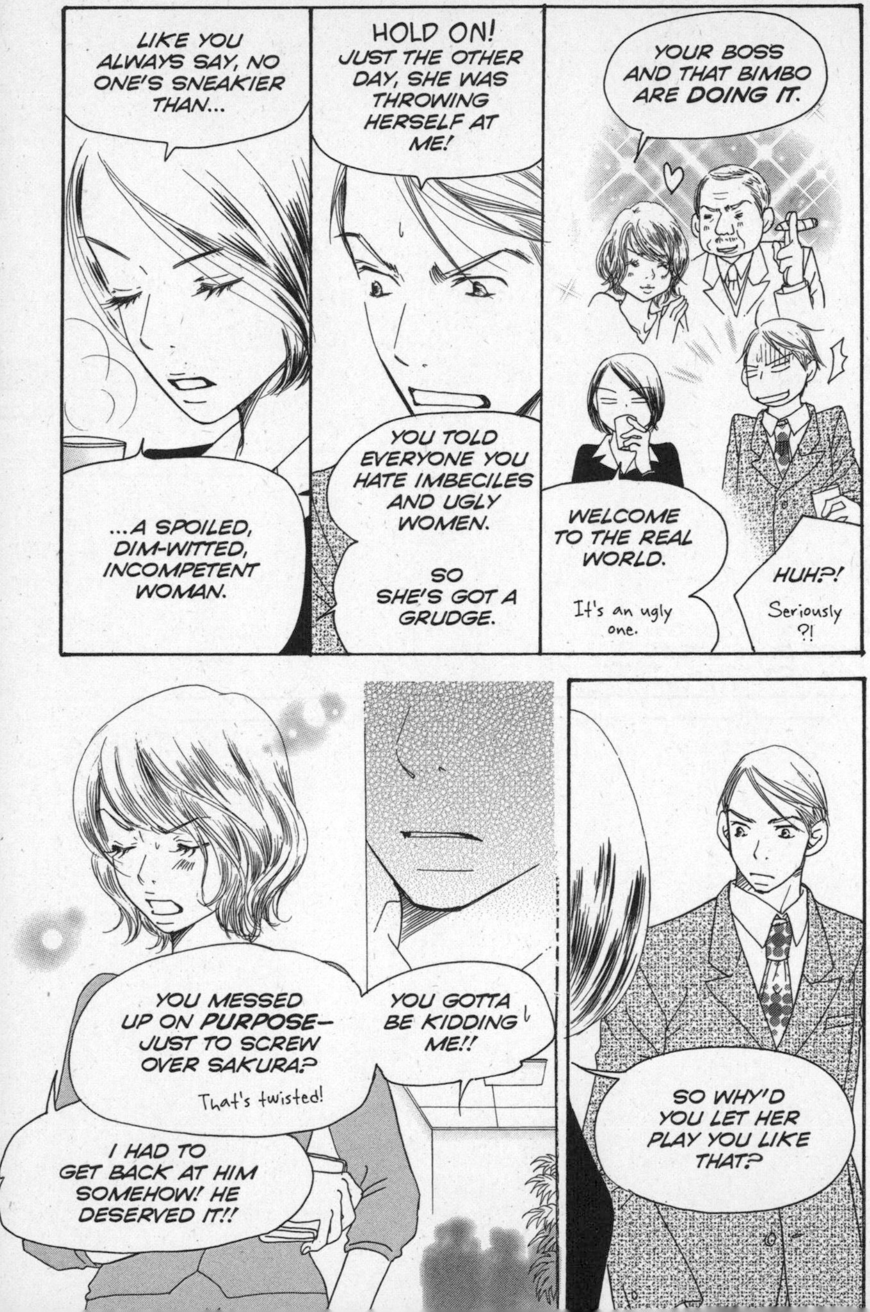
YOUR BOSS AND THAT BIMBO ARE DOING IT.
HUH?!
Seriously?!
WELCOME TO THE REAL WORLD.
It's an ugly one.
HOLD ON! JUST THE OTHER DAY, SHE WAS THROWING HERSELF AT ME!
YOU TOLD EVERYONE YOU HATE IMBECILES AND UGLY WOMEN.
SO SHE'S GOT A GRUDGE.
LIKE YOU ALWAYS SAY, NO ONE'S SNEAKIER THAN...
...A SPOILED, DIM-WITTED, INCOMPETENT WOMAN.
SO WHY'D YOU LET HER PLAY YOU LIKE THAT?
YOU GOTTA BE KIDDING ME!!
YOU MESSED UP ON PURPOSE—JUST TO SCREW OVER SAKURA?
That's twisted!
I HAD TO GET BACK AT HIM SOMEHOW! HE DESERVED IT!!

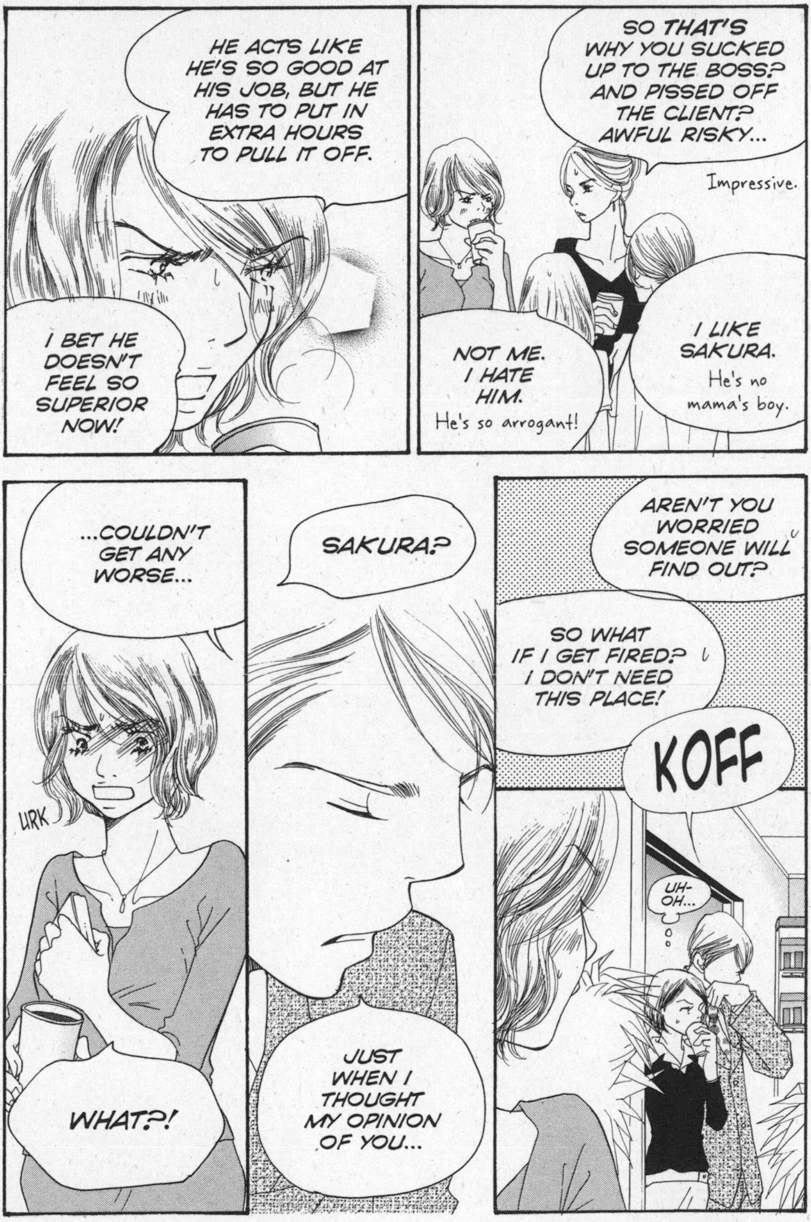
SO THAT'S WHY YOU SUCKED UP TO THE BOSS? AND PISSED OFF THE CLIENT? AWFUL RISKY...
Impressive.
I LIKE SAKURA.
He's no mama's boy.
NOT ME. I HATE HIM.
He's so arrogant!
HE ACTS LIKE HE'S SO GOOD AT HIS JOB, BUT HE HAS TO PUT IN EXTRA HOURS TO PULL IT OFF.
I BET HE DOESN'T FEEL SO SUPERIOR NOW!
AREN'T YOU WORRIED SOMEONE WILL FIND OUT?
SO WHAT IF I GET FIRED? I DON'T NEED THIS PLACE!
KOFF
UH-OH...
SAKURA?
JUST WHEN I THOUGHT MY OPINION OF YOU...
...COULDN'T GET ANY WORSE...
URK
WHAT?!

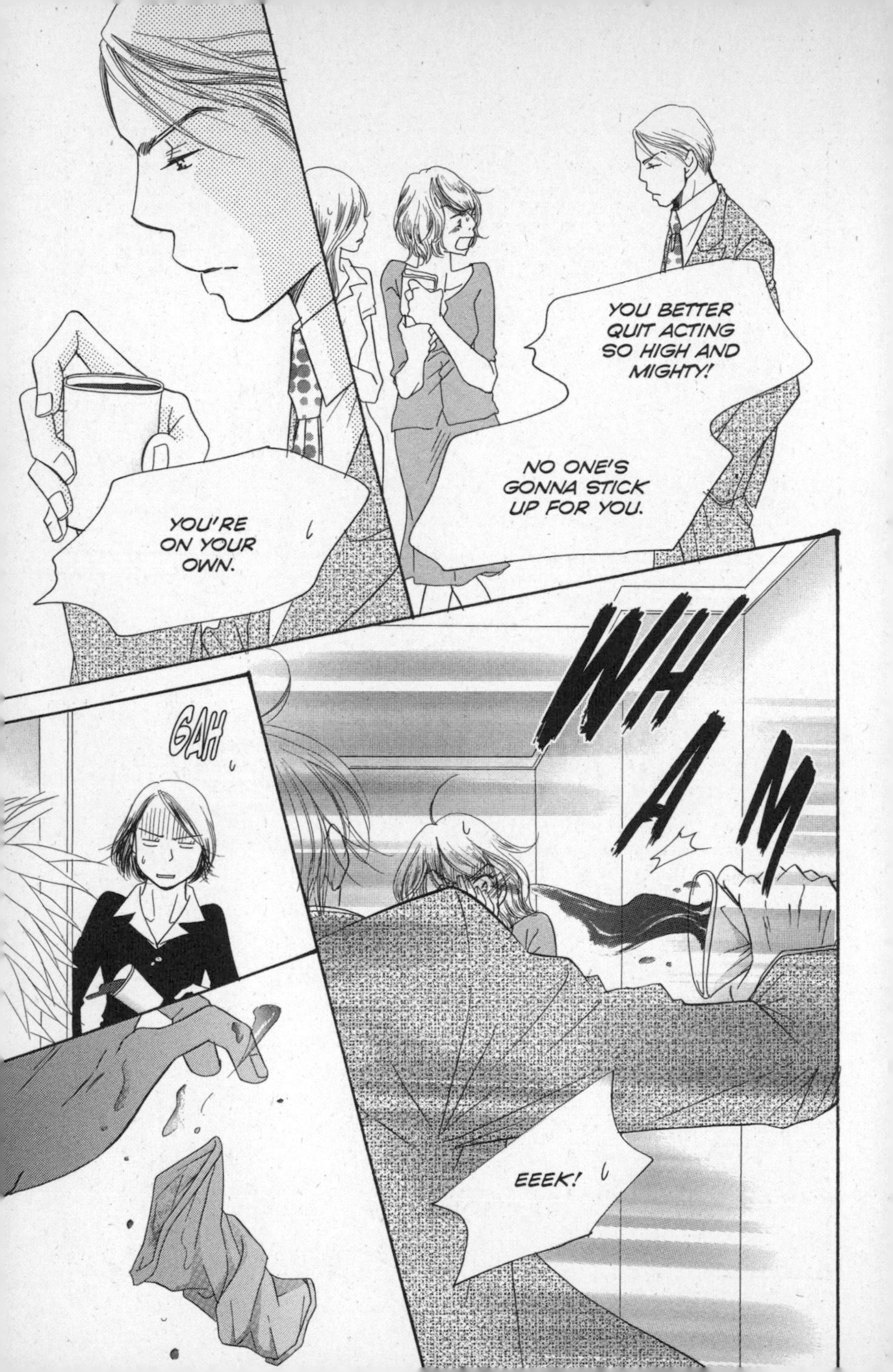
YOU BETTER QUIT ACTING SO HIGH AND MIGHTY!
NO ONE'S GONNA STICK UP FOR YOU.
YOU'RE ON YOUR OWN.
WHAM
EEEK!
GAH

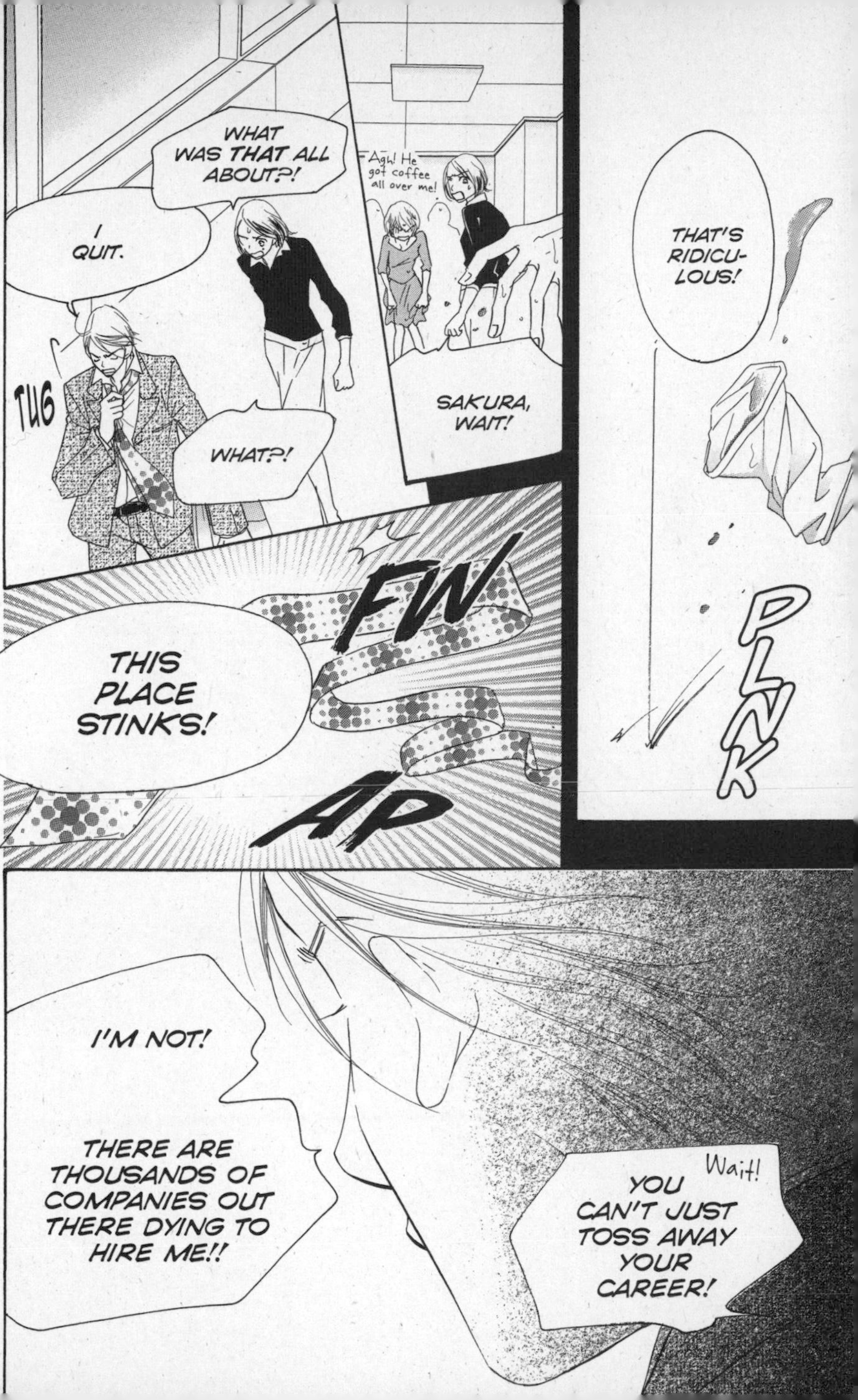
THAT'S RIDICULOUS!
PLNK
Agh! He got coffee all over me!
SAKURA, WAIT!
WHAT WAS THAT ALL ABOUT?!
I QUIT.
TUG
WHAT?!
FW
AP
THIS PLACE STINKS!
Wait!
YOU CAN'T JUST TOSS AWAY YOUR CAREER!
I'M NOT!
THERE ARE THOUSANDS OF COMPANIES OUT THERE DYING TO HIRE ME!!

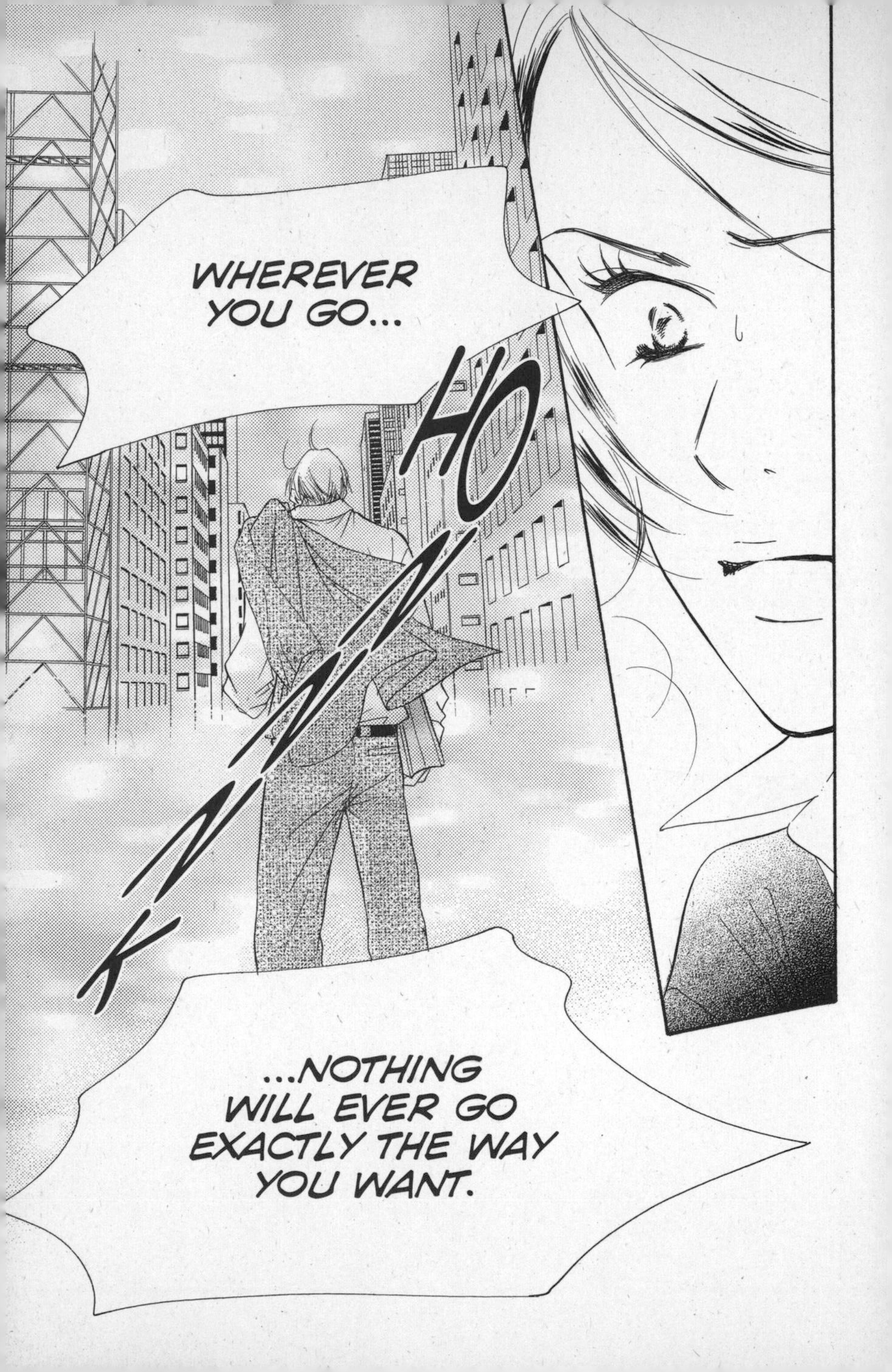
WHEREVER YOU GO...
HONNK
...NOTHING WILL EVER GO EXACTLY THE WAY YOU WANT.

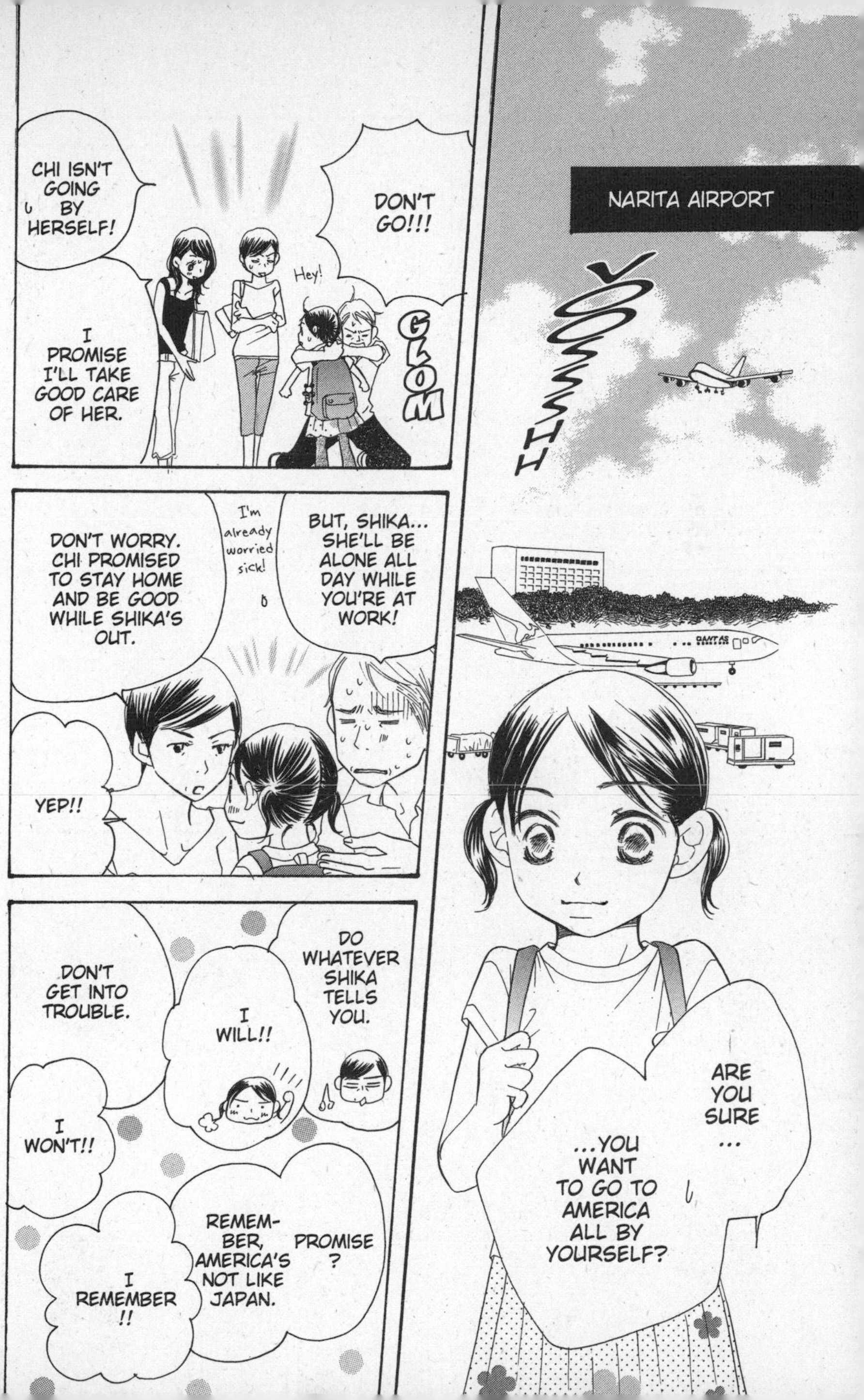
NARITA AIRPORT
VOOSSHH
ARE YOU SURE...
...YOU WANT TO GO TO AMERICA ALL BY YOURSELF?
DON'T GO!!!
Hey!
GLOM
CHI ISN'T GOING BY HERSELF!
I PROMISE I'LL TAKE GOOD CARE OF HER.
BUT, SHIKA... SHE'LL BE ALONE ALL DAY WHILE YOU'RE AT WORK!
I'm already worried sick!
DON'T WORRY. CHI PROMISED TO STAY HOME AND BE GOOD WHILE SHIKA'S OUT.
YEP!!
DO WHATEVER SHIKA TELLS YOU.
I WILL!!
DON'T GET INTO TROUBLE.
I WON'T!!
PROMISE?
REMEMBER, AMERICA'S NOT LIKE JAPAN.
I REMEMBER!!

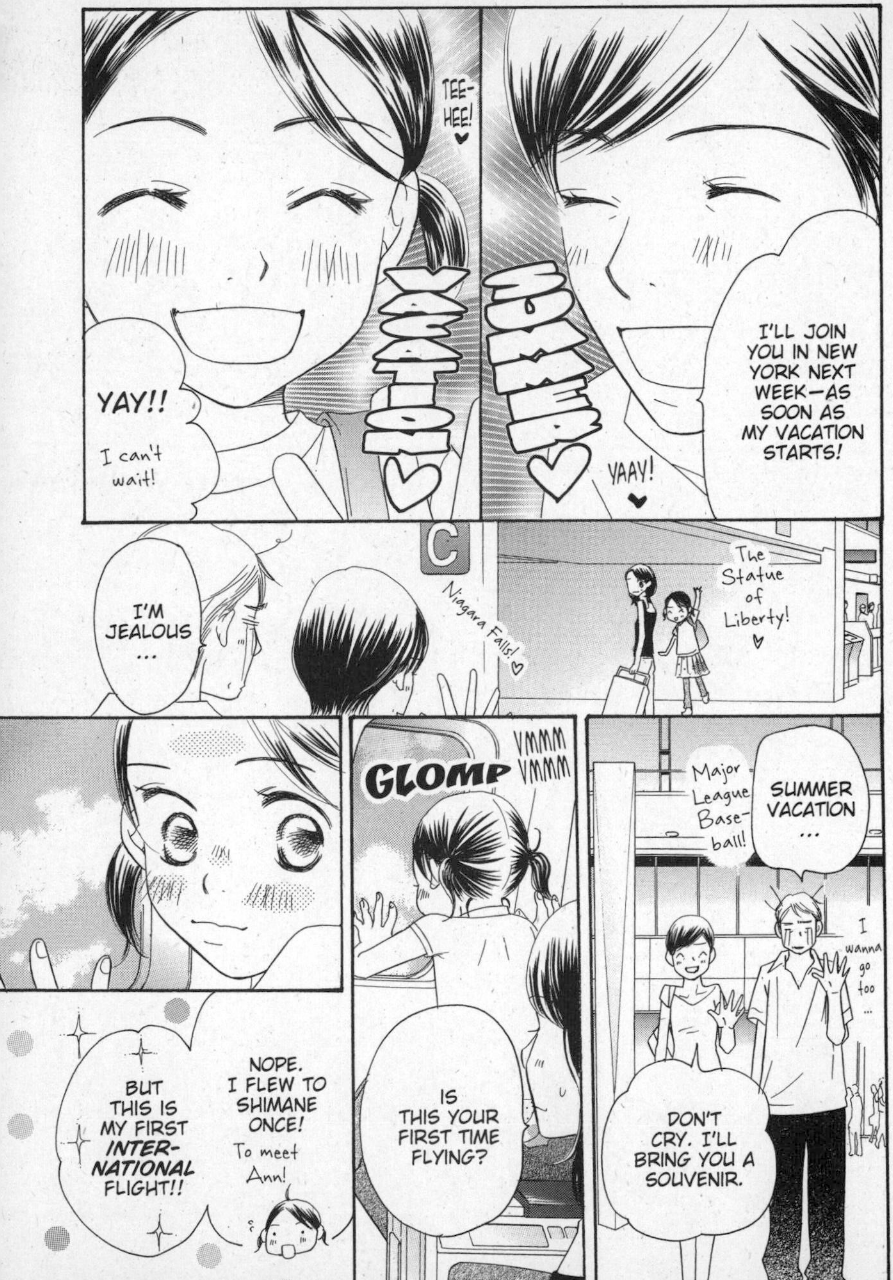
I'LL JOIN YOU IN NEW YORK NEXT WEEK—AS SOON AS MY VACATION STARTS!
SUMMER ♥
YAAY! ♥
TEE-HEE! ♥
VACATION ♥
YAY!!
I can't wait!
The Statue of Liberty! ♥
Niagara Falls! ♥
I'M JEALOUS ...
SUMMER VACATION ...
Major League Base-ball!
I wanna go too ...
DON'T CRY. I'LL BRING YOU A SOUVENIR.
VMMM VMMM
GLOMP
IS THIS YOUR FIRST TIME FLYING?
NOPE. I FLEW TO SHIMANE ONCE!
To meet Ann!
BUT THIS IS MY FIRST INTERNATIONAL FLIGHT!!

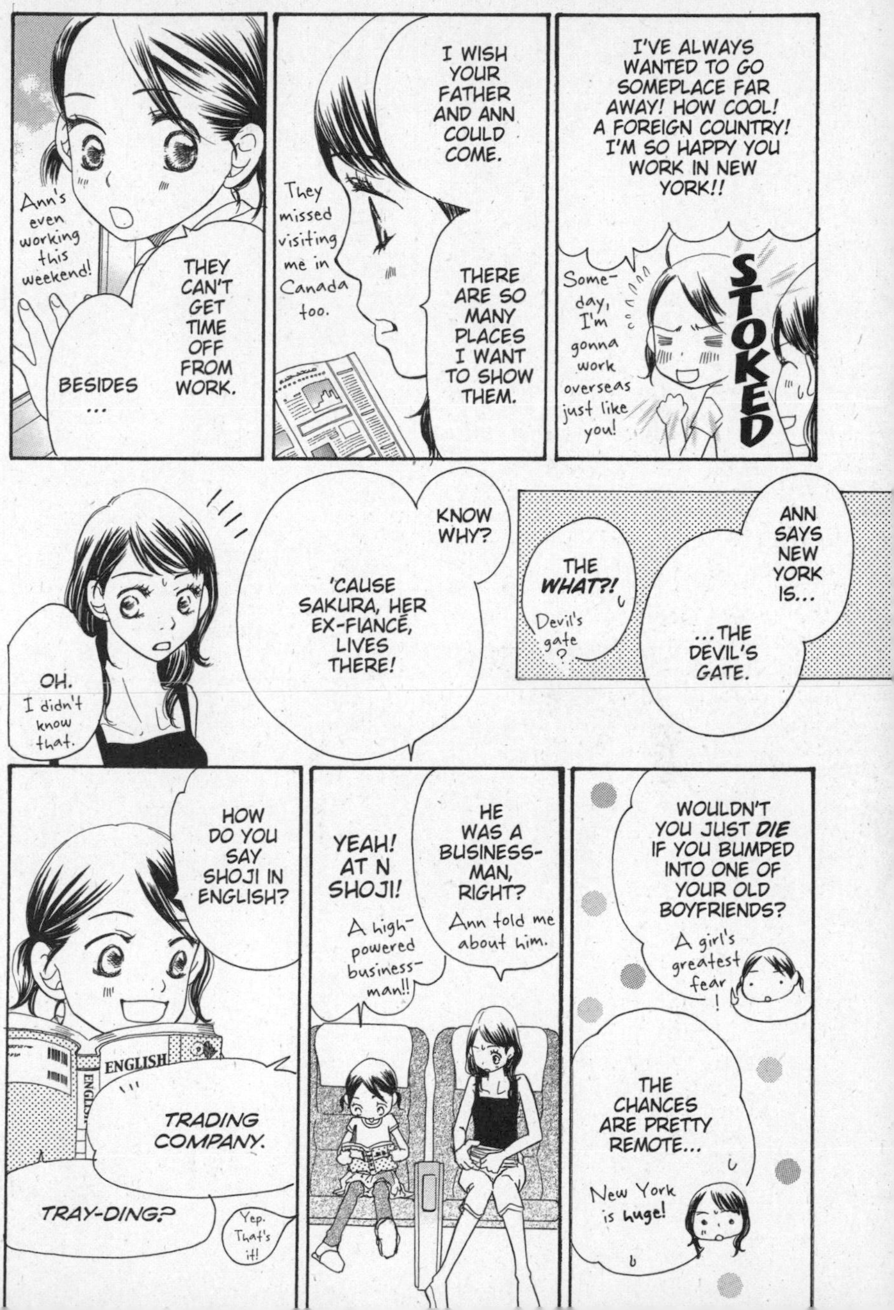

I'VE ALWAYS WANTED TO GO SOMEPLACE FAR AWAY! HOW COOL! A FOREIGN COUNTRY! I'M SO HAPPY YOU WORK IN NEW YORK!!
STOKED
Someday, I'm gonna work overseas just like you!
I WISH YOUR FATHER AND ANN COULD COME.
THERE ARE SO MANY PLACES I WANT TO SHOW THEM.
They missed visiting me in Canada too.
THEY CAN'T GET TIME OFF FROM WORK.
Ann's even working this weekend!
BESIDES...
ANN SAYS NEW YORK IS...
...THE DEVIL'S GATE.
THE *WHAT?!*
Devil's gate?
KNOW WHY?
'CAUSE SAKURA, HER EX-FIANCÉ, LIVES THERE!
OH.
I didn't know that.
WOULDN'T YOU JUST *DIE* IF YOU BUMPED INTO ONE OF YOUR OLD BOYFRIENDS?
A girl's greatest fear!
THE CHANCES ARE PRETTY REMOTE...
New York is huge!
HE WAS A BUSINESS-MAN, RIGHT?
Ann told me about him.
YEAH! AT N SHOJI!
A high-powered business-man!!
HOW DO YOU SAY SHOJI IN ENGLISH?
ENGLISH
TRADING COMPANY.
TRAY-DING?
Yep. That's it!

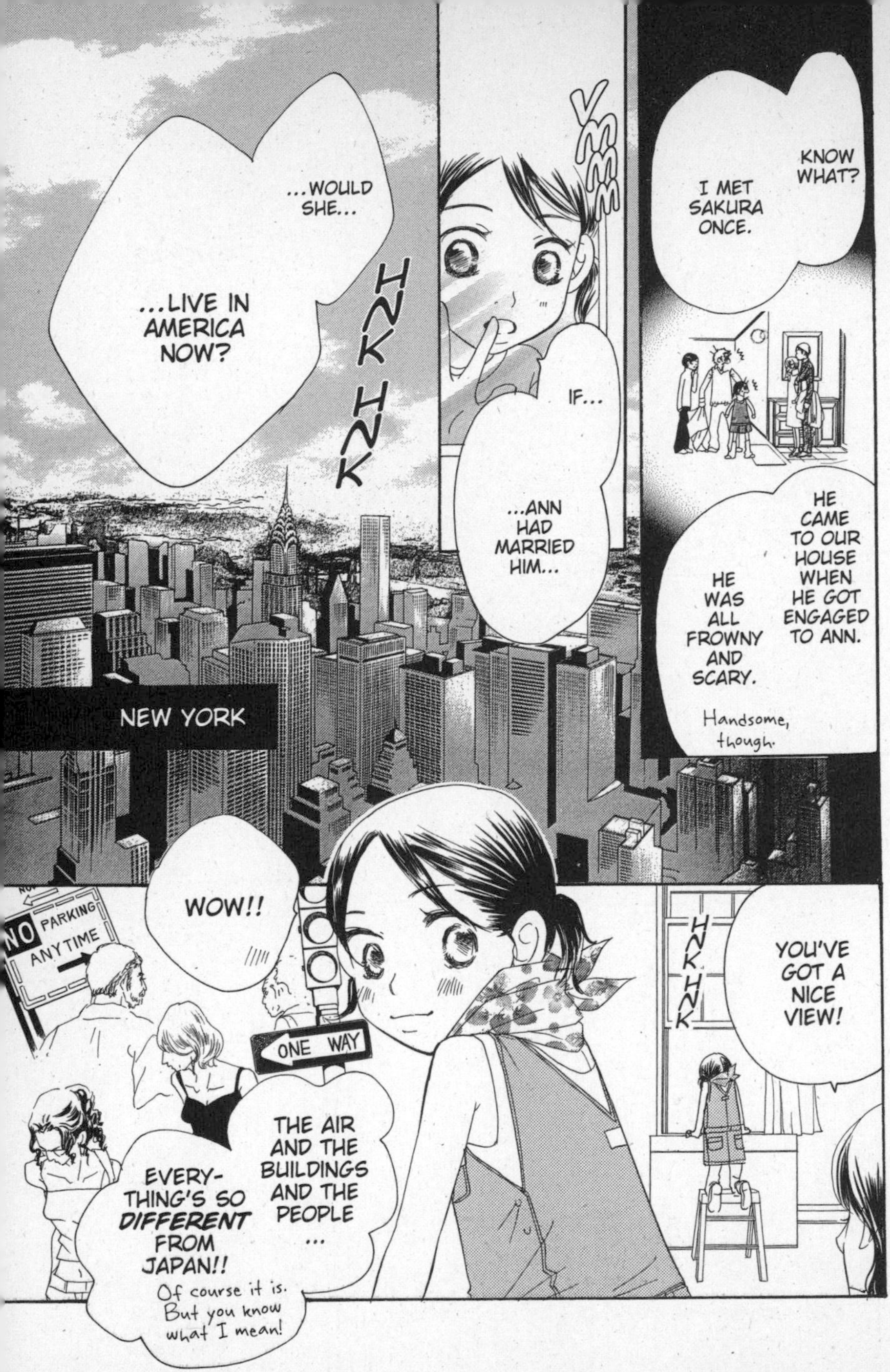
KNOW WHAT?
I MET SAKURA ONCE.
HE CAME TO OUR HOUSE WHEN HE GOT ENGAGED TO ANN.
HE WAS ALL FROWNY AND SCARY.
Handsome, though.
VMMM
IF...
...ANN HAD MARRIED HIM...
...WOULD SHE...
...LIVE IN AMERICA NOW?
HNK HNK HNK
NEW YORK
HNK HNK
YOU'VE GOT A NICE VIEW!
WOW!!
NO PARKING ANY TIME
ONE WAY
THE AIR AND THE BUILDINGS AND THE PEOPLE...
EVERY-THING'S SO ***DIFFERENT*** FROM JAPAN!!
Of course it is. But you know what I mean!

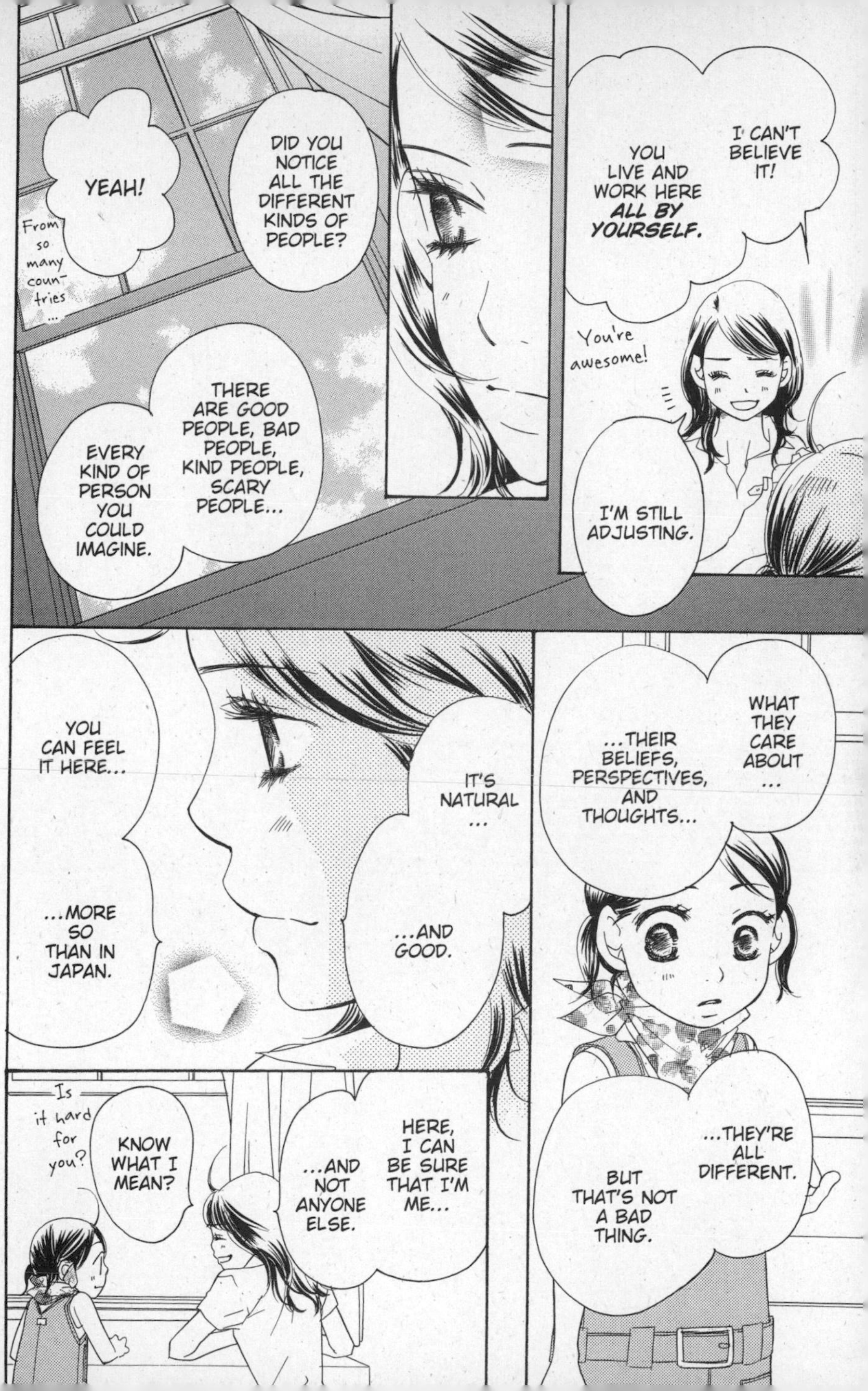
I CAN'T BELIEVE IT!
YOU LIVE AND WORK HERE ALL BY YOURSELF.
You're awesome!
I'M STILL ADJUSTING.
DID YOU NOTICE ALL THE DIFFERENT KINDS OF PEOPLE?
YEAH!
From so many countries...
THERE ARE GOOD PEOPLE, BAD PEOPLE, KIND PEOPLE, SCARY PEOPLE...
EVERY KIND OF PERSON YOU COULD IMAGINE.
WHAT THEY CARE ABOUT...
...THEIR BELIEFS, PERSPECTIVES, AND THOUGHTS...
...THEY'RE ALL DIFFERENT.
BUT THAT'S NOT A BAD THING.
IT'S NATURAL...
...AND GOOD.
YOU CAN FEEL IT HERE...
...MORE SO THAN IN JAPAN.
HERE, I CAN BE SURE THAT I'M ME...
...AND NOT ANYONE ELSE.
KNOW WHAT I MEAN?
Is it hard for you?

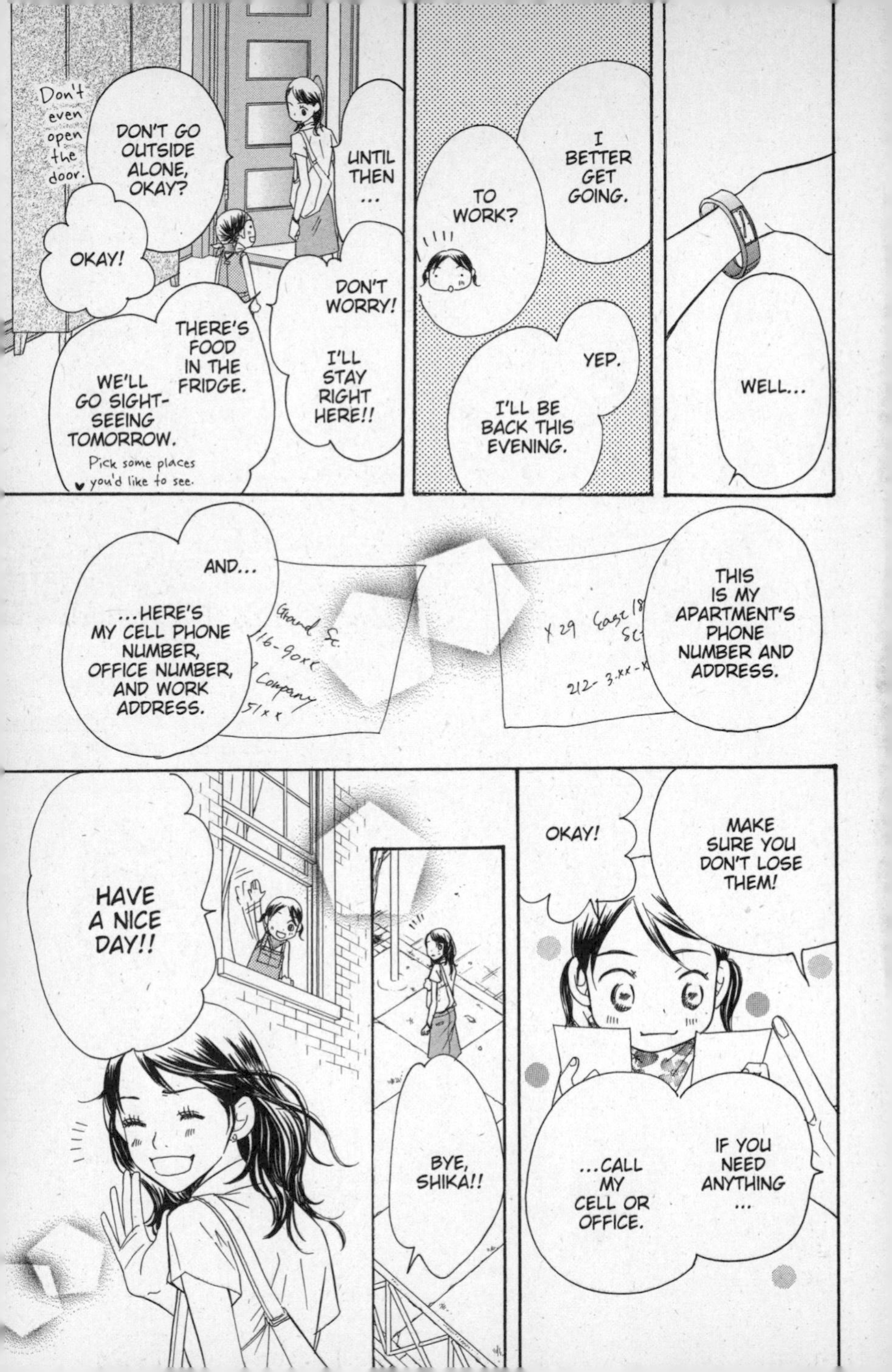
WELL...
I BETTER GET GOING.
TO WORK?
YEP.
I'LL BE BACK THIS EVENING.
UNTIL THEN...
DON'T GO OUTSIDE ALONE, OKAY?
Don't even open the door.
OKAY!
DON'T WORRY!
I'LL STAY RIGHT HERE!!
THERE'S FOOD IN THE FRIDGE.
WE'LL GO SIGHT-SEEING TOMORROW.
Pick some places you'd like to see.
THIS IS MY APARTMENT'S PHONE NUMBER AND ADDRESS.
AND...
...HERE'S MY CELL PHONE NUMBER, OFFICE NUMBER, AND WORK ADDRESS.
MAKE SURE YOU DON'T LOSE THEM!
OKAY!
IF YOU NEED ANYTHING...
...CALL MY CELL OR OFFICE.
BYE, SHIKA!!
HAVE A NICE DAY!!

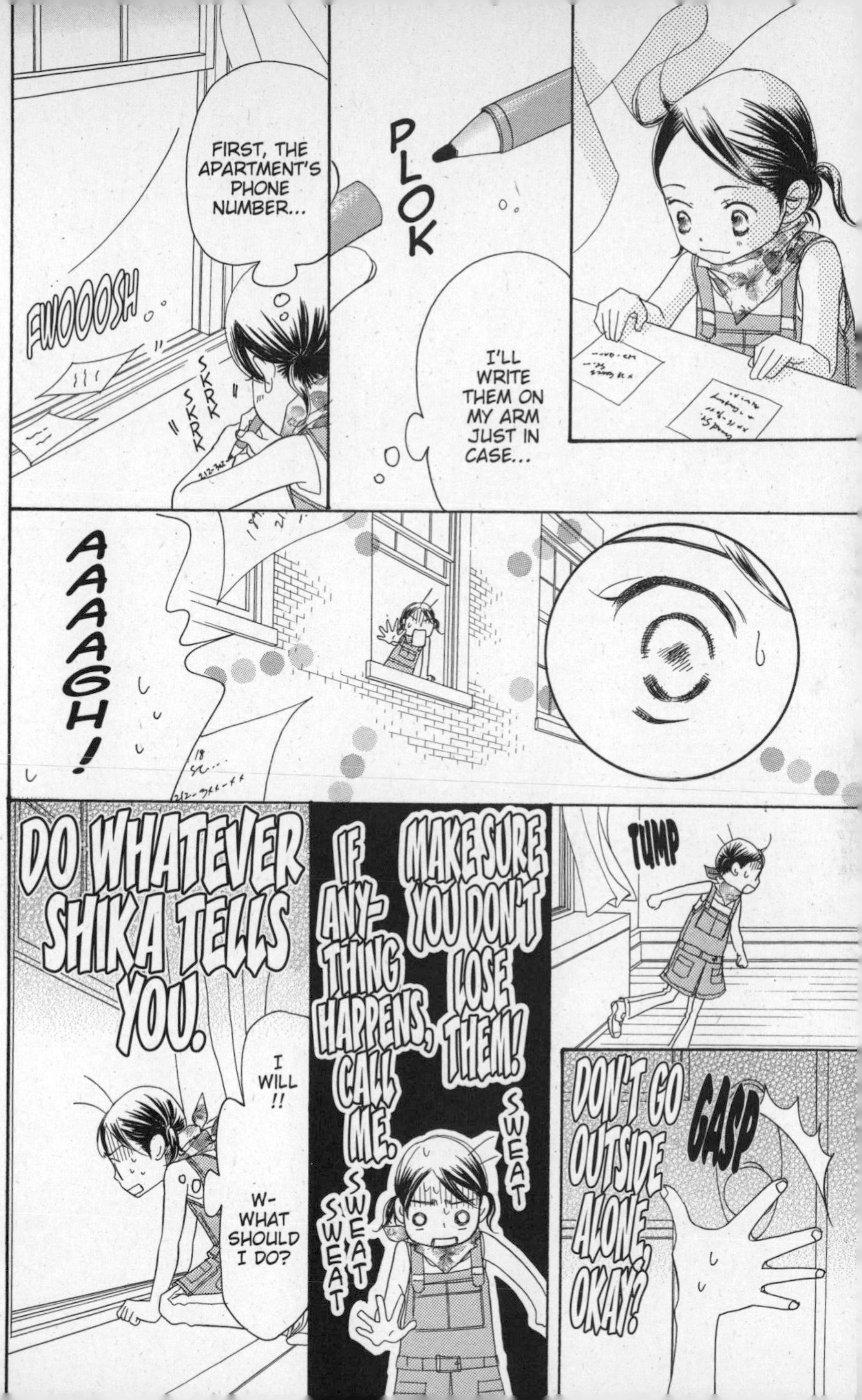
PLOK
I'LL WRITE THEM ON MY ARM JUST IN CASE...
FIRST, THE APARTMENT'S PHONE NUMBER...
FWOOOSH
SKRK SKRK
AAAAGH!
TUMP
DON'T GO OUTSIDE ALONE, OKAY?
GASP
MAKE SURE YOU DON'T LOSE THEM!
IF ANYTHING HAPPENS, CALL ME.
SWEAT SWEAT SWEAT
DO WHATEVER SHIKA TELLS YOU.
I WILL!!
W-WHAT SHOULD I DO?

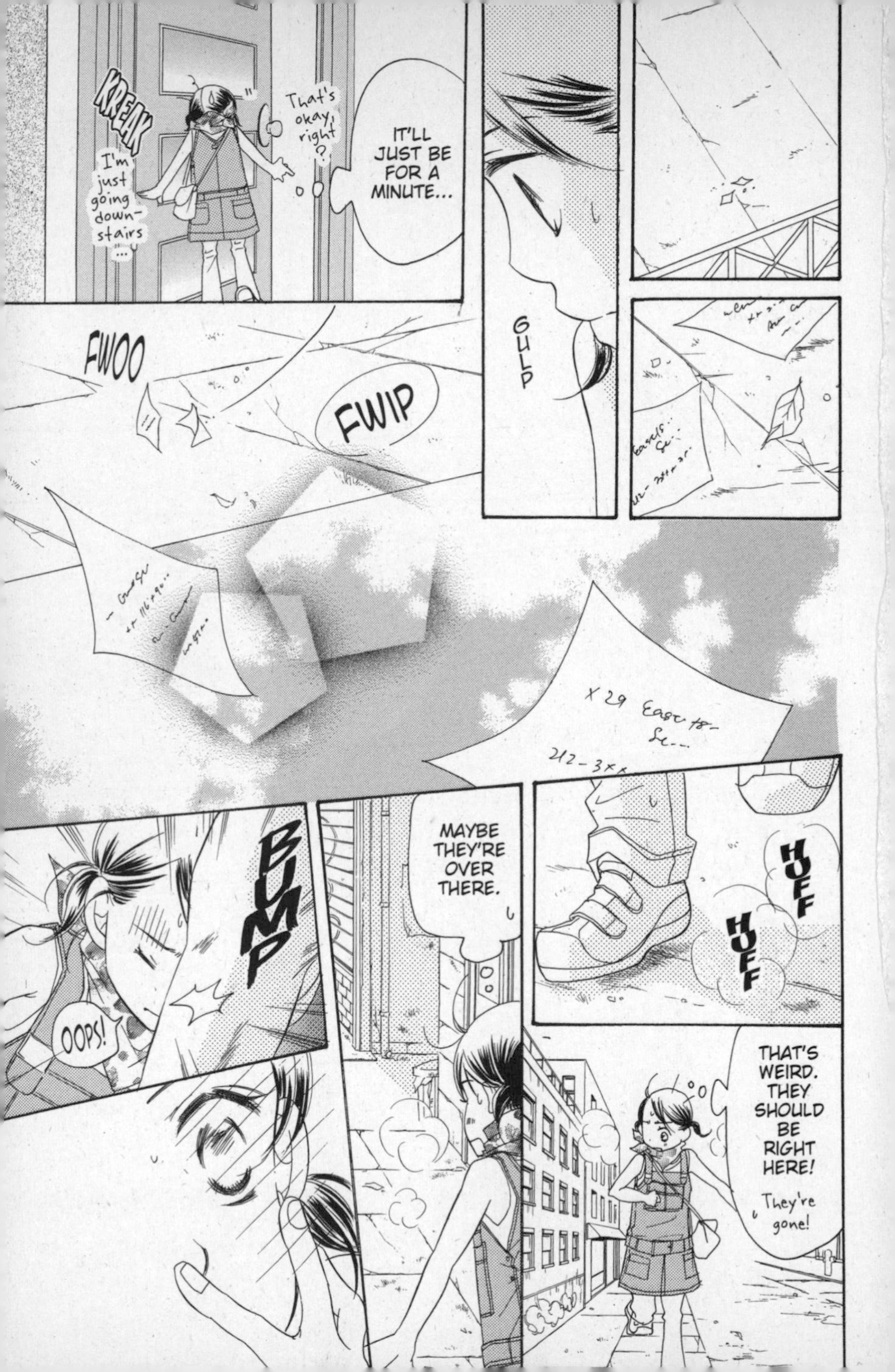
GULP
IT'LL JUST BE FOR A MINUTE...
That's okay, right?
KREAK
I'm just going down-stairs...
FWOO
FWIP
HUFF
HUFF
THAT'S WEIRD. THEY SHOULD BE RIGHT HERE!
They're gone!
MAYBE THEY'RE OVER THERE.
BUMP
OOPS!

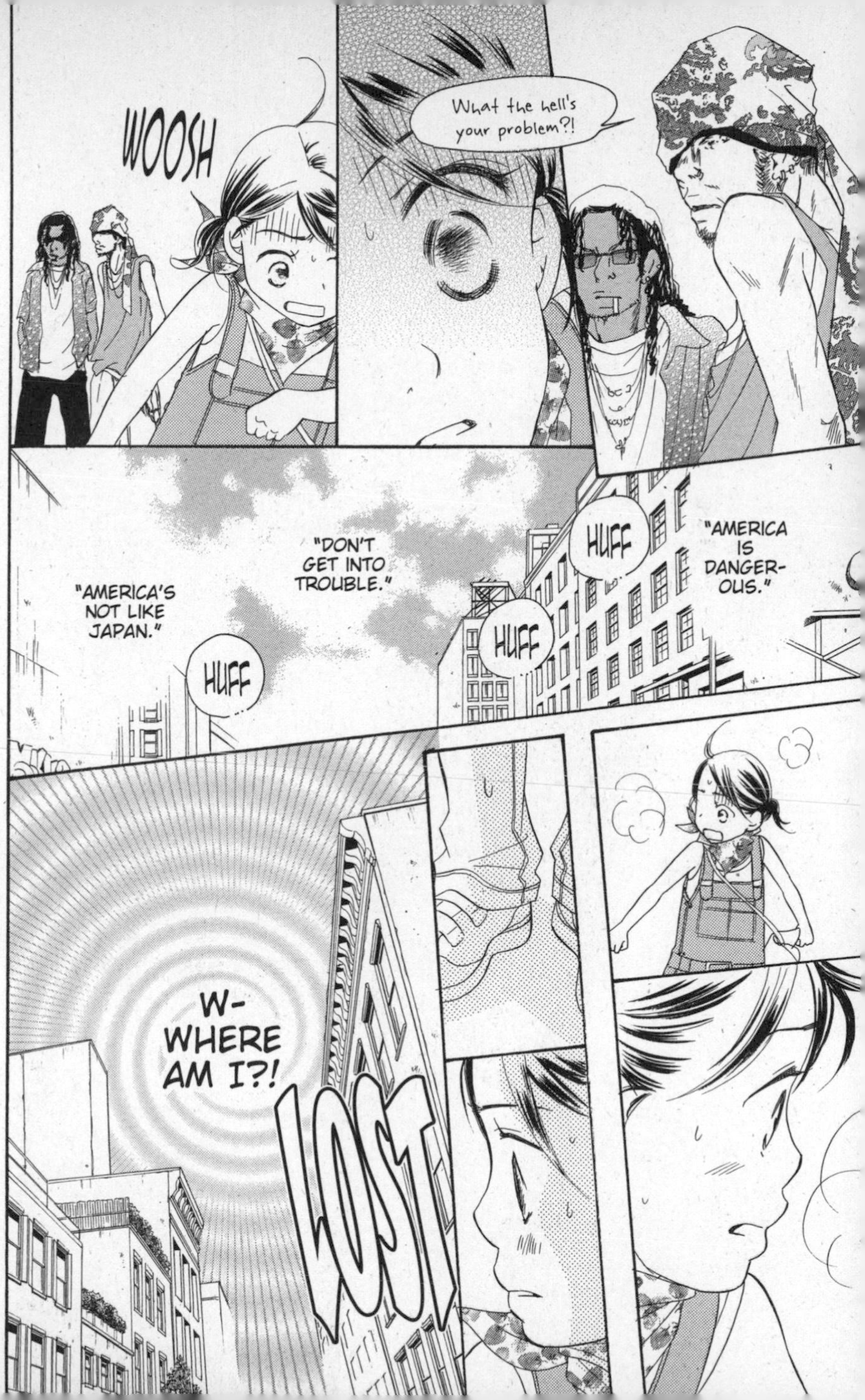
What the hell's your problem?!
WOOSH
"AMERICA IS DANGER-OUS."
HUFF
HUFF
"DON'T GET INTO TROUBLE."
HUFF
"AMERICA'S NOT LIKE JAPAN."
LOST
W-WHERE AM I?!

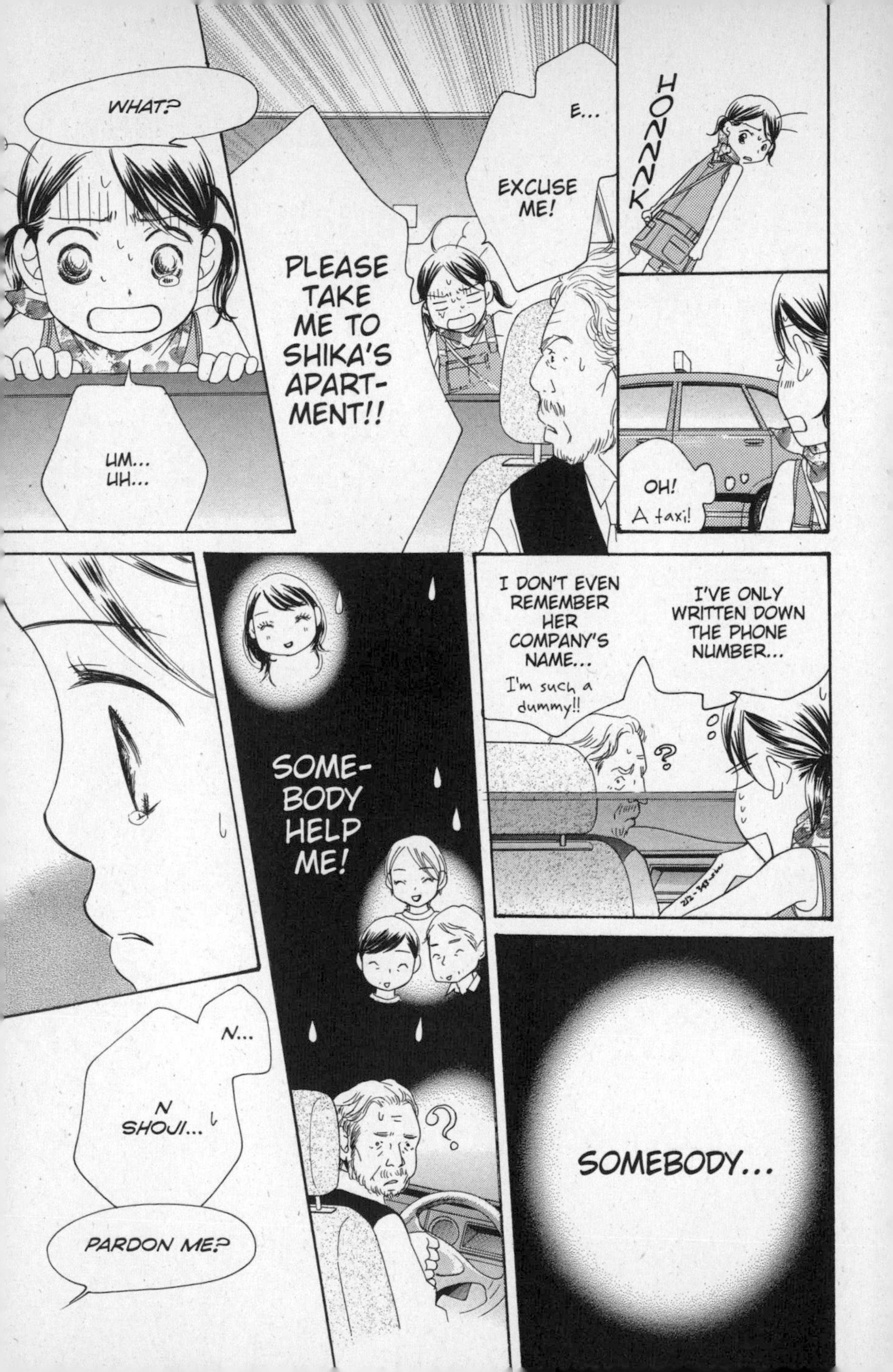
HONNNK
OH!
A taxi!
E...
EXCUSE ME!
PLEASE TAKE ME TO SHIKA'S APARTMENT!!
WHAT?
UM... UH...
I'VE ONLY WRITTEN DOWN THE PHONE NUMBER...
I DON'T EVEN REMEMBER HER COMPANY'S NAME...
I'm such a dummy!!
SOMEBODY...
SOME-BODY HELP ME!
N...
N SHOJI...
PARDON ME?

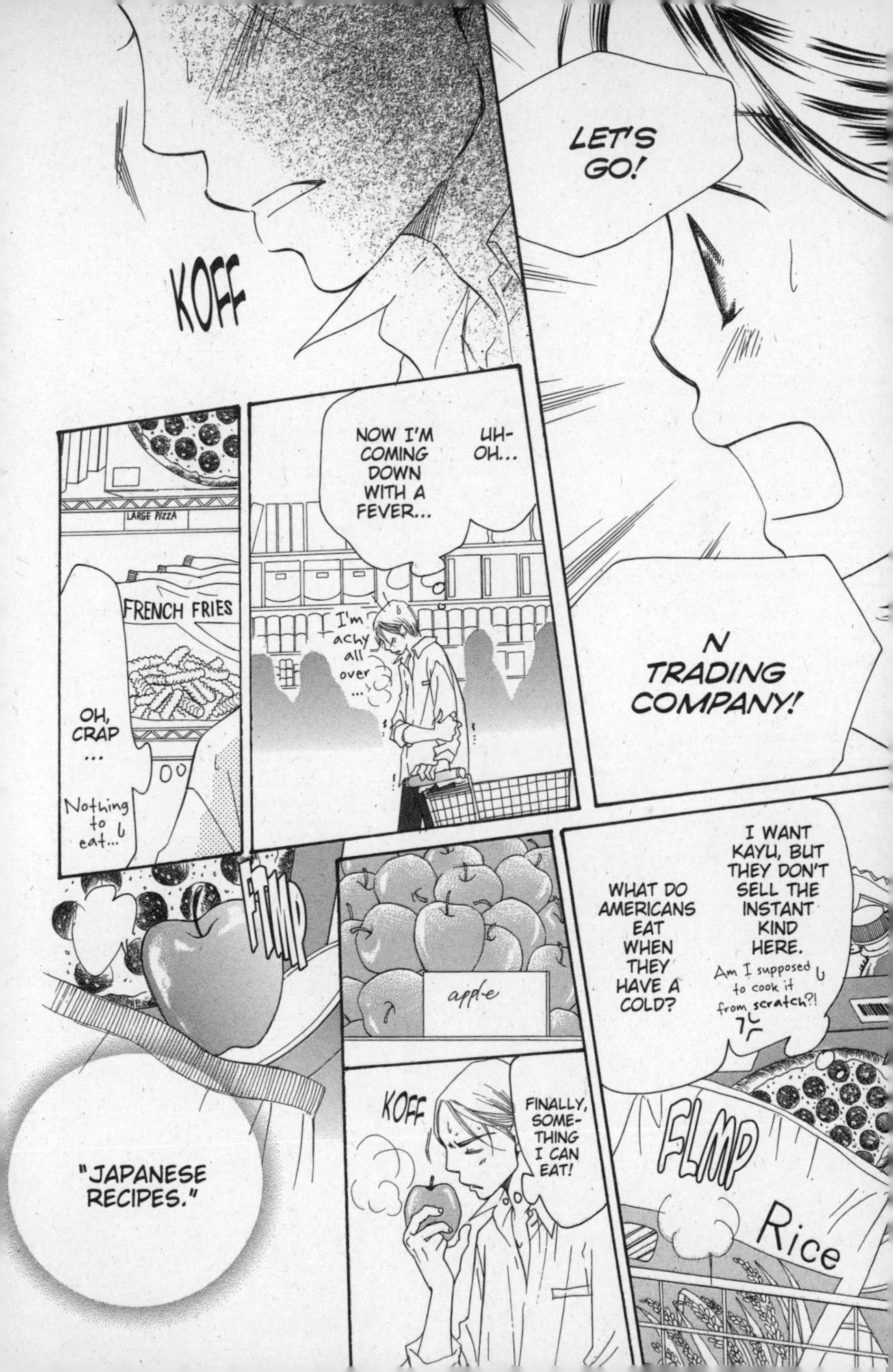
LET'S GO!
N TRADING COMPANY!
KOFF
UH-OH...
NOW I'M COMING DOWN WITH A FEVER...
I'm achy all over...
LARGE PIZZA
FRENCH FRIES
OH, CRAP...
Nothing to eat...
I WANT KAYU, BUT THEY DON'T SELL THE INSTANT KIND HERE.
Am I supposed to cook it from scratch?!
WHAT DO AMERICANS EAT WHEN THEY HAVE A COLD?
FLMP
Rice
apple
KOFF
FINALLY, SOMETHING I CAN EAT!
FLMP
"JAPANESE RECIPES."

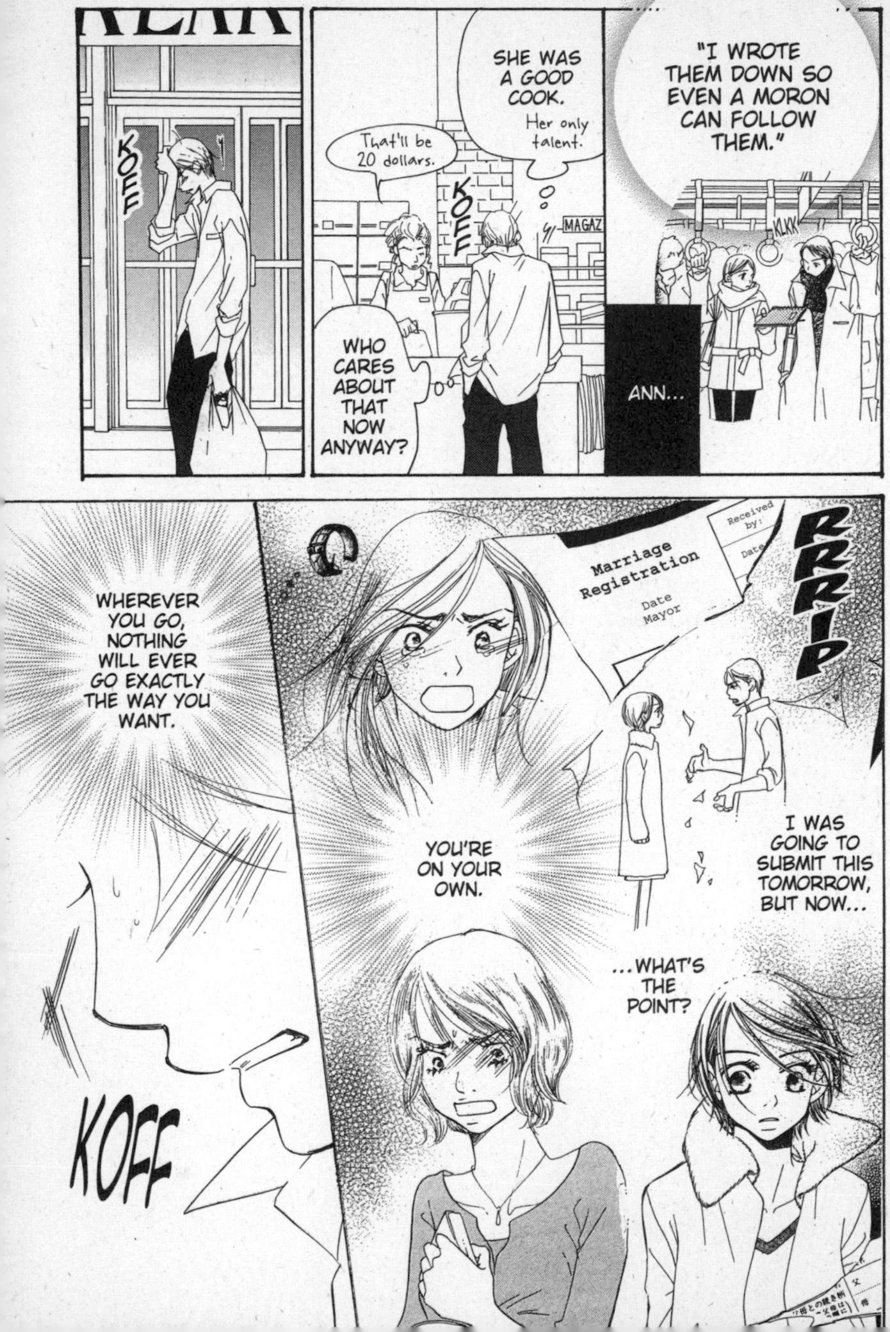
"I WROTE THEM DOWN SO EVEN A MORON CAN FOLLOW THEM."
KLKK
ANN...
SHE WAS A GOOD COOK.
Her only talent.
That'll be 20 dollars.
KOFF
MAGAZ
WHO CARES ABOUT THAT NOW ANYWAY?
KOFF
RRRIP
Received by:
Date
Marriage Registration
Date
Mayor
I WAS GOING TO SUBMIT THIS TOMORROW, BUT NOW...
YOU'RE ON YOUR OWN.
...WHAT'S THE POINT?
WHEREVER YOU GO, NOTHING WILL EVER GO EXACTLY THE WAY YOU WANT.
KOFF

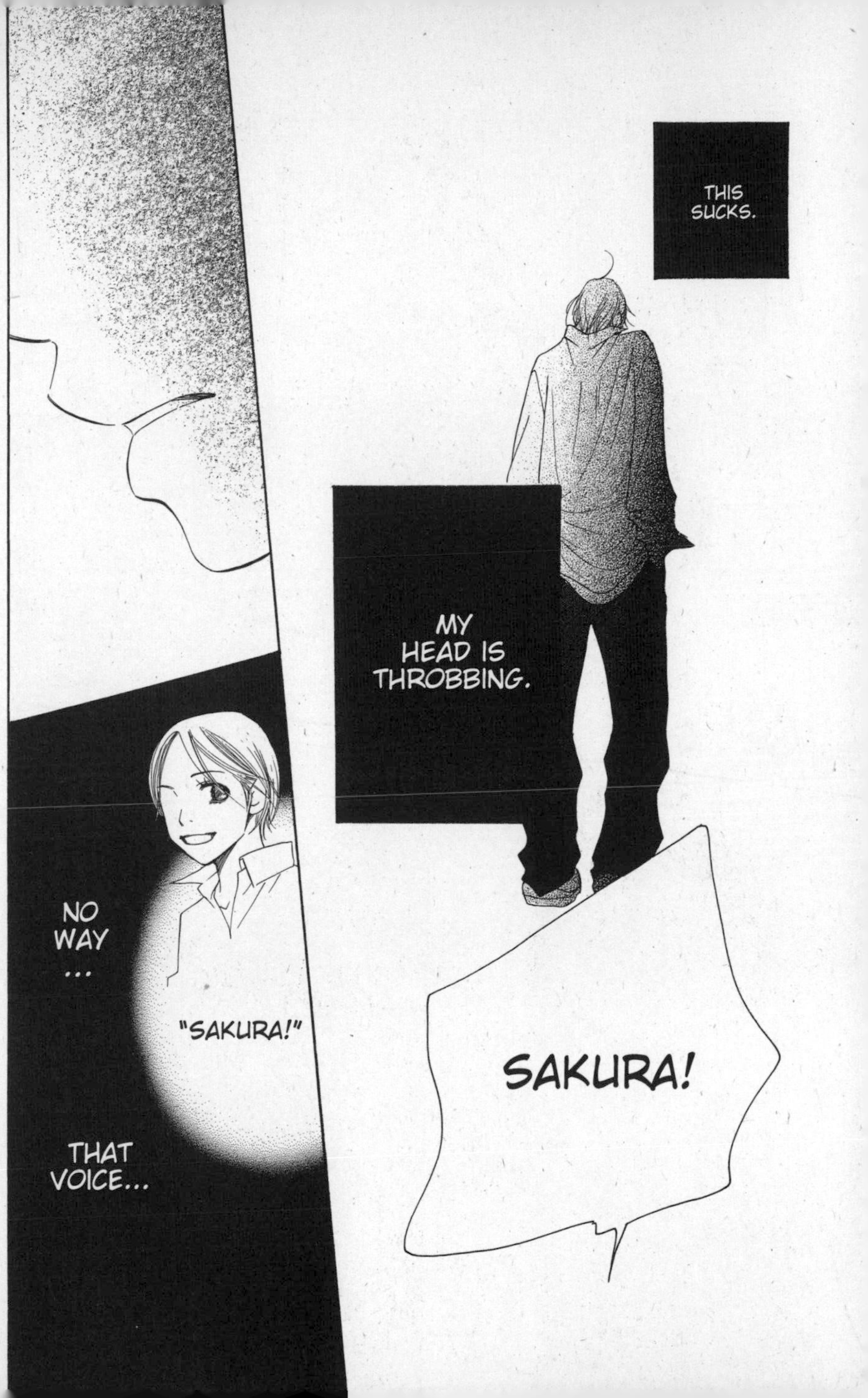
THIS SUCKS.
MY HEAD IS THROBBING.
SAKURA!
NO WAY...
"SAKURA!"
THAT VOICE...

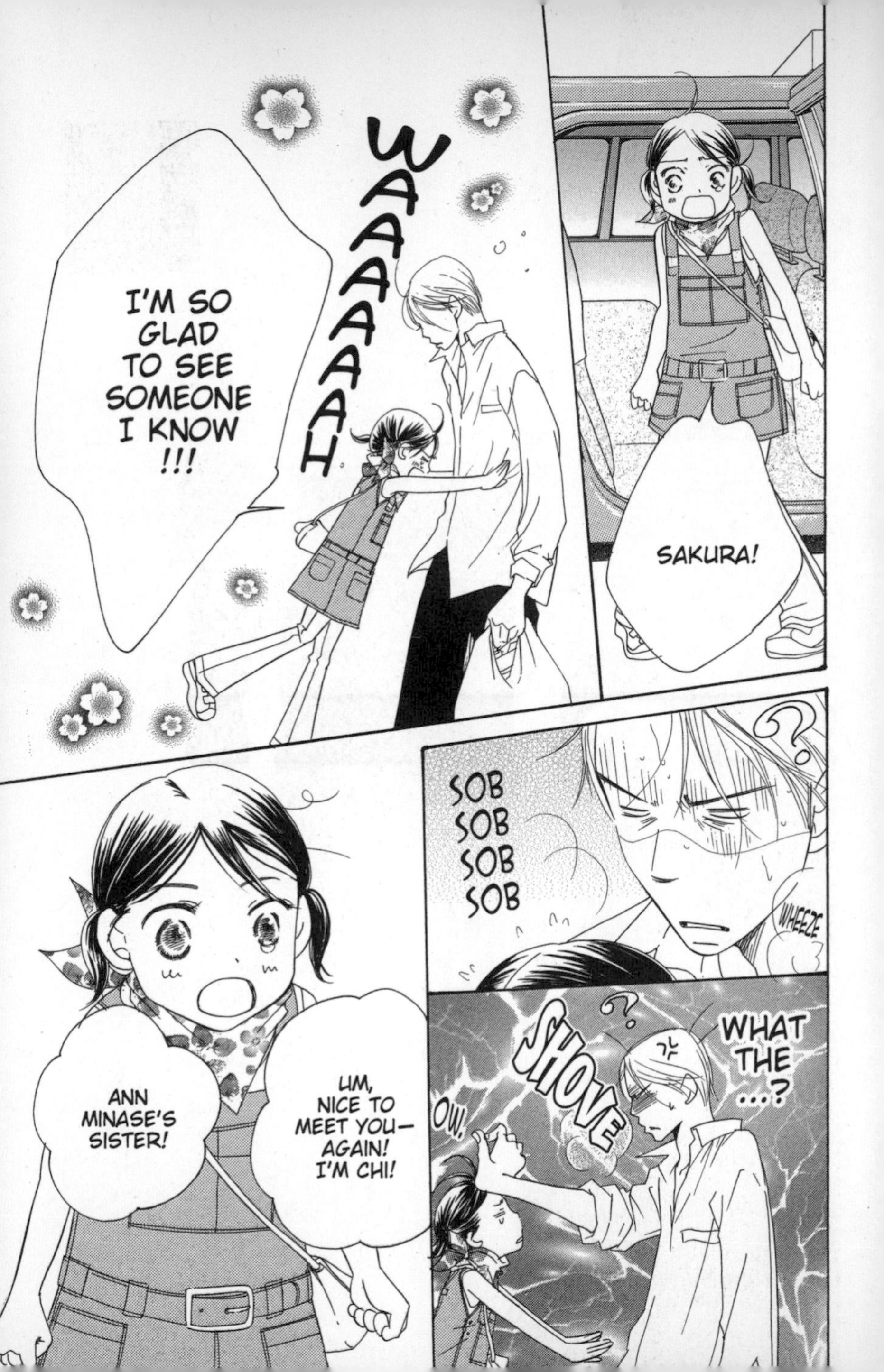
SAKURA!
WAAAAAAH
I'M SO GLAD TO SEE SOMEONE I KNOW!!!
SOB SOB SOB SOB
WHEEZE
WHAT THE ...?
SHOVE
OW!
UM, NICE TO MEET YOU— AGAIN! I'M CHI!
ANN MINASE'S SISTER!

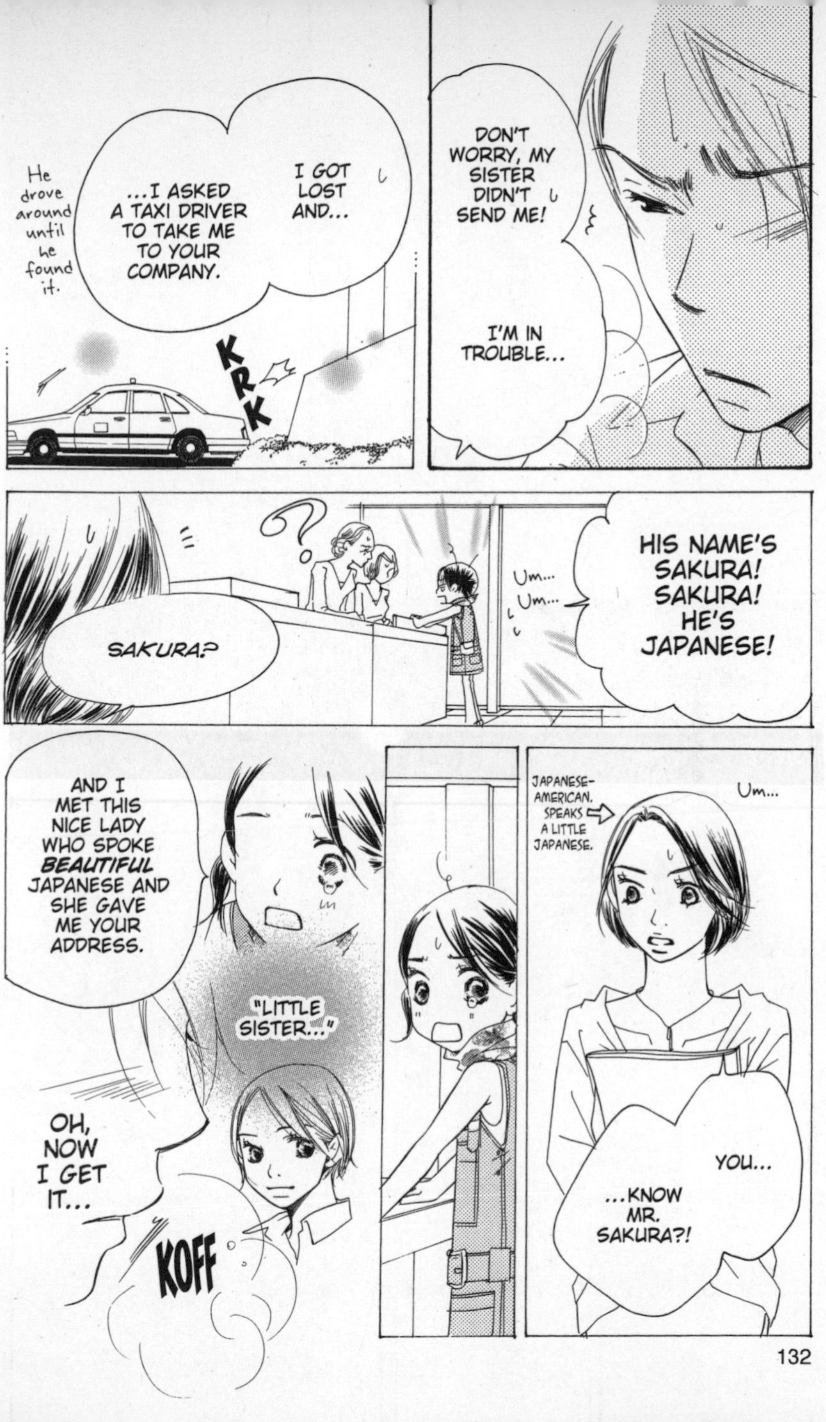
DON'T WORRY, MY SISTER DIDN'T SEND ME!
I'M IN TROUBLE...
I GOT LOST AND...
...I ASKED A TAXI DRIVER TO TAKE ME TO YOUR COMPANY.
He drove around until he found it.
KRK
HIS NAME'S SAKURA! SAKURA! HE'S JAPANESE!
Um... Um...
SAKURA?
Um...
JAPANESE-AMERICAN. SPEAKS A LITTLE JAPANESE.
YOU...
...KNOW MR. SAKURA?!
AND I MET THIS NICE LADY WHO SPOKE BEAUTIFUL JAPANESE AND SHE GAVE ME YOUR ADDRESS.
"LITTLE SISTER..."
OH, NOW I GET IT...
KOFF

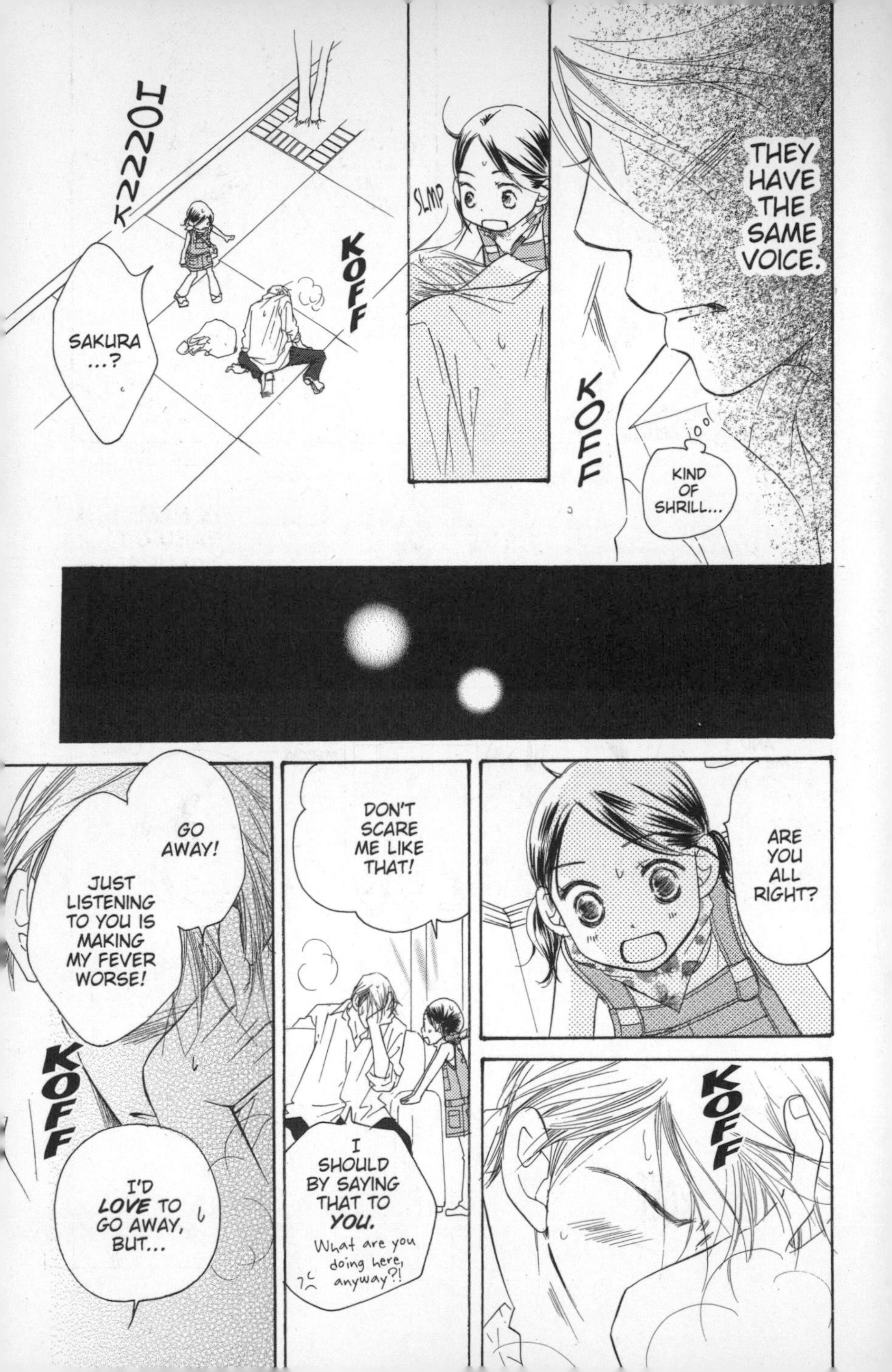
THEY HAVE THE SAME VOICE.
KOFF
KIND OF SHRILL...
SLMP
HONNNK
KOFF
SAKURA ...?
ARE YOU ALL RIGHT?
KOFF
DON'T SCARE ME LIKE THAT!
I SHOULD BY SAYING THAT TO ***YOU.***
What are you doing here, anyway?!
GO AWAY!
JUST LISTENING TO YOU IS MAKING MY FEVER WORSE!
KOFF
I'D ***LOVE*** TO GO AWAY, BUT...

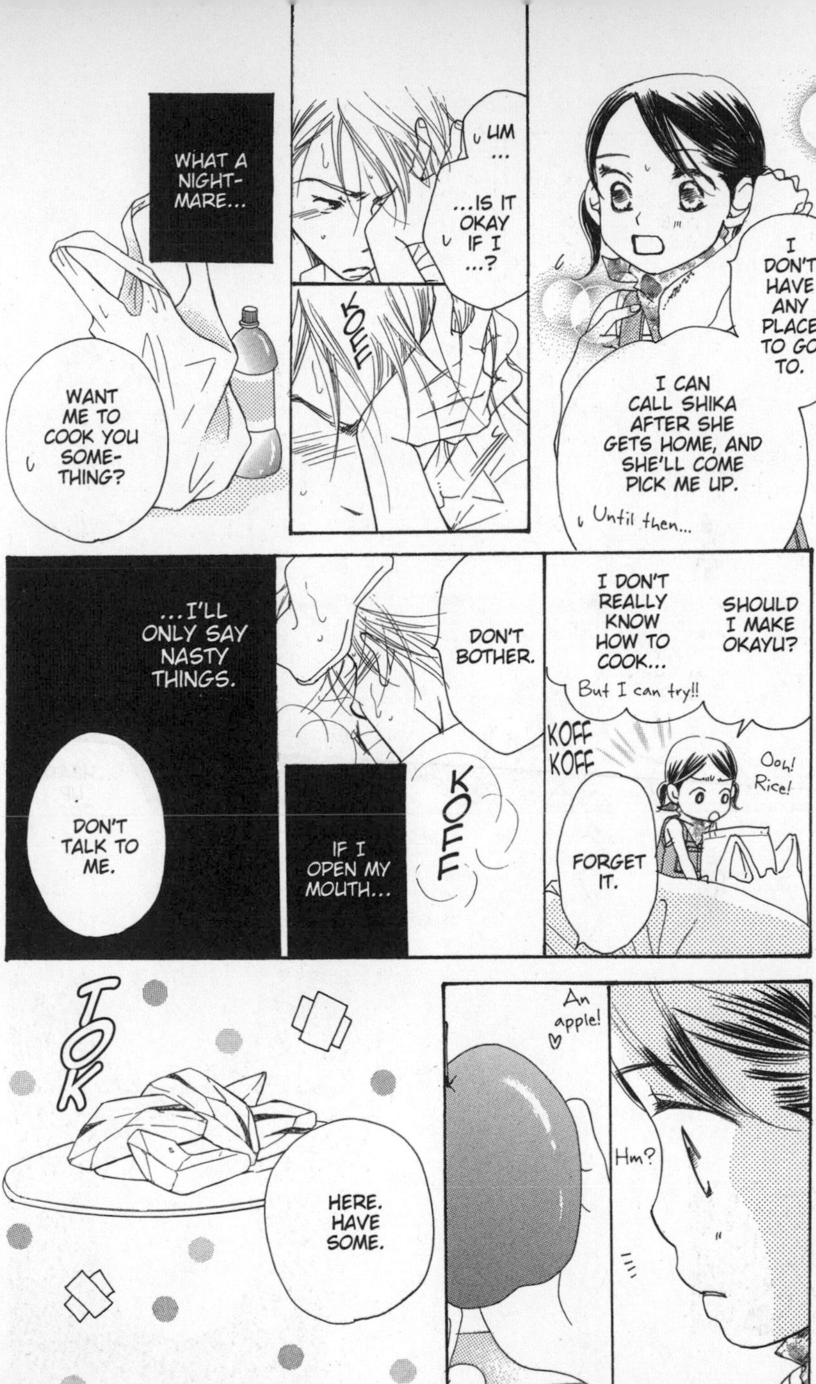
I DON'T HAVE ANY PLACE TO GO TO.
I CAN CALL SHIKA AFTER SHE GETS HOME, AND SHE'LL COME PICK ME UP.
Until then...
UM ...
...IS IT OKAY IF I ...?
KOFF
WHAT A NIGHT-MARE...
WANT ME TO COOK YOU SOME-THING?
SHOULD I MAKE OKAYU?
I DON'T REALLY KNOW HOW TO COOK...
But I can try!!
KOFF KOFF
Ooh! Rice!
FORGET IT.
DON'T BOTHER.
KOFF
IF I OPEN MY MOUTH...
...I'LL ONLY SAY NASTY THINGS.
DON'T TALK TO ME.
Hm?
An apple!
TOK
HERE. HAVE SOME.

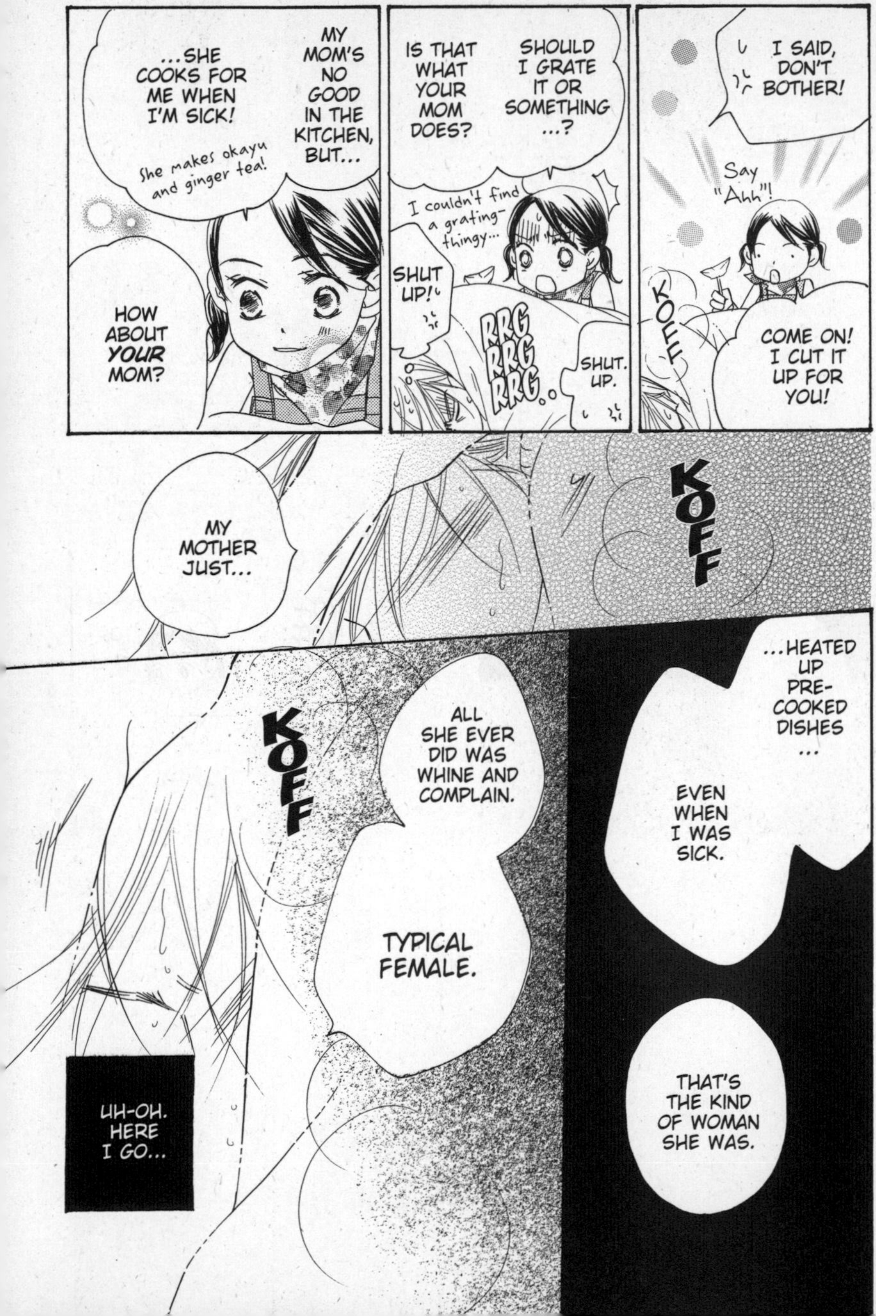
I SAID, DON'T BOTHER!
Say "Ahh"!
KOFF
COME ON! I CUT IT UP FOR YOU!
SHOULD I GRATE IT OR SOMETHING...?
IS THAT WHAT YOUR MOM DOES?
I couldn't find a grating-thingy...
SHUT UP!
RRG RRG RRG
SHUT. UP.
MY MOM'S NO GOOD IN THE KITCHEN, BUT...
...SHE COOKS FOR ME WHEN I'M SICK!
She makes okayu and ginger tea!
HOW ABOUT *YOUR* MOM?
KOFF
MY MOTHER JUST...
...HEATED UP PRE-COOKED DISHES...
EVEN WHEN I WAS SICK.
THAT'S THE KIND OF WOMAN SHE WAS.
ALL SHE EVER DID WAS WHINE AND COMPLAIN.
KOFF
TYPICAL FEMALE.
UH-OH. HERE I GO...

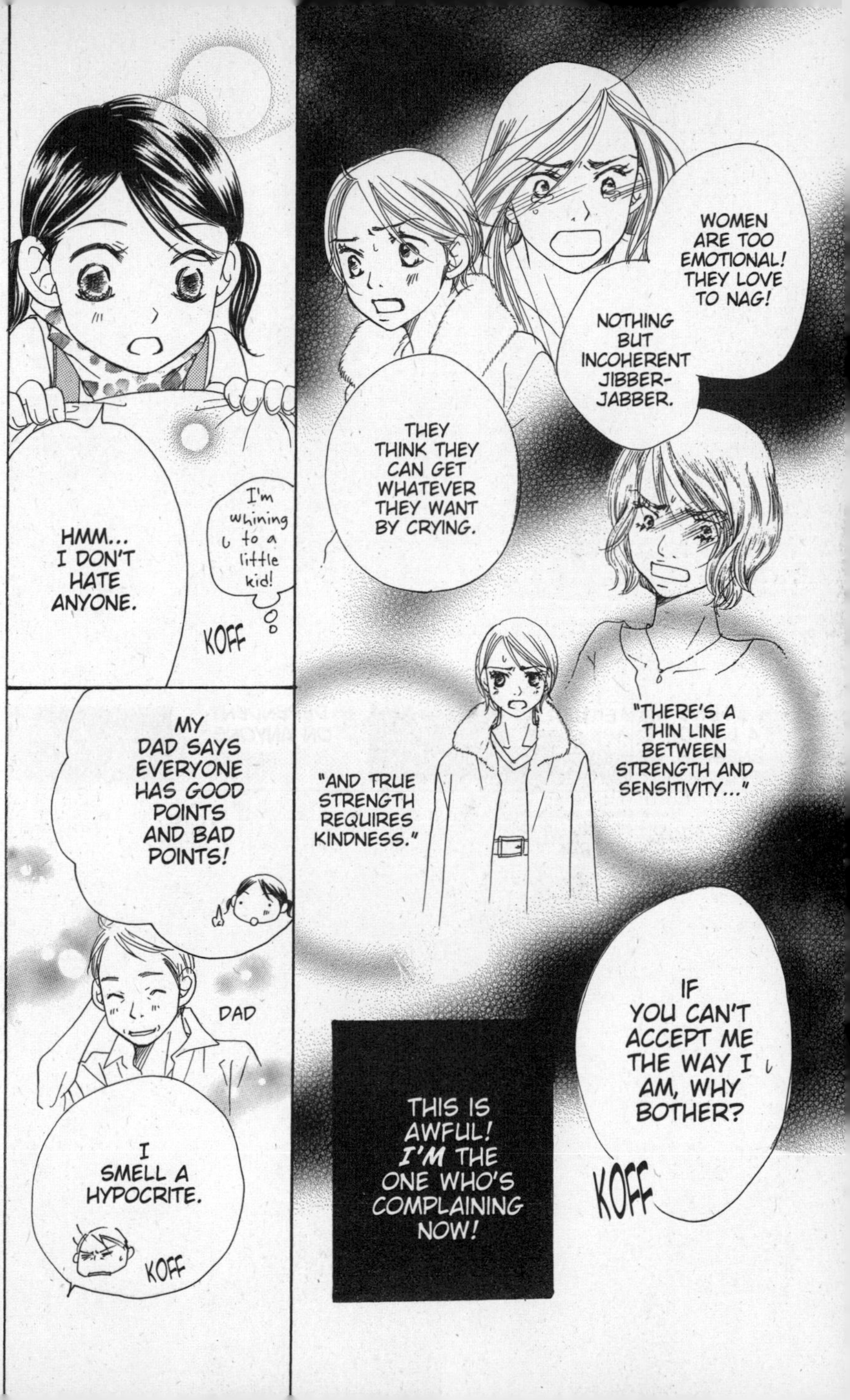
WOMEN ARE TOO EMOTIONAL! THEY LOVE TO NAG!
NOTHING BUT INCOHERENT JIBBER-JABBER.
THEY THINK THEY CAN GET WHATEVER THEY WANT BY CRYING.
"THERE'S A THIN LINE BETWEEN STRENGTH AND SENSITIVITY..."
"AND TRUE STRENGTH REQUIRES KINDNESS."
IF YOU CAN'T ACCEPT ME THE WAY I AM, WHY BOTHER?
KOFF
THIS IS AWFUL! *I'M* THE ONE WHO'S COMPLAINING NOW!
I'm whining to a little kid!
HMM... I DON'T HATE ANYONE.
KOFF
MY DAD SAYS EVERYONE HAS GOOD POINTS AND BAD POINTS!
DAD
I SMELL A HYPOCRITE.
KOFF

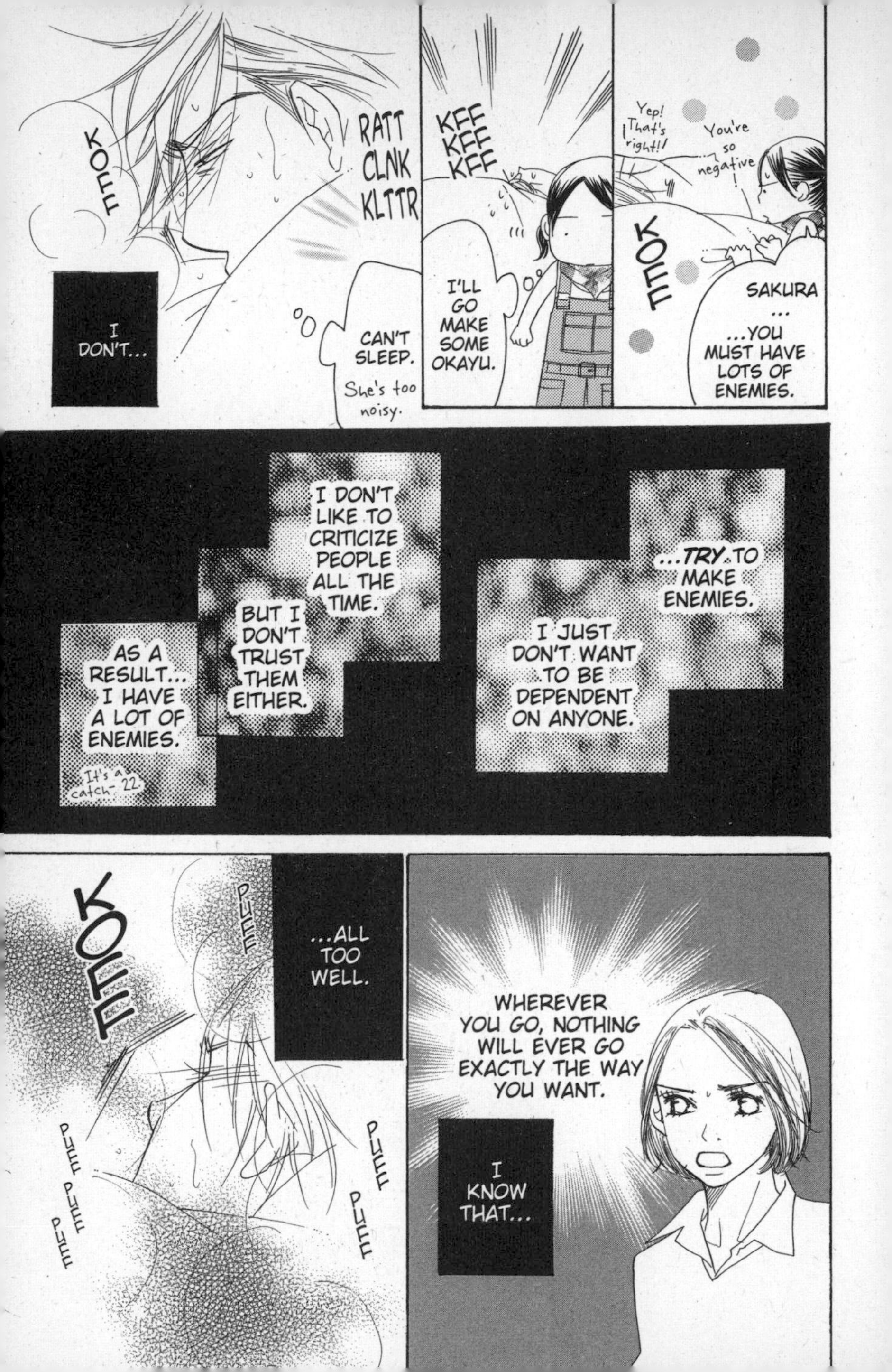
SAKURA...
...YOU MUST HAVE LOTS OF ENEMIES.
Yep! That's right!!
You're so negative!
KOFF
KFF KFF KFF
I'LL GO MAKE SOME OKAYU.
RATT CLNK KLTTR
CAN'T SLEEP.
She's too noisy.
KOFF
I DON'T...
...TRY TO MAKE ENEMIES.
I JUST DON'T WANT TO BE DEPENDENT ON ANYONE.
I DON'T LIKE TO CRITICIZE PEOPLE ALL THE TIME.
BUT I DON'T TRUST THEM EITHER.
AS A RESULT... I HAVE A LOT OF ENEMIES.
It's a catch-22.
WHEREVER YOU GO, NOTHING WILL EVER GO EXACTLY THE WAY YOU WANT.
I KNOW THAT...
...ALL TOO WELL.
KOFF
PUFF
PUFF PUFF
PUFF PUFF PUFF

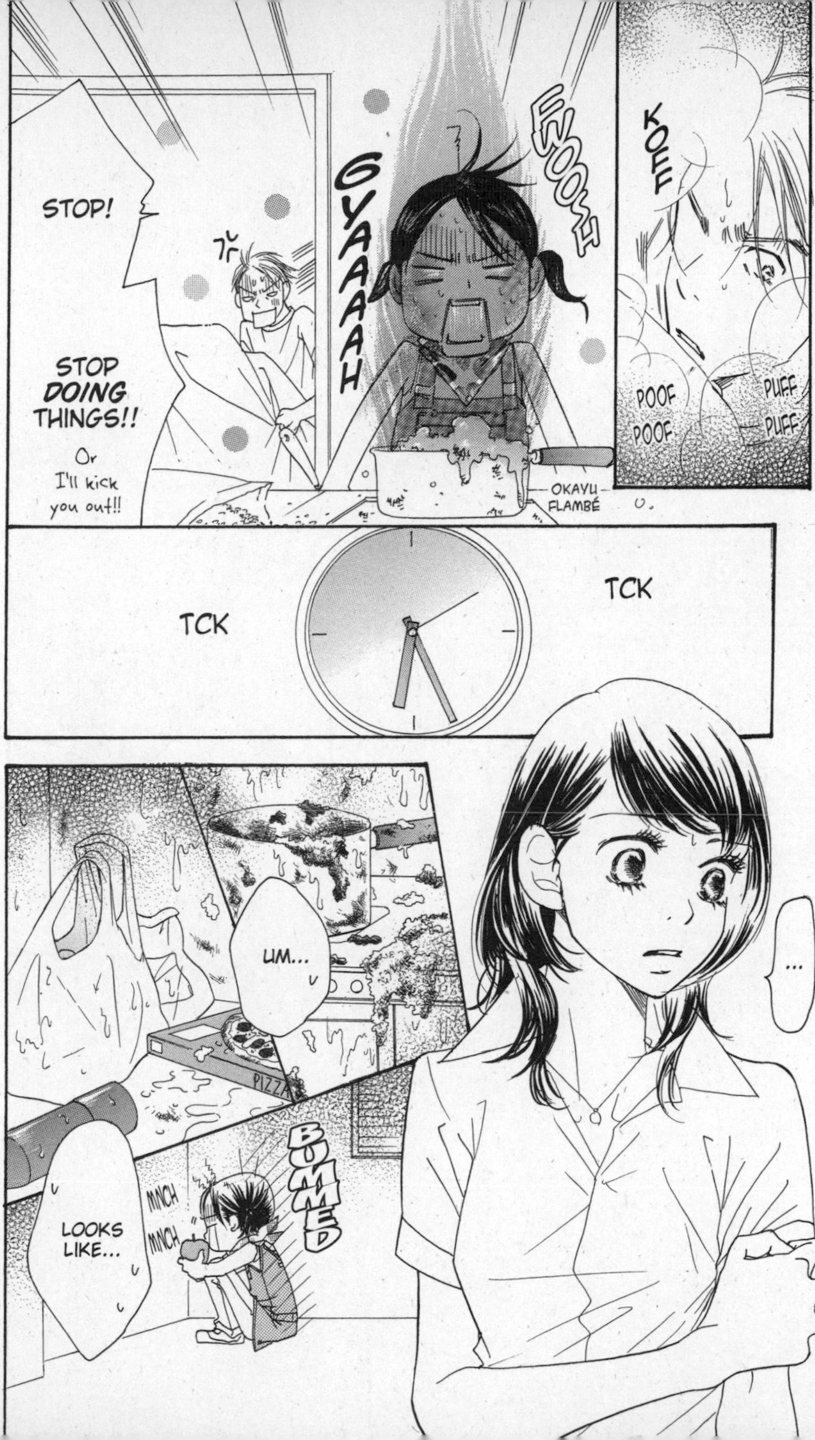
KOFF
POOF POOF
PUFF PUFF
FWOOSH
GYAAAAH
OKAYU FLAMBÉ
STOP!
STOP DOING THINGS!!
Or I'll kick you out!!
TCK
TCK
...
UM...
BUMMED
MNCH MNCH
LOOKS LIKE...

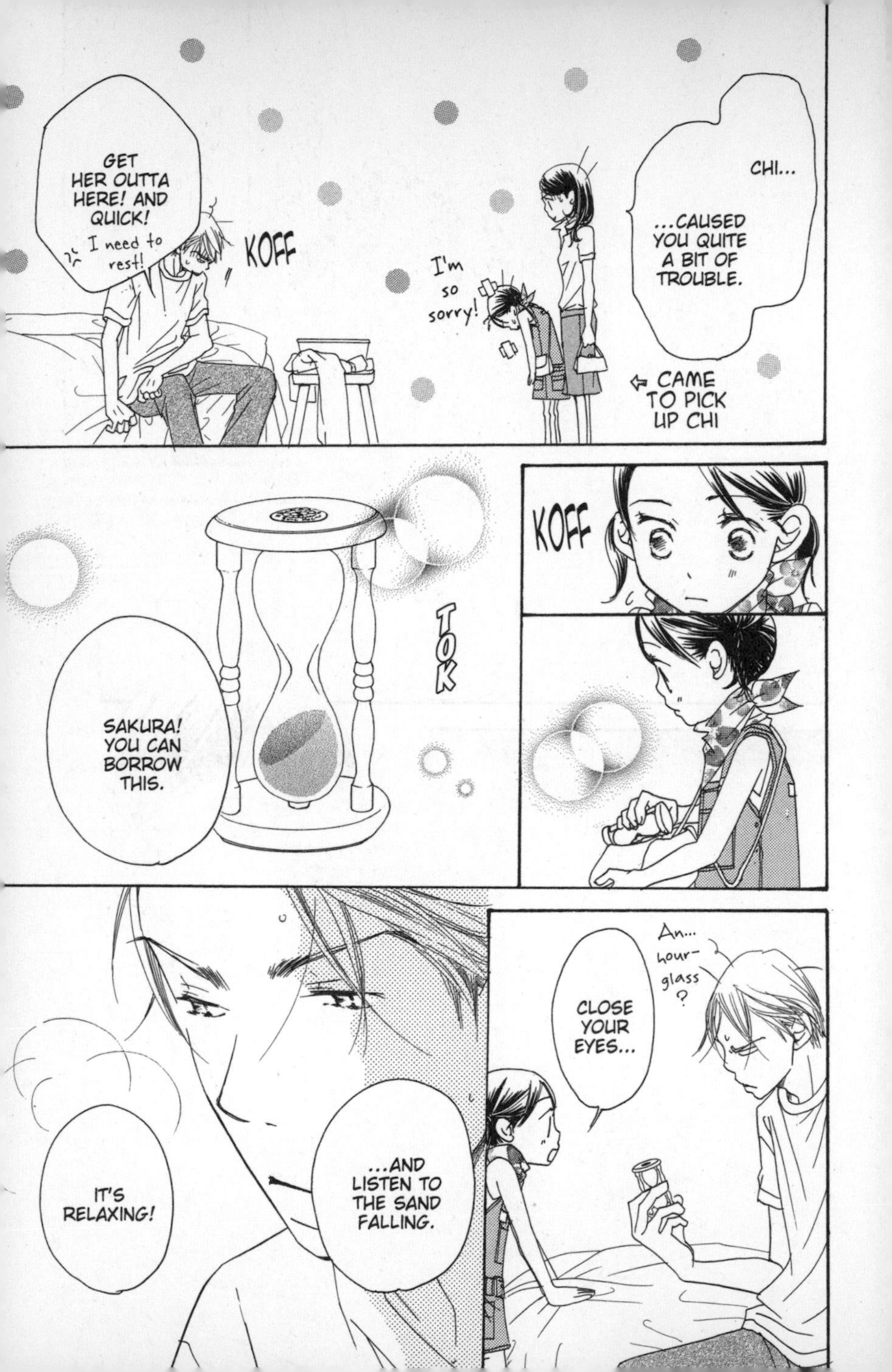
CHI...
...CAUSED YOU QUITE A BIT OF TROUBLE.
CAME TO PICK UP CHI
I'm so sorry!
KOFF
GET HER OUTTA HERE! AND QUICK!
I need to rest!
KOFF
TOK
SAKURA! YOU CAN BORROW THIS.
An... hour-glass?
CLOSE YOUR EYES...
...AND LISTEN TO THE SAND FALLING.
IT'S RELAXING!

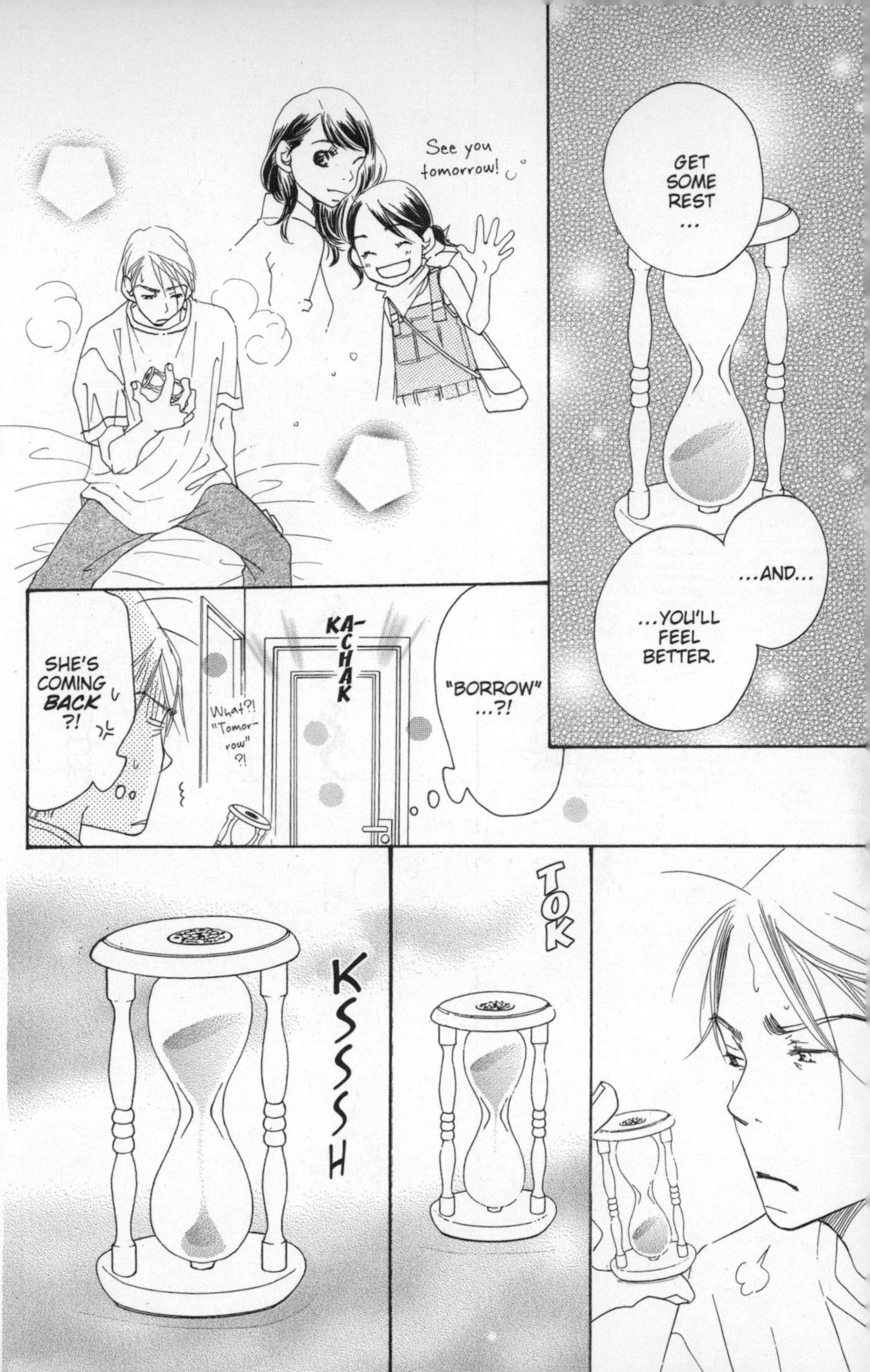
GET SOME REST ...
...AND...
...YOU'LL FEEL BETTER.
See you tomorrow!
"BORROW" ...?!
KA-CHAK
What?! "Tomorrow" ?!
SHE'S COMING BACK ?!
TOK
KSSSH

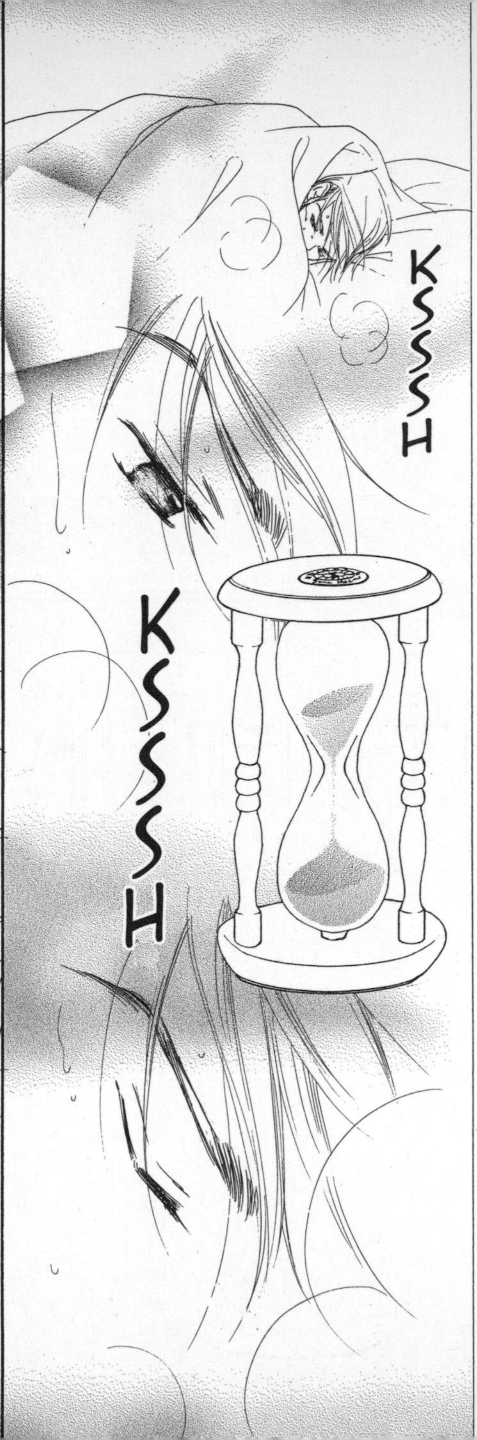
KSSSH
KSSSH
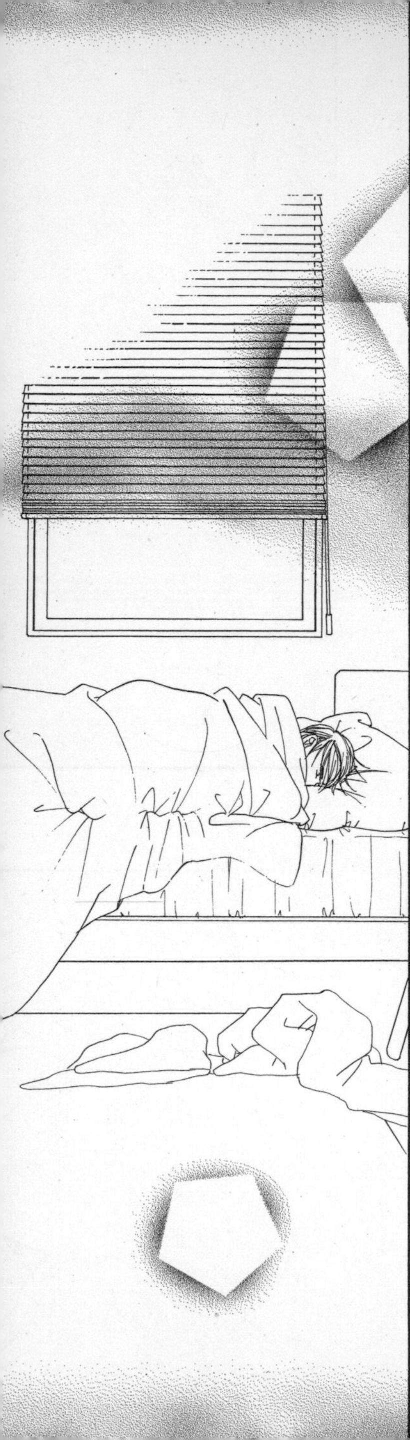

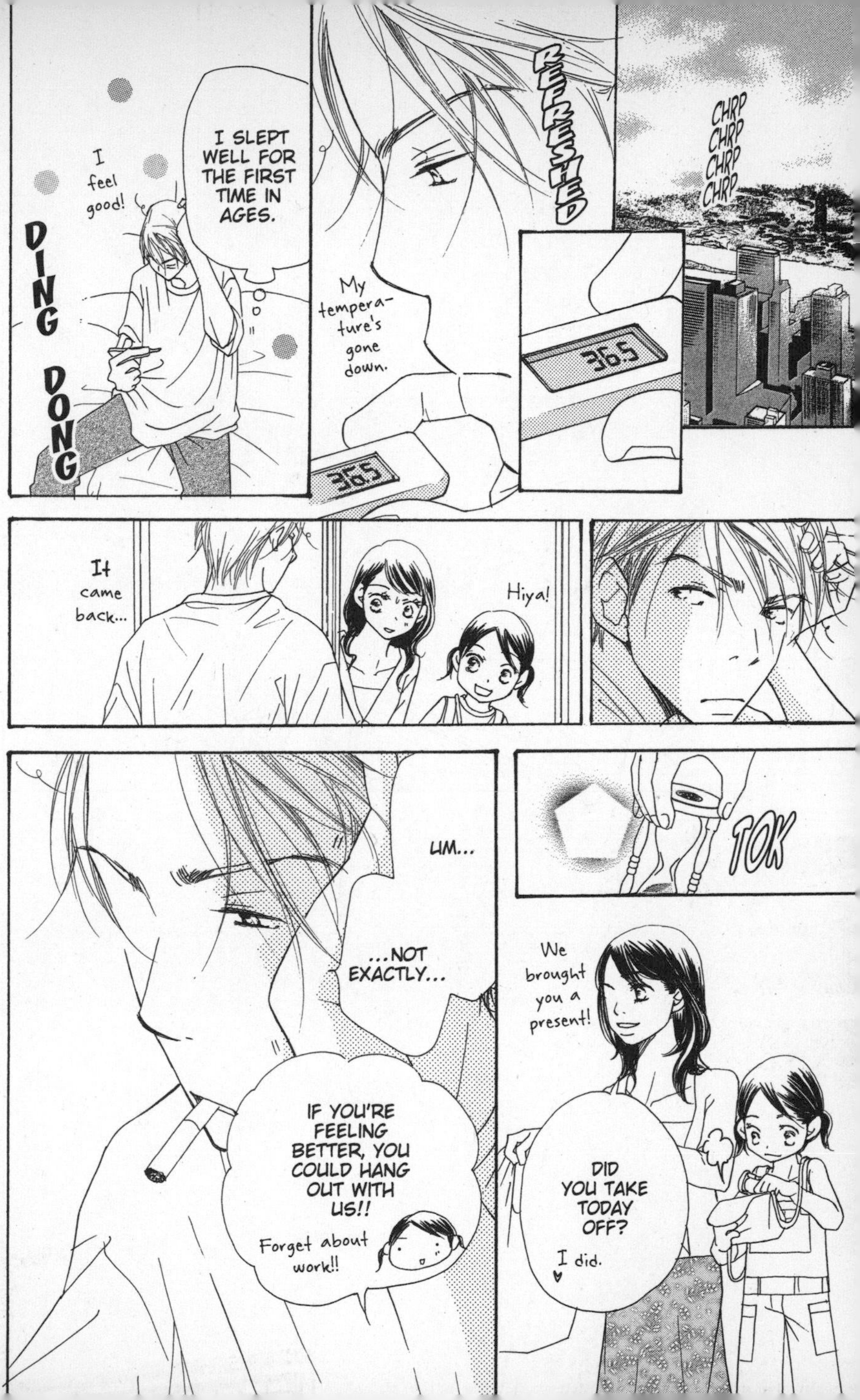
CHRP
CHRP
CHRP
CHRP
36.5
REFRESHED
My temperature's gone down.
36.5
I SLEPT WELL FOR THE FIRST TIME IN AGES.
I feel good!
DING
DONG
Hiya!
It came back...
TOK
We brought you a present!
DID YOU TAKE TODAY OFF?
I did.
UM...
...NOT EXACTLY...
IF YOU'RE FEELING BETTER, YOU COULD HANG OUT WITH US!!
Forget about work!!

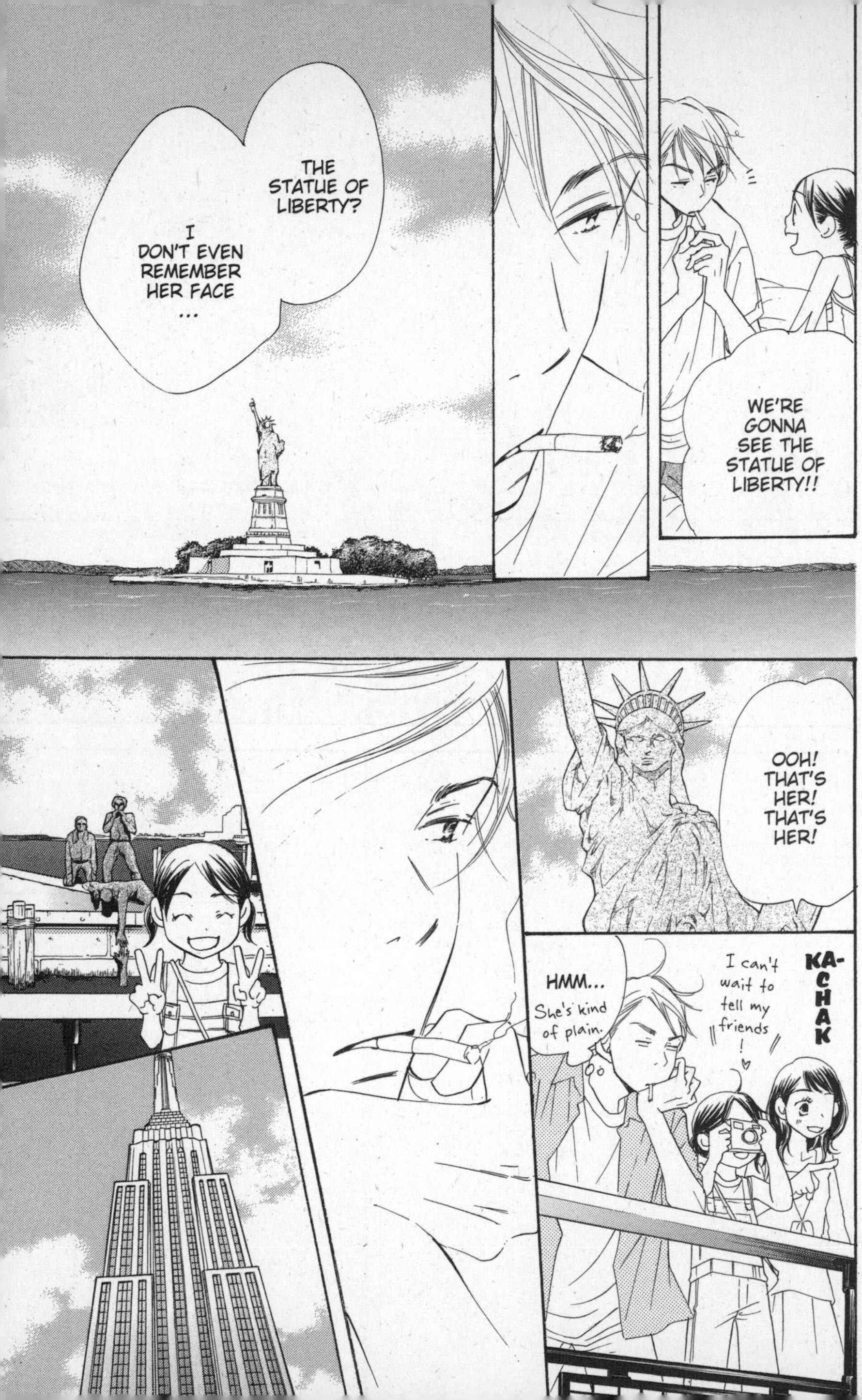
WE'RE GONNA SEE THE STATUE OF LIBERTY!!
THE STATUE OF LIBERTY?
I DON'T EVEN REMEMBER HER FACE ...
OOH! THAT'S HER! THAT'S HER!
KA-CHAK
I can't wait to tell my friends!
HMM...
She's kind of plain.

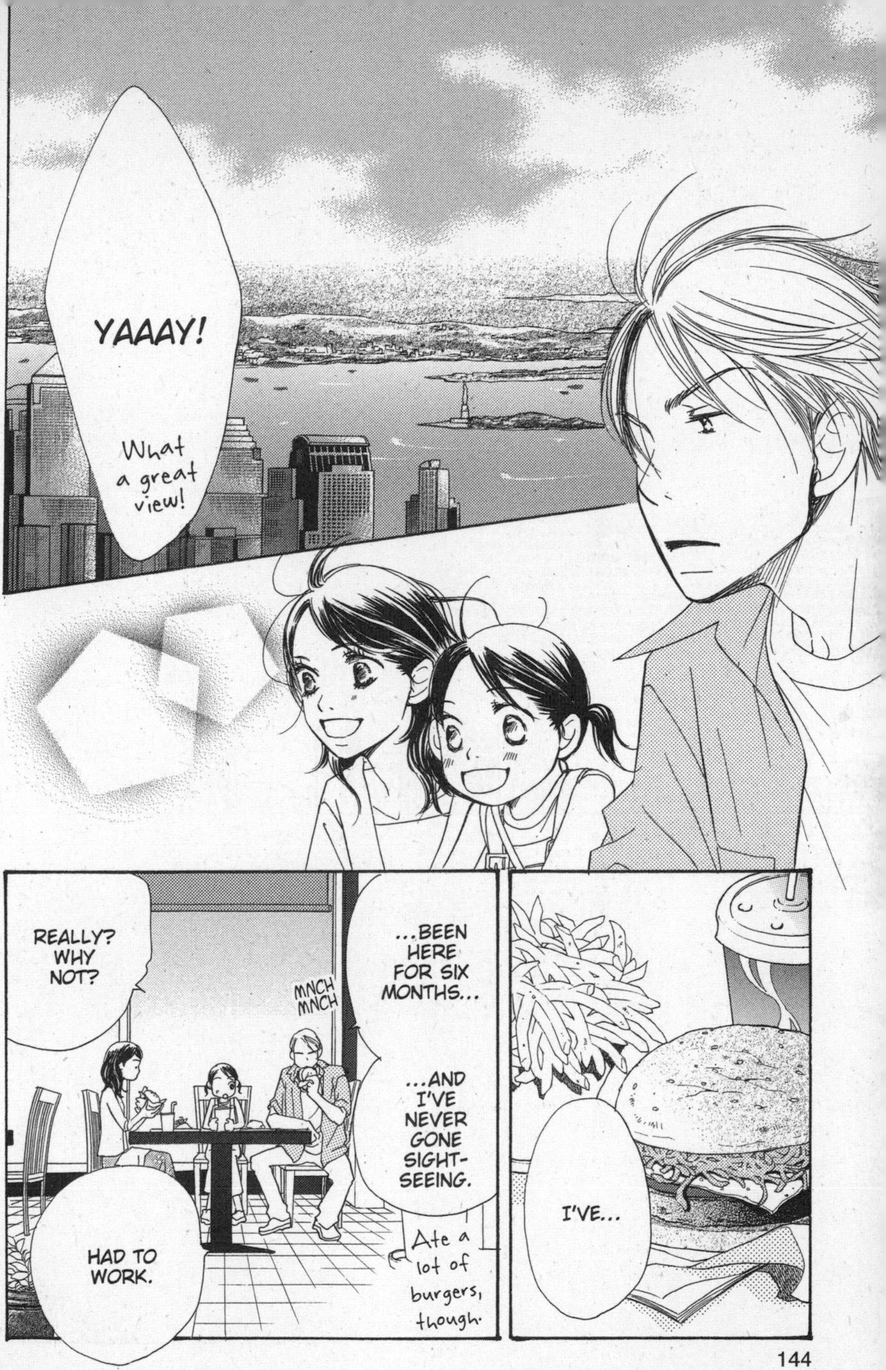
YAAAY!
What a great view!
I'VE...
...BEEN HERE FOR SIX MONTHS...
...AND I'VE NEVER GONE SIGHT-SEEING.
Ate a lot of burgers, though.
MNCH MNCH
REALLY? WHY NOT?
HAD TO WORK.

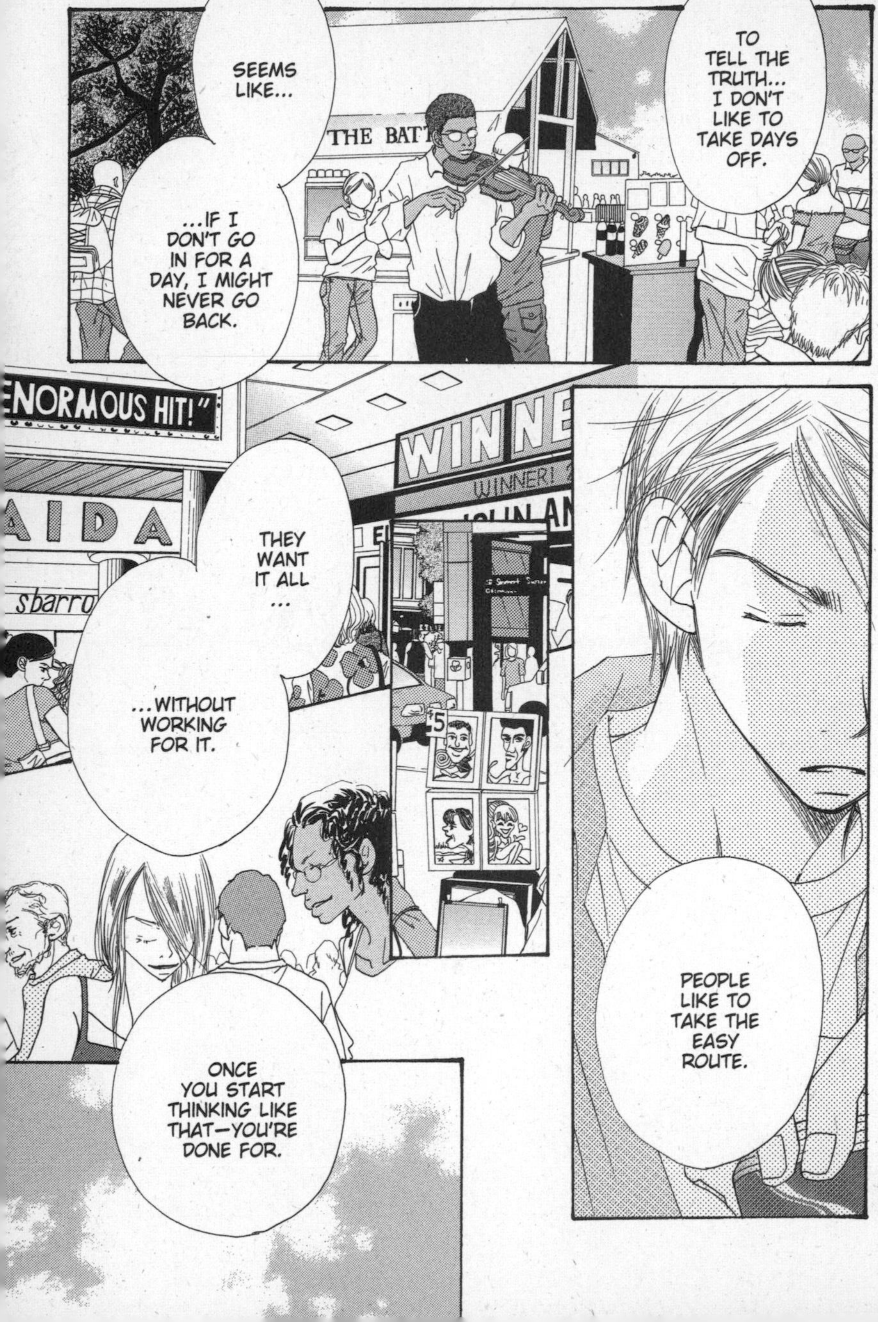
TO TELL THE TRUTH... I DON'T LIKE TO TAKE DAYS OFF.
SEEMS LIKE...
...IF I DON'T GO IN FOR A DAY, I MIGHT NEVER GO BACK.
THE BATT
PEOPLE LIKE TO TAKE THE EASY ROUTE.
ENORMOUS HIT!"
WINNE
AIDA
sbarro
THEY WANT IT ALL...
...WITHOUT WORKING FOR IT.
$5
ONCE YOU START THINKING LIKE THAT—YOU'RE DONE FOR.

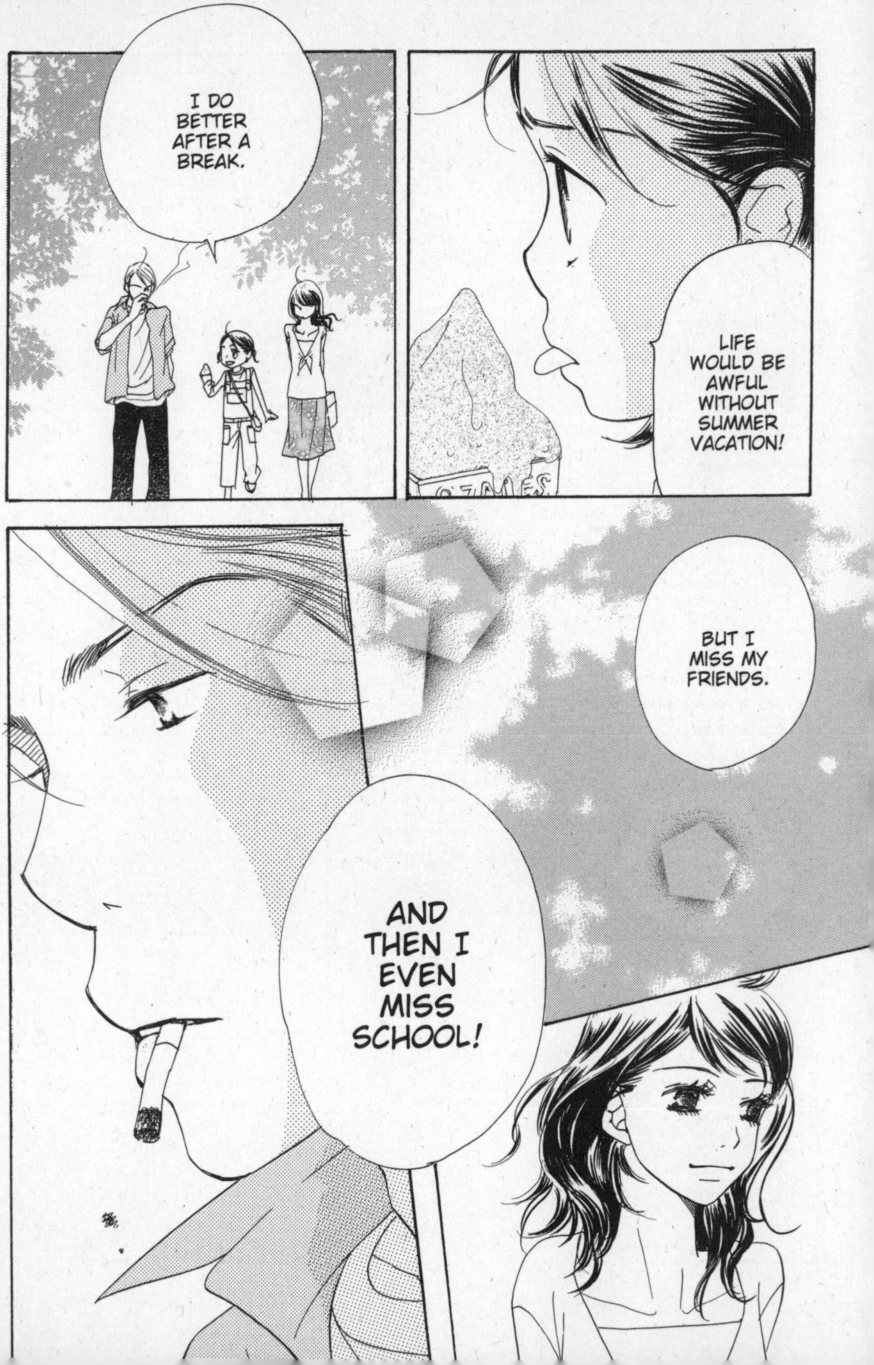
LIFE WOULD BE AWFUL WITHOUT SUMMER VACATION!
I DO BETTER AFTER A BREAK.
BUT I MISS MY FRIENDS.
AND THEN I EVEN MISS SCHOOL!

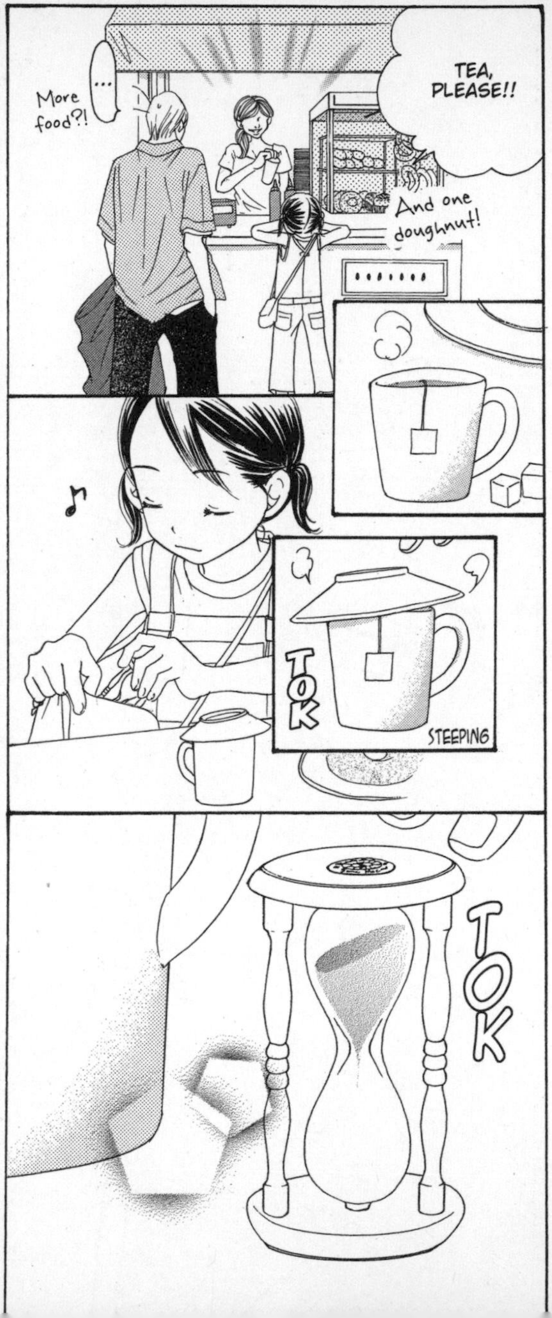
TEA, PLEASE!!
And one doughnut!
...
More food?!
TOK
STEEPING
TOK

"Summer Vacation"

I wanted to go to America to do research for this episode, but I didn't have enough time, so I borrowed a bunch of photos from a friend. I felt like I'd actually gone traveling!

"Present"

I wrote this manga as a short story for Betsucomi. I wanted to run it between volumes 5 and 6, but there weren't enough pages available, so I couldn't. Sorry! And sorry the dimensions are so weird!

There's only one more volume of Sand Chronicles left. I hope you enjoy it!

Thanks!

2/27/06
Hinako Ashihara

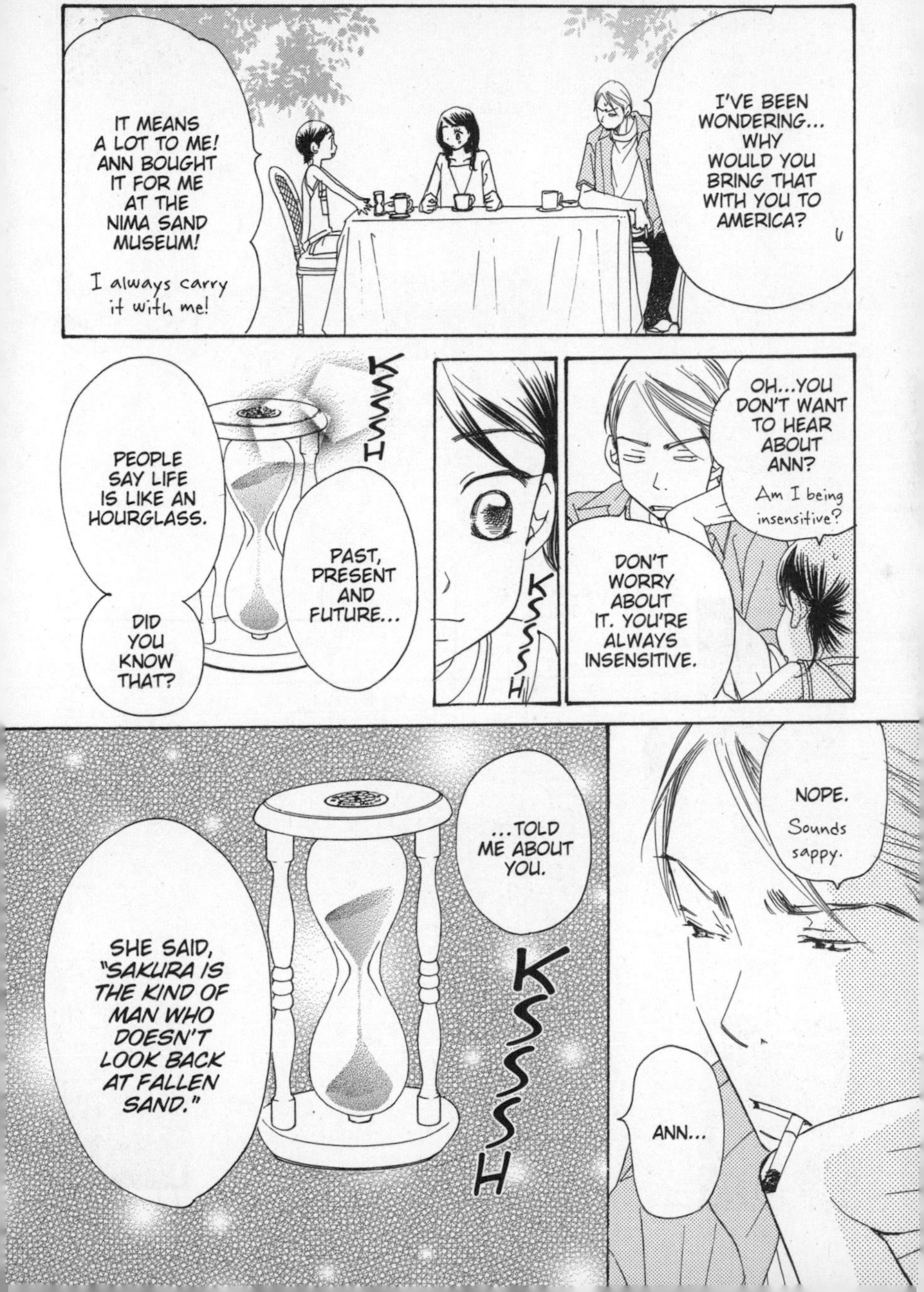
I'VE BEEN WONDERING... WHY WOULD YOU BRING THAT WITH YOU TO AMERICA?
IT MEANS A LOT TO ME! ANN BOUGHT IT FOR ME AT THE NIMA SAND MUSEUM!
I always carry it with me!
OH...YOU DON'T WANT TO HEAR ABOUT ANN?
Am I being insensitive?
DON'T WORRY ABOUT IT. YOU'RE ALWAYS INSENSITIVE.
KSSSH
KSSSH
PEOPLE SAY LIFE IS LIKE AN HOURGLASS.
PAST, PRESENT AND FUTURE...
DID YOU KNOW THAT?
NOPE.
Sounds sappy.
ANN...
...TOLD ME ABOUT YOU.
SHE SAID, "SAKURA IS THE KIND OF MAN WHO DOESN'T LOOK BACK AT FALLEN SAND."
KSSSH

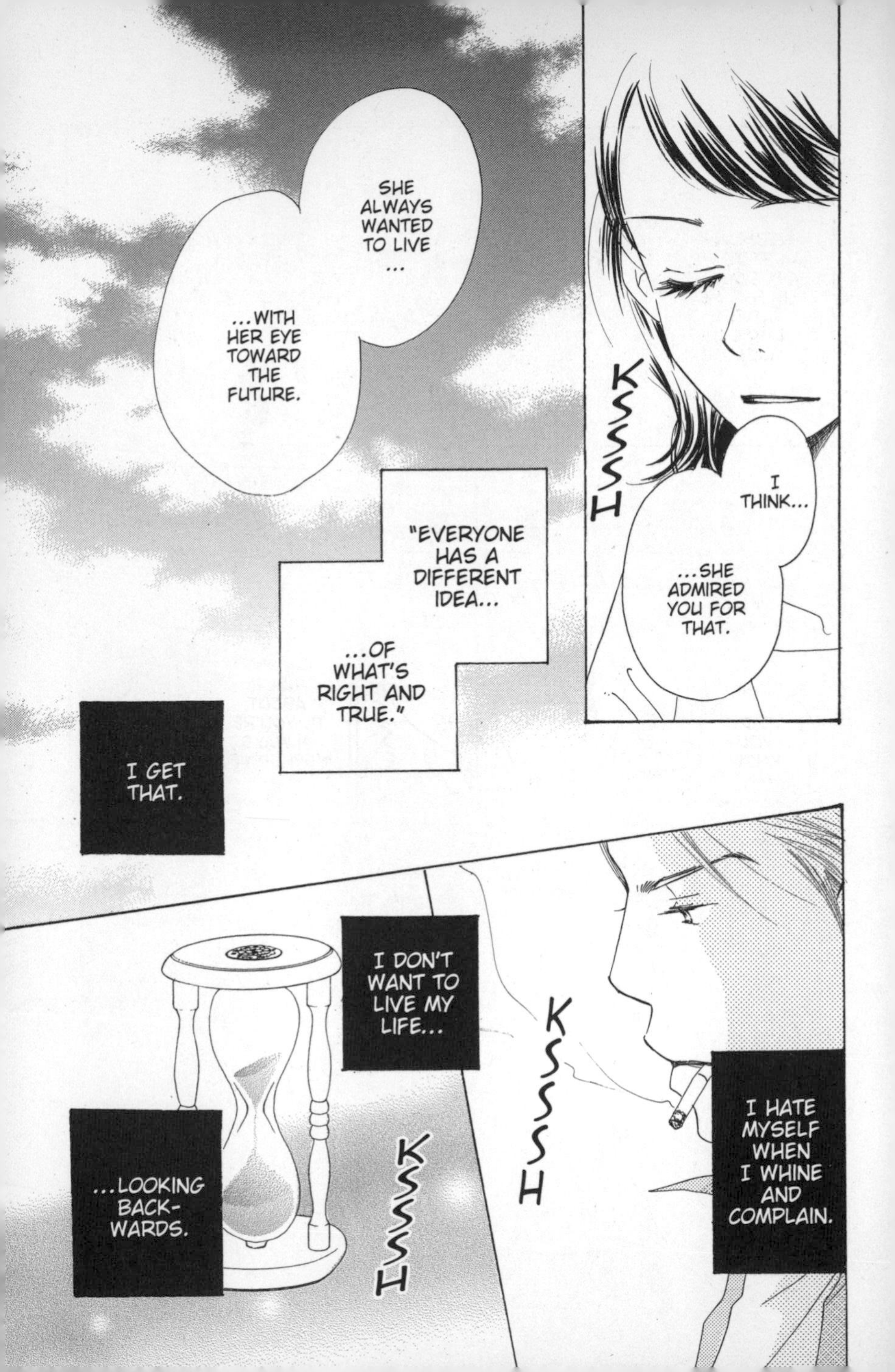
KSSSH
I THINK...
...SHE ADMIRED YOU FOR THAT.
SHE ALWAYS WANTED TO LIVE ...
...WITH HER EYE TOWARD THE FUTURE.
"EVERYONE HAS A DIFFERENT IDEA...
...OF WHAT'S RIGHT AND TRUE."
I GET THAT.
KSSSH
I HATE MYSELF WHEN I WHINE AND COMPLAIN.
I DON'T WANT TO LIVE MY LIFE...
KSSSH
...LOOKING BACKWARDS.

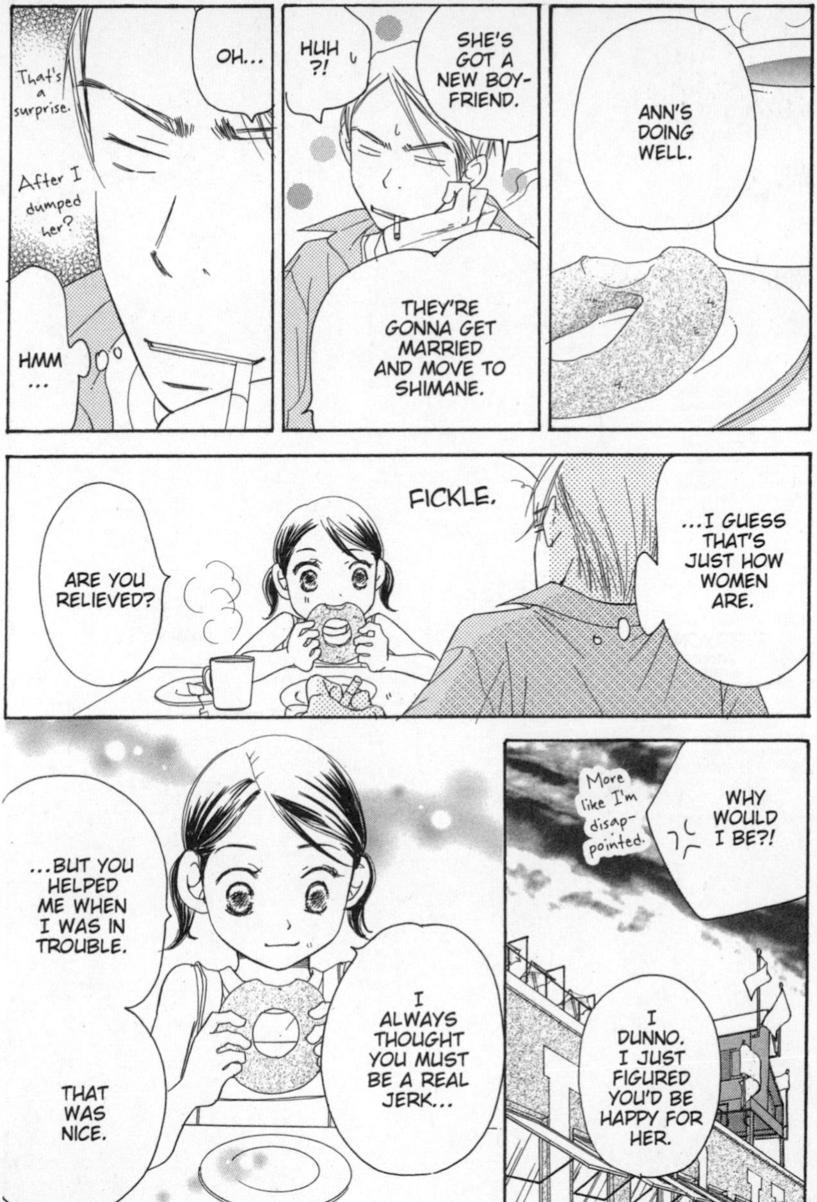
ANN'S DOING WELL.
SHE'S GOT A NEW BOY-FRIEND.
HUH ?!
THEY'RE GONNA GET MARRIED AND MOVE TO SHIMANE.
OH...
That's a surprise.
After I dumped her?
HMM ...
...I GUESS THAT'S JUST HOW WOMEN ARE.
FICKLE.
ARE YOU RELIEVED?
WHY WOULD I BE?!
More like I'm disap-pointed.
I DUNNO. I JUST FIGURED YOU'D BE HAPPY FOR HER.
I ALWAYS THOUGHT YOU MUST BE A REAL JERK...
...BUT YOU HELPED ME WHEN I WAS IN TROUBLE.
THAT WAS NICE.

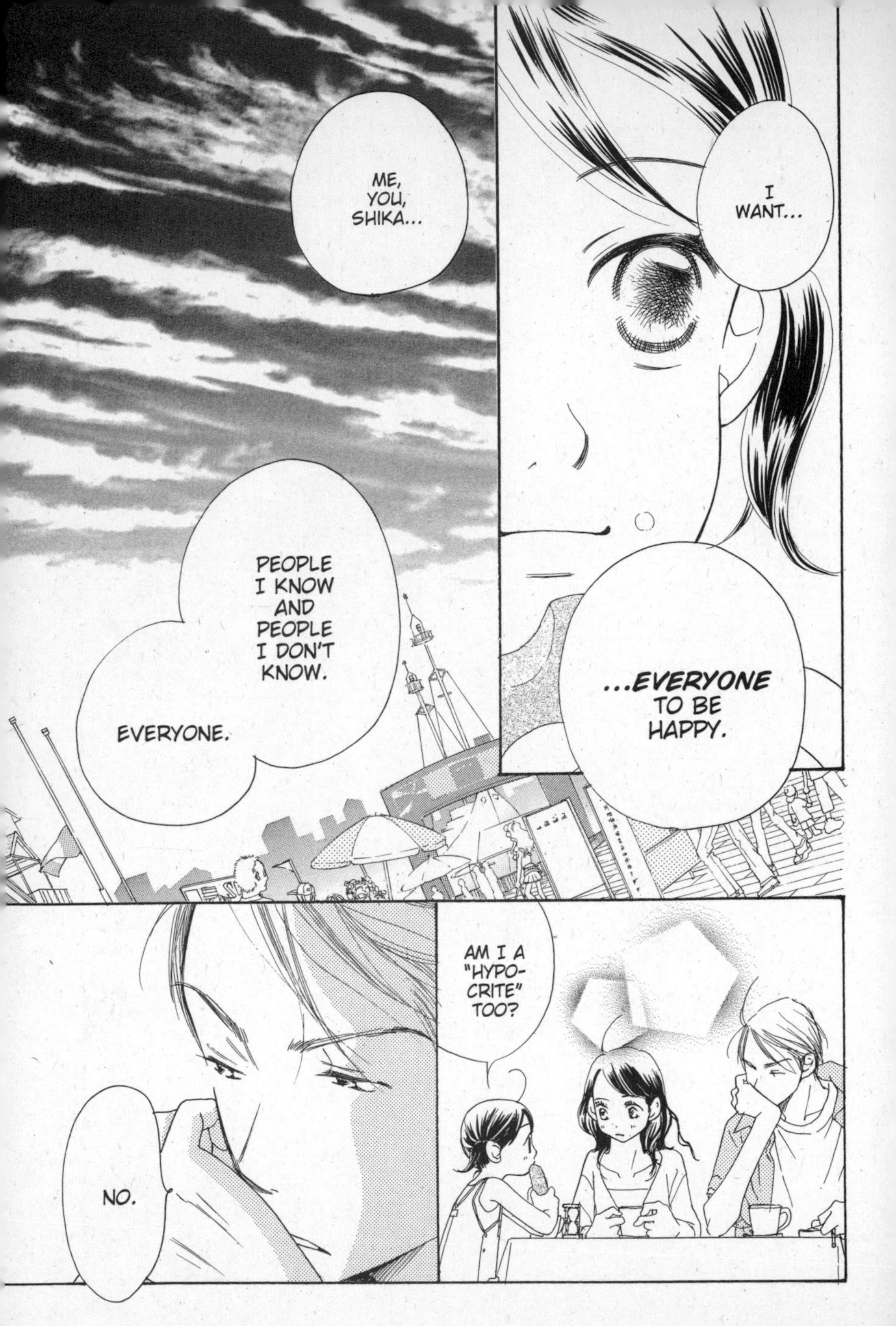
I WANT...
ME, YOU, SHIKA...
PEOPLE I KNOW AND PEOPLE I DON'T KNOW.
EVERYONE.
...EVERYONE TO BE HAPPY.
AM I A "HYPOCRITE" TOO?
NO.

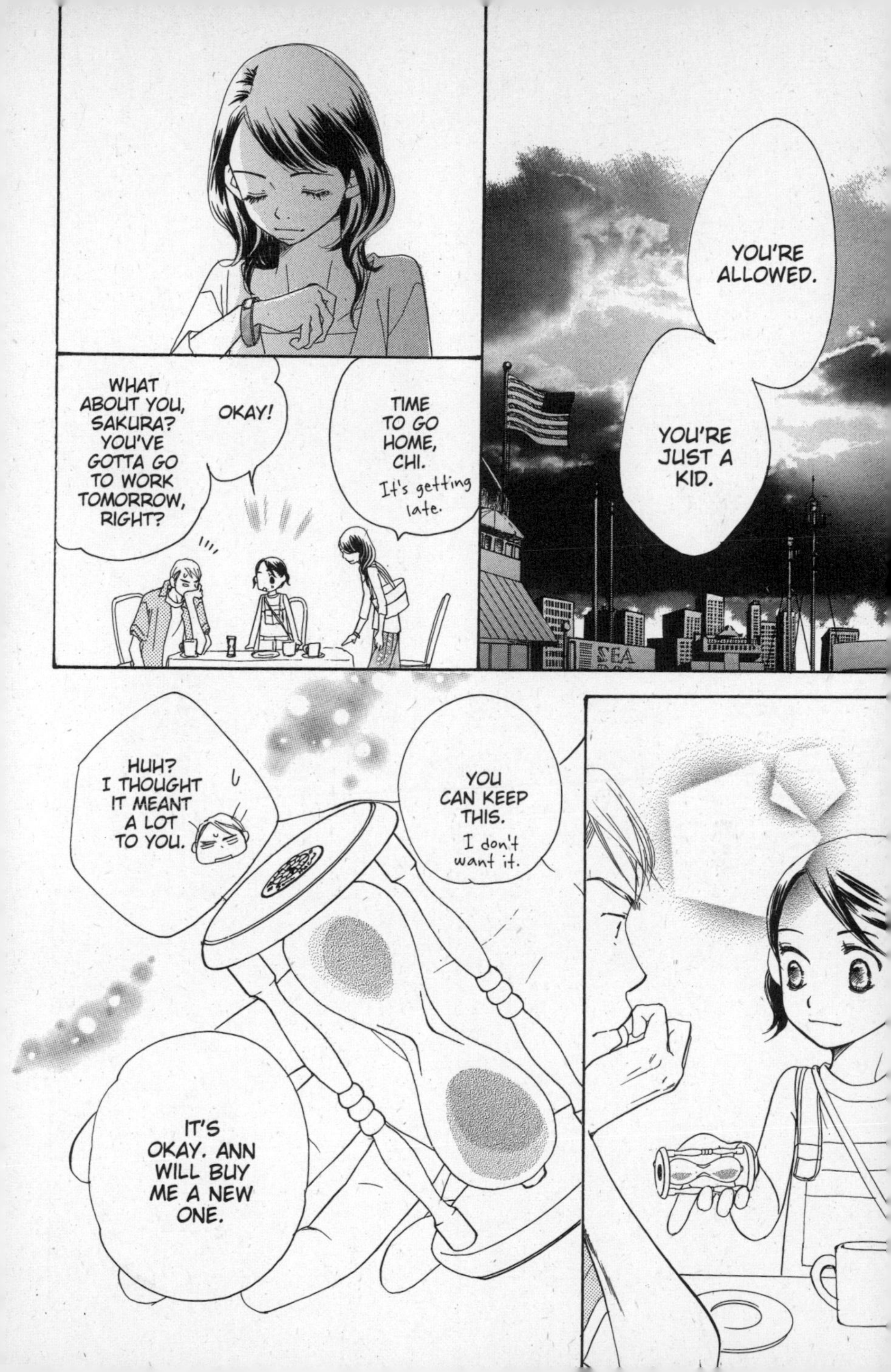
YOU'RE ALLOWED.
YOU'RE JUST A KID.
TIME TO GO HOME, CHI. It's getting late.
OKAY!
WHAT ABOUT YOU, SAKURA? YOU'VE GOTTA GO TO WORK TOMORROW, RIGHT?
YOU CAN KEEP THIS. I don't want it.
HUH? I THOUGHT IT MEANT A LOT TO YOU.
IT'S OKAY. ANN WILL BUY ME A NEW ONE.

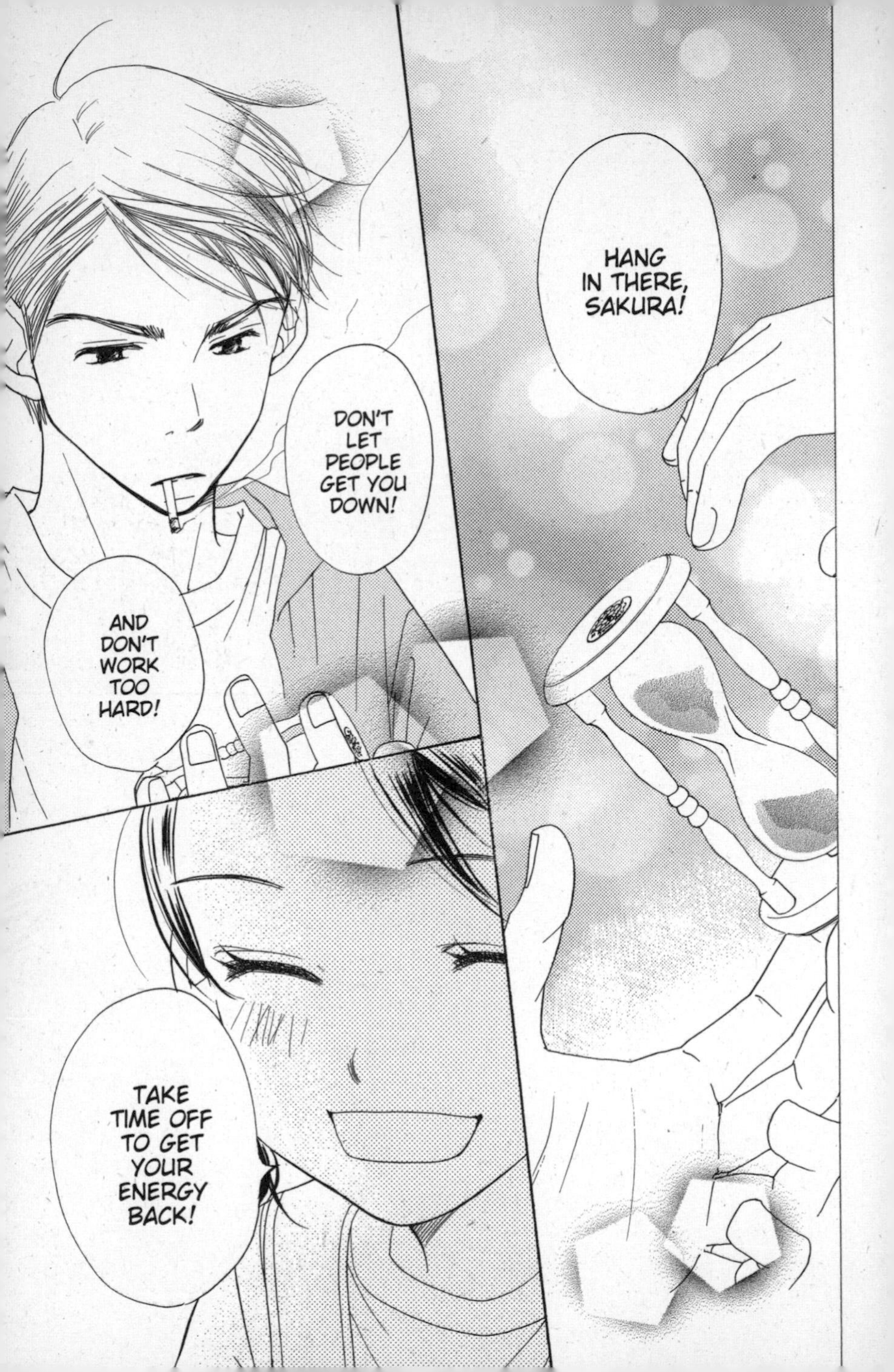
HANG IN THERE, SAKURA!
DON'T LET PEOPLE GET YOU DOWN!
AND DON'T WORK TOO HARD!
TAKE TIME OFF TO GET YOUR ENERGY BACK!

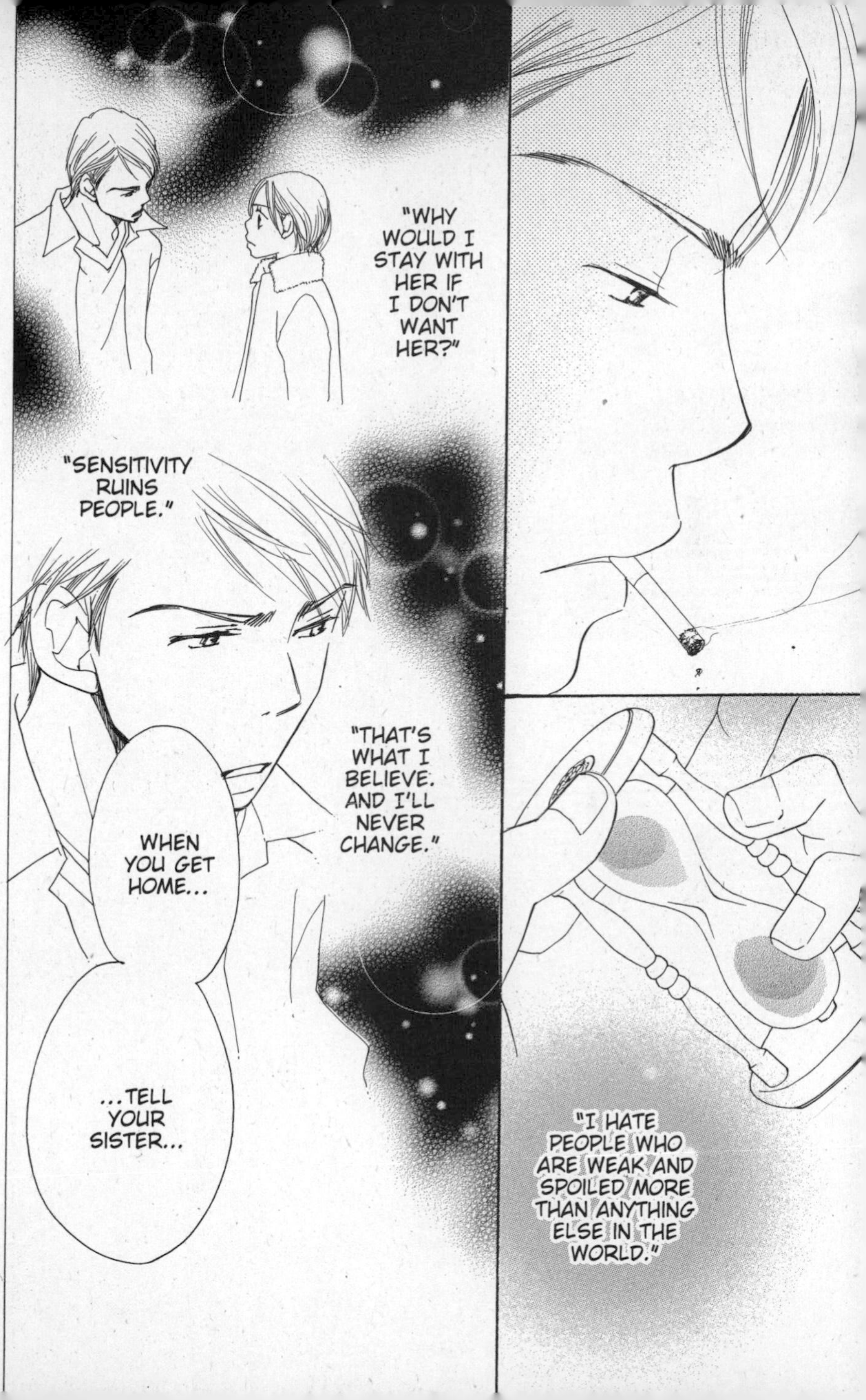
"I HATE PEOPLE WHO ARE WEAK AND SPOILED MORE THAN ANYTHING ELSE IN THE WORLD."
"WHY WOULD I STAY WITH HER IF I DON'T WANT HER?"
"SENSITIVITY RUINS PEOPLE."
"THAT'S WHAT I BELIEVE. AND I'LL NEVER CHANGE."
WHEN YOU GET HOME...
...TELL YOUR SISTER...

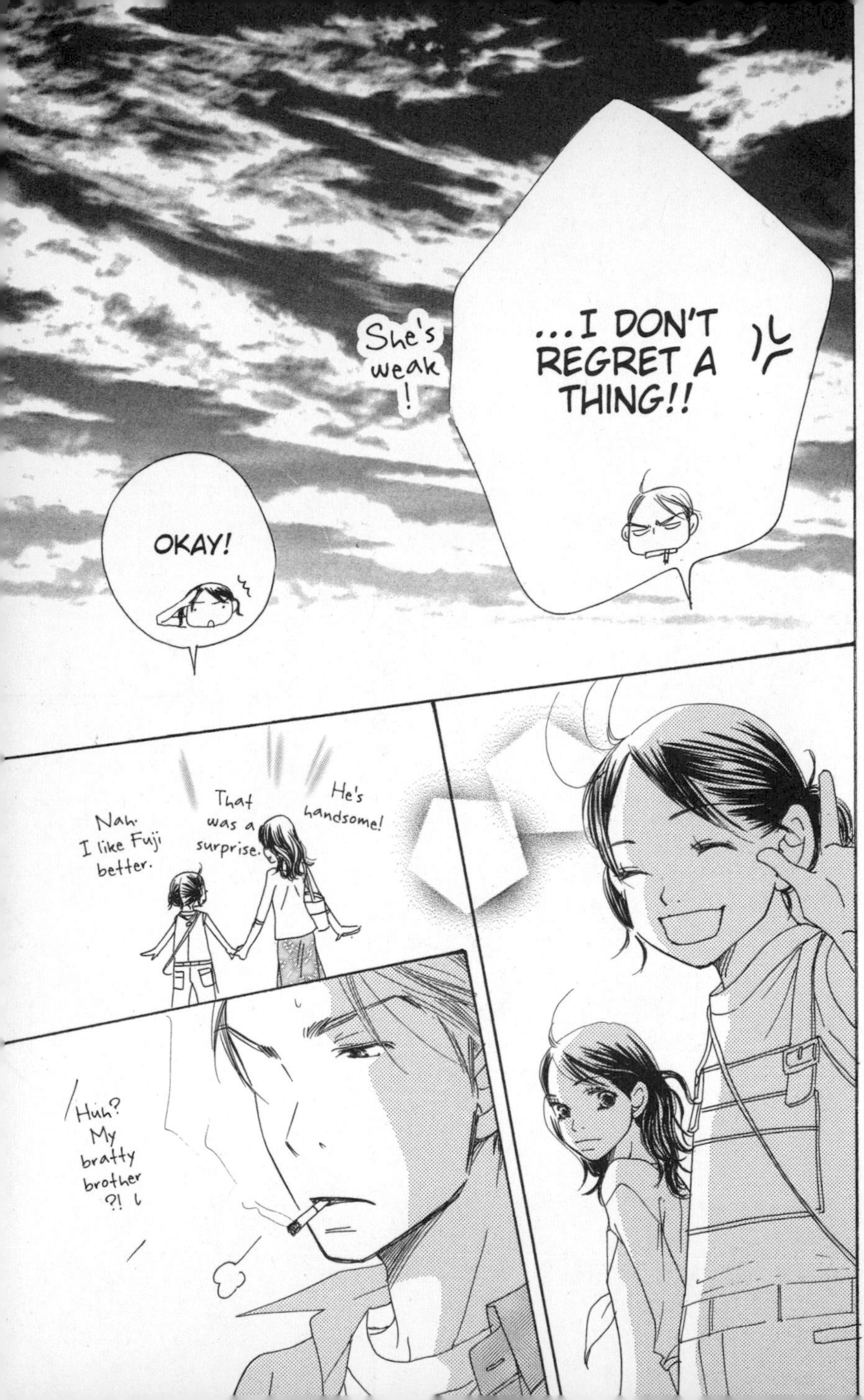
...I DON'T REGRET A THING!!
She's weak!
OKAY!
He's handsome!
That was a surprise.
Nah. I like Fuji better.
Huh? My bratty brother?!

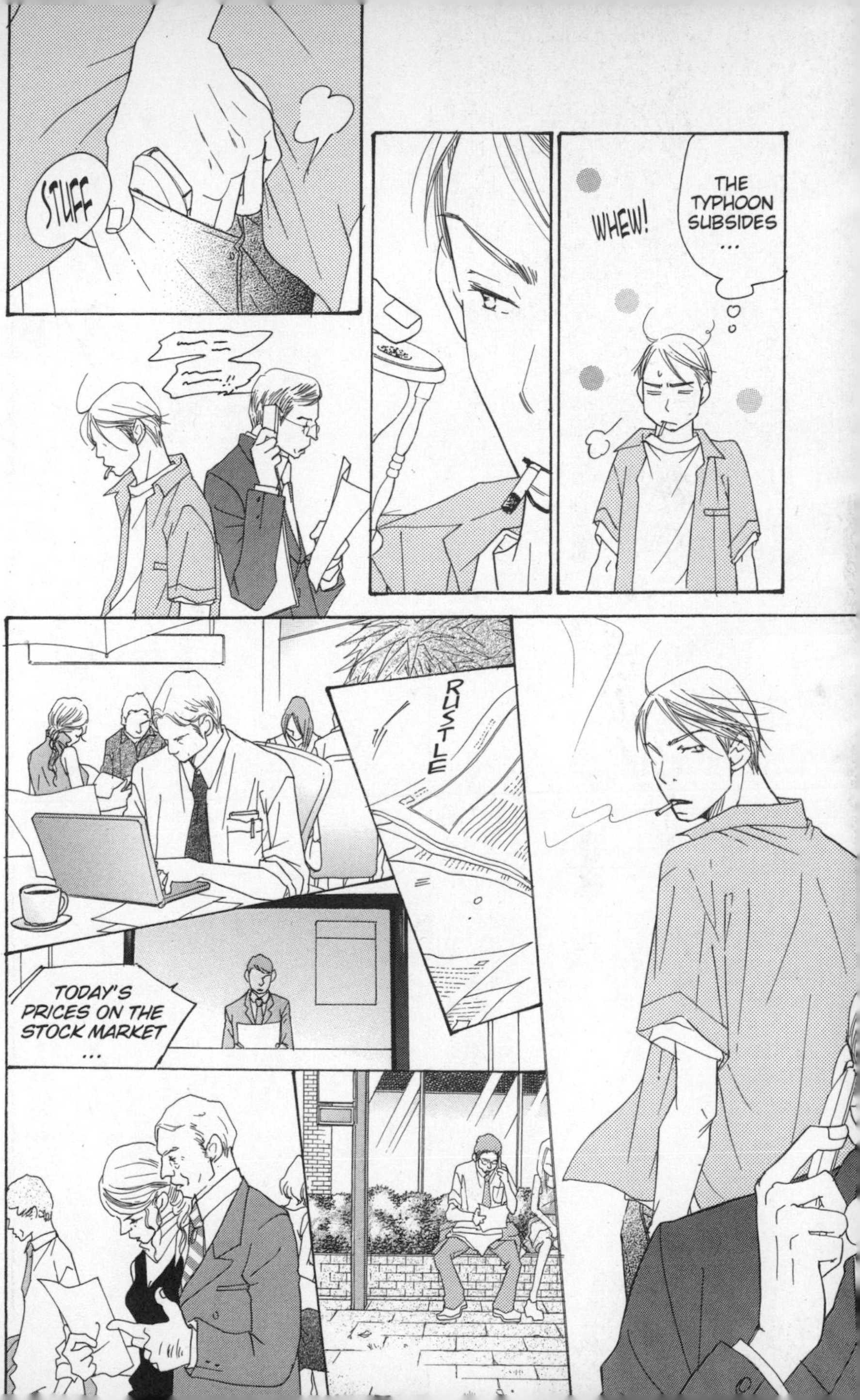
STUFF
THE TYPHOON SUBSIDES ...
WHEW!
RUSTLE
TODAY'S PRICES ON THE STOCK MARKET ...

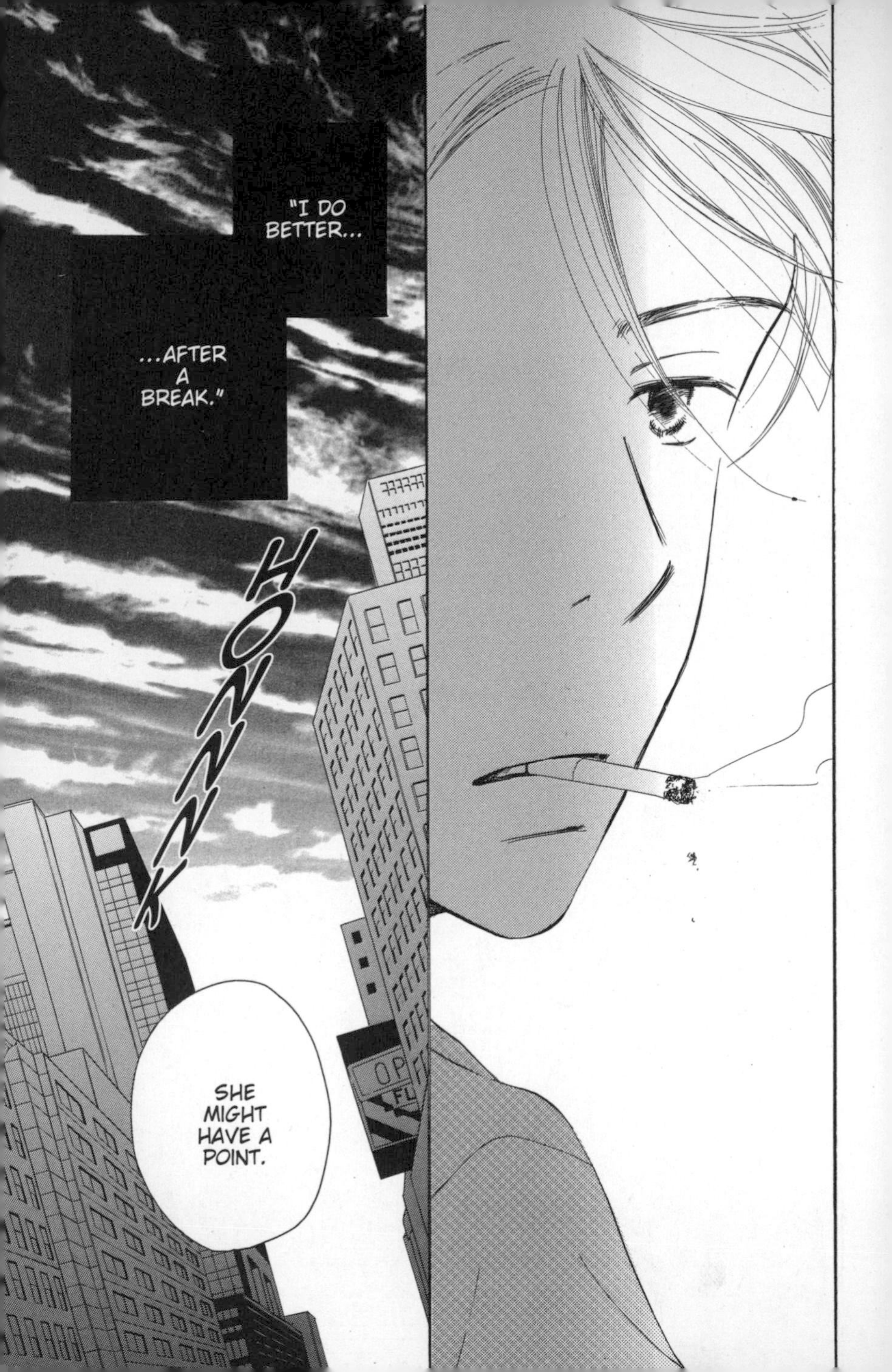
"I DO BETTER...
...AFTER A BREAK."
HONNNK
SHE MIGHT HAVE A POINT.

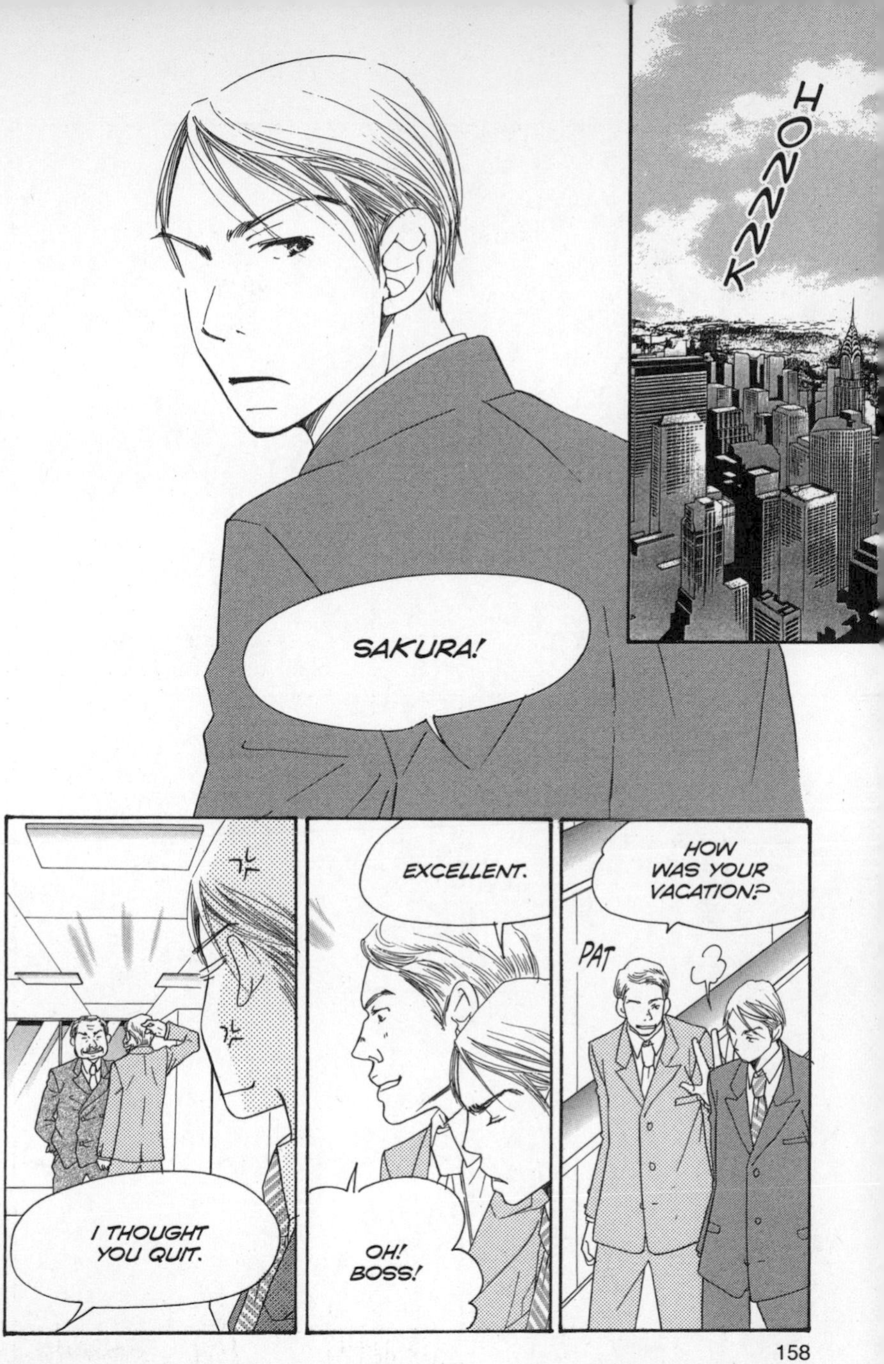
HONNNK
SAKURA!
HOW WAS YOUR VACATION?
PAT
EXCELLENT.
OH! BOSS!
I THOUGHT YOU QUIT.

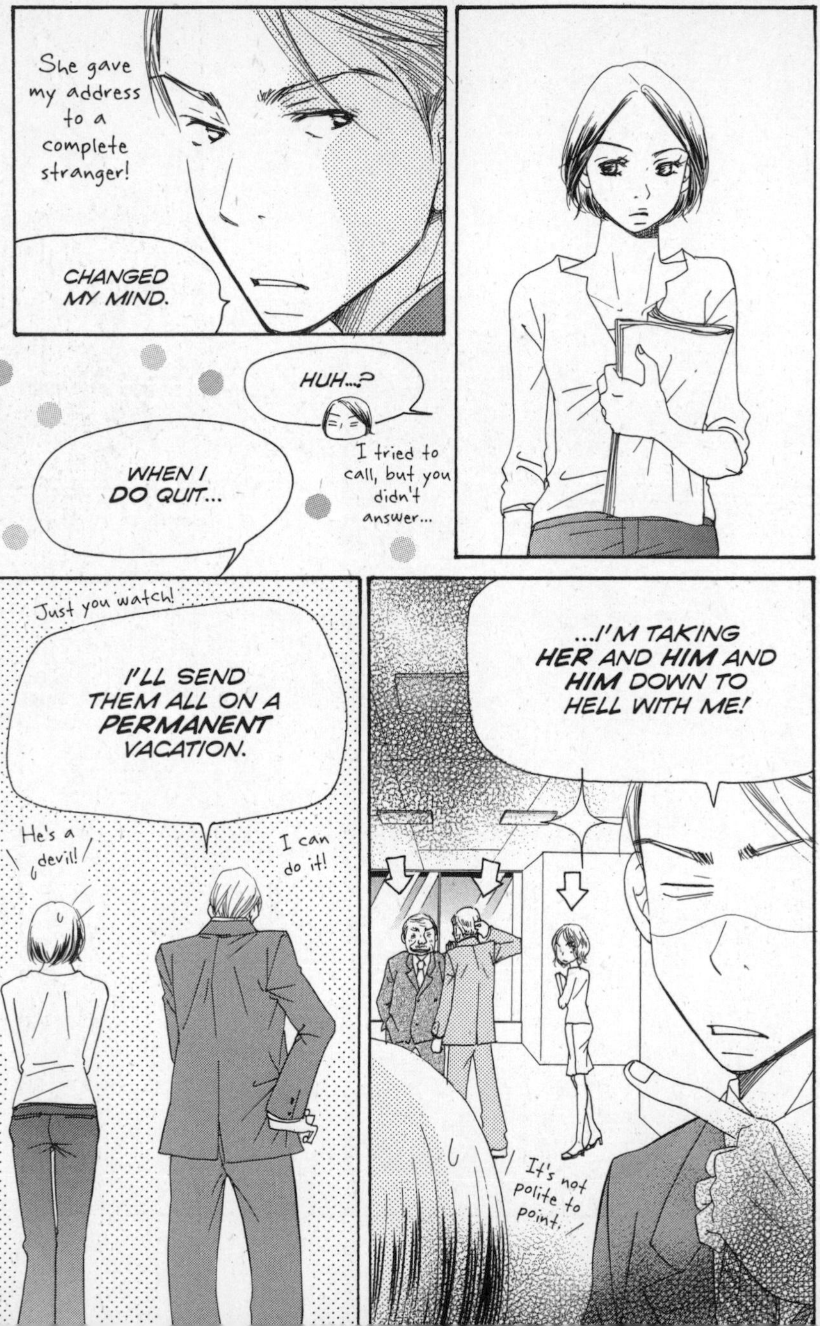
She gave my address to a complete stranger!
CHANGED MY MIND.
HUH...?
I tried to call, but you didn't answer...
WHEN I DO QUIT...
...I'M TAKING HER AND HIM AND HIM DOWN TO HELL WITH ME!
It's not polite to point.
Just you watch!
I'LL SEND THEM ALL ON A PERMANENT VACATION.
I can do it!
He's a devil!

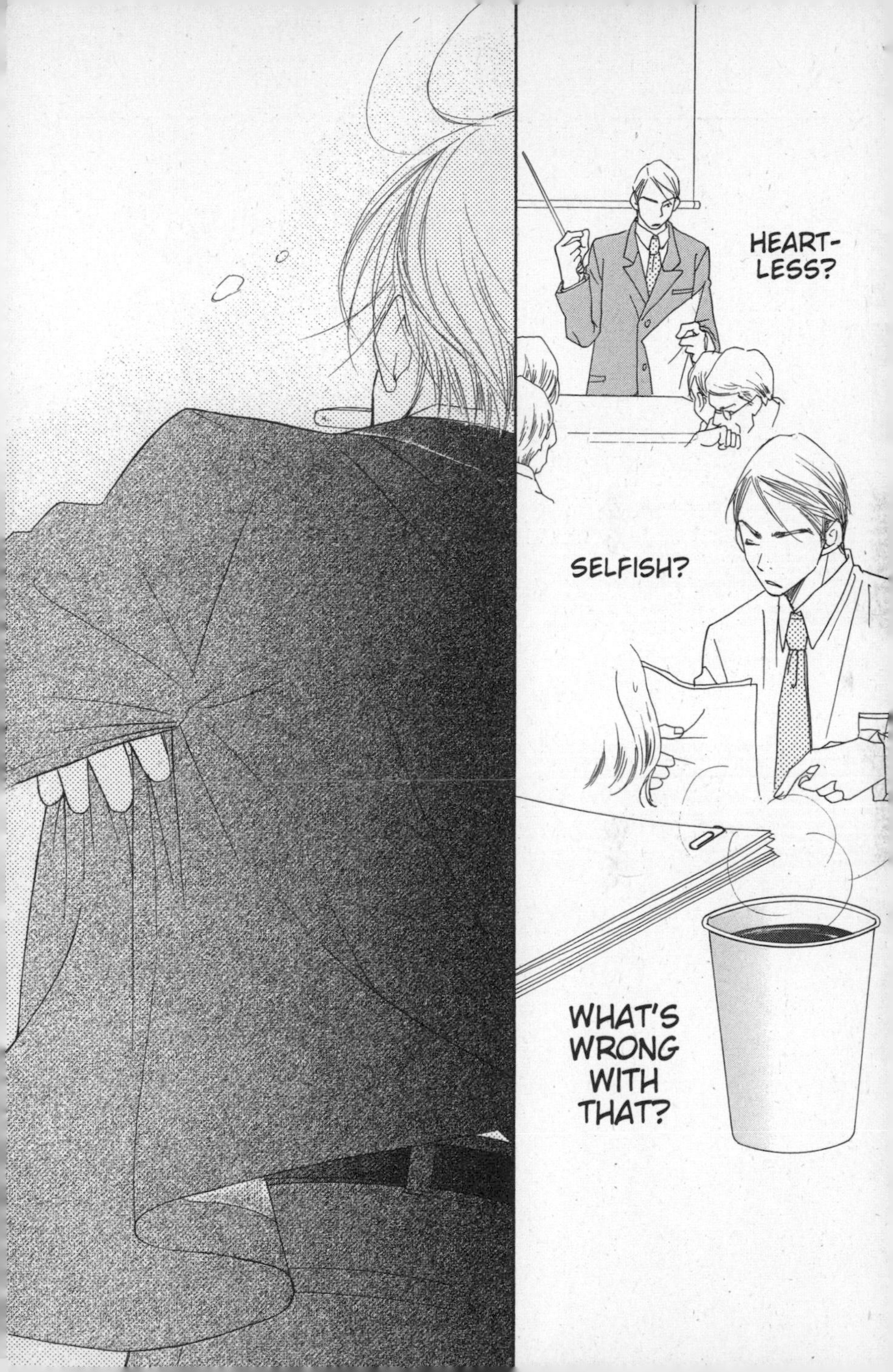
HEART-LESS?
SELFISH?
WHAT'S WRONG WITH THAT?

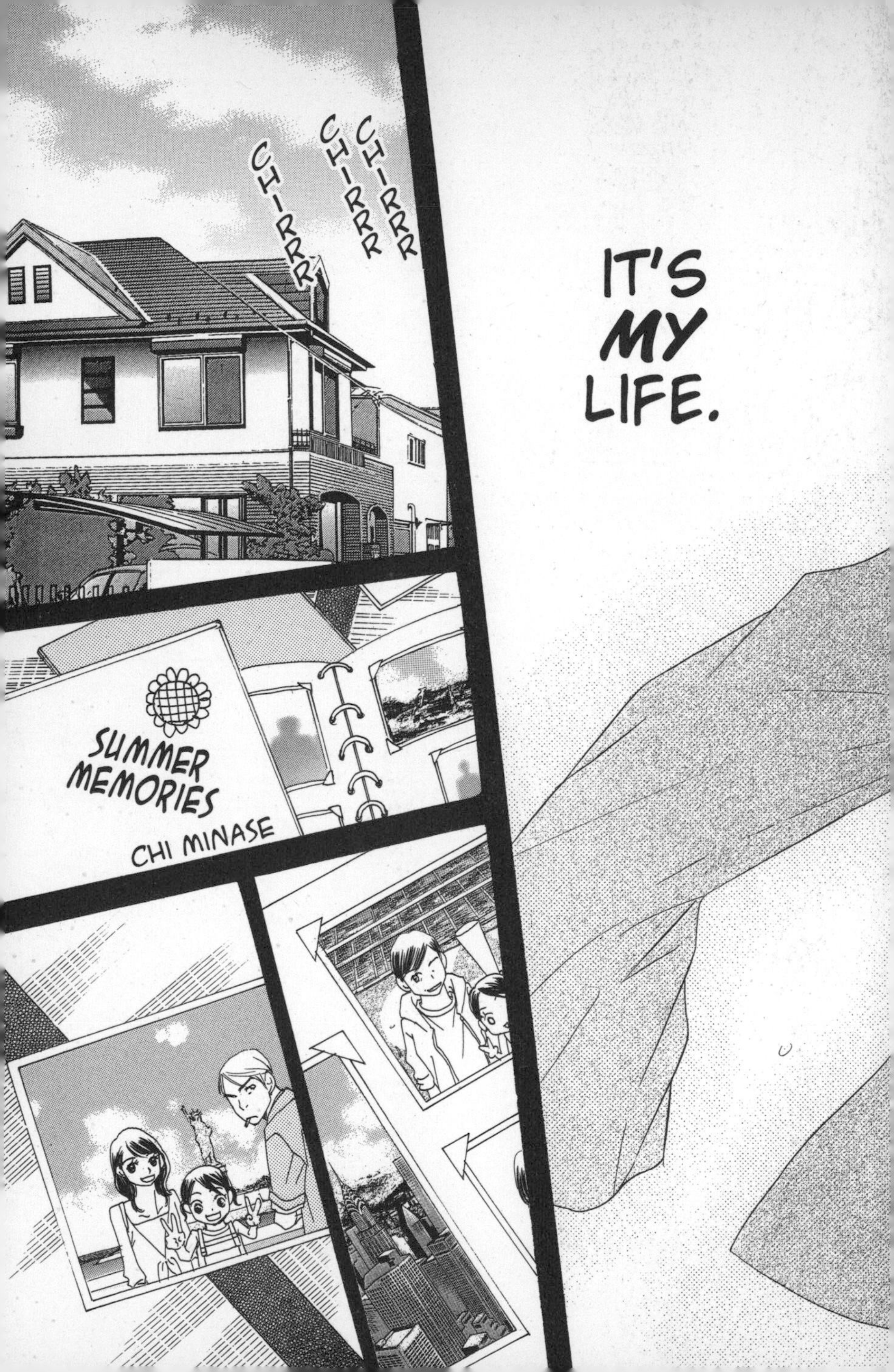
IT'S MY LIFE.
CHIRRR
CHIRRR
CHIRRR
SUMMER MEMORIES
CHI MINASE

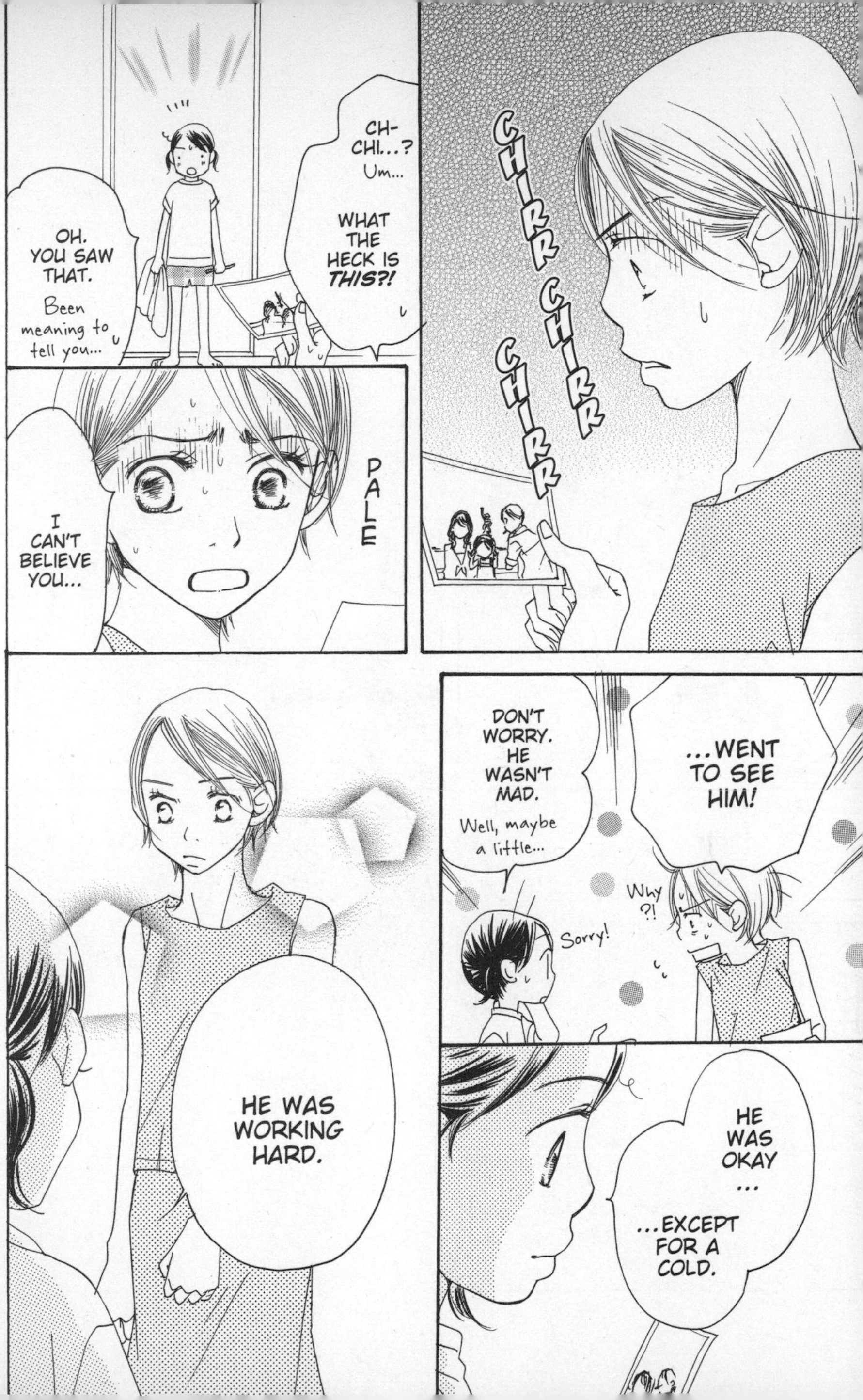
CHIRR CHIRR CHIRR
CH-CHI...? Um...
WHAT THE HECK IS THIS?!
OH. YOU SAW THAT.
Been meaning to tell you...
PALE
I CAN'T BELIEVE YOU...
...WENT TO SEE HIM!
Why ?!
DON'T WORRY. HE WASN'T MAD.
Well, maybe a little...
Sorry!
HE WAS OKAY...
...EXCEPT FOR A COLD.
HE WAS WORKING HARD.

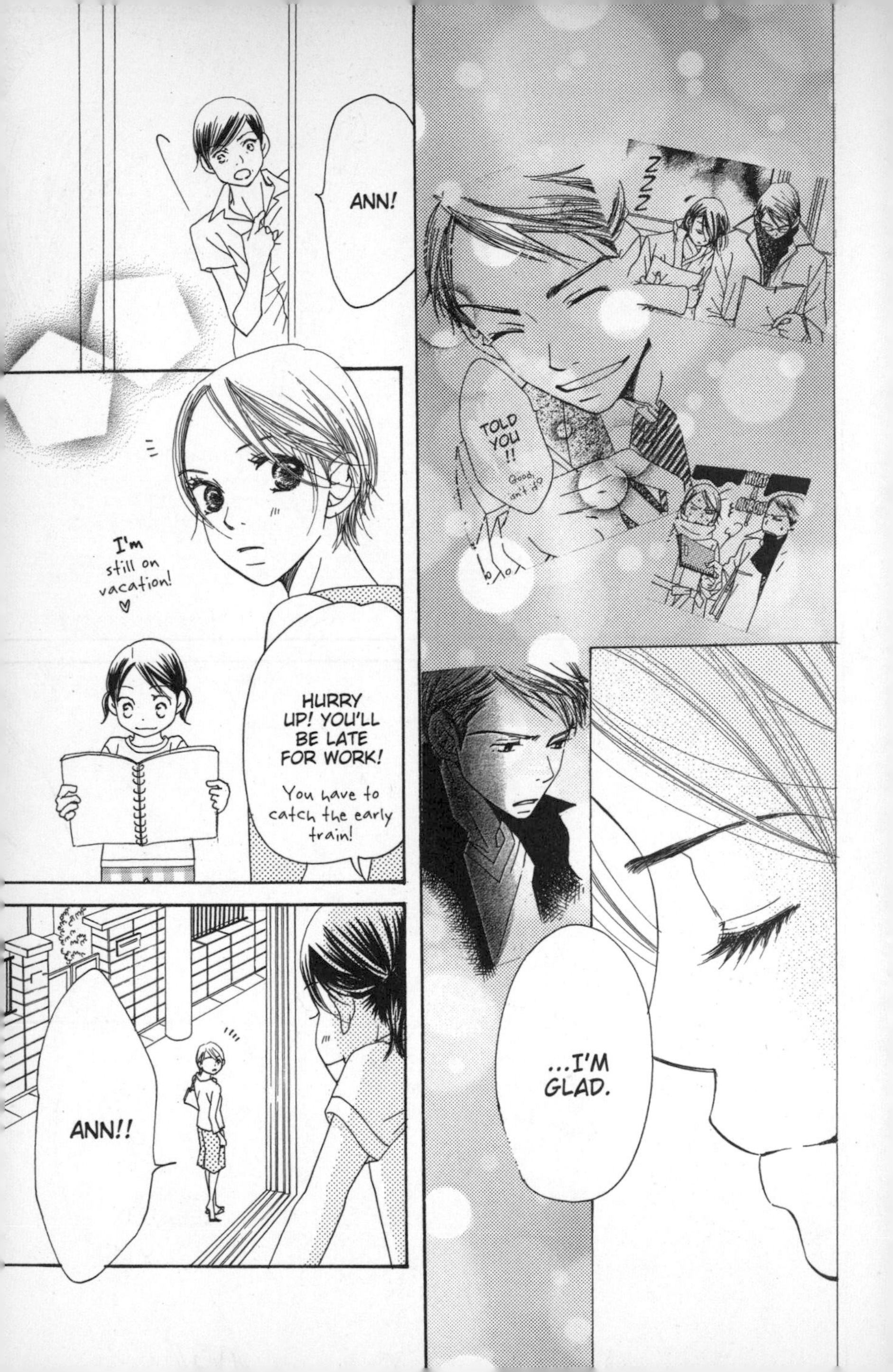
TOLD YOU!! Good, isn't it?
...I'M GLAD.
ANN!
HURRY UP! YOU'LL BE LATE FOR WORK! You have to catch the early train!
I'm still on vacation! ♡
ANN!!

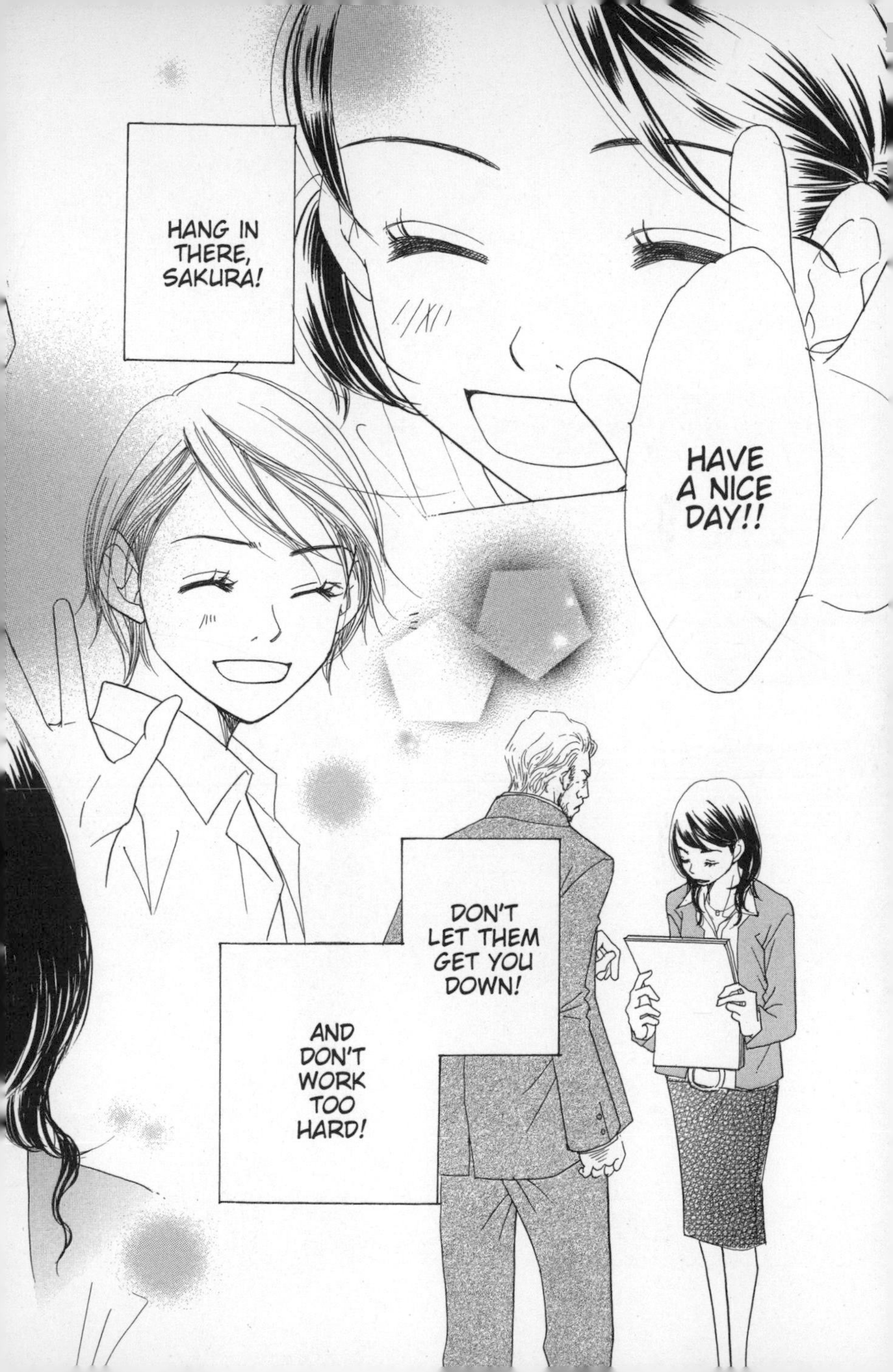
HAVE A NICE DAY!!
HANG IN THERE, SAKURA!
DON'T LET THEM GET YOU DOWN!
AND DON'T WORK TOO HARD!

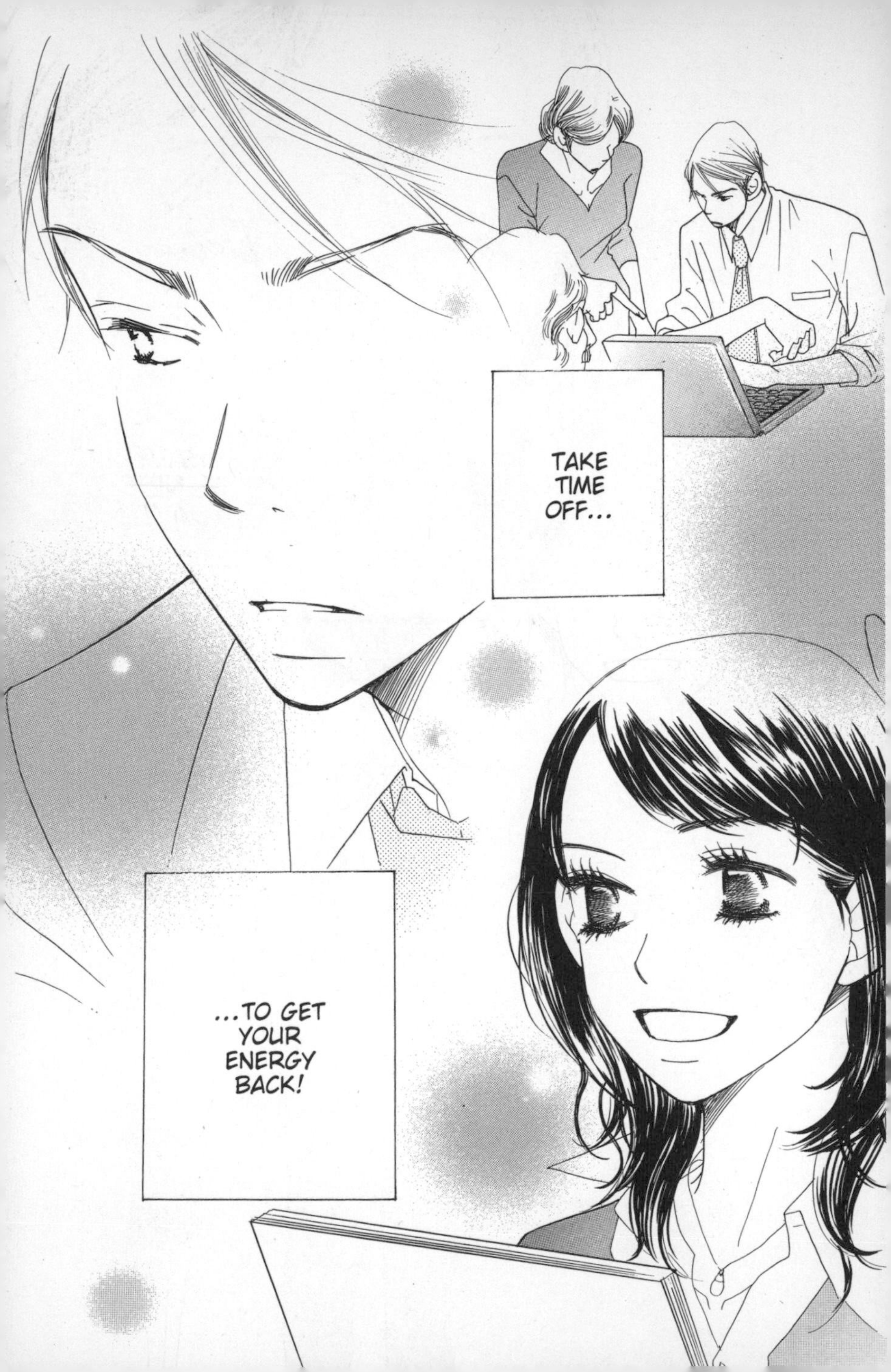
TAKE TIME OFF...
...TO GET YOUR ENERGY BACK!

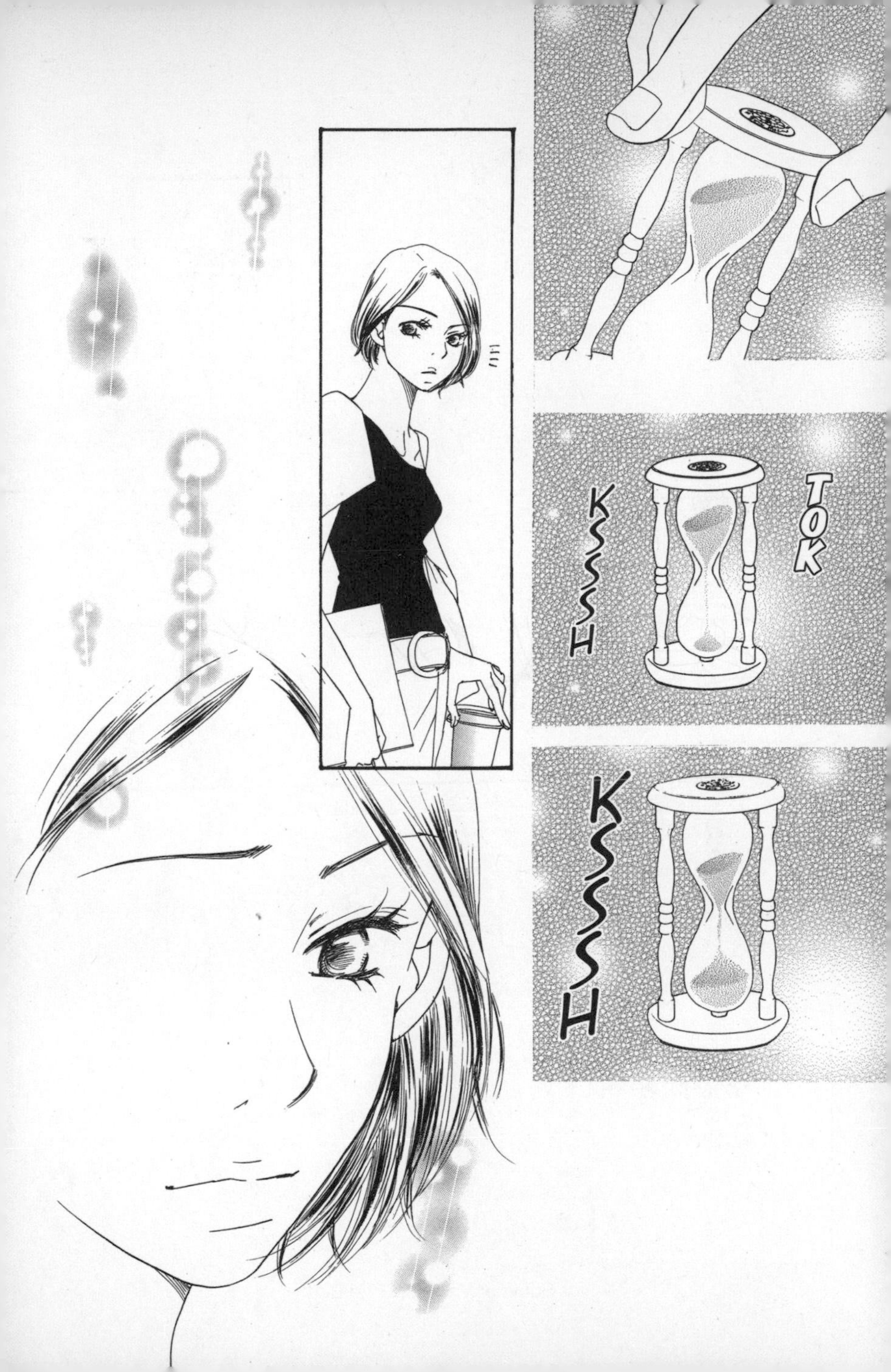
TOK
KSSSH
KSSSH

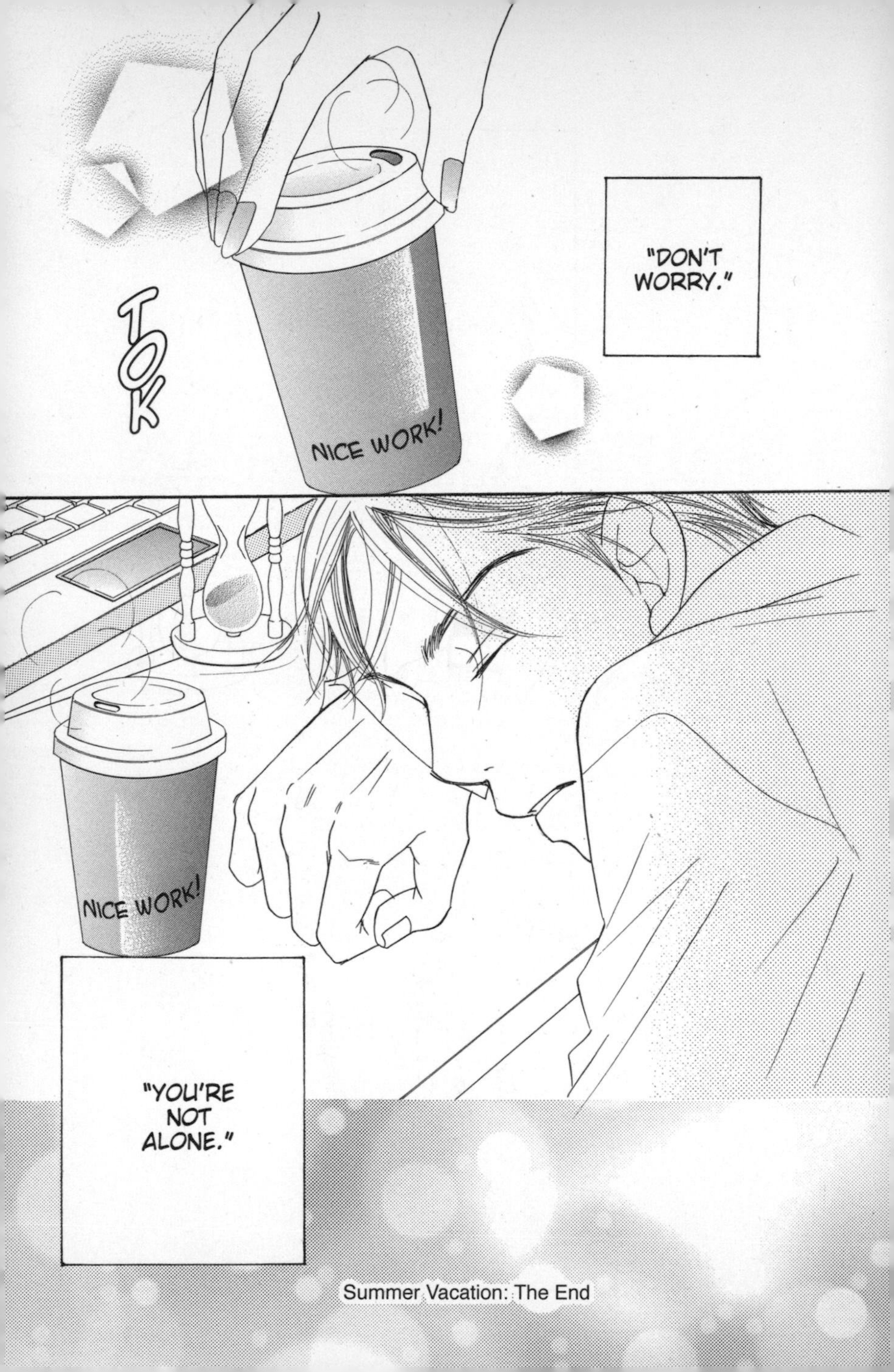
"DON'T WORRY."
TOK
NICE WORK!
NICE WORK!
"YOU'RE NOT ALONE."
Summer Vacation: The End

THE PRESENT

EVERY YEAR...

...I DREADED OPENING MY EYES THAT MORNING...

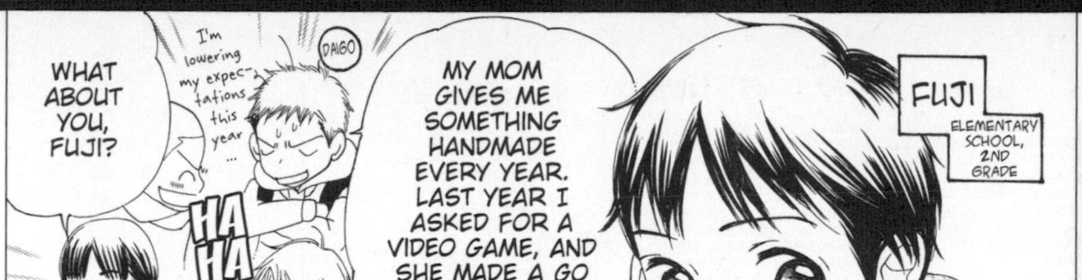
FUJI
ELEMENTARY SCHOOL, 2ND GRADE
CHRISTMAS PRESENTS?
DAIGO
MY MOM GIVES ME SOMETHING HANDMADE EVERY YEAR. LAST YEAR I ASKED FOR A VIDEO GAME, AND SHE MADE A GO BOARD OUT OF CARDBOARD!
I'm lowering my expectations this year...
HA HA
What a cheapskate!
WHAT ABOUT YOU, FUJI?
WHAT DO YOU WANT FOR CHRISTMAS?
You're rich— I bet you get awesome presents!
WE DON'T CELEBRATE CHRISTMAS. IT'S A STUPID HOLIDAY.
HMPH
He's so cool!
Way cool!
What's cool about being a grinch?!
I WASN'T LIKE OTHER KIDS.

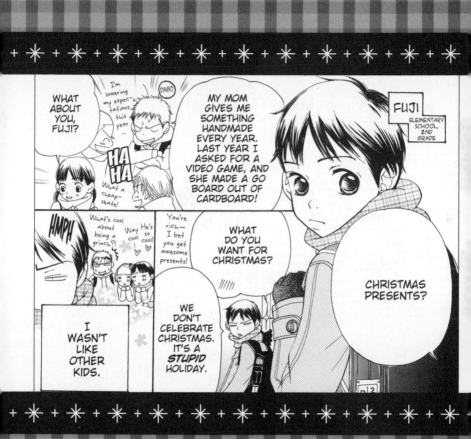

Sand Chronicles "The Present"

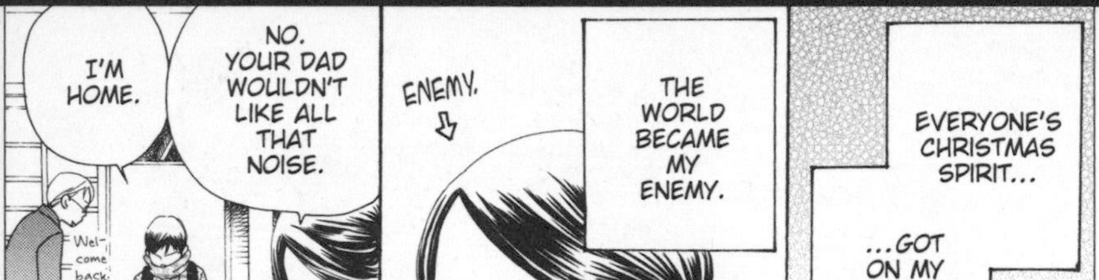
EVERYONE'S CHRISTMAS SPIRIT...
...GOT ON MY NERVES.
CHRISTMAS
SUPER SALE
THE WORLD BECAME MY ENEMY.
ENEMY.
A CHRISTMAS PARTY?
NO. YOUR DAD WOULDN'T LIKE ALL THAT NOISE.
I'M HOME.
Wel-come back!
COME ON!
I wanna have one!
PLEEEEASE!
SETTLE DOWN!
SHIKA'S AT IT AGAIN...

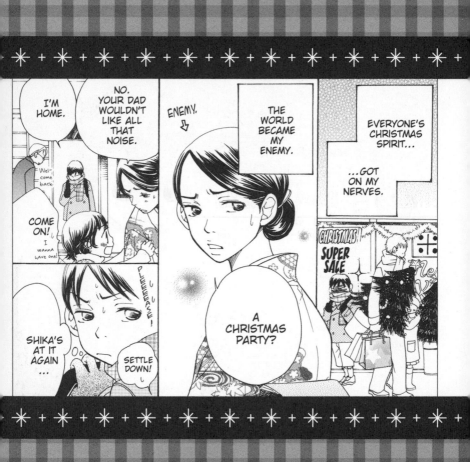

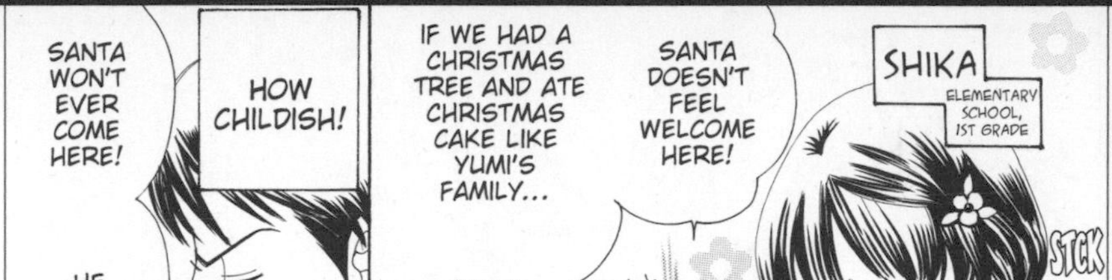
SHIKA
ELEMENTARY SCHOOL, 1ST GRADE
SANTA DOESN'T FEEL WELCOME HERE!
IF WE HAD A CHRISTMAS TREE AND ATE CHRISTMAS CAKE LIKE YUMI'S FAMILY...
...SANTA WOULD VISIT US!!
Santa's a foreigner.
Help me with this, Fuji!!
...
STCK
STCK
OUR FAMILY'S TOO TRADITIONAL ...
STCK
MY SISTER STILL BELIEVES IN SANTA.
HOW CHILDISH!
SANTA WON'T EVER COME HERE!
HE ONLY VISITS HOMES FULL OF LOVE!!
SO?
OUR HOME'S GOT LOVE!

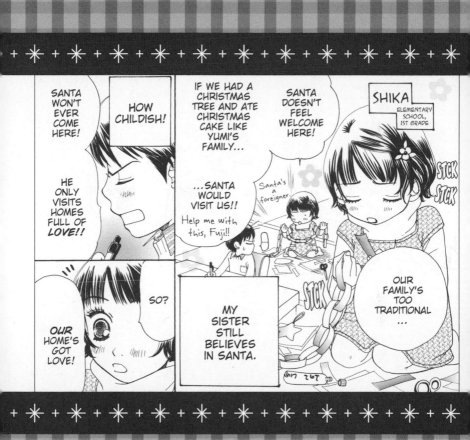

Sand Chronicles "The Present"

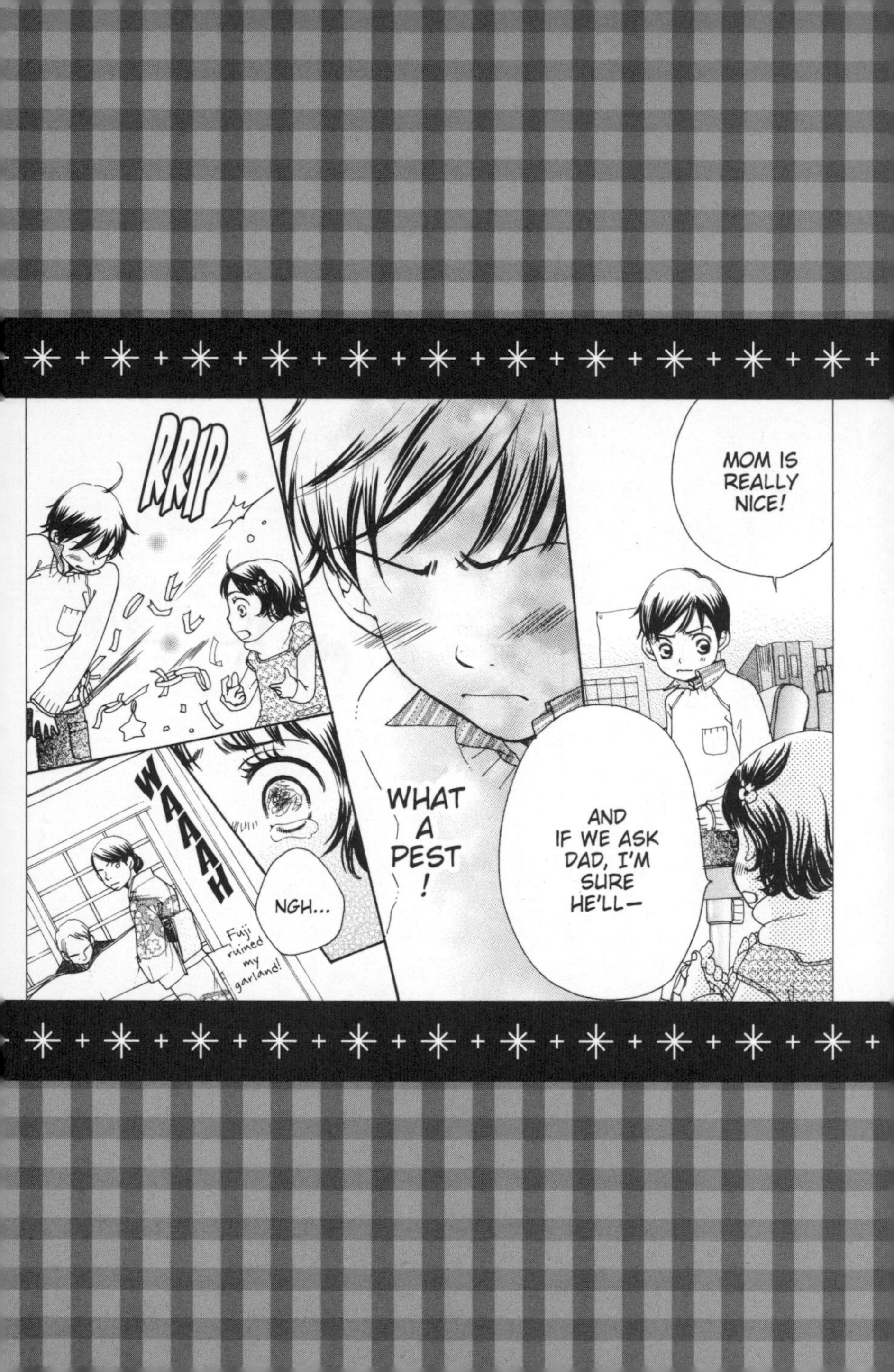
MOM IS REALLY NICE!
AND IF WE ASK DAD, I'M SURE HE'LL—
WHAT A PEST!
RRIP
NGH...
WAAAAH
Fuji ruined my garland!

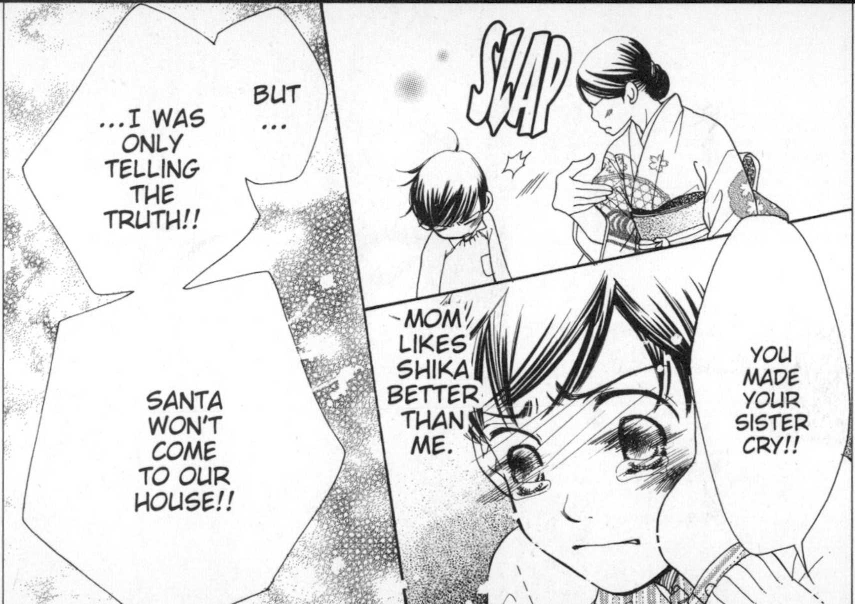
SLAP
YOU MADE YOUR SISTER CRY!!
MOM LIKES SHIKA BETTER THAN ME.
BUT...
...I WAS ONLY TELLING THE TRUTH!!
SANTA WON'T COME TO OUR HOUSE!!

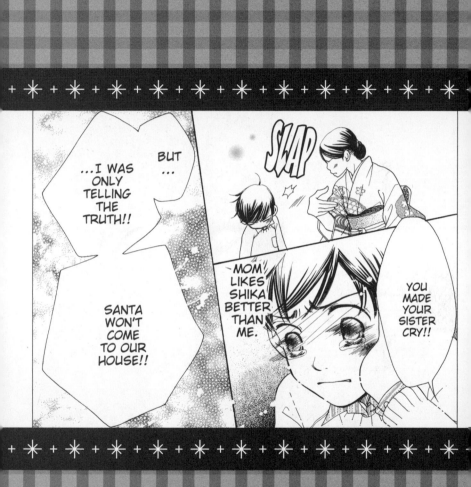

Sand Chronicles "The Present"

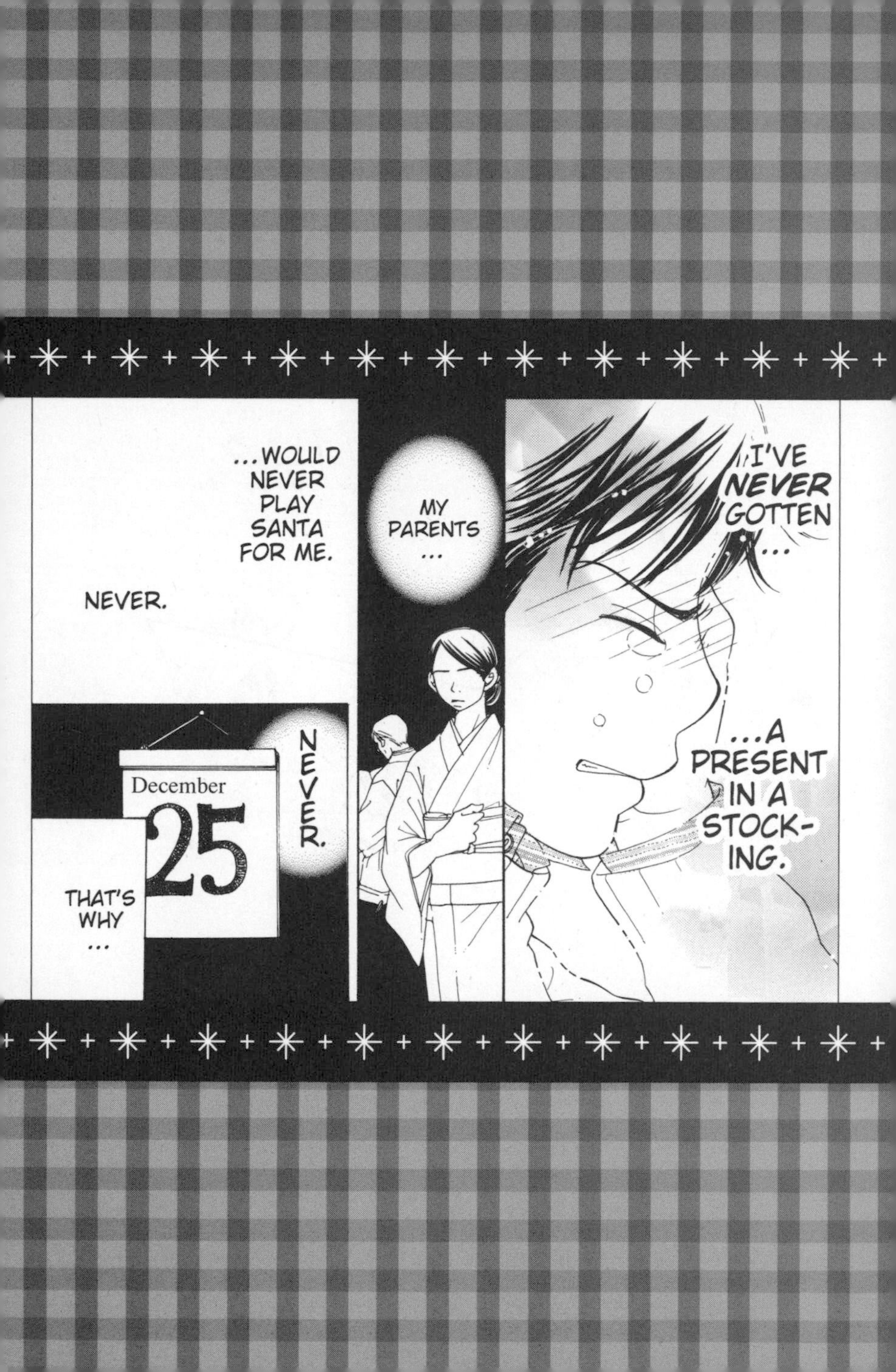
I'VE NEVER GOTTEN ...
...A PRESENT IN A STOCKING.
MY PARENTS ...
...WOULD NEVER PLAY SANTA FOR ME.
NEVER.
NEVER.
December 25
THAT'S WHY ...

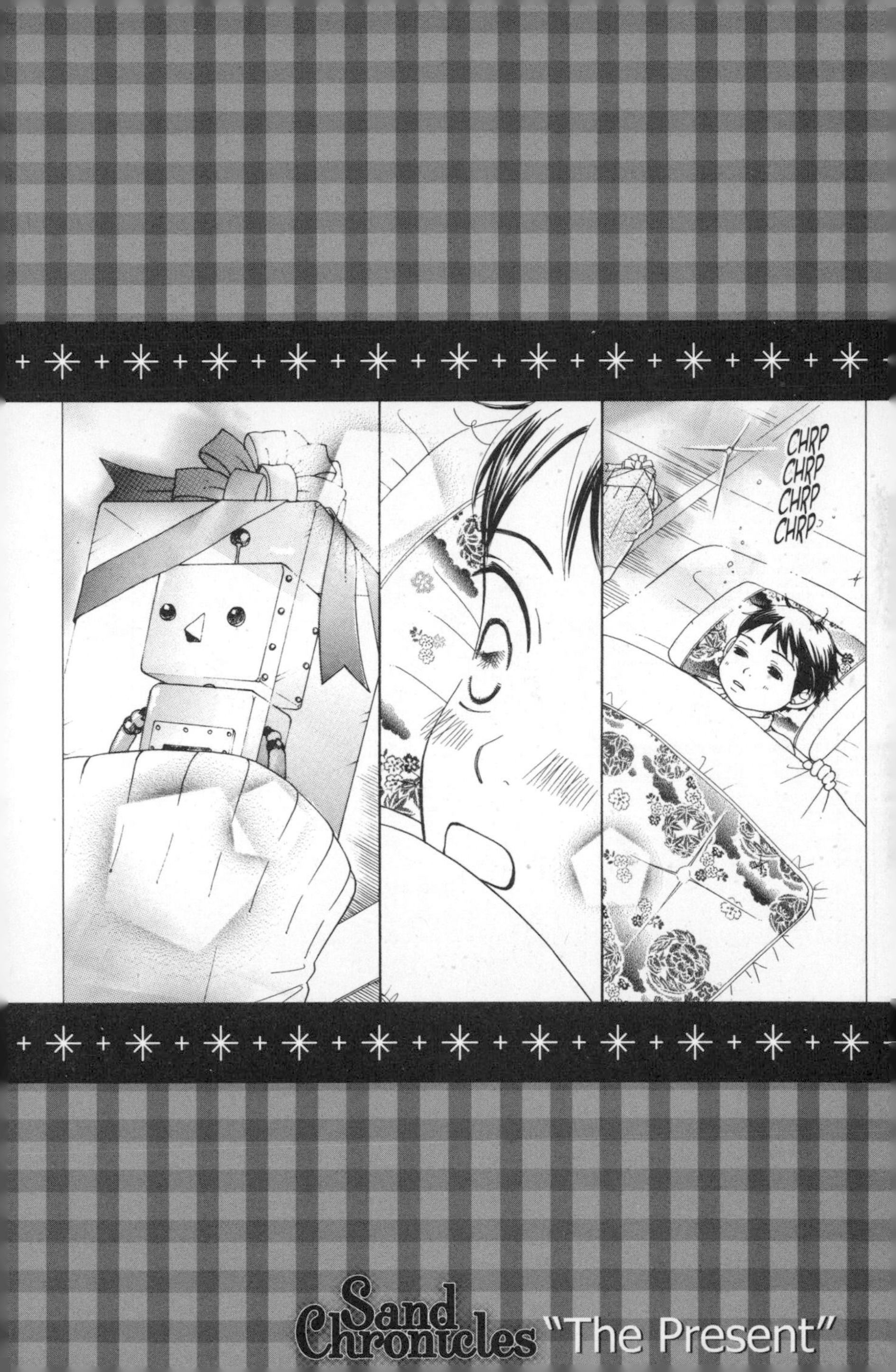
CHRP
CHRP
CHRP
CHRP

Sand Chronicles "The Present"

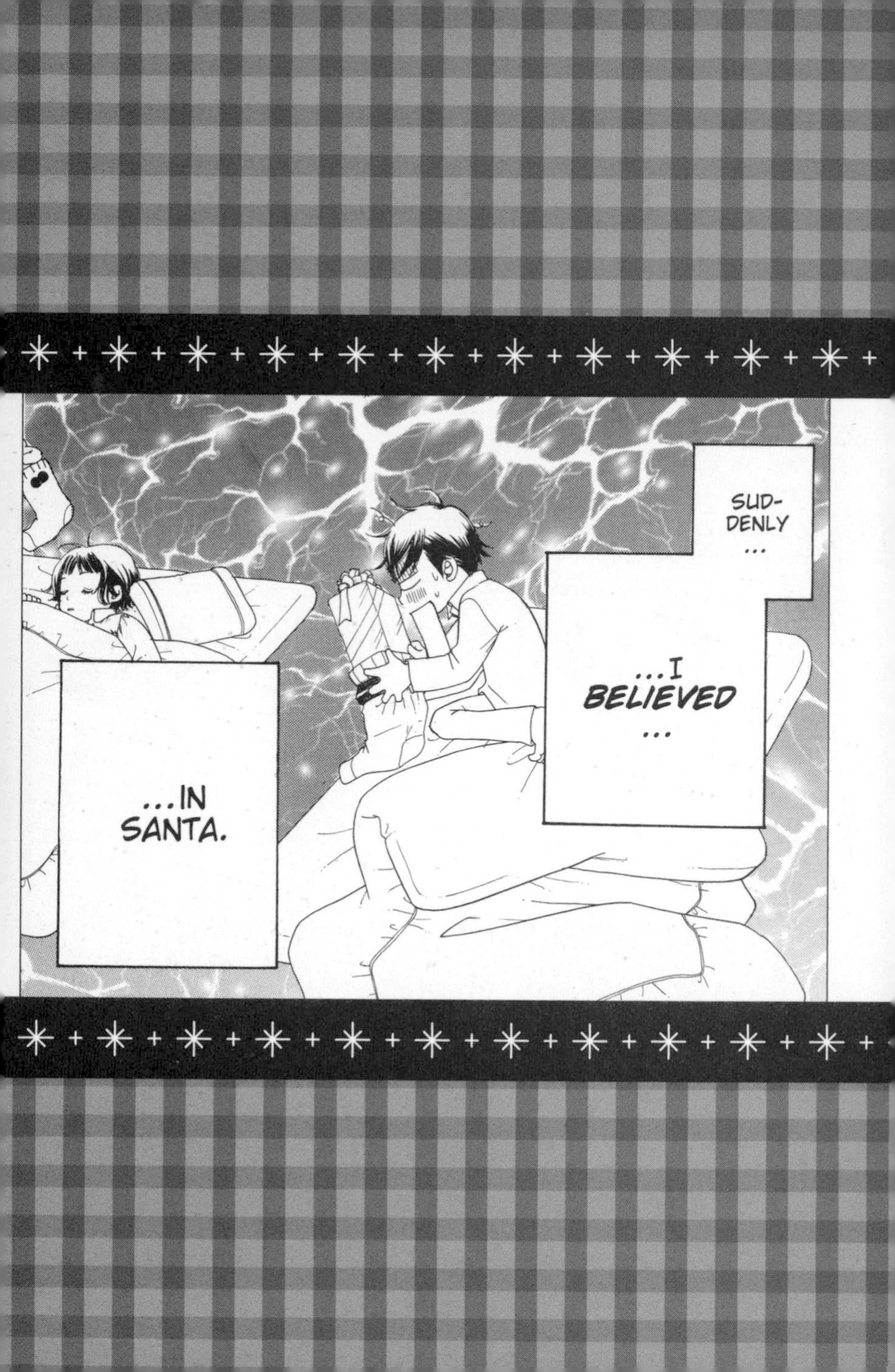
SUD-DENLY ...
...I BELIEVED ...
...IN SANTA.

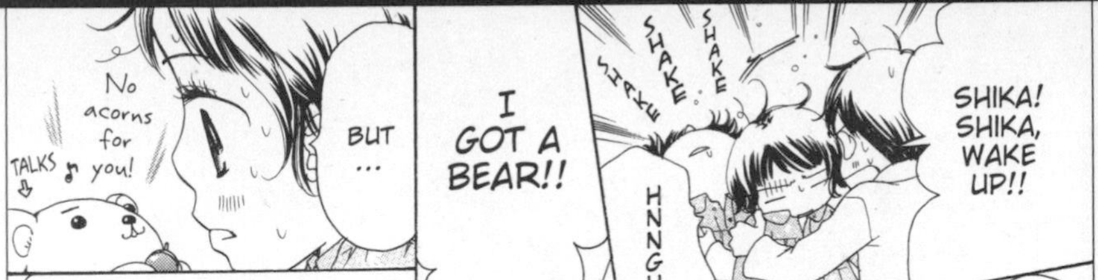
SHIKA! SHIKA, WAKE UP!!
SHAKE
SHAKE
SHAKE
HNNGH?
SANTA CAME!! HE CAME!!
I GOT A BEAR!!
A robot! ♡
BUT...
No acorns for you!
TALKS
YUMI SAID SANTA IS REALLY YOUR MOM AND DAD...
Is that true?
DON'T BE SILLY!
THEY WOULD NEVER DO SOME-THING LIKE THIS!!

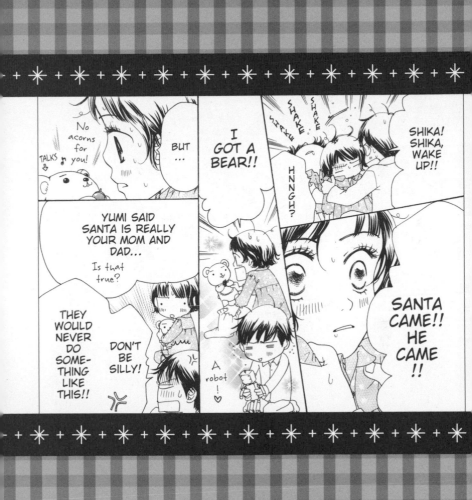

Sand Chronicles "The Present"

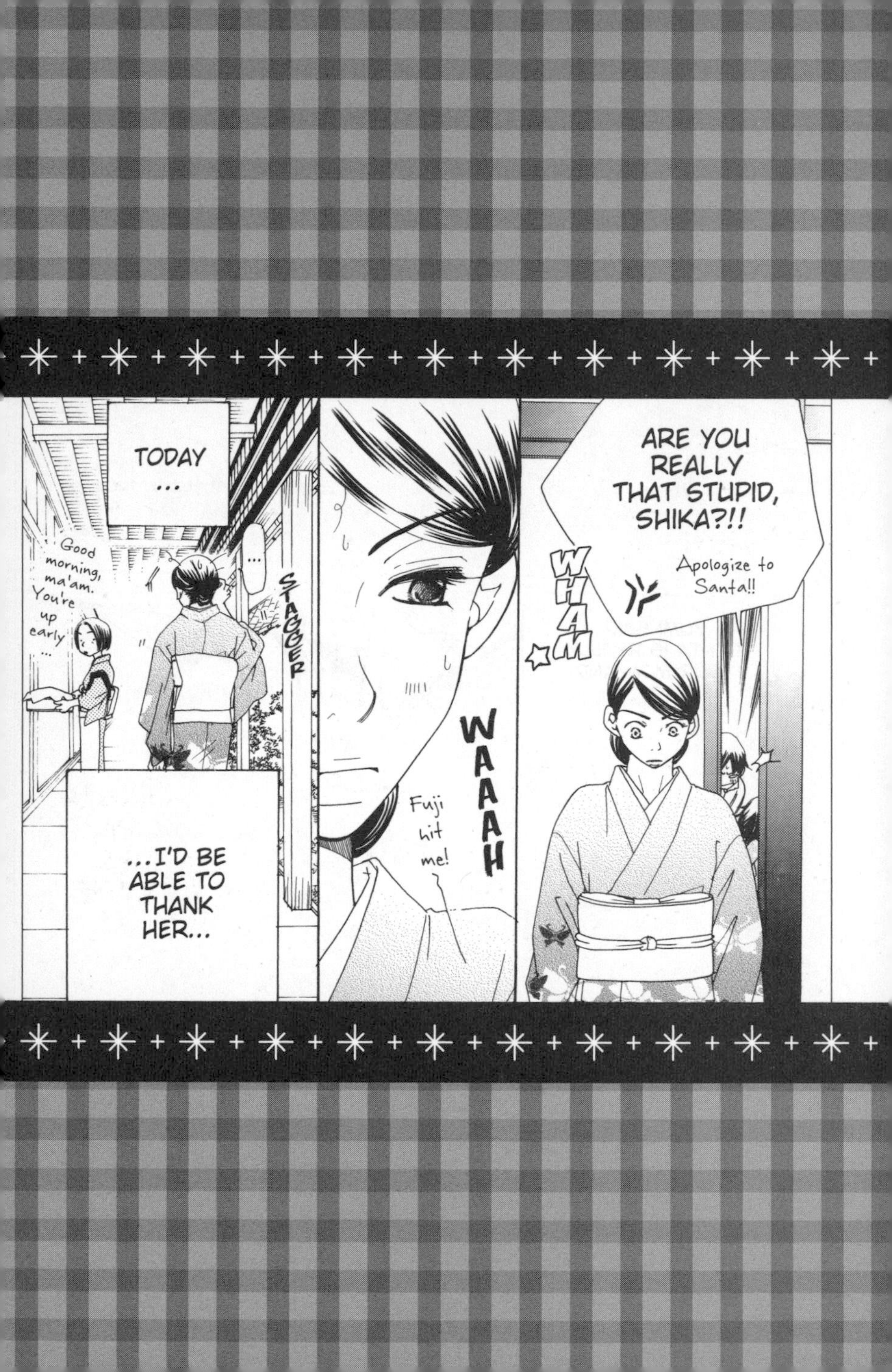
ARE YOU REALLY THAT STUPID, SHIKA?!!
Apologize to Santa!!
WHAM
WAAAAH
Fuji hit me!
TODAY ...
...
STAGGER
Good morning, ma'am. You're up early ...
...I'D BE ABLE TO THANK HER...

YOU DRANK TOO MUCH!

THE PARTY'S OVER.

Everyone went home!

Fell asleep...

NGH ...

AGE 17.

CHRISTMAS EVE, A FEW HOURS AGO...

LET'S GO.

HEAD HURTS ...

FUJI!!

Sand Chronicles "The Present"

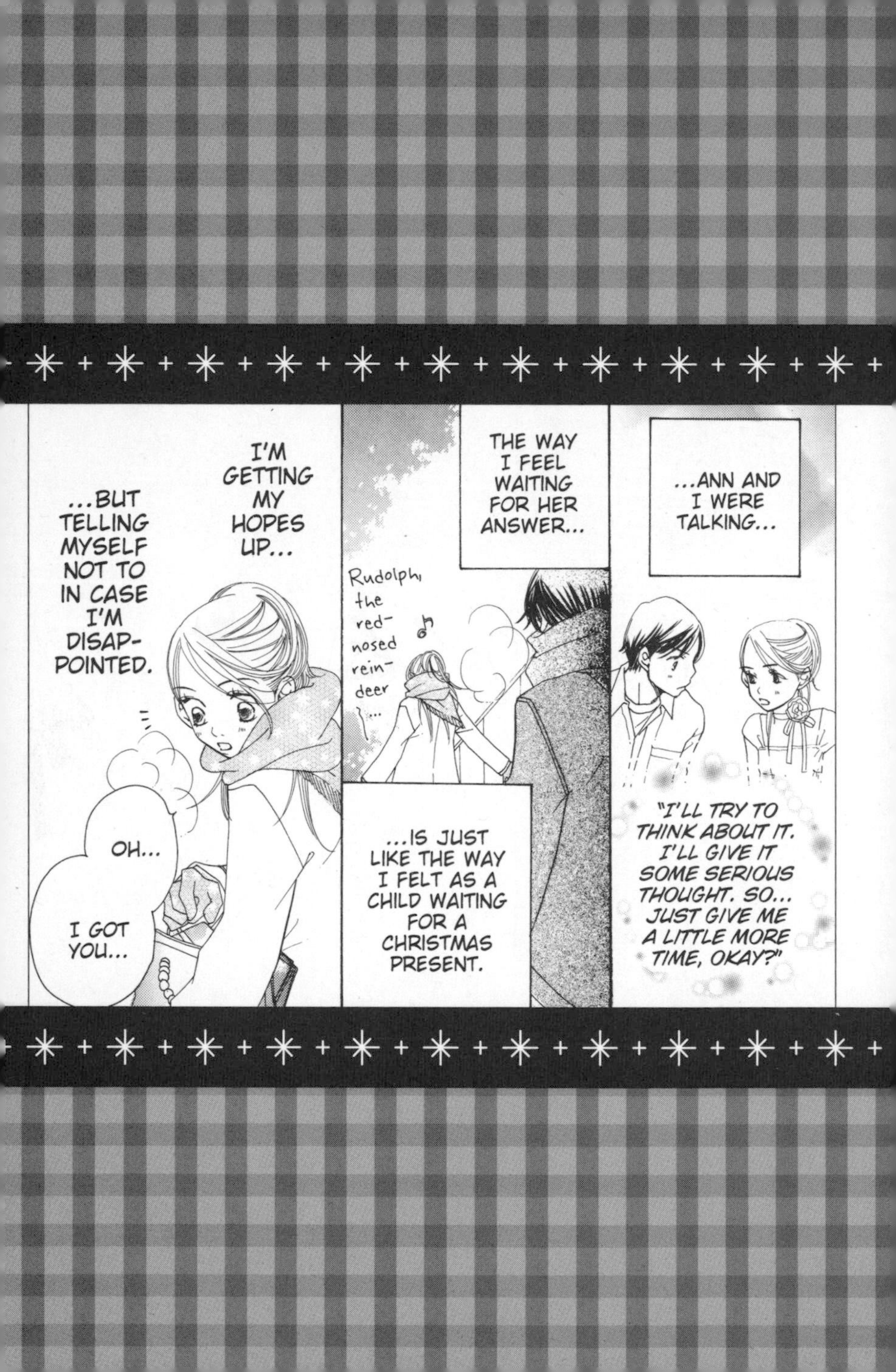
...ANN AND I WERE TALKING...
"I'LL TRY TO THINK ABOUT IT. I'LL GIVE IT SOME SERIOUS THOUGHT. SO... JUST GIVE ME A LITTLE MORE TIME, OKAY?"
THE WAY I FEEL WAITING FOR HER ANSWER...
Rudolph, the red-nosed rein-deer ~...
...IS JUST LIKE THE WAY I FELT AS A CHILD WAITING FOR A CHRISTMAS PRESENT.
I'M GETTING MY HOPES UP...
...BUT TELLING MYSELF NOT TO IN CASE I'M DISAP-POINTED.
OH...
I GOT YOU...

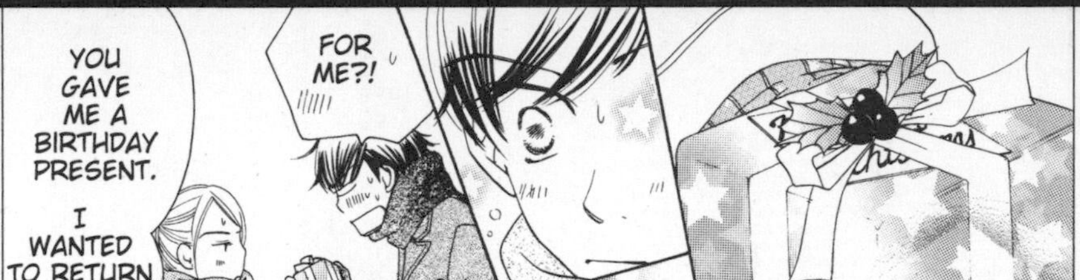
Here!
A CHRISTMAS PRESENT!
FOR ME?!
YOU GAVE ME A BIRTHDAY PRESENT.
I WANTED TO RETURN THE FAVOR.
It's good manners.
RSTL
I NOTICED YOU HAVE A TIN ROBOT ON YOUR BOOKSHELF. SEEMED LIKE IT WAS IMPORTANT TO YOU...
SO I THOUGHT YOU MIGHT LIKE THIS.
10:35

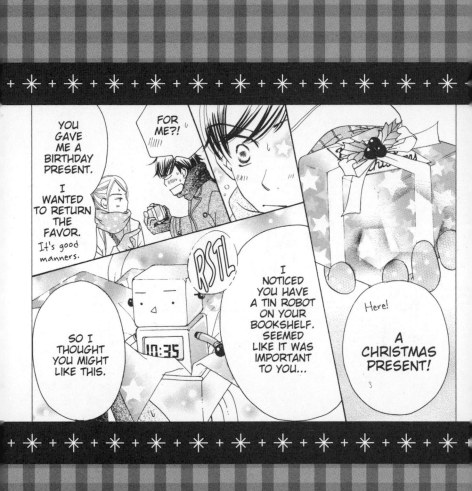

Sand Chronicles "The Present"

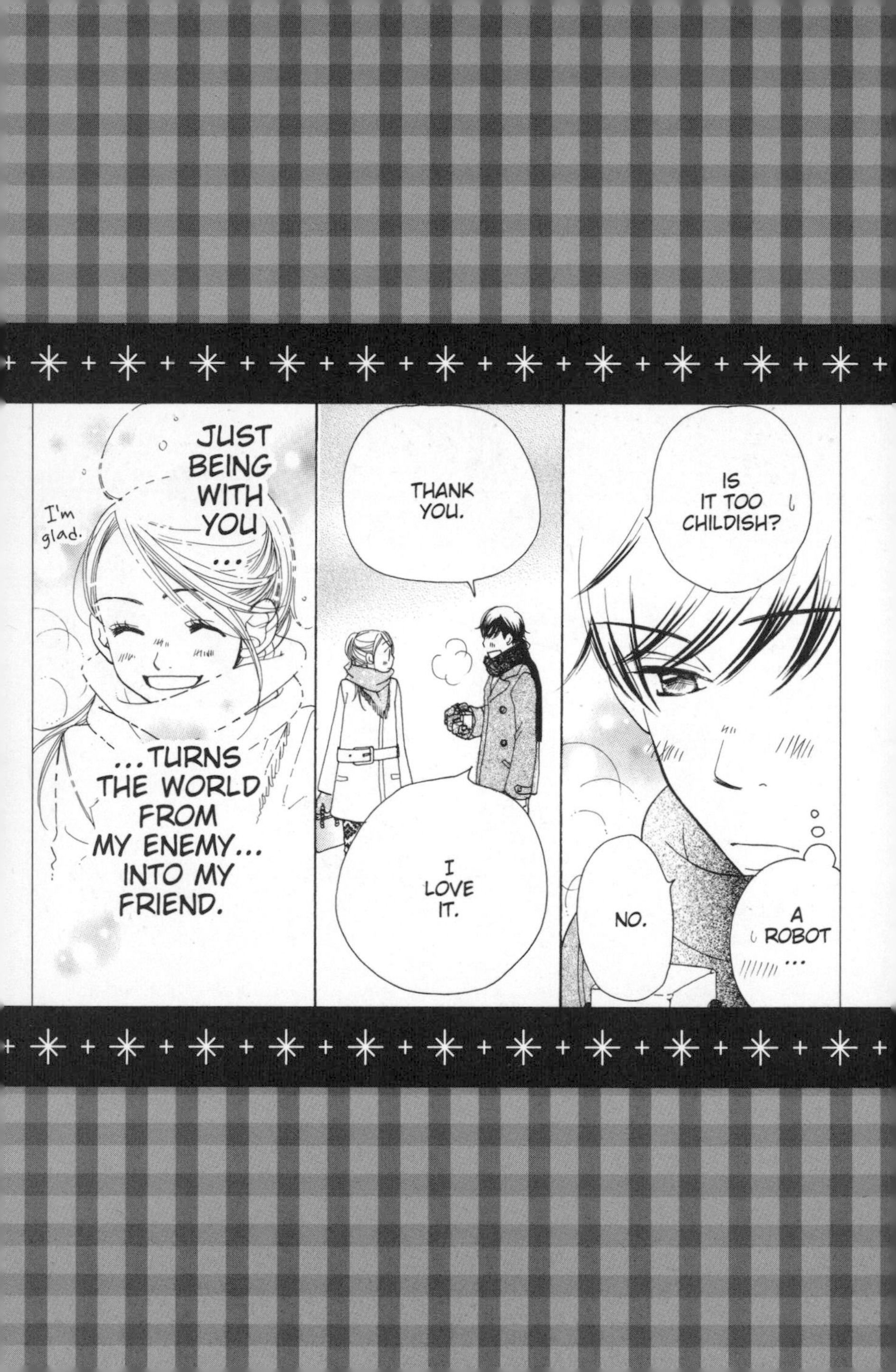
IS IT TOO CHILDISH?
A ROBOT ...
NO.
THANK YOU.
I LOVE IT.
JUST BEING WITH YOU ...
I'm glad.
...TURNS THE WORLD FROM MY ENEMY... INTO MY FRIEND.

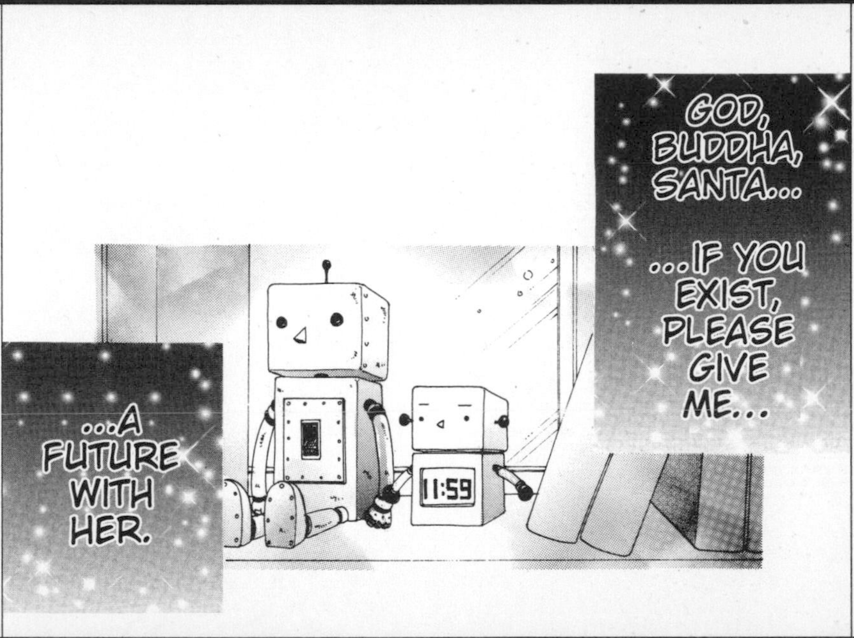
GOD, BUDDHA, SANTA...
...IF YOU EXIST, PLEASE GIVE ME...
...A FUTURE WITH HER.

The Present: The End

Sand Chronicles "The Present"

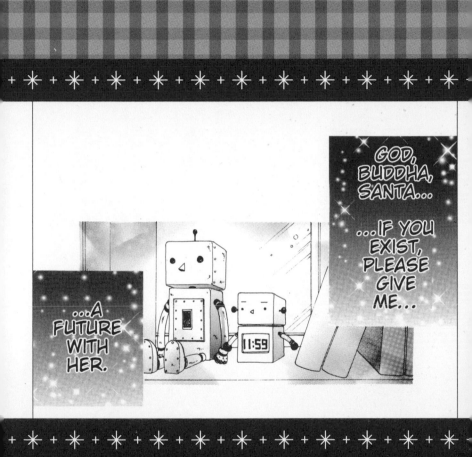

Glossary

If only adolescence came with an instruction manual.
We can't give you that, but this glossary of terms
might prove useful for this volume.

Page 19, panel 2: *koban*
In Japan, police boxes, or *koban*, can be
easily found in every community and are
a place where people can freely stop in to
ask for help.

Page 34, panel 1: *"How many matches can
they hold?"*
A saying about how the longer a girl's
eyelashes are, the more matches can be
stacked on them.

Page 34, panel 2: *"Mummy hunters wind
up as mummies."*
A Japanese proverb that means mummy
hunters end up dying and drying up in a
crypt themselves. An English equivalent
might be, "Go for wool and come home
shorn."

Page 80, panel 1: *"It's thinner than your
legs!"*
Japanese radishes (daikon) are long, thick
and white—not at all like typical small,
round and red radishes popular in the
West. When someone has thick calves, it's
said she has daikon-ashi, or radish-legs.

Page 81, panel 5: *"smitten...mitten"*
The Japanese has a different pun. When
Miwako rushes in out of breath she says,
"*Su!*" This is the first syllable of *suki*,
the "like" in "I met someone I like!!" *Su*
could be taken for the word for vinegar,
among other homonyms. So Hiroko asks,
"Vinegar?"

Page 128, panel 5: *kayu*
Okayu or *kayu* is rice congee.

Profile of Hinako Ashihara

The other day I left some things I'd bought—shopping bag and all—on a bus. I didn't notice until about a week later! Am I losing my memory?

—Hinako Ashihara

Hinako Ashihara won the 50th Shogakukan Manga Award for *Sunadokei*. She debuted with *Sono Hanashi Okotowari Shimasu* in *Bessatsu Shojo Comics* in 1994. Her other works include *SOS*, *Forbidden Dance*, and *Tennen Bitter Chocolate*.

SAND CHRONICLES
Vol. 9
Shojo Beat Edition

STORY AND ART BY **HINAKO ASHIHARA**

© 2003 Hinako ASHIHARA/Shogakukan
All rights reserved.
Original Japanese edition "SUNADOKEI" published by SHOGAKUKAN Inc.

English Adaptation/John Werry
Translation/Kinami Watabe, HC Language Solutions Inc.
Touch-up Art & Lettering/Rina Mapa
Additional Touch-up/Rachel Lightfoot
Cover Design/Deirdre Shiozawa
Interior Design/Daniel Porter
Editor/Annette Roman

VP, Production/Alvin Lu
VP, Sales & Product Marketing/Gonzalo Ferreyra
VP, Creative/Linda Espinosa
Publisher/Hyoe Narita

Printed in Canada

Published by VIZ Media, LLC
P.O. Box 77010
San Francisco, CA 94107

10 9 8 7 6 5 4 3 2 1
First printing, September 2010

www.viz.com www.shojobeat.com

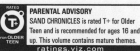

PARENTAL ADVISORY
SAND CHRONICLES is rated T+ for Older
Teen and is recommended for ages 16 and
up. This volume contains mature themes.
ratings.viz.com

Profile of Hinako Ashihara

The other day I left some things I'd bought—shopping bag and all—on a bus. I didn't notice until about a week later! Am I losing my memory?

—Hinako Ashihara

Hinako Ashihara won the 50th Shogakukan Manga Award for *Sunadokei*. She debuted with *Sono Hanashi Okotowari Shimasu* in *Bessatsu Shojo Comics* in 1994. Her other works include *SOS*, *Forbidden Dance*, and *Tennen Bitter Chocolate*.

Shojo Beat

SAND CHRONICLES

Vol. 9

Shojo Beat Edition

STORY AND ART BY HINAKO ASHIHARA

Original Japanese edition "SUNADOKEI" published by SHOGAKUKAN Inc.

English Adaptation/John Werry
Translation/Kinami Watabe, HC Language Solutions Inc.
Touch-up Art & Lettering/Rina Mapa
Additional Touch-up/Rachel Lightfoot
Cover Design/Deirdre Shiozawa
Interior Design/Daniel Porter
Editor/Annette Roman

VP, Production/Alvin Lu
VP, Sales & Product Marketing/Gonzalo Ferreyra
VP, Creative/Linda Espinosa
Publisher/Hyoe Narita

A CIP catalogue record for this book is available from the British Library.

Printed in Canada

VIZ media

SB

www.viz.com www.shojobeat.com

Published by VIZ Media, LLC
P.O. Box 77010
San Francisco, CA 94107

10 9 8 7 6 5 4 3 2 1
First printing, September 2010

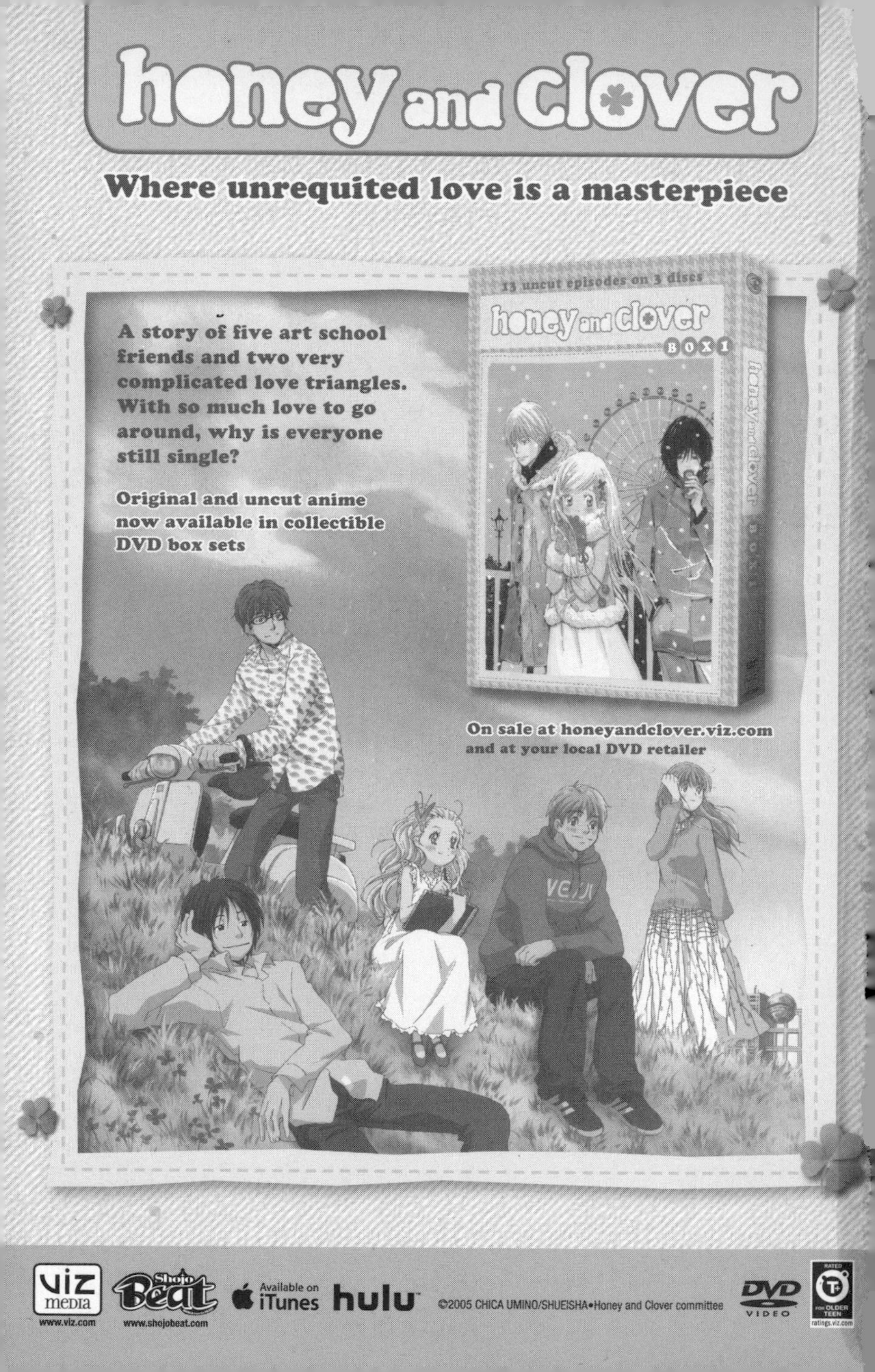
honey and clover
Where unrequited love is a masterpiece
A story of five art school friends and two very complicated love triangles. With so much love to go around, why is everyone still single?
Original and uncut anime now available in collectible DVD box sets
13 uncut episodes on 3 discs
honey and clover
BOX 1
On sale at honeyandclover.viz.com
and at your local DVD retailer
viz media
www.viz.com
Shojo Beat
www.shojobeat.com
Available on iTunes
hulu
©2005 CHICA UMINO/SHUEISHA•Honey and Clover committee
DVD VIDEO
RATED T+ FOR OLDER TEEN
ratings.viz.com